Pro SQL Server 2008 Failover Clustering

Allan Hirt

Apress®

Pro SQL Server 2008 Failover Clustering

Copyright © 2009 by Allan Hirt

Lead Editor: Jonathan Gennick

Technical Reviewer: Uttam Parui

Editorial Board: Clay Andres, Steve Anglin, Mark Beckner, Ewan Buckingham, Tony Campbell, Gary Cornell, Jonathan Gennick, Michelle Lowman, Matthew Moodie, Jeffrey Pepper, Frank Pohlmann, Ben Renow-Clarke, Dominic Shakeshaft, Matt Wade, Tom Welsh

Project Manager: Sofia Marchant

Copy Editors: Damon Larson, Nicole LeClerc Flores

Associate Production Director: Kari Brooks-Copony

Production Editor: Laura Esterman

Compositor: Octal Publishing

Proofreader: April Eddy

Indexer: John Collin

Cover Designer: Kurt Krames

Manufacturing Director: Tom Debolski

Distributed to the book trade worldwide by Springer-Verlag New York, Inc., 233 Spring Street, 6th Floor, New York, NY 10013. Phone 1-800-SPRINGER, fax 201-348-4505, e-mail orders-ny@springer-sbm.com, or visit http://www.springeronline.com.

For information on translations, please contact Apress directly at 2855 Telegraph Avenue, Suite 600, Berkeley, CA 94705. Phone 510-549-5930, fax 510-549-5939, e-mail info@apress.com, or visit http://www.apress.com.

Apress and friends of ED books may be purchased in bulk for academic, corporate, or promotional use. eBook versions and licenses are also available for most titles. For more information, reference our Special Bulk Sales–eBook Licensing web page at http://www.apress.com/info/bulksales.

The source code for this book is available to readers at http://www.apress.com. You will need to answer questions pertaining to this book in order to successfully download the code.

This book is dedicated to my parents, Paul and Rochelle Hirt.

Contents at a Glance

Contents

About the Author

 **ALLAN HIRT** has been using SQL Server since he was a quality assurance intern for SQL Solutions (which was then bought by Sybase), starting in 1992. For the past 10 years, Allan has been consulting, training, developing content, and speaking at events like TechEd and SQL PASS, as well as authoring books, whitepapers, and articles related to SQL Server architecture, high availability, administration, and more. Before forming his own consulting company, Megahirtz, in 2007, he most recently worked for both Microsoft and Avanade, and still continues to work with Microsoft on various projects. Allan can be contacted through his web site, at http://www.sqlha.com.

Acknowledgments

 **UTTAM PARUI** is currently a senior premier field engineer at Microsoft. In this role, he delivers SQL Server consulting and support for designated strategic customers. He acts as a resource for ongoing SQL planning and deployment, analysis of current issues, and migration to new SQL environments; and he's responsible for SQL workshops and training for customers' existing support staff. He has worked with SQL Server for over 11 years, and joined Microsoft 9 years ago with the SQL Server Developer Support team. He has considerable experience in SQL Server failover clustering, performance tuning, administration, setup, and disaster recovery. Additionally, he has trained and mentored engineers from the SQL Customer Support Services (CSS) and SQL Premier Field Engineering (PFE) teams, and was one of the first to train and assist in the development of Microsoft's SQL Server support teams in Canada and India. Uttam led the development of and successfully completed Microsoft's globally coordinated intellectual property for the SQL Server 2005/2008: Failover Clustering workshop. Apart from this, Uttam also contributed to the technical editing of *Professional SQL Server 2005 Performance Tuning* (Wrox, 2008), and is the coauthor of *Microsoft SQL Server 2008 Bible* (Wiley, 2009). He received his master's degree from the University of Florida at Gainesville, and is a Microsoft Certified Trainer (MCT) and Microsoft Certified IT Professional (MCITP): Database Administrator 2008. He can be reached at uttam_parui@hotmail.com.

Acknowledgments

I am not the only one involved in the process of publishing the book you are reading. I would like to thank everyone at Apress who I worked directly or indirectly with on this book: Jonathan Gennick, Sofia Marchant, Damon Larson, Laura Esterman, Leo Cuellar, Stephen Wiley, Nicole LeClerc Flores, and April Eddy. I especially appreciate the patience of Sofia Marchant and Laura Esterman (I promise—no more graphics revisions!).

Next, I have to thank my reviewers: Steven Abraham, Ben DeBow, Justin Erickson, Gianluca Hotz, Darmadi Komo, Scott Konersmann, John Lambert, Ross LoForte, Greg Low, John Moran, Max Myrick, Al Noel, Mark Pohto, Arvind Rao, Max Verun, Buck Woody, Kalyan Yella, and Gilberto Zampatti. My sincerest apologies if I missed anyone, but there were a lot of you!

A very special thank you has to go out to my main technical reviewer, Uttam Parui. Everyone—especially Uttam—kept me honest, and their feedback is a large part of why I believe this book came out as good as it has.

I also would like to thank StarWind for giving me the ability to test clusters easily using iSCSI. The book would have been impossible to write without StarWind. I also would be remiss if I did not recognize the assistance of Elden Christensen, Ahmed Bisht, and Symon Perriman from the Windows clustering development team at Microsoft, who helped me through some of the Windows Server 2008 R2 stuff when it wasn't obvious to me. The SQL Server development team—especially Max Verun and Justin Erickson—was also helpful along the way when I needed to check certain items as well. I always strive in anything I author to include only things that are fully supported by Microsoft. I would be a bad author and a lousy consultant if I put some maverick stuff in here that would put your supportability by Microsoft in jeopardy.

On the personal side, I'd like to thank my friends, family, and bandmates for putting up with my crazy schedule and understanding when I couldn't do something or was otherwise preoccupied getting one thing or another done for the book.

Allan Hirt
June, 2009

Preface

If someone had told me 10 years ago that writing a whitepaper on SQL Server 2000 failover clustering would ultimately lead to me writing a book dedicated to the topic, I would have laughed at them. I guess you never know where things lead until you get there.

When I finished my last book (*Pro SQL Server 2005 High Availability*, also published by Apress), I needed a break to recharge my batteries. After about a year of not thinking about books, I got the itch to write again while I was presenting a session on SQL Server 2008 failover clustering with Windows Server 2008 at TechEd 2008 in Orlando, Florida. My original plan was to write the update to my high availability book, but three factors steered me toward a clustering-only book:

1. Even with as much space as clustering got in the last book, I felt the topic wasn't covered completely, and I felt I could do a better job giving it more breathing room. Plus, I can finally answer the question, "So when are you going to write a clustering book?"

2. Both SQL Server 2008 failover clustering and Windows Server 2008 failover clustering are very different than their predecessors, so it reinforced that going wide and not as deep was not the way to go.

3. Compared to failover clustering, the other SQL Server 2008 high-availability features had what I'd describe as incremental changes from SQL Server 2005, so most of the other book is still fairly applicable. Chapter 1 of this book has some of the changes incorporated to basically bring some of that old content up to date.

This book took a bit less time to do than the last one—about 8 months. Over that timeframe (including some blown deadlines as well as an ever-expanding page count), Microsoft made lots of changes to both SQL Server and Windows, which were frustrating to deal with during the writing and editing process because of when the changes were released or announced in relation to my deadlines, but ultimately made the book much better. Some examples include the very late changes in May 2009 to Microsoft's stance on virtualization and failover clustering for SQL Server, Windows Server 2008 R2, Windows Server 2008 Service Pack 2, and SQL Server 2008 Service Pack 1. Without them, I probably would be considering an update to the book sooner rather than a bit later.

The writing process this time around was much easier; the book practically wrote itself since this is a topic I am intimately familiar with. I knew what I wanted to say and in what order. The biggest challenge was setting up all of the environments to run the tests and capture screenshots. Ensuring I got a specific error condition was sometimes tricky. It could take hours or even a day to set up just to grab one screenshot. Over the course of writing the book, I used no less than five different laptops (don't ask!) and one souped-up desktop.

Besides authoring the book content, I also have completed some job aids available for download. You can find them in the Source Code section of the Apress web site (http://www.apress.com), as well as on my web site, at http://www.sqlha.com. Book updates will also be posted to my web site. Should you find any problems or have any comments, contact me through the web site or via e-mail at sqlhabook@sqlha.com.

I truly hope you enjoy the book and find it a valuable addition to your SQL Server library.

CHAPTER 1

Failover Clustering Basics

Deploying highly available SQL Server instances and databases is more than a technology solution, it is a combination of people, process, and technology. The same can be said for disaster recovery plans. Unfortunately, when it comes to either high availability or disaster recovery, most people put technology first, which is the worst thing that can be done. There has to be a balance between technology and everything else. While this book is not intended to be the definitive source of data center best practices, since it is specifically focused on a single feature of SQL Server 2008—failover clustering—I will be doing my best to bring best practices into the discussion where applicable. People and process will definitely be touched upon all throughout the book, since I live in the "real world" where reference architectures that are ideal on paper can't always be deployed. This chapter will provide the foundation for the rest of the book; discuss some of the basics of high availability and disaster recovery; and describe, compare, and contrast the various SQL Server availability technologies.

A Quick High Availability and Disaster Recovery Primer

I find that many confuse high availability and disaster recovery. Although they are similar, they require two completely different plans and implementations. *High availability* refers to solutions that are more local in nature and generally tolerate smaller amounts of data loss and downtime. *Disaster recovery* is when a catastrophic event occurs (such as a fire in your data center), and an extended outage is necessary to get back up and running. Both need to be accounted for in every one of your implementations. Many solutions lack or have minimal high availability, and disaster recovery often gets dropped or indefinitely shelved due to lack of time, resources, or desire. Many companies only implement disaster recovery after they encounter a costly outage, which often involves some sort of significant loss. Only then does a company gain a true understanding of what disaster recovery brings to the proverbial table.

Before architecting any solution, purchasing hardware, developing administration, or deploying technology, you need to understand what you are trying to make available and what you are protecting against. By that, I mean the *business* side of the house—you didn't really think you were considering options like failover clustering because they are nifty, did you? You are solving a business problem—ensuring the business can continue to remain functioning. SQL Server is only the data store for a large ecosystem that includes an application that connects to the SQL Server instance, application servers, network, storage, and so on—without one component working properly, the entire ecosystem feels the pain. The overall solution is only as available as its weakest link.

For example, if the application server is down but the SQL Server instance containing the database is running, I would define the application as unavailable. Both the SQL Server database and the instance housing it are available, but no one can use them. This is also where the concept of *perceived unavailability* comes into play—as a DBA, you may get calls that users cannot access the database. It's a database-driven application, so the problem *must* be at the database level, right? The reality is that the actual problem often has nothing to do with SQL Server. Getting clued into the bigger picture and having good communication with the other groups in your company is crucial. DBAs are often the first blamed for problems related to a database-based application, and have to go out of their way to prove it is not their issue. Solving these fundamental problems can only happen when you are involved before you are told you've got a new database to administer. While it rarely happens, DBAs need to be involved from the time the solution or application (custom or packaged) is first discussed—otherwise, you will always be playing catch-up.

The key to availability is to calculate how much downtime actually means to the business. Is it a monetary amount per second/minute/hour/day? Is it lost productivity? Is it a blown deadline? Is it health or even the possibility of a lost human life (e.g., in the case of a system located in a hospital)? There is no absolute right or wrong answer, but knowing how to make an appropriate calculation for your environment or particular solution is much better than pulling a number out of a hat. This is especially true when the budget comes into play. For example, if being down an entire day will wind up costing the company $75,000 plus the time and effort of the workers (including lost productivity for other projects), would it be better to spend a proportional amount on a solution to minimize or eliminate the outage? In theory, yes, but in practice, I see a lot of penny-wise, pound-foolish implementations that skimp up front and pay for it later. Too many bean counters look at the up-front acquisition costs vs. what spending that money will actually save in the long run.

A good example that highlights the cost vs. benefit ratio is a very large database (VLDB). Many SQL Server databases these days are in the hundred-gigabyte or terabyte range. Even with some sort of backup compression employed, it takes a significant amount of time to copy a backup file from one place to another. Add to that the time it takes to restore, and it can take anywhere from a half a day to two days to get the SQL Server back end to a point where the data is ready for an application. One way to mitigate that and reduce the time to get back up and running is to use hardware-based options such as clones and snapshots, where the database may be usable in a short amount of time after the restore is initiated. These options are not available on every storage unit or implemented in every environment, but they should be considered prior to deployment since they affect how your solution is architected. These solutions sometimes cannot be added after the fact. Unfortunately, a hardware-based option is not free—there is a disk cost as well as a special configuration that the storage vendor may charge a fee for, but the benefits are immeasurable when the costs associated with downtime are significant.

There are quite a number of things that all environments large or small should do to increase availability:

- Use solid data center principles
- Employ secure servers, applications, and physical access
- Deploy proper administration and monitoring for all systems and databases
- Perform proactive maintenance such as proper rebuilding of indexes when needed
- Have the right people in the right roles with the right skills

If all of these things are done with a modicum of success, availability will be impacted in a positive way. Unfortunately, what I see in many environments is that most of these items are ignored or put off for another time and never done. These are the building blocks of availability, not technology like failover clustering.

Another fundamental concept for both high availability and disaster recovery is *nines*. The term *nines* refers to the number of nines in a percentage that will represent the uptime of a system, network, solution, and so on. Based on that definition, 99.999 percent is five nines of availability, meaning that the application is available 99.999 percent of the year. To put it in perspective, five nines translates into 5.26 minutes of downtime a year. Even with the best people and excellent processes, achieving such a low amount of downtime is virtually impossible. Three nines (99.9 percent) is 8.76 hours of downtime per year. That number is much easier to achieve, but is still out of reach for many. Somewhere between three and two (87.6 hours per year) nines is arguably a realistic target to strive for. I want to add one caveat here: I am not saying that five nines could never be achieved; in all of my years in the IT world, I've seen one IT shop achieve it, but they obviously had more going for them than just technology. When you see a marketing hype saying a certain technology or solution can achieve five nines, ask tough questions.

There are two types of downtime: planned and unplanned. *Planned downtime* is exactly what it sounds like—it is the time in which you schedule outages to perform maintenance, apply patches, perform upgrades, and so on. I find that some companies do not count planned downtime in their overall availability number since it is "known" downtime, but in reality, that is cheating. Your true uptime (or downtime) numbers have to account for every minute. You may still show what portion of your annual downtime was planned, but being down is being down; there is no gray area on that issue. *Unplanned downtime* is what high availability and disaster recovery is meant to protect against: those situations where some event causes an unscheduled outage.

Unplanned downtime is further complicated by many factors, not the least of which is the size of your database. As mentioned earlier, larger databases are less agile. I have personally experienced a copy process taking 24 hours for a 1 TB backup file. If you have some larger databases, agreeing to unrealistic availability and restore targets does not make sense. This is just one example of where taking all factors into account helps to inform what you need and can actually achieve.

All availability targets (as well as any other measurements, such as performance) must be formally documented in service-level agreements (SLAs). SLAs should be revisited periodically and revised accordingly. Things do change over time. For example, a system or an application that was once a minor blip on the radar may have evolved into the most used in your company. That would definitely require a change in how that system is dealt with. Revising SLAs also allows you to reflect other changes (including organizational and policy) that have occurred since the SLAs were devised.

SLAs are not only technically focused: they should also reflect the business side of things, and any objectives needed to be agreed upon by both the business and IT sides. Changing any SLA will affect all plans that have that SLA as a requirement. All plans, either high availability or disaster recovery, must be tested to ensure not only that they meet the SLA, but that they're accurate. Without that testing, you have no idea if the plan will work or meet the objectives stated by the SLA.

You may have noticed that some documentation from Microsoft is moving away from using nines (although most everyone out there still uses the measurement). You will see a lot of Microsoft documentation refer to recovery point objectives (RPOs) and recovery time objectives (RTOs). Both are measurements that should be included in SLAs. With any kind of disaster recovery (or high availability for that matter), in most cases you have to assume some sort of data loss, so how much (if any) that can be tolerated must be quantified.

Without formally documented SLAs and tests proving that you can meet them, you can be held to the fire for numbers you will never achieve. A great example of this is restoring a database, which, depending on the size, can take a considerable amount of time. This speaks to the RTO mentioned in the previous paragraph. Often, less technical members of your company (including management) think that getting back up and running after a problem is as easy as flicking a switch. People who have lived through these scenarios understand the 24-hour days and overnight shifts required to bring production environments back from the brink of disaster. Unless someone has a difficult discussion with management ahead of any disaster that may occur, they may expect IT (including the DBAs) to perform Herculean feats with an underfunded and inadequate staff. This leads to problems, and you may find yourself between a rock and a hard place. Have your resume handy since someone's head could roll, and it may be yours.

If you want to calculate your actual availability percentage, the formula is the following:

$$\text{Availability} = (\text{Total Units of Time} - \text{Downtime}) / \text{Total Units of Time}$$

For example, there are 8,760 hours (365 days × 24 hours) in a calendar year. If your environment encounters 100 hours of downtime during the year (which is an average of 8 1/3 hours per month), this would be your calculation:

$$\text{Availability} = (8760 - 100) / 8,760$$

The availability in this case is .98858447, or 98.9 percent uptime (one nine). For those "stuck" on the concept of nines, only claiming one nine may be a bitter pill to swallow. However, look at it another way: claiming your systems are only down 1.1 percent of the entire calendar year is nothing to sneeze at. Sometimes people need a reality check.

Politics often comes into play when it comes to high availability and disaster recovery. The ultimate goal is to get back up and running, not point fingers. Often, there are too many chiefs and not enough workers. When it comes to a server-down situation, everyone needs to pitch in—whether you're the lead DBA or the lowest DBA on the ladder. Participation could mean anything from looking at a monitoring program to see if there are any abnormalities, to writing Transact-SQL code for certain administrative tasks. Once you have gone through any kind of downtime or disaster, always have a postmortem to document what went right and what went wrong, and then put plans into place to fix what was wrong, including fixing your disaster plans.

Finally, I feel that I should mention one more thing: testing. It is one thing to implement high availability and/or disaster recovery, but if you never test the plans or the mechanisms behind them, how do you know they work? When you are in the middle of a crisis, the last thing you want to be doing is crossing your fingers praying it all goes well. You should hold periodic drills. You may think I'm crazy since that actually means downtime (and maybe messing up your SLAs)—but at the end of the day, what is the point of spending money on a solution and wrapping some plans around it if you have no idea if it works or not?

■**Tip** I would be remiss if I did not place a shameless plug here and recommend you pick up another book (or books) on high availability and/or disaster recovery. My previous book for Apress, *Pro SQL Server 2005 High Availability*, has more information on the basics of availability and other topics that are still relevant for SQL Server 2008. The first two chapters go into more detail on what I've just summarized here in a few pages. Disaster recovery gets its own chapter as well. Many of the technology chapters (log shipping, database mirroring, and replication) that are not focused on failover clustering are still applicable. Some of the differences between what I say in my earlier book and what you find in SQL Server 2008 are pointed out in the next section.

Understanding the SQL Server Availability Technologies

Microsoft ships SQL Server 2008 with five major availability features: backup and restore, failover clustering, log shipping, database mirroring, and replication. This section will describe and compare failover clustering with log shipping, database mirroring, and replication, as well as show how they combine with failover clustering to provide more availability.

Backup and Restore

Many people don't see backup and restore as a feature designed for availability, since it is a common feature of SQL Server. The truth is that the cornerstone of any availability and disaster recovery solution *is* your backup (and restore) plan for your databases and servers (should a server need to be rebuilt from scratch). None of the availability technologies—including failover clustering—absolve you from performing proper SQL Server database backups. I have foolishly heard some make this claim over the years, and I want to debunk it once and for all. Failover clustering does provide excellent protection for the scenarios and issues it fits, but it is not a magic tonic that works in every case. If you only do one thing for availability, ensure that you have a solid backup strategy.

Relying on backups either as a primary or a last resort more often than not means data loss. The reality is that in many cases (some of which are described in the upcoming sections on SQL Server availability technologies), some data loss is going to have to be tolerated. Whenever I am assisting a client and ask how much data loss is acceptable, the answer is always none. However, with nearly every system, there is at least some minimal data loss tolerance. There are ways to help mitigate the data loss, such as adding functionality to applications that queue transactions, but those come in before the implementation of any backup and restore strategy, and would be outside the DBA's hands. I cannot think of one situation over the years that I have been part of that did not involve data loss, whether it was an hour or a month's (yes, a month's) worth of data that will never be recovered. When devising your SLAs and ensuring they meet the business needs, they should be designed to match the backup scheme that is desired.

It is important to test your backups, as this is the only true way to ensure that they work. Using your backup software to verify that a backup is considered valid is one level of checking, but nothing can replace actually attempting to restore your database. Besides guaranteeing the database backup is good, testing the restore provides you with one piece of priceless information: how long it takes to restore. When a database goes down and your only option is restoring the database, someone is inevitably going to ask the question, "How long will it take to get us back up and running?" The answer they do not want to hear is, "I don't know." What would exacerbate the situation would be if you do not even know where the latest or best backup is located, so where backups are kept is another crucial factor, since access to the backups can affect downtime.

If you have tested the restore process, you will have an answer that will most likely be close to the actual time, including acquiring the backup. Testing backups is a serious commitment that involves additional hardware and storage space. I would even recommend testing the backups not only locally, but at another site. What happens if you put all of your backups on tape type A at site A, but you have a disaster and try to restore from tape, only to find that site B only has support for tape type B?

Many companies use third-party or centralized backup programs that can do things like back up a database across the network. These solutions are good as long as they integrate and utilize the SQL Server Virtual Device Interface (VDI) API. The same holds true for storage-based backups. VDI ensures that a backup is a proper and correct SQL Server backup, just like if you were not using any additional software or hardware. So, if you are unsure of your backup solution's support for SQL Server, ask the vendor. The last thing you want to find out is that your backups are not valid when you try to restore them.

Note The features *attach* and *detach* are sometimes lumped in with backup and restore. However, they are not equivalent. Attach and detach do exactly what they sound like: you can detach a database from a SQL Server instance, and then attach it. After you detach it, you can even copy the data and log files elsewhere. Attach and detach are not substitutes for backup and restore, but in some cases, they may prove useful in an availability situation. For example, if your failover cluster has problems and you need to reinstall it, if your data and log files on the shared drive were fine, after rebuilding, you could just attach the data and log files to the newly rebuilt SQL Server instance.

Windows Clustering

The basic concept of a cluster is easy to understand as it relates to a server ecosystem; a *cluster* is two or more systems working in concert to achieve a common goal. Under Windows, two main types of clustering exist: scale-out/availability clusters known as *Network Load Balancing (NLB) clusters*, and strictly availability-based clusters known as *failover clusters*. Microsoft also has a variation of Windows called Windows Compute Cluster Server. SQL Server's failover clustering feature is based upon a Windows failover cluster, not NLB or Compute Cluster Server.

Network Load Balancing Cluster

This section will describe what an NLB cluster is so you understand the difference between the two types of clustering. An NLB cluster adds availability as well as scalability to TCP/IP-based services, such as web servers, FTP servers, and COM+ applications (should you still have any deployed). NLB is also a non-Windows concept, and can be achieved via hardware load balancers. A Windows feature–based NLB implementation is one where multiple servers (up to 32) run independently of one another and do not share any resources. Client requests connect to the farm of servers and can be sent to any of the servers since they all provide the same functionality. The algorithms behind NLB keep track of which servers are busy, so when a request comes in, it is sent to a server that can handle it. In the event of an individual server failure, NLB knows about the problem and can be configured to automatically redirect the connection to another server in the NLB cluster.

NLB is not the way to scale out SQL Server (that is done via partitioning or data-dependent routing in the application), and can only be used in limited scenarios with SQL Server, such as having multiple read-only SQL Server instances with the same data (e.g., a catalog server for an online retailer), or using it to abstract a server name change in a switch if using log shipping or one of the other availability features. NLB cannot be configured on servers that are participating in a failover cluster, so it can only be used with standalone servers.

Failover Cluster

A Windows failover cluster's purpose is to help you maintain client access to applications and server resources even if you encounter some sort of outage (natural disaster, software failure, server failure, etc.). The whole impetus of availability behind a failover cluster implementation is that client machines and applications do not need to worry about which server in the cluster is running a given resource; the name and IP address of whatever is running within the failover cluster is *virtualized*. This means the application or client connects to a single name or IP address, but behind the scenes, the resource that is being accessed can be running on any server that is part of the cluster. A server in the failover cluster is known as a *node*. To allow virtualization of names and IP addresses, a failover cluster provides or requires redundancy of nearly every component—servers, network cards, networks, and so on. This redundancy is the basis of all availability in the failover cluster. However, there is a single point of failure in any failover cluster implementation, and that is the single *shared cluster disk array*, which is a disk subsystem that is attached to and accessible by all nodes of the failover cluster. See later in this section, as *shared* may not be what you think when it comes to failover clustering.

Note Prior to Windows Server 2008, a Windows failover cluster was known as a *server cluster*. Microsoft has always used the term *failover clustering* to refer to the clustering feature implemented in SQL Server. It is important to understand that SQL Server failover clustering is configured on top of Windows failover clustering. Because Microsoft now uses the same term (failover clustering) to refer to both a Windows and a SQL Server feature, I will make sure that it is clear all throughout the book which one I am referring to in a given context. It is also important to point out at this juncture that SQL Server failover clustering is the only high-availability feature of SQL Server that provides instance-level protection.

Depending on your data center and hardware implementation, a failover cluster can be implemented within only one location or across a distance. A failover cluster implemented across a distance is known as a *geographically dispersed cluster*. The difference with a geographically dispersed cluster is that the nodes can be deployed in different data centers, and it generally provides both disaster recovery as well as high availability. Every storage hardware vendor that supports geographically dispersed clusters implements them differently. Check with your preferred vendor to see how they support a geographically dispersed cluster. A failover cluster does not provide scale-out abilities either, but the solution can scale up as much as the operating system and hardware will allow. It must be emphasized that SQL Server can scale out as well as up (see the second paragraph of the preceding "Network Load Balancing Cluster" section), but the scale-out abilities have nothing to do with failover clustering.

A clustered application has individual *resources*, such as an IP address, a physical disk, and a network name, which are then contained in a *cluster resource group*, which is similar to a folder on your hard drive that contains files. The cluster resource is the lowest unit of management in a failover cluster. The resource group is the unit of failover in a cluster; you cannot fail over individual resources. Resources can also be a *dependency* of another resource (or resources) within a group. If a resource is dependent upon another, it will not be able to start until the top-level resource is online. For example, in a clustered SQL Server implementation, SQL Server Agent is dependent upon SQL Server to start before it can come online. If SQL Server cannot be started, SQL Server Agent will not be brought online either.

SQL Server requires a one-to-one ratio from instance to resource group. That means you can install only one instance of SQL Server per resource group. Resources such as disks cannot be shared across resource groups, and are dedicated to that particular instance of SQL Server residing in a resource group. For example, if you have disk S assigned to SQL Server instance A and want to configure another SQL Server clustered instance within the same Windows failover cluster, you will need another disk for the new instance.

A failover cluster works on the principle of a shared-nothing configuration; however, this is a bit of a misnomer. A shared-nothing cluster in the Microsoft world is one where only a single node can utilize a particular resource at any given time. However, a resource can be configured to work on only certain nodes, so it is not always the right assumption that a given cluster resource can be owned by all nodes. A given resource and its dependencies can only be running on a single node at a time, so there is a direct one-to-one ownership role from resource to node.

For an application like SQL Server to work properly in a Windows failover cluster, it must be coded to the clustering application programming interface (API) of the Windows Platform software development kit (SDK), and it must have at least three things:

- One or more disks configured in the Windows failover cluster

- A clustered network name for the application that is different from the Windows failover cluster name

- One or more clustered IP addresses for the application itself, which are not the same as the IP addresses for either the nodes or the Windows failover cluster

SQL Server failover clustering requires all of these elements. Depending on an application and how it is implemented for clustering, it may not have the same required elements as a clustered SQL Server instance.

Note Prior to Windows Server 2003, an application with the preceding three characteristics was known as a *virtual server*, but since the release of Microsoft Virtual Server, that terminology is no longer valid and will not be used anywhere in this book to refer to a clustered SQL Server instance.

Once SQL Server is installed in a cluster, it uses the underlying cluster semantics to ensure its availability. A Windows failover cluster uses a *quorum* that not only contains the master copy of the failover cluster's configuration, but also serves as a tiebreaker if all network communications fail between the nodes. If the quorum fails or becomes corrupt, the failover cluster shuts down, and you will not be able to restart it until the quorum is repaired. There are now four quorum types in Windows Server 2008. Chapter 2 describes the different quorum models in detail, and also gives advice on when each is best used. Some can be manually brought online.

Failover Cluster Networks

A failover cluster has two primary networks:

- A *private cluster network*: Sometimes known as the *intracluster network*, or more commonly, the *heartbeat network*, this is a dedicated network that is segregated from all other network traffic and is used for the sole purpose of running internal processes on the cluster nodes to ensure that the nodes are up and running—and if not, to initiate failover. The private cluster network does not detect process failure. The intervals these checks happen at are known as *heartbeats*.

- A *public network*: This is the network that connects the cluster to the rest of the network ecosystem and allows clients, applications, and other servers to connect to the failover cluster.

Finally, two other processes, sometimes referred to as checks, support the semantics of a failover cluster and are coded specifically by the developer of the cluster-aware application:

- *LooksAlive* is a lightweight check initiated by the Windows failover cluster that basically goes out to the application and says, "Are you there?" By default, this process runs every 5 seconds.

- *IsAlive* is a more in-depth application-level check that can include application-specific calls. For a clustered SQL Server instance, the IsAlive check issues the Transact-SQL query SELECT @@SERVERNAME. The query used by the IsAlive check is not user configurable. IsAlive requires that the failover cluster has access to SQL Server to issue this query. IsAlive has no mechanism for checking to see whether user databases are actually online and usable; it knows only if SQL Server (and the master database) is up and running. By default, the IsAlive process runs every 60 seconds and should never be changed, unless directed by Microsoft Support.

Figure 1-1 represents a failover cluster implementation. You can see both networks represented.

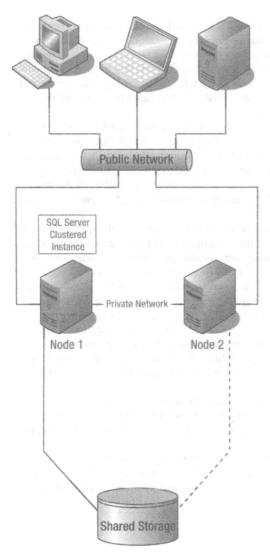

Figure 1-1. *Sample failover cluster*

Failover Cluster Semantics

The Windows service associated with the failover cluster named Cluster Service has a few components: an event processor, a database manager, a node manager, a global update manager, a communication manager, and a resource (failover) manager. The resource manager communicates directly with a resource monitor that talks to a specific application DLL that makes an application cluster-aware. The communication manager talks directly to the Windows Winsock layer (a component of the Windows networking layer).

All nodes "fight" for ownership of resources, and an arbitration process governs which node owns which resource. In the case of disks (including one that may be involved as part of a quorum model), for Windows Server 2003, three SCSI-2 commands are used under the covers: reserve to obtain or maintain ownership, release to allow the disk to be taken offline so it can be owned by another node, and reset to break the reservation on the disk. Windows Server 2008 use SCSI-3's persistent reservation commands, and is one reason there is more stringent testing before nodes are allowed to take part in a failover cluster (see the "Cluster Validation" section of Chapter 2 for more information on the tests). For more information about the types of drivers and the types of resets done by them, see the section "Hardware and Drivers" later in this chapter. Key to clustering is the concept of a disk signature, which is stored in each node's registry. These disk signatures must not change; otherwise, you will encounter errors. The Cluster Disk Driver (clusdisk.sys) reads these registry entries to see what disks the cluster is using.

When a failover cluster is brought online (assuming one node at a time), the first disk brought online is one that will be associated the quorum model deployed. To do this, the failover cluster executes a disk arbitration algorithm to take ownership of that disk on the first node. It is first marked as offline and goes through a few checks. When the cluster is satisfied that there are no problems with the quorum, it is brought online. The same thing happens with the other disks. After all the disks come online, the Cluster Disk Driver sends periodic reservations every 3 seconds to keep ownership of the disk.

If for some reason the cluster loses communication over all of its networks, the quorum arbitration process begins. The outcome is straightforward: the node that currently owns the reservation on the quorum is the defending node. The other nodes become challengers. When a challenger detects that it cannot communicate, it issues a request to break any existing reservations it owns via a bus-wide SCSI reset in Windows Server 2003 and persistent reservation in Windows Server 2008. Seven seconds after this reset happens, the challenger attempts to gain control of the quorum. If the node that already owns the quorum is up and running, it still has the reservation of the quorum disk. The challenger cannot take ownership and it shuts down the Cluster Service. If the node that owns the quorum fails and gives up its reservation, then the challenger can take ownership after 10 seconds elapse. The challenger can reserve the quorum, bring it online, and subsequently take ownership of other resources in the cluster. If no node of the cluster can gain ownership of the quorum, the Cluster Service is stopped on all nodes.

Note both the solid and dotted lines to the shared storage shown earlier in Figure 1-1. This represents that for the clustered SQL Server instance, only one node can own the disk resources associated with that instance at time, but the other could own it should the resources be failed over to that node.

You never want to find yourself with a failover cluster scenario called *split brain*. This is when all nodes lose communication, the heartbeats no longer occur, and each node tries to become the primary node of the cluster, independent of the others. Effectively, you would have multiple nodes thinking they are the CEO of the cluster.

The Failover Process

The failover process is as follows:

1. The resource manager in failover clustering detects a problem with a specific resource.

2. Each resource has a specific number of retries within a specified window in which that resource can be brought online. The resources are brought online in dependency order. This means that resources will attempt to be brought online until the maximum number of retries in the window have been attempted. If all the resources cannot be brought online at this point, the group might come online in a partially online state with the others marked as failed; any resource that has a failed dependency will not be brought online and will remain in a failed state. However, if any resource that failed is configured to affect the resource group, things are escalated and the failover process (via the failover manager) for that resource group is initiated. If the resources are not configured to affect the group, they will be left in a failed state, leaving you with a partially online group.

3. If the failover manager is contacted, it determines based on the configuration of the resource group who the best owner will be. A new potential owner is notified, and the resource group is sent to that owner to be restarted, beginning the whole process again. If that node cannot bring the resources online, another node (assuming there are more than two nodes in the cluster) might become the owner. If no potential owner can start the resources, the resource group as a whole is left in a failed state.

4. If an entire node fails, the process is similar, except that the failover manager determines which groups were owned by the failed node, and subsequently figures out which other node(s) to send them to start again.

Figure 1-2 shows the cluster during the failover process before the clustered SQL Server instance has changed ownership.

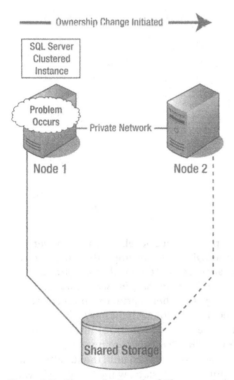

Figure 1-2. *Cluster during the failure process*

Figure 1-3 shows what a SQL Server failover cluster looks like after the instance fails over to another node. It is important to understand one thing when it comes to understanding the process of failover as it relates to SQL Server: SQL Server considers itself up and running after the master database is online. All databases go through the normal recovery process since a failover is a stop and a start of SQL Server. However, how big your transaction log is, what is in there, the size of each transaction, and so on, will impact how long it takes for each individual user database to come online. Pruning the transaction log via transaction log backups is one method to keep the number of transactions manageable in the transaction, and to also keep the size of the transaction log reasonable. If you never backed up your transaction log and are using the full or bulk-logged recovery models for that database, SQL Server will potentially go through every transaction since day one of the database's implementation when the recovery process starts.

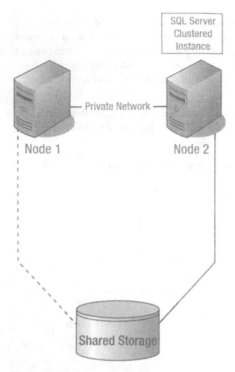

Figure 1-3. *Cluster after the failover process*

Log Shipping

Log shipping provides protection on a per-database, not a per-instance, level. Its concept is very simple: take transaction log backups from a database on one SQL Server and apply them to a copy of the database on another server. The source SQL Server instance is called the *log shipping primary* (or just *primary*), and the destination SQL Server instance is called the *log shipping secondary* (or just *secondary*). The secondary is also known as the *warm standby*. Together, a primary and secondary are known as a *log shipping pair*. There can be multiple secondaries for each primary.

To initiate the process, a full database backup that represents a point in time must be restored on the secondary using one of two options (WITH STANDBY or WITH NORECOVERY) to put the restored database into a state that allows the transaction log backup files to be applied until the standby database needs to be brought online for use. NORECOVERY is a pure loading state, while STANDBY allows read-only access to the secondary database. You can do this task manually or via the configuration wizard for the built-in log shipping feature. The process of bringing the secondary online is called a *role change* since the primary server will no longer be the main database used to serve requests. There are two types of role changes: *graceful* and *unplanned*. A graceful role change is one where you have the ability to back up the tail of the log on the primary, copy it, and apply it to the secondary. An unplanned role change is when you lose access to the primary and you need to bring your secondary online. Since you were not able to grab the tail of the log, you may encounter some data loss.

If you implement log shipping using the built-in feature of SQL Server 2008, it utilizes three SQL Server Agent jobs: the transaction log backup job on the primary, the copy job on the secondary, and the restore job on the secondary.

TERMINOLOGY: ROLE CHANGE VS. FAILOVER

A pet peeve of mine is the use of the word *failover* for the process of changing from one instance to another for log shipping. To me, *failover* implies something more automatic. There is a reason different SQL Server technologies have different terminology. If you think about the way log shipping works, you really are switching places, or roles, of the servers. I know many of you will still use the term *failover* in conjunction with log shipping and I won't be able to change it, but I felt I had to say my piece on this subject.

After the secondary database is initialized, all subsequent transaction log backups from the primary can be copied and applied to the secondary. Whether this process is manual or automatic depends on your configuration for log shipping. The transaction logs must be applied in order. Assuming the process is manual, the secondary will only be a short time behind the primary in terms of data. The log shipping flow is shown in Figure 1-4.

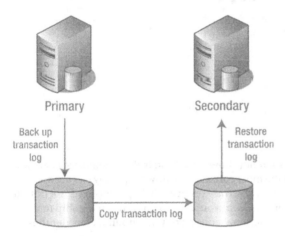

Figure 1-4. *Log shipping flow*

Improvements to Log Shipping in SQL Server 2008

The only major change to log shipping in SQL Server 2008 is the support for backup compression, as shown and highlighted in Figure 1-5. Backup compression is a feature of Enterprise Edition only, but you can restore a compressed backup generated by Enterprise Edition on any other edition of SQL Server 2008. That means you can configure log shipping from a primary that is Enterprise Edition to a secondary that is Standard Edition, while taking advantage of all the benefits (smaller files, shorter copy times) that come along with compression. Outside of this, log shipping is the same as it was in SQL Server 2005, so Chapter 10 of *Pro SQL Server 2005 High Availability* will still be useful to you should you own that book.

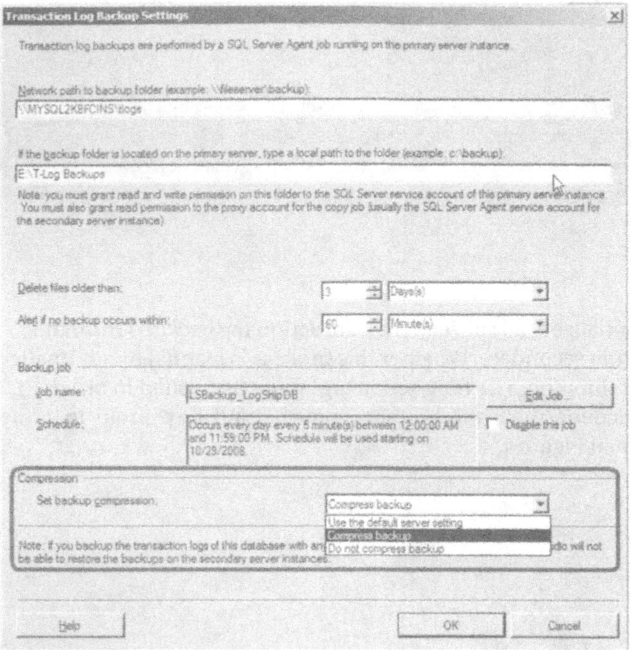

Figure 1-5. *New compression option in log shipping*

Log Shipping Timeline

One concern many have around log shipping is latency: how far behind is the secondary? There are numerous factors affecting latency, but some of the most common are how frequently you are backing up your transaction log, copying it to the secondary, and then restoring it. Log shipping is not bound by any distance, so as long as your network supports what you want to do, you can log ship to a server all the way around the planet. From a transactional consistency standpoint, consider these four transaction "states":

- *The last transaction completed on the primary database*: This transaction may just have been written to the primary database's transaction log, but not backed up yet. Therefore, if disaster strikes at this moment, this newly committed transaction may be lost if a final transaction log backup cannot be generated and copied to the secondary.

- *The last transaction log backed up for that database*: This transaction log backup would be the newest point in time that a secondary database could be restored to, but it may not have been copied or applied to the secondary database. If disaster strikes this server before this transaction log backup can be copied (automatically or manually), any transactions included in it may be lost if the server containing the primary database cannot be revived.

- *The last transaction log backup copied from the primary instance to the secondary instance*: This transaction log backup may not be the newest transaction log generated, which would mean that there is a delta between this copied transaction log backup and the latest transaction log backup available for being copied on the primary. This newly copied transaction log backup may not yet have been applied to the secondary. Until it is applied, the secondary will remain at a larger delta between the primary and the secondary.

- *The last transaction log backup restored to the database on the secondary.* This is the actual point in time that the secondary has been restored to. Depending on which transaction log backup was next in line, it could be closer or farther away from the primary database.

Take the example of a database that has log shipping configured with automated processes. There is a job that backs up the transaction log every 5 minutes and takes 2 minutes to perform. Another process runs every 10 minutes to copy any transaction logs generated, and on average takes 4 minutes. On the secondary, a process runs every 10 minutes to restore any transaction logs that are waiting. Each transaction log takes 3.5 minutes to restore. Based on this configuration, a sample timeline is shown in Table 1-1.

Table 1-1. *Log Shipping Timeline Example*

Time	Action Performed on Server 1	Action Performed on or for Server 2
10:00 a.m.	Transaction log 1 backed up	
10:02 a.m.	Transaction log 1 backup complete	
10:05 a.m.	Transaction log 2 backed up	
10:07 a.m.	Transaction log 2 backup complete	
10:10 a.m.	Transaction log 3 backed up	Transaction logs 1 and 2 copied to the secondary
10:12 a.m.	Transaction log 3 backup complete	
10:14 a.m.		Copy of transaction logs 1 and 2 complete
10:15 a.m.	Transaction log 4 backed up	
10:17 a.m.	Transaction log 4 backup complete	
10:20 a.m.	Transaction log 5 backed up	Transaction log 1 restore begins; copy of transaction logs 3 and 4 begins
10:22 a.m.	Transaction log 5 backup complete	
10:24 a.m.		Transaction log 1 restore complete; copy of transaction logs 3 and 4 complete; transaction log 2 restore started
10:25 a.m.	Transaction log 6 backed up	

What this example translates into is that the secondary will be approximately 24 minutes behind the one on the primary, even though you are backing up your transaction logs every 5 minutes. The reason for this is that you need to take into account not only the actual times the automated jobs run, but how long each one takes to complete. An example of this would be that the copy process is affected by such issues as network speed and the speed of the disks at both the primary and the secondary. This timeline demonstrates one important point around latency and log shipping: if your SLA dictates that you can only have 5 minutes of data loss, just doing transaction log backups every 5 minutes will not get you there. If that SLA requires that another database has those transactions and is considered up to date, there's much more you have to do to meet that SLA.

Earlier I mentioned that there was one major change in SQL Server 2008's implementation of log shipping: backup compression. This is technically true. However, a big change in SQL Server 2008 is that a job can now be scheduled with a timing of seconds as well (not just hours and minutes). This change is huge, but don't get too excited: the same limitations apply as they would if you were doing minutes or hours. It would be unrealistic to think that you can actually generate a transaction log backup in under a minute consistently on a heavily used database unless you had some extremely fast disk subsystems. The same could be said for the copy and restore processes. Here are the considerations for doing subminute log shipping:

- If you set the transaction log backup job to run every 10 seconds, the next execution will not start until the previous one is complete.

- You run the risk of filling the error log in SQL Server with a ton of "backup completed" messages. While this can be worked around by using trace flag 3226, if you enable that trace flag, you will suppress all messages denoting a successful backup message; failures will still be written. This is not something you want to do in a mission-critical environment where you need to know if backups were made or not, since not only will they not be written to the SQL Server logs, but the messages will also not appear in the Windows event log.

- msdb will grow faster and larger than expected because of the frequent backup information that is being stored. This can be pruned with sp_delete_backuphistory, but again, that information may prove useful and be needed.

- If you do subminute transaction log backups or restores in conjunction with backup compression, you may adversely affect CPU utilization. The SQL Server Customer Advisory Team has written two blog entries that address how to tune performance with backup compression in SQL Server 2008 (see http://sqlcat.com/technicalnotes/archive/2008/04/21/tuning-the-performance-of-backup-compression-in-sql-server-2008.aspx and http://sqlcat.com/technicalnotes/archive/2009/02/16/tuning-backup-compression-part-2.aspx).

Best Uses for Log Shipping

There are a few scenarios that best fit the use of log shipping. Not all may be applicable in your environment.

Disaster Recovery and High Availability

The most common use for log shipping is in disaster recovery. Log shipping is a relatively inexpensive way of creating a copy of your database in a remote location without having to worry about getting tied into a specific hardware configuration or SQL Server edition. Considerations such as network latency and the ability to redirect your application to the new database server, as well as your SLAs, will dictate how effective your disaster recovery solution is, but this has been log shipping's main use over the years, going back to version 4.21a of SQL Server. It was not until SQL Server 2000 Enterprise Edition that Microsoft made log shipping an official feature of the SQL Server engine. All prior implementations were either homegrown or utilized the version that Microsoft provided with the old BackOffice Resource Kit quite a few years ago.

Log shipping is also a very effective high-availability solution for those who can only use a low-tech solution (for whatever reason). I know some of you are probably saying to yourselves that log shipping is not a high-availability solution since there is a lot of latency. But not everyone has the budget, need, or expertise to deploy other technologies to make their databases available.

I would argue that most people out there who started with log shipping employed it in a high-availability capacity. Log shipping certainly is not the equivalent of a supermodel you drool over, but may be much more attractive in other ways. It is for the most part "set and forget," and has very little overhead in terms of administration outside of monitoring the transaction log backups and restores.

One of the things that isn't mentioned a lot with log shipping is that it can help out with the "fat finger" problem (i.e., when someone does something stupid and screws up the data in the database), or if database corruption gets into the data. Since the transaction log loads are done on a periodic/delayed basis, if the errors are caught, they may not make it to the standby server.

Intrusive Database Maintenance

Assuming that you have no issues with your application after a role change, and the secondary has enough capacity to handle the performance needed, another possible use of log shipping is to create your warm standby and switch to it when you need to perform maintenance on your primary database. This would allow minimal interruption to end users in a 24/7 environment. For example, if reindexing your 30-million-row table takes 2 hours on the primary, but a log shipping role change only takes 10 minutes (assuming you are up to date in terms of restoring transaction logs), what sounds better to you? Having the application unavailable for 2 hours, or 10 minutes? Most people would say 10 minutes. This does mean that you will be switching servers, and you may need to have a mechanism for switching back to the primary database at some point, since the primary database should be optimized for performance after the index rebuild. In this case, you would also need a process to get the data delta from the secondary back into the primary. At the end of the day, users do not care about where the data lives; you do. They only care about accessing their information in a timely manner. Log shipping may be too much hassle and work for some to consider for this role, but for others it may be a lifesaver where SLAs are very tight.

Tip To avoid having to reinitialize log shipping if you want to make the original primary the primary again, make sure that you make the last transaction log backup, or tail of the log, before the role change using the WITH NORECOVERY clause of BACKUP LOG. If this is done, log shipping can be configured in reverse, and any transaction log backups from the new primary (the former secondary) can be applied. If NORECOVERY is set via a final transaction log backup, the database will not be in an online state, so you could not use this feature to assist with intrusive database maintenance.

Migrations and Upgrades

My favorite use of log shipping is to facilitate a server move or upgrade a SQL Server database from one version to another when you are log shipping from old hardware to new hardware. It is possible to restore a full backup as well as subsequent transaction log backups from a previous version of SQL Server (2000 and 2005) to SQL Server 2008. The reason this works so well is that you can start the process at any given point before the switch to the new hardware. At some point, you stop all traffic going to the primary, take the last transaction log backup, make sure it is copied and applied to the secondary, recover the database, and do whatever else you need to do (such as redirecting the application) to make that new database a full copy of your current production database. The switch itself should take under 10 minutes, assuming your transaction logs are caught up.

There are two big pluses of doing a migration or upgrade this way: first, it provides a fallback/backout plan where you can go back to your old configuration; and second, you can start the process way before you do the actual switch—that is why it only takes about 10 minutes of planned downtime during your upgrade. Other methods, including using the upgrade that is part of the SQL Server setup, may have much greater actual downtime, measured in hours. You can take your full backup, restore it on the new hardware, and start log shipping hours, days, or months in advance of your actual cutover date. What is even better is that the process is based on the tried-and-true method of backup and restore; there is no fancy technology to understand. As the log shipping applies the actual transactions, this also helps test the newer version for compatibility with your application during your run-up to the failover. A log shipping–based migration or upgrade is not for every scenario, but there are very few I have found where it is not applicable.

USING LOG SHIPPING AS A REPORTING SOLUTION

One of the questions I am asked the most when it comes to log shipping is, "Can I use the secondary as a reporting database?" Technically, if you restore the secondary database using WITH STANDBY, which allows read-only access while still allowing transaction log loads, you can. You can also stick a fork in your eye, but it does not make it a superb idea. Since sticking a fork in your eye will most likely cause you permanent damage, I would even go so far as to say it is a dumb idea and the pain you will feel is not worth whatever momentary curiosity you are satisfying. Similarly, I would tell you that thinking you can use a log-shipped database for reporting will cause great pain for your end users.

Another huge consideration for using log shipping as a reporting solution is licensing. According to Microsoft's rules for a standby server (http://www.microsoft.com/sqlserver/2008/en/us/licensing-faq.aspx), "Keeping a passive server for failover purposes does not require a license as long as the passive server has the same or fewer processors than the active server (under the per-processor scenario). In the event of a failover, a 30-day grace period is allowed to restore and run SQL Server on the original active server." If you use that secondary for any *active* use, it must fully be licensed. That could mean considerable cost to the business. As a pure availability or disaster recovery solution, log shipping will not cost you anything (up to the stated 30 days).

A reporting solution is supposed to be available for use. To be able to use the secondary for reporting, as part of your transaction log loading process, you need to make sure that all users are kicked out of the database. Restoring transaction log backups requires exclusive access to the database. If you do not kick the users out, the transaction log backups will not be applied and your data will be old (and most likely leave you exposed from an availability perspective, since you are most likely using the secondary for disaster recovery or high availability). If you can tolerate a larger delta for availability and less frequent data (i.e., not close to real time), you could technically choose to queue the transaction log backups and apply them once a day (say, at midnight). That would have minimal impact on end users, but may not be optimal for availability.

Consider the example with the timeline shown in Table 1-1 earlier in this chapter. Every 10 minutes, transaction logs will be restored, and take 3.5 minutes on average. That leaves 6.5 minutes out of those 10 that the database is available for reporting. Multiply that by 6, and you get at best 39 minutes of reporting per hour if you are only loading one transaction log backup per 10-minute interval. Most likely you will have much less availability for reporting, since you may want to set the restore job to run more frequently than every 10 minutes to ensure that the secondary is more up to date in the event of a failure. Does that sound like an ideal reporting solution to you?

If you want to use log shipping as a reporting solution, knock yourself out. It can work. But I bet you could come up with a better alternative.

Combining Failover Clustering and Log Shipping

Combining log shipping with failover clustering is arguably the most common configuration I have seen for years at customer sites, and looks something like Figure 1-6.

Until database mirroring was introduced in SQL Server 2005, it was my favorite solution, and continues to remain a no-brainer, even though database mirroring is available. The only caveat to take into account is that if your primary and/or secondary are failover clustering instances, the locations where transaction log backups are made on the primary and then copied to and restored from on the secondary must reside on one of the shared disks associated with their respective instances. Other than that, log shipping should "just work"—and that is what you want. It is based on technology (backup and restore, copying files) that is easy to grasp. There's no magic. One of the reasons that log shipping is so popular with clustered deployments of SQL Server is that it may also balance out the cost of buying the cluster, which can be considerable for some, depending on the implementation. And why not? You have to back up your databases anyway, and chances are you have to do transaction log backups, so it is a natural fit.

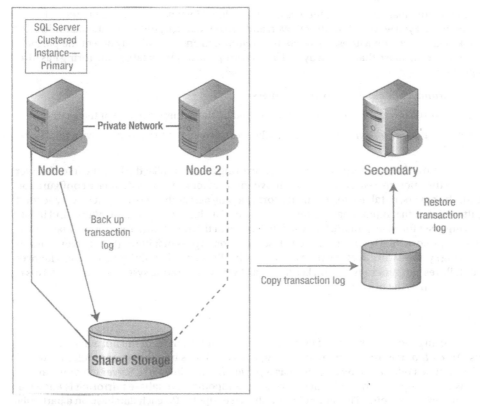

Figure 1-6. *Failover clustering with log shipping*

Database Mirroring

Like log shipping, database mirroring provides protection on a per-database, not a per-instance, level. The easiest way to describe database mirroring is that it is transactional replication meets log shipping, with a touch of clustering thrown in for good measure. Similar to log shipping, you take a point-in-time backup of your database and restore it using WITH NORECOVERY to put it in a state that will allow it to load transactions. Restoring the mirror database using WITH STANDBY is not supported. Database mirroring does not work by sending individual transaction log backups—it sends each individual transaction log record to the standby database, which is transactional replication-like behavior. Therefore, anything written to the source database's transaction log will be applied to the copy of the database on the other server. The action of sending transaction log records can happen synchronously or asynchronously. The switch to the other database can happen either manually or automatically, depending on your configuration. Like log shipping, you can only mirror user databases, not system databases. Unlike log shipping, mirroring is a one-to-one affair: one source database to a single mirrored database.

Most of the terminology for database mirroring is different from the other SQL Server availability technologies. You have a source database, or the *principal*, that then sends the transaction log records to the *mirror*, which is the target database. The instance with the principal and the instance with the mirror are *partners* in a *database mirroring session*. One significant difference from log shipping is that the relationship between the principal database and the mirror database is a one-to-one ratio—you cannot have multiple mirrors for every principal.

Besides the principal and mirror, there is a third optional instance, named the *witness*. The witness is required if you want automatic failover, and can be shared by different database mirroring sessions. Like clustering, the witness helps create a *quorum* to ensure that only one of the partners currently owns the database that is used by end users and applications. Database mirroring has three types of quorum:

- *Full quorum*: A principal, mirror, and witness

- *Witness-to-partner quorum*: Quorum established by the witness and one of the partners

- *Partner-to-partner quorum*: Quorum established between the two partners, with no witness involved

The quorum mechanisms used by database mirroring are not unlike the heartbeat for failover clustering, and the quorum assists during the failover process for a mirrored database configuration. Underneath the covers, database mirroring performs a ping across the network once every second. The default setting is that if ten pings are returned as missed, this is considered a failure, and if database mirroring is set for an automatic failover, it will occur at this point. Otherwise, a manual failover will need to be performed. However, as you will see, different types of failures (SQL Server or hardware/operating system) will affect the time required—it will not necessarily be a 10-second failover. SQL Server failures can generally be quicker than hardware or operating system failures in terms of the ability to switch to the mirror.

Endpoints

Database mirroring requires the use of endpoints that are different from the normal instance endpoints. An *endpoint* is an object created by SQL Server that is bound to a particular network protocol (sometimes referred to by Microsoft as a *payload*) that allows SQL Server to communicate on your network to applications and other servers. An endpoint for database mirroring is known as a *database mirroring endpoint*. This endpoint is a shared endpoint for each database on a particular SQL Server instance, so once it is configured, until you change it, all databases that will use database mirroring will use the same endpoint. The database mirroring endpoint is used for SQL Server–to–SQL Server communication, and that communication uses TCP/IP exclusively. The endpoint must have a port number that is different from that of any other TCP/IP service on the server. This functions not unlike the cluster private network in a failover clustering configuration.

Improvements to Database Mirroring in SQL Server 2008

There are two major improvements in SQL Server 2008's implementation of database mirroring: log compression and automatic page repair. With SQL Server 2005, it was more difficult to scale database mirroring due to the amount of traffic it potentially put on your network (load dependent, of course). SQL Server 2008 (Enterprise or Standard Edition) compresses the log stream between the principal and the mirror. The new compression ability will not solve underlying networking issues, but it will certainly help reduce contention, since there will be less traffic on the network from database mirroring.

If you've ever seen 823, 824, or 829 errors—which are usually related to data corruption—when using database mirroring, you know that dealing with those can be a frustrating experience. SQL Server 2008 introduces automatic page repair. That means that if a page is detected to be corrupted at either the principal or mirror, SQL Server will attempt to repair that page with the copy of the page (mirror or principal) on the other end of the wire. Unlike executing DBCC CHECKDB with the option REPAIR_ALLOW_DATA_LOSS, the automatic page repair feature actually results in no data loss. However, you should still investigate the underlying issue, as it may be indicative of a hardware problem that must be resolved. If it is a hardware problem, the automatic page repair in SQL Server is more like a Band-Aid, not a permanent solution.

One thing that should be mentioned in this section is the filestream data type. Filestream is another new feature of SQL Server 2008. It is a new data type that can be used for a database schema. Unfortunately, database mirroring does not support databases that use the filestream data type.

Transaction Safety

Database mirroring introduces the concept of transaction safety. Transaction safety controls if a database mirroring session is synchronous or asynchronous. There are two ways this can be set: FULL (synchronous) and OFF (asynchronous). The value for transaction safety controls which mode will be used by the database mirroring session. The default value is FULL.

Mirroring State

A database participating in database mirroring can have one of the following *mirroring states*, or statuses:

- SYNCHRONIZING: This is when the mirror is not caught up to the principal. This status is most commonly seen when database mirroring is first started and is in high-performance mode, as described in the next section.

- SYNCHRONIZED: This is when the mirror is caught up to, or nearly caught up to, the principal. Your transaction safety setting will govern whether there may be data loss. If your transaction safety is set to FULL, there will be no data loss. If it is set to OFF, there is the potential for data loss.

- SUSPENDED: This means that the mirror is unavailable and is not receiving transactions from the principal.

- PENDING_FAILOVER: This state will only occur once a failover from the principal to the mirror is initiated and before the mirror becomes the new primary.

- DISCONNECTED: This is when one partner cannot connect to the other partner.

Database Mirroring Modes

There are two modes for database mirroring: *high-performance* and *high-safety*. Both are related to the combination of the safety level set for the mirroring session and whether a witness is required.

High-Performance Mode

High-performance mode of database mirroring is simply mirroring asynchronously. This means that any transactions created on the principal will not necessarily be immediately applied to the mirror. This is much like log shipping, where there is a delta between the primary and the secondary. If you are mirroring asynchronously, you will see better performance and arguably less overhead, but you are trading some availability for that performance. High-performance mode requires that transaction safety has a value of OFF. It is important to note that high-performance mode is only supported if you deploy SQL Server 2008 Enterprise Edition.

The witness serves no purpose in high-performance mode—only the principal and mirror are needed. In fact, adding the witness to a high-performance mode configuration will add risk since its addition to this setup will enforce quorum, which requires two or more SQL Server instances. I would not use a witness in a high-performance scenario, as it provides no value. If quorum is lost, there are two scenarios: when the principal is down, you will only be able to manually force the mirror to become the new primary if it can connect to the witness; and when the mirror is down, the principal will be taken offline if it cannot connect to the witness. Therefore, it makes no sense to configure a witness with high-performance mode.

The sequence of events that happens in high-performance mode is as follows, and is represented in Figure 1-7:

1. An application or end user submits a transaction for the principal, and SQL Server writes that transaction to the transaction log file.

2. SQL Server commits the data on the principal and acknowledges to the application or end user that it "has" the transaction.

3. The principal contacts the mirror, and the transaction is sent.

4. The transaction is written to the transaction log of the mirror.

5. The mirror "handshakes" with the principal to acknowledge that the mirror has the transaction.

6. The data is committed on the mirror.

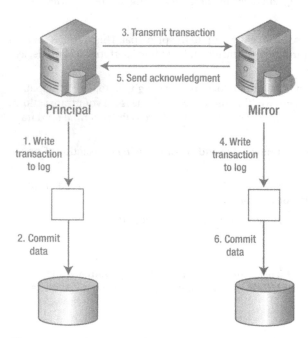

Figure 1-7. *High-performance mode database mirroring*

As you may have already deduced, the process is a variant of a two-phase commit where you have the possibility of incurring data loss. A *two-phase commit* is a transaction initiated by a host that waits for acknowledgement from the receiver before it is completed.

High-performance mode works similarly to log shipping. You are only as current as the last transaction sent from the principal, committed, and then acknowledged on the mirror. Depending on factors such as your network, distance, and disk speed, the latency could be a subsecond response or something much larger than that.

Since high-performance mode does not support automatic failover, you have three options if the principal is unavailable:

- Assuming nothing catastrophic has happened on the principal, you can wait for it to come back online (e.g., if someone has just rebooted it after performing normal maintenance).

- If something has happened to the principal database itself, but the instance that is home to the principal has no damage, you can reinitialize database mirroring by restoring the database from backups.

- You can force the mirror to become the new primary. The mirroring state should be DISCONNECTED or SUSPENDED to allow this to happen. You may lose some data in the process.

High-Safety Mode

High-safety mode is when database mirroring is operating synchronously. The process is similar to high-performance mode, except that this is a "proper" two-phase commit: the transaction cannot be committed on the principal until it has been committed on the mirror as well. This ensures both partners are completely in sync. High-safety mode requires the use of an instance to contain the witness if you want an automatic failover.

The sequence of events that happens in high-safety mode is as follows and is represented in Figure 1-8:

1. An application or end user submits a transaction for the principal, and SQL Server writes that transaction to the transaction log file on the principal.

2. The principal contacts the mirror, and the transaction is written to the transaction log of the mirror.

3. The mirror "handshakes" with the principal to acknowledge that the mirror has the transaction.

4. SQL Server acknowledges to the application or end user that SQL Server "has" the transaction.

5. SQL Server commits the data on the principal.

6. SQL Server commits the data on the mirror.

Like failover clustering, high-safety mode can support automatic failover from the principal to the mirror if it is configured to do so. This requires not only that the mirror database is synchronized, but that the witness and mirror are still connected when the failure on the principal occurs. Once the automatic failover occurs, the mirror is the new principal database, and when or if the principal comes back online, it will assume the mirror role. If the principal and witness are lost, you will have to force the mirror to become the primary database.

The automatic failover time should take less than 30 seconds in most cases, but it depends on a few factors. The first is when the failure is detected on the principal. This is governed by the database mirroring TIMEOUT value, which defaults to 10 seconds. However, depending on the failure (such as a disk failure on the principal), this may actually take longer than the value specified for TIMEOUT. If the witness cannot get the principal to respond in the time set by TIMEOUT, it is considered to be down. The next factor is ensuring that the principal and mirror are in sync. If they are, there will be no transactions to roll forward on the mirror when the redo process begins to bring the database online. If there are transactions to roll forward, they will be applied and will take as long as necessary to complete. If the principal comes online before the redo phase completes, the mirror does not assume the principal role. Once the mirror is designated as the principal, all incomplete transactions are rolled back and the database comes online.

If the witness is lost in high-safety mode, you lose the ability to do an automatic failover, and there is no impact on the application or client. The principal will continue on as if nothing happened.

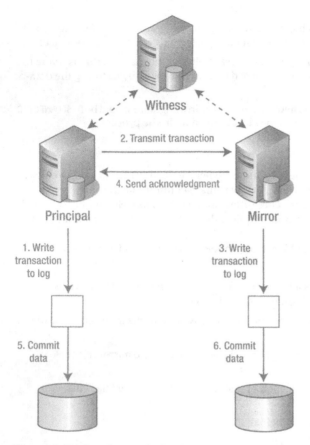

Figure 1-8. *High-safety mode database mirroring*

■Tip You may want to consider implementing high-safety database mirroring to use a dedicated private network for its traffic. When creating your endpoints, you can specify the LISTENER_IP to force database mirroring to use a specific endpoint to listen on.

Best Uses for Database Mirroring

There are a few scenarios that best fit the use of database mirroring. Not all may be applicable in your environment.

Disaster Recovery and High Availability

Database mirroring supports disaster recovery since it is not bound by distance or a specialized configuration, and it supports high availability when you are in the same data center. Synchronous database mirroring can assist in cases where your SLAs dictate that there is minimal data loss and very little downtime. Asynchronous database mirroring may work in situations where some data loss could be accepted and the overall SLA is not as tight in terms of time.

Migration to New Hardware

Database mirroring can facilitate moving from one server to another when both are using the same edition and version of SQL Server. That means you cannot mirror from SQL Server 2005 to SQL Server 2008 or vice versa, nor can you mirror from Standard to Enterprise. Assuming the proper conditions, if you configure server A as the principal and server B as the mirror, at some designated point you can stop all traffic to server A and then manually fail over to the mirror.

Reporting

Database mirroring was designed to take into account the desire to have a place to potentially do some reporting, unlike log shipping. To use database mirroring as a reporting database, you can create a database snapshot with SQL Server on the mirrored database. This is a point-in-time snapshot, so if you would need updated data, you will need to drop and re-create the snapshot if you need to keep the same name for the snapshot. So you still need a process to automate the snapshot recreation.

There is a big caveat to using database mirroring for reporting. As noted earlier, if you use the server that is technically for a high availability/disaster recovery purpose as an active server for reporting, you must fully license the server and instance containing the mirror and the snapshot. It is up to you to determine if this cost is worth the price of admission.

Combining Failover Clustering and Database Mirroring

While failover clustering and database mirroring complement each other, there are some things you should look out for. The main problem with using database mirroring for a database in a clustered instance of SQL Server is that if you are using high-safety mode and have automatic failover set up for mirroring, database mirroring may wind up conflicting with the failover mechanism for the cluster. This happens because if the instance itself must fail over to another node, mirroring may detect the problem and fail that particular database to the mirror. This behavior is not what most people want. The desired scenario is that the failover of the instance should occur, and if the instance cannot come online in the cluster, only then do you want mirroring to pick up the slack. If this is what you want to achieve, you will most likely have to set database mirroring to not allow an automatic switch to the mirror (i.e., no witness).

There is one potential way to avoid database mirroring kicking in first using high-safety mode with automatic failover for both the failover cluster and database mirroring. Database mirroring has a TIMEOUT value (described earlier), which is the number of seconds that must consecutively fail by the ping process from the mirror to the principal for the automatic failover process to be initiated. The default value is 10 seconds. If you change the default PARTNER TIMEOUT value to be something larger than the time it takes for the instance to complete the failover process to another node, database mirroring will not kick in first. This means that you must test how long it takes to fail the instance from one node to another under load. To change the value, use the command ALTER DATABASE dbname SET PARTNER TIMEOUT x, where x is a valid number of seconds. To see the value currently set, execute SELECT [mirroring_connection_timeout] FROM master.sys.database_mirroring WHERE [database_id] = DB_ID ('dbname'). I generally do not recommend doing this because the failover time for the instance may change depending on what is going on prior to the failure that initiated the failover in the cluster.

Additionally, when you are configuring your endpoints, and one or both of the instances participating in database mirroring are configured as clusters, remember to use the clustered IP address, not one of the IP addresses from the nodes. If you are using name resolution such as a DNS server, this will not apply, but it is something to keep in mind. Figure 1-9 shows what this architecture may look like.

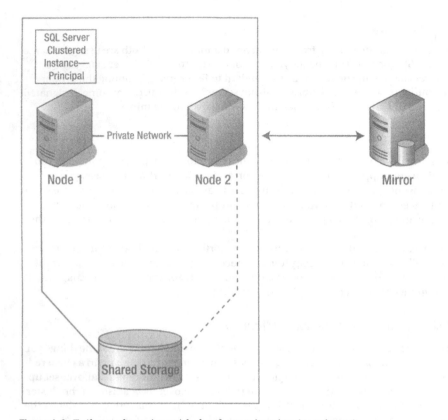

Figure 1-9. *Failover clustering with database mirroring (no witness)*

This combination is starting to emerge as a popular choice, since your remote data center will be potentially synchronized with your principal database at a fairly low cost. Either this configuration or failover clustering with log shipping will most likely be your starting point for combination high-availability/disaster recovery solutions.

Replication

Simply put, replication allows you to take some of your data and make it available elsewhere. Replication works at a data level. There are three main types of replication within SQL Server:

- Snapshot
- Merge
- Transactional

Each of these types of replication has the same common components: a Publisher, a Distributor, and one or more Subscribers. The *Publisher* is your source database that has a *publication* and a set of *articles* (the actual selections of data that will be replicated) defined on it to denote what data will be published to the *Subscribers* of that data. The *subscription* that the Subscriber uses can be either *push* or *pull*, meaning data can be sent from the Publisher to the Subscriber, or the Subscriber can grab the data itself. The *Distributor* keeps track of the subscriptions and is the hub for the activity between the Publisher and the Subscriber. In reality, each of these components may not be separate servers. For example, some replication architectures will have the Publisher and Distributor configured on the same SQL Server instance. For discussion purposes, treat them as different bits of functionality.

As part of its configuration, replication configures various SQL Server Agent jobs, and some forms of replication create triggers on the Publisher to capture when changes occur to the data in the publication database. The reason I mention this is that as a DBA, you will have to be aware of what is added to each SQL Server instance participating in replication. Objects such as triggers can certainly affect the overall performance of your database and the instance containing it. If you have a very heavily used OLTP database with many inserts, you have to account for the overhead of replication in the sizing of your server; otherwise, you may have serious problems down the road.

Replication is similar to log shipping and database mirroring since it offers some protection on a per-database level. With database mirroring and log shipping, you get everything that hits the transaction log at the standby server; with replication, you generally only get what data is defined in the publication. This may be all the data in a table or a database (assuming it does not exceed any limitations of replication), but there is no guarantee (e.g., if a subscription exceeds the row limit size for a particular form of replication). It is usually only possible to replicate a subset of data from a table or a database, which is really all you should strive to do anyway. The ability to be much more focused and deliver a granular set of data to a standby server can be a very helpful feature, but it may not be right for you. When disaster strikes and you need to have business continuity, replication is a great way to make crucial data available elsewhere to allow the business to run while you are solving the bigger issue. On the flip side, if you need your entire database at your standby site, replication is not the best or most efficient way to go about achieving that goal; database mirroring and log shipping are far better technologies for that.

Caution Never update or change objects such as the triggers configured during replication unless directed to by Microsoft. I know many people out there do so, but you will not only be in an unsupported position if you need support, you will also need to maintain whatever customizations you deploy. If replication doesn't do what you want, maybe it is the wrong technology for you. Think about it.

Snapshot Replication

Snapshot replication completely refreshes the data of the Subscriber each time a push or pull occurs (according to the subscription that is configured). If any data is updated at the Subscriber, it will be completely overwritten when the snapshot is republished to the Subscriber. Snapshot replication is not for those who need to update data at the Subscriber.

Snapshot replication is generally helpful where data changes infrequently, and it is easier to refresh everything instead of just a portion of it. Snapshot replication is also ideal when a database changes so much that it is easier to refresh the Subscriber periodically, and the in-between changes are not needed sooner. A good example of the use of snapshot replication is a catalog for an online e-commerce site. Since this database is read-only, you could do a full refresh at a scheduled time each day across all instances.

Arguably, the most important use of snapshot replication is to seed the other forms of replication via the initial snapshot. While there are other methods by which this can be achieved in some cases, even if you are using merge or transactional replication, chances are you may use snapshot replication in some way.

When it comes to availability, snapshot replication will most likely not be appropriate unless you have a small dataset and refresh frequently enough to meet your SLAs. Since each push and pull is a one-off, there is a lot of autonomy on both sides, and there could be a large delta between the

Publisher and the Subscriber. The whole goal of availability is to have small deltas of difference. Keep in mind that pushing a snapshot of an entire published database will put quite a resource hit on both Publisher and Subscriber, and may take some time to complete. If you have the option available to you, and the servers participating in replication are attached to the same storage unit, using a hardware-based solution such as a split mirror to initialize via the snapshot may be worth it. The hardware configuration would take time and planning, and would not be an inexpensive option.

Figure 1-10 shows the architecture for snapshot replication.

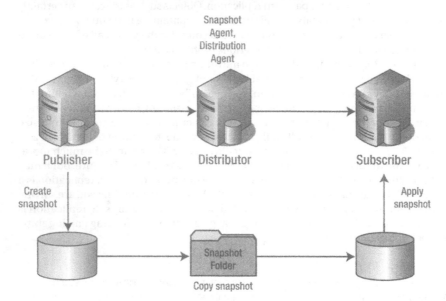

Figure 1-10. *Snapshot replication architecture*

Merge Replication

Merge replication is slightly different from snapshot replication. After the initial subscription is in place, you replicate only the changes made, and you can schedule the interval at which those changes are pushed to or pulled by the Subscriber. In this way, merge replication is not unlike a differential backup or applying incremental transaction logs. However, one main difference is that with merge replication, you do have the possibility of updating Subscribers along with the ability to take advantage of conflict resolution.

Merge replication works when a transaction occurs at the Publisher or Subscriber; that change is written to change-tracking tables by utilizing triggers. The merge agent checks those change-tracking tables. Distribution only stores synchronization history and tracking information in the case of merge replication. If you have a very high-use OLTP system, there could be a fair amount of overhead associated with merge replication due to the triggers and tracking tables involved.

It is not a requirement of deploying merge replication that the Subscribers have the ability to update data. Merge replication can be a one-way send of data from the Publisher to the Subscriber. Clearly, a one-way data send is a much easier topology to deal with. However, the ability to have autonomous Subscribers (who are in turn Publishers of data back to the central server, which would be a Subscriber to the data; these are also known as *republishers*) can be very beneficial in an availability scenario.

Let's look at an example in which bidirectional merge replication is a benefit. You have a retail store with 1,000 locations across North America. There is a central data warehouse that has all the data from all the stores. Each local retail store has a scaled-down version of that database with all of the relevant lookup and company data, and the store's local sales information. This architecture allows each individual store to be autonomous in its operation. An individual store is not dependent on the home office (or other stores) for anything other than updates. Periodically during the day, each store sends updated sales figures and other information to the central server. In the event that the central server fails and has a total meltdown, not only can the data be reconstructed from the data in each store, but the largest portion of the business—the retail outlets serving customers nearly 12 hours a day—is unaffected and is able to keep going despite the outage.

If you are updating data, merge replication provides a mechanism to deal with data conflicts. You need to set up rules that define whether a change made at the Subscriber and sent back to the Publisher will be resolved and allowed. There is a great explanation of this in the SQL Server Books Online article "How Merge Replication Detects and Resolves Conflicts" (see http://msdn.microsoft.com/en-us/library/ms151749.aspx). Conflict detection and resolution occur either by the default conflict detection in SQL Server, or a custom component coded by you in managed code. Many customers write their own conflict resolution code since the rules are very specific to their business. Custom conflict resolution is the most powerful feature of merge replication because you can author any conflict resolution logic you can think of. In practice, implementing custom conflict resolution logic is not straightforward. If you need it, conflict resolution can provide a ton of flexibility since transactional replication is limited to three choices in case of a conflict (Publisher wins, Subscriber wins, or log an error and let a human resolve it).

Figure 1-11 shows the architecture for merge replication.

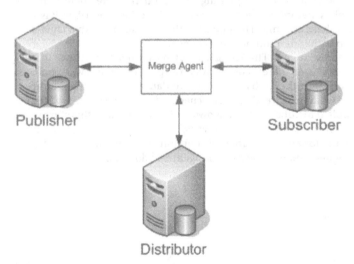

Figure 1-11. *Merge replication architecture*

Transactional Replication

Transactional replication is arguably the most popular form of replication, especially when it comes to availability. It is also the most granular and gives you the lowest latency and often the best throughput. Like its feature name, transactional replication replicates the data from the Publisher to the Subscriber each time a transaction completes at the Publisher. If you have a very high-use OLTP system, this could add significant overhead to your instance, which you would need to take into account. There are other impacts to the publication database, such as the inability to truncate/back up the transaction log until the transaction is written to the Distributor.

When the transaction is written to the transaction log, the log reader agent reads it from the transaction log and writes it to the distribution database. The distribution agent will then be aware of the new data, which will either be pushed to or pulled by the Subscriber.

Figure 1-12 shows the architecture for transactional replication.

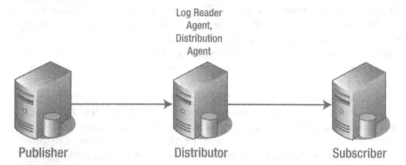

Figure 1-12. *Transactional replication architecture*

Updateable Subscriptions

Like merge replication, you can also have Subscribers that can update data. The two main types of updateable subscriptions are ones that do immediate updating and ones that queue updates. *Immediate* updating is exactly what it implies: before the data change is made at the Subscriber, it is sent back to the Publisher through a two-phase commit. The Publisher then redistributes that change to other Subscribers, including the Subscriber that initiated the change.

Queued updating Subscribers allow latency. The Publisher and Subscriber do not have to be connected. Updates are queued and sent when there is connectivity. The problem comes with conflicts. Since the process can be asynchronous, another Subscriber could update the data in the interim. The data that is sent would overwrite what was already sent. Queued updating Subscribers work best if the transactional replication is applied to Subscribers that own their own data and therefore work within the available conflict resolution choice of "Subscriber wins."

Figure 1-13 shows the architecture for an updateable subscription with immediate updates. Immediate updates use MSDTC. Queued updates use a queue agent and do not use MSDTC.

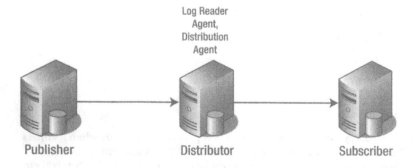

Figure 1-13. *Updateable subscription with immediate updates*

Bidirectional Transactional Replication

Bidirectional transactional replication is a specific form of transactional replication that allows both the Publisher and the Subscriber to send data to each other. However, this is a "dumb" send; there is no validation. When data changes at one end, it is sent to the other, where it overwrites the data at the Subscriber.

Peer-to-Peer Replication

Peer-to-peer replication is a specific variation of transactional replication and is very similar to bidirectional transactional replication. One limitation is that there is no conflict resolution, so you need to really think about how data will be inserted into the application to avoid conflicts. SQL Server 2008 does introduce conflict detection, which did not exist in SQL Server 2005, so it is at least improved. It allows you to update data at both a Publisher and a Subscriber, and send the updated data to each other. Where peer-to-peer differs from bidirectional is that if any of the servers hosting the databases fail, your application (assuming it is properly programmed) can use any one of the other databases participating in peer-to-peer as its primary database. This means that all copies of the data at all Publishers and Subscribers are exactly the same. This is also another case where NLB can be used to abstract the name of the servers to provide a single name/virtual IP address to your application.

One of the challenges with peer-to-peer is that you will have a hard time knowing where any given transaction is within the replication process at the moment of failure. If you are considering peer-to-peer replication, I would recommend periodically issuing some sort of custom check to see where your databases are in terms of consistency. Figure 1-14 shows a high-level peer-to-peer configuration that has three geographically dispersed locations, all of which are replicating to each other.

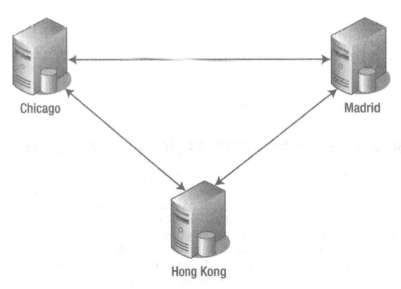

Figure 1-14. *Example peer-to-peer replication topology*

Combining Failover Clustering and Replication

Using replication with failover clustering is also a standard configuration. SQL Server does not care whether your Publisher, Distributor, and Subscriber are clustered; whether only some are clustered; or whether none are. The only thing you need to make sure is that any kind of directory, such as one for snapshots, is accessible by the clustered instance (meaning it may need to be placed on one of the shared cluster disks if it is not a network share). If you are planning a remote Distributor, you may want to think about whether to put it in another instance on the same cluster with your Publisher or Subscriber if each are clustered, put it on the same instance, or put it in a completely separate location. All are valid architectures. It boils down to what you think gives you the most flexible deployment and best performance while maintaining availability. Figure 1-15 shows a sample architecture containing both failover clustering and replication. The Distributor does not need to be remote, as shown; it can reside on a clustered instance of SQL Server.

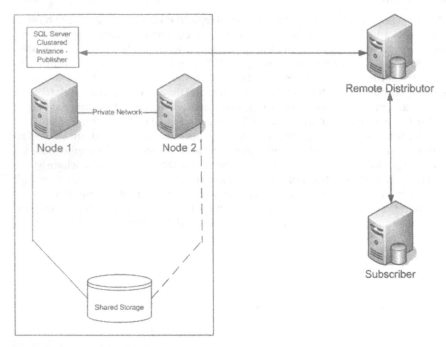

Figure 1-15. *Example of failover clustering with replication and a remote Distributor*

Applications, Availability, and Failover Clustering

Last, but certainly not least, there is the linchpin of the entire operation: the application. Without the application, all we would have to do as IT professionals is stare at the blinking lights on the servers and disk arrays. Too often, developers and third-party application vendors assume that availability is only the problem of the IT department implementing that solution. Once the application is in production, all responsibility is no longer their problem. Nothing could be further from the truth. The application has everything to do with how available that solution will be. Unfortunately, IT is often the last to know the application is coming ("Hey, we're deploying this application next month; can you guys get some servers up and running for us?"), and the DBAs often find out later than that. I have seen this in action time and time again over the years at clients big and small, and it is a recipe for disaster. IT (and by proxy, the DBAs) often has to perform the miracle of trying to fit a square peg into a round hole because the current administrative processes or technologies cannot support whatever they are trying to deploy, which leads to a domino effect on cost and time of the implementation. Solutions and applications need to be designed or purchased with your environment in mind.

Application Availability Issues

The biggest problem with applications is that they can be inflexible, which ensures that IT has to compensate somewhere on the back end for an application's shortcomings. I apologize to any developers or third-party vendors who are reading this and do not follow "worst practices," but such practices are still very much alive and well in most application development shops.

- Many application developers (in-house or third-party) *still* do the most boneheaded thing known to developer-kind: hard-coding object names and other parameters (databases names, SQL Server instance names, IP addresses, administrative account names, paths for files, default directories, etc.) right in the application. This wreaks havoc on those who have to support those applications and makes it nearly impossible to do any kind of reasonable (and non-messy) disaster recovery. Whether it is in a database, a configuration file, or something completely different, an application should have configurable parameters that allow whatever is done on the back end to be as transparent as possible to the application. This is especially troublesome in a disaster recovery scenario, where it may be much more efficient to bring up a new server with a new IP address instead of having to create a near-replica of the original server.

- As a follow-up to the previous bullet point, an application needs to be user friendly. Remember that applications are not for IT or the developer: they are for end users. The last thing that should happen is for end users to get back cryptic messages when something goes wrong. Cryptic messages lead to panic, which in turn prompts the users to flood IT with phone calls.

- Applications should take into account the back end technologies it will ultimately support, or that customers may want. For example, if database mirroring is going to be supported, the application should support the concept of the failover partner to allow an automatic failover that would be nondisruptive to the application or end users. Specific failover clustering considerations will be discussed in the next section, "Client Connections and Clustered SQL Server–Based Applications."

- In this world of GUIs and rapid application development, I find the use of requirements documents has become lackadaisical since it is just so quick and easy to crank out code (a good deal of which may not even be written by hand) or buy an off-the-shelf package. There is something to be said for having a document that governs all aspects of development or the qualifications for the application that will be purchased, and this document needs to be aligned with the business and its needs as well. IT should be involved in the review of the requirements document. Having said that, remember that there is the spirit of the law and the letter of the law. Things change over the course of planning and deployment, and a requirements document should reflect that. Both junior and senior developers should ask questions, because assumptions can lead to fatal flaws; no one is immune to making a mistake.

- Performance is not just an IT problem. Performance is a crucial availability factor, since downtime to fix a performance problem is often downtime that can be prevented or avoided altogether. Throwing all the hardware in the world at a poorly written query will not solve the issue. It may mask some of the side effects, but it will never be eliminated and will rear its ugly head at the most inopportune time. Designing an application for performance is not an easy task, but it reaps huge rewards if done correctly.

- Applications must be secure from the word "go." I still see applications that want full system administrator privileges or other escalated privileges within SQL Server and Windows. Stop the madness! Every single application and its databases need to be designed with the concept of least privilege in mind. Those of you who need to be compliant with standards such as SOX or HIPAA know this well. If you fail an audit, there may be dire consequences for the company. This is a completely preventable situation; all it would have taken was a developer spending time to figure out the exact privileges needed. Instead, the developer took the lazy route and coded with escalated privileges because it was easy.

- Consolidation is a hotbed topic for nearly every customer I have talked to since about 2005. Many applications (and subsequently their databases) have designs that assume separate application servers and SQL Server instances for *everything*. This is no longer a feasible business model to strive for with most applications, and adds not only a lot of monetary cost for supporting the application, but quite a bit of administrative burden. Applications need to be designed to play nicely with the other kids in the sandbox. There are exceptions, of course—for example, mission-critical, data-sensitive human resources applications should still be completely isolated, as should applications with significantly different (and conflicting) availability SLAs.

Client Connections and Clustered SQL Server–Based Applications

As noted earlier, in a cluster, the IP address and name are "virtualized" so that an application connection does not need to worry about which node owns the resources being used. The clustered SQL Server instance will appear the same as a regular, standalone SQL Server instance to the end user or application. All clients will access the IP address and name configured during the SQL Server installation, not the name of one of the nodes, nor the Windows failover cluster. For example, say you have the following configuration:

- Three nodes: JOHN, with an IP address of 197.100.101.5; CHUCK, with an IP address of 197.100.101.6; and JAMES, with an IP address of 197.100.101.7

- A Windows failover cluster with the name TW4 with an IP address of 197.100.101.8

- A clustered SQL Server 2008 default instance with the name MIRACLES with an IP address of 197.100.101.9

Any client or application will connect to that instance using the name of MIRACLES or via 197.100.101.9 (and its associated TCP/IP port). Never connect using CHUCK, JAMES, or JOHN, either by name or IP address, since there is no concept of "local."

How your application behaves in a failover will differ depending on how it is coded. During the failover process from one node to another, the resources are stopped on one node and started on another. From a SQL Server perspective, this means that all client connections will need to deal with a stop and a start of the SQL Server service, since the client connections will be dropped and broken.

The best way to handle the stop and start is to use a cluster-aware application. A cluster-aware application is one that is coded to the clustering API, which is part of the aforementioned Platform SDK. There is an SDK released for each specific version of Windows. SQL Server itself is a cluster-aware application, as are many of its tools, such as Management Studio. A cluster-aware application detects the failover of the back end service and gracefully handles the failover to minimize or hide the impact to the end user. How each application deals with that can be different; some may reconnect automatically, and others may disconnect without throwing up an error in the application and require the end user to reconnect. If you are coding your own applications, this is a capability you want to think about building in from the start.

Tip You can find the latest version of the Platform SDK by going to http://www.microsoft.com/downloads and searching for "Platform SDK."

Most applications are not coded to be cluster-aware. There are a few extra steps to make an application cluster-aware. The most important is to build in a retry for the situation where the application is talking to one node and a failover to the other node occurs. Even though the new node will take on both the network name and IP address of the failed node, your application users will actually be talking across IP using MAC addresses, which cannot fail over (they are tied to the actual NIC hardware); so the application needs to simply retry the connection, and TCP/IP will naturally re-resolve the address and connect to the new node.

Since there is a stop and a start of SQL Server, the best approach, if you do not want to code to the Platform SDK, is to put some sort of retry logic into the application that will poll to see whether SQL Server is up, and then automatically reconnect when SQL Server comes back up after the failover. Some web-based applications might not need to take into account that the back end is clustered. In many cases, a simple refresh of the browser will do. Sometimes a middle-tier or queuing application such as Microsoft BizTalk, when incorporated into an overall solution, might also help abstract a clustered SQL Server failover, but that is something that would need to be evaluated based on your requirements. A final approach could be implementing some sort of time-out value in the application and then returning a friendly message to the end user.

What you do not want to do is something that will impede an application from being able to connect to a clustered back end after a failover. Years ago, I was working with a client who encountered a failover of SQL Server on a cluster. SQL Server failed over just fine, but for some reason, the client could not get the application to reconnect. As it turns out, the application was ODBC-based and was using a persistent connection to the database back end. When the SQL Server instance failed over, the connections knew nothing about it. The client had to reset the persistent connection.

An important point to remember is that an application that requires some form of state, or memory, of the user's session will have to be taken into account in the context of a clustered SQL Server back end. SQL Server will always remain consistent in a failover, since in the stop and start process, the transaction logs will be rolled back or forward depending on what is there. Incomplete transactions will be rolled back, and any completed transactions that are not yet committed will be rolled forward. All committed transactions will already be in the database. Your user databases will be in the same state as they were at the point of failure. This is why it is important to always code and use transactions within your statements to ensure database consistency.

Ports are another issue in terms of client connectivity. SQL Server 2008 by default will dynamically be assigned a port number. The first instance will generally take the well-known 1433, but if it is in use, another will be used. If you have more than one instance of SQL Server running, they will all have unique port values. The SQL Server native client knows this. However, from a pure security standpoint, setting a static port is the best way to ensure consistency, and you can avoid known ports such as 1433 that might be security risks. This means the application will need to know about the static port. However, if the static port is unavailable in the event of a failover to another node, SQL Server will use another port. Make sure you take this into account in your overall planning. I explain how to set a manual port number for a clustered SQL Server 2008 instance in Chapter 7.

One step you will definitely have to take is to test your application against a clustered SQL Server back end to see how it will behave. Part of measuring your availability is to understand the impact to your end users when something like a failover event happens. Knowing the behavior of your application when you implement a failover cluster will help you manage expectations of your end users and assist in troubleshooting any problems.

Note Although slightly out of the scope of this section, it is important to know that database mirroring has a programmatic mechanism to assist in abstracting a server change with automatic failover only. In the connection string, you can specify the failover partner, which is the instance that contains the mirrored database.

Comparing Failover Clustering to Other Availability Technologies

Table 1-2 provides a high-level comparison of failover clustering to the other SQL Server availability features. Following the table is a more in-depth comparison based on the table, as well as a comparison of failover clustering to non-Microsoft technologies.

Table 1-2. *SQL Server High Availability Technology Comparison*

Attribute	Failover Clustering	Log Shipping	Database Mirroring	Replication
Distance	Limited[1]	No distance limitations[2]	No distance limitations[2]	No distance limitations[2]
Server switch	Automatic or manual	Manual	Automatic or manual	Manual
Server switch time (average)	30 seconds–2 minutes	Minutes	10 seconds–1 minute (+/−)	Minutes
Protects	Full instance of SQL Server	Individual database	Individual database	Individual database
Granularity	Entire instance	Per transaction log	Per transaction	Depends on type of replication
Individual database restrictions	None	Bulk-logged or full recovery only	Full recovery only	Depends on type of replication
Special hardware considerations	Yes[3]	No	No	No
Data loss in server switch	No[4]	Likely[5]	Maybe[6]	Likely[7]
Single point of failure	Disk subsystem	None	None	None
Worry about objects that reside outside the database	No	Yes	Yes	Yes
Redundant server(s) can be used for reporting	No[8]	Maybe[9]	Yes[10]	Yes[11]
Coexists/works with prior versions of SQL Server	Yes[12]	Yes[13]	No	Yes[14]

Table 1-2. *SQL Server High Availability Technology Comparison*

Attribute	Failover Clustering	Log Shipping	Database Mirroring	Replication
Works with other SQL Server 2008 editions	N/A	Yes[15]	No[16]	Yes[17]
Number of possible failover/mirror/standby servers	Up to 16	Unlimited	1	Unlimited
Configuration	Setup	Post-setup	Post-setup	Post-setup
Schema dependencies	No	No	No	Yes[18]
Editions supported	Developer, Enterprise, Standard	Developer, Enterprise, Standard, Workgroup	Developer, Enterprise, Standard	All
Server name change abstracted	Yes	No	Maybe[19]	No

[1] *Limited by any restrictions of fiber, which is generally around 100 miles for synchronous disk replication.*

[2] *Limited by your network as well as your disk subsystem.*

[3] *See the "Cluster Validation" section of Chapter 2 for more details on what constitutes a valid Windows failover cluster with either Windows Server 2003 or Windows Server 2008.*

[4] *Databases are always consistent to the point of failover, meaning any transactions completed will be rolled forward, and any incomplete transactions will be rolled back.*

[5] *Unless it is a graceful role change where you back up the tail of the log, you will only be able to restore to the last transaction in the last transaction log backup available.*

[6] *If you are in high-safety mode, you should not have any data loss. If you are mirroring asynchronously, there is a chance you will lose data.*

[7] *When using replication, you are most likely not replicating your entire database, and if you are not using transactional replication, you are most likely losing data.*

[8] *One node owns all resources associated with a particular instance.*

[9] *Technically, the secondary, if it is restored using* WITH STANDBY, *can be used for reporting purposes, but it would be unavailable during transaction log restores.*

[10] *If you create a database snapshot, the mirror can be used for reporting.*

[11] *This is most likely the purpose for using replication in the first place.*

[12] *A SQL Server 2008 failover cluster can be configured in a side-by-side configuration with a SQL Server 2000 or SQL Server 2005 failover cluster.*

[13] *You can log ship using custom scripts from SQL Server 2000 or SQL Server 2005 to SQL Server 2008, but not from SQL Server 2008 to SQL Server 2000 or SQL Server 2005.*

[14] *Replication can populate older versions of SQL Server.*

[15] *Log shipping has no restrictions on the edition of the primary or secondary.*

[16] *While technically you can mirror if you are in high-safety mode from Standard to Enterprise or vice versa, it is not recommended.*

[17] *Replication has no edition restrictions.*

[18] *Some forms of replication require that primary keys are configured within a schema.*

[19] *If you are using high-safety mode and your application is coded properly, the server name change during the server switch will be abstracted.*

Database Mirroring vs. Failover Clustering

Database mirroring is most often compared with failover clustering since to the untrained ear, as they sound similar. However, they are fundamentally different. In some of its early marketing material for SQL Server 2005 (the first version with database mirroring), Microsoft gave the impression that it was positioning database mirroring to replace failover clustering. Database mirroring is by no means a cluster killer, though—at least how it is currently implemented.

Architecturally, both have the concept of quorum. Endpoints in database mirroring are similar to the cluster's private network. Both require that the servers participating are using the same edition of SQL Server. Both support automatic and manual failover options. By default, failover clustering is designed to take advantage of an automatic failover, whereas database mirroring depends on which mode is implemented. Depending on how the application is coded, whether you are using failover clustering or database mirroring, it may or may not force you to reconnect after an automatic failover. Both technologies provide ways to minimize impact on the end users, but it is up to the developer to implement them.

Both give you excellent availability, but their main difference is that failover clustering protects your entire instance, while database mirroring protects a single database. This is a huge difference. It means that in a failover for a clustered instance, you will have to worry about reconnecting to the instance, but everything will still be there. With database mirroring, logins will need to be added and synchronized, and anything that resides outside of the database that is not captured as a transaction (such as jobs, maintenance plans, etc.) will need to be created on the mirror. However, the storage in failover clustering is a single point of failure, whereas with database mirroring, you have two separate copies of a particular database.

The one major advantage that database mirroring has over failover clustering is that the whole implementation can be done on commodity hardware with no specific validation requirements around a solution. Clustering has specific hardware requirements (although they are somewhat relaxed in Windows Server 2008 compared to the way things used to be) that are documented in the "Cluster Validation" section in Chapter 2. In the past, this aspect of clustering has been a sore point.

The complexity of clustering is one reason why I think most people will look for an "easier" solution, even if it may not totally meet their needs. Clustering is perceived as being difficult, and some may have had a bad experience with it in the past for one reason or another. This is not the right way to evaluate a technology. Where it may have been wrong in the past, it may be right now. As your needs change, so does technology (and usually for the better). It is never a bad thing to reevaluate clustering again if you need to implement a new solution.

Another aspect that is easier with database mirroring is spanning distance. With failover clustering, you need a specialized, geographically dispersed cluster solution that most likely has some sort of physical limitation (e.g., fiber is only rated at certain distances) that you cannot avoid. Database mirroring involves two separate installations that can reside on any supported hardware (clustered or not), and is not bound by distance, but by the limitations of your network bandwidth and the speed of applying the transactions.

The time it takes to get back up and running after a problem is different with database mirroring and failover clustering. Failover clustering is generally measured in minutes by the time user databases are available, and database mirroring could be seconds. After the database has failed over to the mirror, you still may have to perform other steps such as creating SQL Server Agent jobs or synchronizing logins to ensure that it is a fully working copy of the original, so there may be a net savings of zero time.

Failover clustering has no limitations in terms of what features it supports with SQL Server, whereas database mirroring, as an example, supports different modes on different editions of SQL Server and does not support the filestream data type. If you have an application or a related set of applications that use multiple databases, those are generally more suited to failover clustering, since they can be configured in the same instance and all fail over at once, creating a consistent failover point for each database. Last but not least, with failover clustering, you have a definite single point of failure in your disk subsystem. Configuring your disks with some sort of RAID gives you some redundancy, but if you are not deploying a geographically dispersed failover cluster, your disks are all part of the same set of enclosures in one data center and become your single point of failure. Database mirroring's architecture enables redundancy across distance to another data center.

Log Shipping vs. Failover Clustering

Log shipping is hard to compare to failover clustering in a meaningful way, as it does not act or feel like clustering at all. Log shipping is based on a core functionality of the SQL Server engine: backup and restore. It only protects a single database, it has no options for automatic failover, and the server switch is not abstracted from the client connections. The one thing that log shipping has on failover clustering is that it is easy to implement over long distances. Can log shipping provide the same availability as failover clustering? In some cases, the answer is absolutely yes, but your deployment would need to know all the caveats that go along with log shipping. Log shipping works much better as a disaster recovery technology than as a high-availability technology, and can complement failover clustering in this capacity, especially since it can assist with the "fat finger" scenario.

Replication vs. Failover Clustering

Replication is an effective data availability solution that allows you to possibly take all of the data in your database or a subset of the data and make it available elsewhere. Failover clustering defends your databases as a whole since its unit of protection is the entire instance. Like database mirroring and log shipping, replication can be configured on an instance that is deployed as a failover cluster. Like log shipping, you really cannot directly compare replication to failover clustering because the mechanisms and what they provide are two completely different things, and depending on what type of replication you are using, things change even more. The main differences are similar to those of log shipping.

Third-Party Clustering vs. Failover Clustering

Third-party clustering products are now being used by some to "cluster" SQL Server. By the strictest definition of a cluster, which I define in the first paragraph of the "Windows Clustering" section, what they do is absolutely correct. However, these solutions use a completely different mechanism and approach than a standard SQL Server failover cluster. Some are hardware-only. Some are purely software-based. Others are tied into both a hardware and a software solution in one way or another, and act more like Microsoft's implementation, but they have a few features that companies may find desirable. Some are widely used, others are up-and-coming. They all work fairly well and as advertised, and you should do your homework to see if they will meet your needs.

The biggest issue with most third-party products is that if you encounter a problem, the manufacturers will be the first point of contact—not Microsoft—since any third-party solution is most likely not a Microsoft-certified solution. As a consultant, one of my biggest responsibilities to my customers is to identify risk and mitigate it. I certainly cannot force a customer to use or not use a technology or a solution (Microsoft or non-Microsoft), but supportability is a concern, since the last thing you want to hear from a support engineer is, "Sorry, have a nice day," when your system is down. You know your organization better than I ever will. You know what risks your business is willing to accept and what it won't tolerate.

As you go through the process of evaluating products, especially ones that would be a primary form of availability or disaster recovery, keep supportability in mind. You should consult with those in the trenches—the administrators who live, eat, sleep, and breathe your SQL Server administration and implementations. They will most likely be able to tell you if they have firsthand knowledge of the technology in question, and whether the vendor you are considering is good. You may have implemented another product from a vendor and had a bad experience, either with the technology, or worse, the support. Know all of your facts before you spend a lot of money on something that could be the equivalent of a technology paperweight.

As noted in the chapters on clustering, for a geographically dispersed failover cluster solution, it is always best to consider solutions that are certified and appear in the Windows Server Catalog. Any other solution—no matter how reputable the vendor—may cause you some support headaches down the road.

Oracle's Real Application Clusters vs. Failover Clustering

The debate over how Microsoft implements clusters vs. how Oracle does it is an age-old fight and borders on a religious battle for some. Simply put, Microsoft and other software vendors have different design approaches to availability and clusters. Microsoft's approach is just as valid as any other out there. Whether you agree with it or not is a completely different story.

I've described in detail earlier in this chapter how failover clustering works, and how it is based on a shared-nothing architecture. A fully shared architecture would mean that the vendor coding the software to run on the cluster would have to devise some sort of locking mechanism to ensure that things like write order are preserved, so that a request coming in from one end user or application to a database does not somehow trump a request from another at the same time. There cannot be chaos at a low level. The other thing to consider is that while such shared architectures allow multiple servers to be able to process transactions at the same time, there is still only one copy of the data. That means the shared disk, which contains the database and its associated files, is a single point of failure, as well as a potential bottleneck for scalability if the disk design is not optimal. The shared disk single point of failure is similar to the disk being a single point of failure with Microsoft's failover clustering.

Microsoft took its first strides into the shared database arena with SQL Server 2005, and the same story remains in SQL Server 2008. SQL Server 2005 introduced support for read-only, shared scale-out databases even on clusters. For more information and the steps on how to implement such a solution, consult Microsoft Knowledge Base Article 910378, "Scalable shared databases are supported by SQL Server 2005" (http://support.microsoft.com/kb/910378/en-us).

Oracle's implementation of clustering is known as Real Application Clusters (RAC), and while it can increase the availability of your database implementation, it is more of a performance offering. It allows you to scale out by having multiple Oracle servers hitting a single shared database on the back end. This means the workload is distributed among the multiple servers, but your single point of failure and potential bottleneck will become your shared database (as well as your disk subsystem). A locking mechanism is also employed to ensure that the multiple servers hitting the single database do not corrupt or somehow mess up your data. So while the perception of customers is that the Oracle architecture on paper provides better availability and scalability, the reality is that you do not necessarily get better availability or scalability than from implementing a traditional Microsoft SQL Server failover cluster and using the methods available to you within SQL Server to scale out. Oracle just gives you an easier scale-out solution out of the box. It must also be noted that implementing RAC is not a cheap solution. Your basic Oracle implementations generally do not utilize RAC. Like Microsoft's failover clustering, RAC is an advanced configuration that may require special attention and skilled administrators who can support the solution.

THE "I HATE SQL SERVER FAILOVER CLUSTERING" SYNDROME

I used this sidebar topic in my previous book, *Pro SQL Server 2005 High Availability*, and I am recycling and updating it since the topic is still relevant. Even in SQL Server 2008, failover clustering still has a bad reputation for some of the sins committed back in failover clustering's dark days—namely, involving SQL Server 6.5 and SQL Server 7.0 with Windows NT 4.0 and direct attached storage using SCSI. The fear, uncertainty, and doubt (FUD) still spread by word of mouth in 2008 as I am writing this astounds me. The categories outlined in this sidebar tend to reflect the profile of those who actively resist implementing failover clusters in their environment. I have noticed five different variations.

Variation One

Many customers have had a bad experience clustering SQL Server with either version 6.5 or version 7.0. My experience with clustering SQL Server goes back to SQL Server 7.0, and I can tell you that clustering 10 years ago was an iffy proposition at best: to do things like apply a SQL Server service pack with SQL Server 6.5 or 7.0, you had to uncluster the nodes, apply the service pack, and then recluster the nodes. Talk about having to cross your fingers! In those days, you were also more likely than not using SCSI-based direct attached storage, which could prove problematic on its own, let alone when used in conjunction with clustering. Then add in the seemingly weird dependence on specific versions of MDAC. Believe it or not, having the right version of MDAC was one of the factors that determined whether failover clustering was able to work. Until SQL Server 2000, which was a fully cluster-aware application, all previous versions of SQL Server failover clustering used a "shim" layer that replaced some DLLs on the server to allow SQL Server 6.5 and 7.0 to work in a clustered configuration. So if you did something to replace one of the DLLs, like install an unsupported version of MDAC, you would break your cluster. Since those early days of clustering with SQL Server, both the hardware and software aspects have improved immensely. While you may have had extremely bad experiences with SQL Server and clustering years ago, you should still consider it for new implementations (if it meets your requirements), because it has changed quite a bit. If your company has a bias due to previous bad experiences, you may want to ask what versions of SQL Server and Windows they are referring to, because the experience of clustering both Windows and SQL Server has improved immensely over the years.

Variation Two

Implementing a cluster is not something you decide to do off the cuff—it takes quite a lot of planning and involves what I refer to as "moving parts." It is human nature that people tend to like simpler, more straightforward implementations and shy away from the complexity of a cluster. While I would agree, you should not undertake implementing clusters as an afterthought—with the right guidance, planning, and *time*, you will get it right. The end may justify the means if failover clustering meets your availability needs. If need be, for at least your first implementation, find a good consultant to help you, and become a sponge—soak up their experience. Just because this book is dedicated to failover clustering doesn't mean you'll turn you into an expert overnight. Gaining experience—especially on your first implementations with someone else more qualified to assist—will help you acquire the practical experience to any "book" learning you may do.

Variation Three

Many people are seemingly forced into using SQL Server failover clustering because it is the only high-availability method supported by an application vendor for the program their business chooses to deploy. There is nothing you can do about this, other than venting at the decision-maker who wanted the application in the first place, and then contacting the vendor who designed the solution to support other things. No one held a gun to the vendor's head to only support failover clustering, so it is not Microsoft's fault. If you have to implement failover clustering, and it is the right thing for your situation, my advice is to find a way to make it work. Fighting it will only make the end implementation more difficult than it has to be. Over the years, I have had the occasional client try to fight me every step of the way when implementing clusters (Why do we need a specific firmware version on our SAN? Why are we spending so much time planning? We cannot give the service accounts these rights!). It adds time (and cost if you are paying a consultant for assistance) because you spend more time spinning wheels in "we don't do things this way" arguments than you do just planning it and getting on with things. Consultants who are working with you onsite should be trusted advisors, not mortal enemies. Speaking from experience, when I'm faced with a resistant customer who is in this specific predicament, I want to get their production environment up and running just as quickly as they do. It isn't any more fun for the consultant to have constant delays, when in some cases they could be prevented by just going with the flow. There has to be a middle ground that everyone can come to that pushes the implementations forward.

Variation Four

Clustering is scary to some, and it should be approached with the proper respect it deserves. If clustering is new to your organization, it is something that the application and IT teams will have to support and understand inside and out. Clustering changes everything—how you deploy, how you troubleshoot, how you do maintenance, and so on. While it's still just an installation of SQL Server when all is said and done, there are still some cluster-specific things you will need to worry about (which will be outlined throughout the rest of this book). The best way to combat growing pains is to deploy test or staging environments that are clustered to provide a good training ground and sandbox for your staff.

Variation Five

Needing to have certified solutions from the servers to the HBAs, shared disks, and drivers has been a long-standing pain point for Windows-based failover clusters. However, this restriction goes away for the most part with Windows Server 2008, and will be discussed in Chapter 2.

Summary

It is important to understand what you are trying to protect before you choose and possibly implement failover clustering as a solution. It is also imperative to understand how failover clustering works, as well as its pros and cons, to determine whether it is the right technology for your implementations, or whether you should use something else (or even combine multiple supporting technologies). Each of the SQL Server availability technologies is beneficial in its own way, but there are rarely absolutes when it comes to scenarios where a specific technology would be used in each and every case. There are always exceptions to the rule, so as long as what you ultimately wind up deploying is fully supported by the hardware vendors, as well as any developers or third-party vendors, it is the right solution for you.

This chapter wrapped some perspective around failover clustering, but now it is time to deep dive into the implementation of a SQL Server 2008 failover cluster, starting with its most fundamental building block: Windows.

■■■

CHAPTER 2

Preparing to Cluster Windows

Now that you understand the basics of availability, the difference in the SQL Server availability options, and how the application fits into the mix, it's time to get down to work. Before clustering SQL Server, there is a whole other layer to consider before you even think about running SQL Server 2008's installation program: Windows. Windows failover clustering was completely rewritten from the ground up in Windows Server 2008. The components that have been changed and improved will be dealt with in their appropriate sections in this chapter and throughout the upcoming two chapters.

It is absolutely crucial to understand that what is done—or not done—in Windows will affect the stability and reliability of a SQL Server 2008 failover cluster. This chapter, along with Chapters 3 and 4, is Windows-centric but written from a SQL Server point of view. If you are unfamiliar with what is being presented, or you are a DBA who is only responsible for SQL Server, but need to ensure that your failover clusters are built properly, work with the appropriate resources or groups in your company. Even if you are ultimately not responsible for Windows (either administration or deployment), it is in your best interests to understand the Windows configuration. It will not only help you be a better administrator, but you can work better with your counterparts, especially if something goes wrong.

VARIATIONS NOT COVERED IN THIS BOOK

If you plan on using Windows Server 2003 to deploy SQL Server 2008, refer to Chapters 4 through 6 of *Pro SQL Server 2005 High Availability* because all of the considerations, as well as how to configure and administer, will be the same as if you were deploying SQL Server 2005. Ensure that you are using at least Windows Server 2003 with Windows Server 2003 Service Pack 2 applied.

Similarly, SQL Server 2005 is supported on Windows Server 2008 if SQL Server 2005 has SQL Server 2005 Service Pack 2 or later applied to it. Figure 2-1 shows the message that pops up when you first start the SQL Server 2005 setup, alerting you to the fact you need to patch SQL Server 2005 immediately after installation. This chapter, along with Chapters 3 and 4, should be able to help you with the Windows Server 2008 portion of your SQL Server 2005 failover clustering deployments, but refer to Chapters 7 through 9 of *Pro SQL Server 2005 High Availability* to learn how to plan, deploy, and administer SQL Server 2005 failover clustering. I have also posted some differences not covered in the last book that pertain to installing SQL Server 2005 failover clusters on Windows Server 2008 on my blog, which can be found at http://www.sqlha.com/blog.

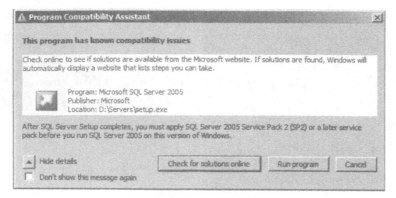

Figure 2-1. *Message shown if SQL Server 2005 is installed on Windows Server 2008*

Choosing a Version and Edition of Windows Server 2008

This section will help you decide which variation of Windows Server 2008 you should deploy in your environments. Microsoft maintains a good page for differentiating between the versions of Windows Server 2008: http://www.microsoft.com/windowsserver2008/en/us/differentiated-features.aspx.

Failover clustering is only a feature of the Datacenter and Enterprise editions of Windows Server 2008. Depending on what processor architecture you choose, there is a different maximum number of nodes. Microsoft Knowledge Base article 288778 (http://support.microsoft.com/kb/288778) will always be kept up to date with the maximum number of nodes for each version of Windows, and covers all editions going back to Windows NT 4.0. Table 2-1 shows the number of nodes currently supported per edition of Windows Server 2008. SQL Server supports up to the operating system maximum.

Table 2-1. *Nodes Supported per Edition of Windows Server 2008*

Edition	Maximum Nodes (SQL Server 2008 Enterprise Edition)	Maximum Nodes (SQL Server 2008 Standard Edition)
All x64	16	2
All x86 and Itanium	8	2

It is important to know that the released-to-manufacturing (RTM) version of Windows Server 2008 shipped as Service Pack 1, which is shown in Figure 2-2. The first full update for Windows Server 2008 is Windows Server 2008 Service Pack 2. During the course of writing this book, Microsoft announced that they will be releasing Windows Server 2008 R2 (no release date available), which will also have some improvements to clustering. When possible, those improvements will be noted where appropriate throughout the rest of the book.

Windows edition ——

Windows Server® Enterprise without Hyper-V

Copyright © 2007 Microsoft Corporation. All rights reserved.

Service Pack 1

Figure 2-2. *Windows Server 2008 RTM version showing Service Pack 1*

32- or 64-Bit?

Although SQL Server 2000 released a 64-bit version late in its cycle for Intel's Itanium (IA64) processor, SQL Server 2005 and Windows Server 2003 were the first versions of Microsoft's key products that fully supported 32- and 64-bit across the entire product line from the moment they were released. Windows Server 2008 and SQL Server 2008 continue this tradition and support both 32-bit (x86) and 64-bit (the aforementioned IA64 in addition to x64, which is short for Extended 64 and refers to AMD's AMD64 or Intel's EMT64T technology). For clusters, you cannot mix 32- and 64-bit nodes in the same failover cluster, and all nodes must be of the same type, major version, and edition. For example, in a two-node cluster, you cannot have one node be Windows Server 2008 Enterprise Edition 32-bit and the other be 64-bit; pick one or the other. The edition of Windows is the same, but that does not mean you can deploy a cluster in that configuration.

My strong recommendation at this point is for any new SQL Server 2008 deployment to use 64-bit, and preferably x64. Most of the newer servers you would have purchased over the past few years are probably 64-bit capable. There are differences that may push you toward IA64, but the reality is that x64 has become ubiquitous and inexpensive. One of the major differences between x64 and IA64 is that x64 is backward compatible with x86 since the x64 architecture utilizes 64-bit extensions on top of the x86 instruction set. Whether you buy an AMD-based or Intel based x64 processor, you have the ability to deploy x86 or x64 versions of Windows. Itanium is not backward compatible (but now has an emulation layer), which is arguably why it may have had a tougher time gaining market share. Itaniums have historically been in larger servers, such as the Unisys ES7000 and the Hewlett-Packard Superdome, but even those support x64 now. Itaniums are based upon Explicitly Parallel Instruction Computing (EPIC).

The biggest gain for SQL Server when 64-bit support came into the picture was the ability to use much larger amounts of memory. In the "old" days, with 32-bit Windows, to scale beyond 2 GB of memory, you had to configure settings in boot.ini (/3GB to allow SQL Server to use memory up to 3 GB, and reserve 1 GB for Windows; /PAE to allow use above 4 GB). Then, depending on how much memory you needed (and Windows supported), you had to enable a special setting in SQL Server called AWE. While 32-bit SQL Server 2005 on Windows Server 2003 could access large amounts of memory dynamically, prior to that scenario, a fixed amount of memory needed to be configured in addition to the other settings. It made scalability a lot tougher, especially if you were looking to use multiple instances on a single server or cluster. Another good reason to go 64-bit is that the 64-bit versions of Windows and SQL Server can use threads more efficiently and can handle I/O much better. SQL Server may be your reason to start pushing a 64-bit agenda within your company.

■**Tip** To see how memory works under Windows, see the topic "About Memory Management" at `http://msdn.microsoft.com/en-us/library/aa366525(VS.85).aspx`. Another good read is "Supporting Systems That Have More Than 64 Processors," which can be found at `http://www.microsoft.com/whdc/system/Sysinternals/MoreThan64proc.mspx`. It is a developer-focused paper, but may prove useful. For more information about processors and threads in Windows, see the topic "Processors and Threads" at `http://msdn.microsoft.com/en-us/library/ms684841(VS.85).aspx`.

Table 2-2 shows the maximum processor and memory limitations of the versions of Windows Server 2008 RTM that support failover clustering.

Table 2-2. *Maximum Specifications of Windows Server 2008 RTM*

Windows Server 2008 Edition	Memory	Processor
Datacenter RTM (x86)	64 GB	32 physical sockets or cores
Datacenter RTM (x64)	2 TB	64 physical sockets or cores
Datacenter RTM (IA64)	2 TB	64 physical sockets or cores
Enterprise RTM (x86)	64 GB	8 physical sockets or 32 cores
Enterprise RTM (x64)	2 TB	8 physical sockets or 64 cores
Enterprise RTM (IA64)	2 TB	8 physical sockets or 64 cores

However, making the switch to 64-bit is not a guaranteed win. The issue is not SQL Server; SQL Server 2008 works just fine on a 64-bit platform. The entity holding up adoption of 64-bit Windows is not what you would think: it's most likely your IT department. Many companies are still heavily invested in the 32-bit world for their Windows environments. From deployment and administration to drivers and the skills of the IT shop, switching to a 64-bit version of Windows is a fundamental change that has to be embraced and planned for. Since SQL Server 2005, most DBAs would have loved to take advantage of a 64-bit platform, but, in many cases, IT is not there yet.

To assist in the preparation to go to 64-bit Windows, here are some suggestions:

- Building servers will be different. All existing builds and build processes will need to be updated accordingly for your 64-bit Windows deployments. This is not a trivial task, since it is not just Windows you need to worry about. You also need to worry about 64-bit drivers for hardware components such as network interface cards (NICs) and host bus adapters (HBAs). You need to find out whether you can even use 64-bit on existing hardware you may want to repurpose, or whether you need new servers. Thankfully, drivers are rarely an issue now for 64-bit, but it always pays to do your homework before getting too far down the planning and implementation road. It is very costly to find out at the last minute that something will not work, and that you have to change your plans completely. I have been there with customers, and more often than not the only fix is to spend more money, which you may not have.

- Ensure that there are 64-bit equivalents to all of the administration software you currently use. This will include but is not limited to backup utilities, antivirus programs, monitoring tools, security policy enforcers, and possibly the application software used by end users. Do not assume that you can use whatever you are using now. You may even need 64-bit-specific editions of some products, whereas others may work in their current incarnation—it will be a case-by-case basis. The real problem is that if you do need a new version or an upgrade, is it going to cost something? It may not be in the budget to update your other software to be able to deploy 64-bit Windows.

- Update all administration processes, documentation, and skill sets of administrators. While most skills should be the same or variations on the same theme, never assume that what you did on 32-bit servers will always work on the newly deployed 64-bit servers. There may be some subtle differences (e.g., the memory model) where you did one thing in 32-bit land, but may have to do something else in the 64-bit world. One good example of this is that if you are using SQL Server Integration Services, there may be a lack of availability of 64-bit drivers for non–SQL Server sources (especially older software with no hope of any updates).

Caution SQL Server 2008 is *not* supported in Windows-on-Windows (WOW) mode in a clustered configuration. If you need to deploy a 32-bit version of SQL Server, you must deploy a 32-bit operating system. WOW gives you the ability to install 32-bit software so it can run under a 64-bit operating system. This limitation even applies to upgrades, so if you currently have SQL Server 2000 or SQL Server 2005 running in WOW with Windows Server 2003 and you want to upgrade to 64-bit Windows Server 2008, you will have to deploy a new, full 64-bit installation version of SQL Server 2008 and migrate your databases. The irony is that a lot of the SQL Server tools and utilities are still 32-bit and run under WOW.

Windows Server 2008 With and Without Hyper-V

Windows Server 2008 has two additional major "flavors" besides the various editions (Datacenter, Web, Enterprise, and so on): with Hyper-V and without Hyper-V. The choice will show up when you run the Windows install media, as shown in Figure 2-3. Hyper-V is Microsoft's new hypervisor-based virtualization technology that allows you to run multiple virtual machines under a single Windows Server 2008 deployment.

A SQL Server 2008 clustered deployment is supported on cluster nodes with or without Hyper-V. Unless you are actually going to use Hyper-V to virtualize other servers in addition to deploying SQL Server 2008 failover clustering, use the versions of Windows Server 2008 without Hyper-V. The reason is that a mission-critical deployment of SQL Server should not potentially be affected by anything else unless there is a good reason for that configuration. That means that if Hyper-V is not used but just configured, in terms of patching and possible security risks, it is one more thing to worry about. However, on the flip side, going without Hyper-V may limit future deployments in terms of architecture if failover clustering does become supported, so think about your choice carefully. Chapter 9 will talk more about virtualization and how it fits in with failover clustering.

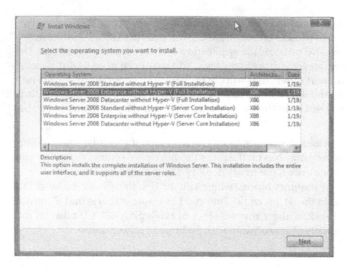

Figure 2-3. *Options showing the edition of Windows available to install*

Server Core

As you may have noticed in Figure 2-3, there is also another new variation of Windows Server 2008: Server Core. Server Core is a stripped-down edition of Windows that has no interface; it is just for command line use. It also does not support the installation of many applications since it does not support the installation of the .NET Framework. For this main reason, even though Server Core can be clustered, it is not supported for any version of SQL Server in either a clustered or standalone capacity.

Windows Server 2008 R2

Windows Server 2008 will have more than scalability improvements. First and foremost, R2 will be the first 64-bit-only version of Windows Server. If you need to deploy x86, the current branch (RTM) of Windows Server 2008 will be the end-of-line platform for those deployments. Failover clustering also changes for the better in Windows Server 2008 R2. Microsoft is getting away from using the command line cluster.exe and moving toward PowerShell for script-based management of failover clusters. A preview of what this will look like is shown in Chapters 4 and 8. One of the biggest improvements in Windows Server 2008 R2 is the ability to take advantage of failover clustering to improve the availability of virtualized guests running under Hyper-V. This feature will be explored more in Chapter 9.

Cluster Validation

Anyone who has deployed a Windows Server 2003 (or earlier) server cluster knows what a pain it was in one sense: the entire solution had to either be in the old Windows Hardware Compatibility List (HCL) or, later in the Windows Server 2003 cycle, in the Windows Server Catalog as a complete solution (down to firmware, BIOS, and storage driver versions). Otherwise, a server cluster was not considered valid and would not be supported by Microsoft. This aspect of planning a server cluster has historically been a bone of contention with customers and has definitely impeded some cluster deployments.

With Windows Server 2008, you are no longer bound by the HCL or Windows Server Catalog. There is a new process to follow: *cluster validation.* Cluster validation is implemented as the Validate a Cluster Wizard in the new administration tool Failover Cluster Management. It is reminiscent of the Microsoft Cluster Configuration Validation Wizard, which shipped post–Windows Server 2003 (and pre-Windows Server 2008). Cluster validation does exactly what it sounds like: it validates that the hardware and operating system settings you intend to use for your failover cluster are suitable. You do not get off completely from some hardware requirements, though. All intended hardware must be specifically marked "Certified for Windows Server 2008." This means that if you want to repurpose a Windows Server 2003 server as a new Windows Server 2008 cluster node, it needs this certification. If not, that hardware component cannot be used for a Windows Server 2008 deployment even if it passes cluster validation. The easiest place to check for compliant hardware is in the Windows Server Catalog (http://www.windowsservercatalog.com).

There are four main categories of tests run as part of cluster validation:

- *Inventory.* This is a series of tests to catalog the various components (hardware, software, settings, storage) on each potential cluster node. For a full list of inventory tests, go to http://technet.microsoft.com/en-us/library/cc733033.aspx.

- *Network.* This is a series of tests to validate the network configuration on each potential cluster node. For a full list of network tests, go to http://technet.microsoft.com/en-us/library/cc771323.aspx.

- *Storage.* This is a series of tests that validates if the storage is properly configured, supports the requirements for a failover cluster, and can be used by each potential cluster node. These tests can take a considerable amount of time, depending on how many disks and nodes you will be using. Some storage tests may take disks offline for various purposes, including failover, so plan accordingly if these tests need to be run after the nodes are in production. For a full list of storage tests, go to http://technet.microsoft.com/en-us/library/cc771259.aspx.

- *System configuration.* This is a series of tests to confirm that the system software and configuration settings are compatible across all of the potential nodes. For a full list of system configuration tests, go to http://technet.microsoft.com/en-us/library/cc770399.aspx.

With Windows Server 2008 RTM, there are a total of 39 tests. The reason I provide links and do not list each specific test is that the links cover both Windows Server 2008 RTM and Windows Server 2008 R2, so if tests are added or change by the time R2 is released, the most up-to-date documentation will be easy to find.

In addition to cluster validation, there is the Failover Cluster Configuration Program (FCCP). The FCCP is similar to the old HCL or Windows Server Catalog, with a slight twist: it is essentially a list each vendor maintains of configurations that have already passed through cluster validation. You still have to run cluster validation during the actual configuration process, but buying solutions from a vendor who has qualified it under the FCCP will ensure that you have a proper cluster.

Technically, the cluster validation process permits you to mix and match servers from different vendors, or servers with different configurations (such as processor or memory), and allows you to configure them as a failover cluster. I do not recommend doing that—you should still strive to use the same vendor, model, and configuration for each node where possible. It makes administration and supportability much easier. Maybe you would consider mixing and matching in a test environment, but never do it in production.

Caution Since the HCL/Windows Server Catalog requirement has been lifted for Windows Server 2008 failover clustering deployments, Microsoft no longer maintains a list of supported drivers, firmware, and BIOS versions for failover clustering hardware such as servers, storage units, and HBA cards. You must now do additional homework with each individual component's manufacturer/vendor to ensure that the versions you are deploying are compatible with Windows Server 2008 failover clustering. Sometimes the versions the vendor has tested and certified for failover clustering are lower than the "latest and greatest" version. Do not assume that the most updated version is the one to deploy.

If you ever make a change to the hardware configuration, rerun validation. All validation reports are saved to the %windir%\Cluster\Report folder, and they can also be found in the Temp directory for the user that ran it (see Chapter 4). Cluster validation allows you to run selective tests. However, to be fully supported, the solution must pass each test. Selectively filtering out validation tests may generate a false positive and get you around an immediate issue you do not feel like dealing with, but will most likely come back and haunt you later on. The best part about cluster validation is that it is a full test that can root out problems in your configurations well before you even cluster Windows and SQL Server.

Cluster validation takes on additional importance beyond Windows itself; the SQL Server 2008 installation process also checks the report generated, and if it reports any failures, it will block the SQL Server 2008 install. Consider the following example: you encounter an issue and fail cluster validation. You discover the issue is fixed by installing a hotfix, SQL Server Cumulative Update, or a service pack (SQL Server or Windows), and you correct the problem. Instead of rerunning validation, you skip validation (see Figure 2-4) and proceed to cluster the nodes, which completes with no errors. If you try to cluster SQL Server 2008, it will fail, as shown in Figure 2-5, due to the fact that validation was not run again.

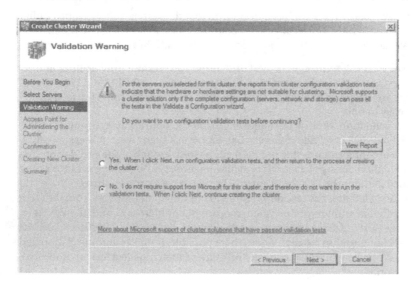

Figure 2-4. *Skipping validation*

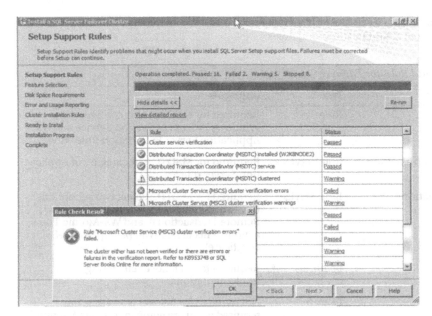

Figure 2-5. *SQL Server 2008's install fails if cluster validation has errors.*

■ **Tip** The official Microsoft support policy for Windows Sever 2008 failover clusters can be found in Knowledge Base article 943984 (http://support.microsoft.com/kb/943984). In addition to the Windows article, there is a specific one for SQL Server (Knowledge Base article 327518, at http://support.microsoft.com/kb/327518).

Security

This section will describe the security-related concerns for deploying Windows Server 2008 failover clusters. The focus will be on Windows-specific security issues. SQL Server–specific security issues are covered in Chapter 5.

Kerberos

If you will be using Kerberos authentication with SQL Server 2008, follow the instructions in Knowledge Base article 319723 (http://support.microsoft.com/kb/319723/en-us) to configure Kerberos properly. If you do things correctly, it will eliminate errors and ensure the SPNs are properly registered.

Server Features and Server Roles

Windows Server 2008 is more secure out of the box than previous versions of Windows. There is very little functionality that is enabled by default, including failover clustering. To control what the server can do, Microsoft introduced *server features* and continued with the concept of *server roles* in Windows Server 2008. In RTM, there are 16 roles and 35 features from which to choose. Until you disable it, the Initial Configuration Tasks dialog, shown in Figure 2-6, will be displayed. It is an easy way to check which features and roles are defined for that particular server. In this particular example, no features or roles have been configured yet. Table 2-3 shows what features and roles need to be configured for failover clustering. How to add features and roles is documented in the Chapter 3 section "Step 3: Add Features and Roles."

Table 2-3. *Features and Roles for Failover Clustering*

Name	Type	Comments
Application Server	Role	Required for MSDTC; also configures the Windows Process Activation Service and the Application Server Foundation Role Service.
Application Server Foundation	Role Services	Required for MSDTC; subcategory of Application Server role.
Distributed Transactions	Role Services	Required for MSDTC; select two suboptions (Incoming Remote Transactions, Outgoing Remote Transactions), and WS-Atomic Transactions if necessary (will prompt for an SSL certificate).
Failover Clustering	Feature	Required for all failover clustering implementations.
Multipath I/O	Feature	Not required for failover clustering, but required if you are going to be using Multipath I/O with your storage.
Storage Manager for SANs	Feature	Optional; new tool to manage storage on SANs.
Windows PowerShell	Feature	New way to manage servers; optional in Windows Server 2008 RTM and installed by default on Windows Server 2008 R2.
Windows System Resource Manager	Feature	Optional; will also install a dependency, which is the Windows Internal Database feature.

Figure 2-6. *Initial Configuration Tasks dialog*

Domain Connectivity

Failover clustering has always required that the nodes be part of a Windows domain. For Windows Server 2008 nodes, the domain must be Active Directory–based, not the older-style Windows NT 4.0 domains. If you are still using older, non–Active Directory domains, you will not be able to deploy Windows Server 2008 failover clustering until those domains are upgraded. All nodes must be part of the same domain. You must also have redundant domain controllers to prevent a single point of failure. In fact, all aspects of your back end (DNS, etc.) should be redundant. It would be counterproductive to take out a cluster due to the fact another component brought it down.

CLUSTER NODES AS DOMAIN CONTROLLERS

One bone of contention with many customers is the domain requirement. In some cases, SQL Server failover clustering is the only reason that would require the use of domains in a customer's environment, so customers want to make the nodes domain controllers as well. The recommendation from the Windows development team at Microsoft is that the nodes be only member servers. Can you install a domain controller on a node? Yes; there are no mechanisms in place to prevent it, and it should work. However, be aware that SQL Server 2008's installer specifically checks to see if any of the nodes are domain controllers, and will block the installation of SQL Server 2008. Therefore, you will need separate (and redundant) servers to function as domain controllers. I apologize if this is a sticking point with anyone reading this section, but if you cannot meet the requirement that SQL Server 2008 not run on a domain controller, then do not deploy failover clusters, and choose an alternative technology to make your SQL Server instances and databases available. Also, do not think you can fake the installer out by installing SQL Server and then configuring a node as a domain controller. Even if this were possible to do, doing so would mean invalidating a cluster configuration that previously would have been supported.

Cluster Administration Account

A big change to failover clustering in Windows Server 2008 is the way failover clustering uses the domain-based account usually configured for the cluster. Unlike previous versions of Windows where you would create a domain account that would be used to run the cluster on each node, Windows Server 2008 does not require a domain account for this purpose. Windows Server 2008 failover clustering runs in a special context that has the permissions and rights necessary. This is similar to the local system context, but with reduced privileges.

You still need to create a domain-based account that will be used to install and then administer the failover cluster. This account must be added to the local Administrators group on each node. The account must also be given the Create Computer Objects right in Active Directory.

If you do not give this right, you will see an error similar to the one in Figure 2-7. Technically, you can use any domain-based account that is configured in the local Administrators group on each node and assigned the Create Computer Objects right to install and administer a Windows Server 2008 failover cluster, but it makes sense to create a dedicated account for these purposes so you know that there are limited users who can perform cluster-related tasks.

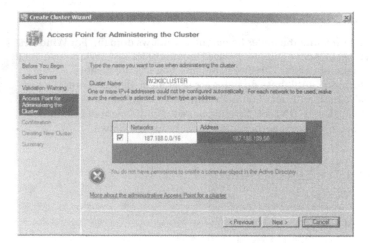

Figure 2-7. *Windows failover cluster error when the account does not have the Create Computer Objects privilege*

Cluster Name Object

At the domain level, you now have something called the Cluster Name Object (CNO). The CNO is a Network Name resource in the Windows failover cluster that acts as the identity for the cluster and owns all of the Virtual Computer Objects (VCOs) configured in the failover cluster. A VCO is one of the names (such as the name given to a virtual SQL Server).

Networking

One of the key components to deploying a successful server cluster is your networking, since clustering relies on the network to ensure node availability. You must have a minimum of two physically separate NICs in each server that will participate as a node in a server cluster. One NIC will be used for the public network and another for the private network. Many motherboards in servers now include built-in NICs. While you do not have to, for serviceability, it may be better to use NICs that utilize expansion slots in the server, not built-in network ports on the motherboard. It is much quicker, easier, and less risky to replace a single bad NIC than it is to replace a motherboard. Consider your NICs from another standpoint: your chances of availability go up if at least one will work in the event that there is a driver problem with one of your NICs (and assuming they are separate [one in a slot, one on board]). One reviewer for this chapter did point out that he had seen private IP conflicts when using blades in a chassis using all on-board NICs.

Cluster Networks

In Chapter 1, you learned that a failover cluster relies on both a public and a private network to work. For a server cluster to be able to provide the availability it is designed for, redundant physical networks and paths must be used. For example, do not plug every node into the same network switch. Redundant DNS servers must exist in your network ecosystem, and your DNS must support dynamic registration. WINS is not required.

Private Cluster Network

The private cluster network must be separate from the public network. This means it must be running on its own and physically must connect through its own switches, hubs, and routers. If all the networks on your cluster are plugged into the same switches, hubs, and routers, your network could be a single point of failure. You need to ensure that even at the physical layer, there is appropriate redundancy and separation. When configuring the private cluster network, the following rules apply:

- If you are only deploying two nodes located in the same data center near each other, a crossover cable can be used for the primary private network. If more than two nodes are used, a crossover cable cannot be used between the nodes.

- NIC teaming, which is the ability to provide fault tolerance by "binding" network cards together to allow failover and failure of one without bringing the entire network on the server down, is not supported on the dedicated adapters for the private cluster network.

- Never configure a gateway or DNS server in the TCP/IP settings for the network adapter used for the private cluster network.

- Disable NetBIOS for all network adapters that are participating in the private cluster network.

- The private cluster network needs to have redundancy, or a backup network in the event the primary private network fails. This can be another dedicated private network or the public network.

- The private cluster network cannot have a network latency of greater than 500 milliseconds.

- The private cluster network, if not on the main network, should use a unique subnet available to only nodes of the cluster you are configuring. The private cluster network can use the following blocks of IP addresses since they are related to private usage; do not use them for the public network configuration:

  - 10.0.0.0 to 10.255.255.255 (class A)

  - 172.16.0.0 to 172.31.255.255 (class B)

  - 192.168.0.0 to 192.168.255.255 (class C)

■**Tip** For a primer on subnets and subnet masks, refer to http://technet.microsoft.com/en-us/library/cc958832.aspx, or, for a more academic approach, http://tools.ietf.org/html/rfc4632. With the switch to support IPv6 in Windows Server 2008, you may have noticed some places using the traditional subnet masks, and other places (PowerShell New-Cluster or Add-Cluster cmdlets when the -IgnoreNetwork switch is used in R2) using the shortcuts (i.e., /8, /16). Understanding the shorthand will serve you well far into the future if you learn it now.

- Although it might support higher speeds from the physical network, the private cluster network does not require high bandwidth.

Public Network

The public network does not have as many strict rules imposed on it as the private network, but there are still some considerations:

- You might configure more than one public network as long as you have the IP addresses available and slots to put additional NICs in the servers.

- You must configure both a gateway and a primary and secondary DNS for each network adapter configured for use with the public network.

- The public network must be on a completely different subnet than the private network (or any other network) configured as part of the failover cluster.

- In Windows Server 2008, by default, all networks are enabled for use in the failover cluster. One network must provide redundancy for the private network. The public network should serve as that redundant network for private communications.

- NIC teaming is technically supported on the externally facing NICs used by the public network. Do not use NIC teaming unless you test the failover capabilities of the NIC to ensure it will not cause any problems with the failover cluster. An example of a problem would be a false failover of resources if an interruption in network service is detected. If you are encountering problems on your cluster where NIC teaming is enabled on the public network, should you call Microsoft Support, be aware that they may ask you to disable NIC teaming.

- Each network (and this includes the private cluster network) must be configured as a distinct subnet that differs from all other networks being used. The same subnet mask is fine, but, for example, configuring two networks to use 195.222.x.x would be invalid.

Dedicated TCP/IP Addresses or Dynamic TCP/IP Addresses

When deploying a SQL Server 2008 failover cluster, there is a minimum number of IP addresses that you will need. How many you need will depend on a few factors, not the least of which is the number of nodes. Consider the following example: you will be deploying a four-node cluster that will also require MSDTC.

The TCP/IP addresses needed are as follows:

- One TCP/IP address for each cluster node, for a total of four

- One for the private network on each cluster node, for a total of four

- One for the Windows failover cluster itself

- Any networking required for storage

- One for MSDTC

- One for each SQL Server failover clustering instance

Windows Server 2008 adds support for IPv6 addresses as well as the old-style IPv4 addresses. Most, if not all, of your current networks probably use the old style of IP addressing, or IPv4. Only deploy an IPv6-based addressing scheme if your infrastructure is prepared to support it. However, you should start talking about when it may make sense to consider transitioning to IPv6-based networks to get it in your planning roadmap.

New to Windows Server 2008 failover clustering is the ability to utilize DHCP for TCP/IP addresses. Both the nodes and the Windows Server 2008 failover cluster can use DHCP. Even SQL Server 2008 supports DHCP for its instances (SQL Server 2005 does not support DHCP). However, I would not recommend using DHCP for any SQL Server 2008 deployment, since part of installing a reliable, dependable server is predictability, and you would hopefully want to ensure that even after a failover, a SQL Server instance will retain its TCP/IP address.

Network Ports

Various ports both on Windows and in network-based firewalls must be opened for both Windows Server 2008 and SQL Server 2008 failover clustering to work properly. Table 2-4 shows the ports with an explanation of what each covers.

Table 2-4. *TCP and UDP Ports Required for Failover Clustering*

Affected	Port Number	Port Type	Comments
Analysis Services	2383	TCP	2383 is the default dynamic port that an instance of Analysis Services will attempt to use. See Chapter 5 for more information.
Cluster Service	3343	UDP	This is the port used by Windows failover clustering.
Database Mirroring Endpoints	TBD	TCP	This is only configured when database mirroring is enabled for a database.
Failover Cluster Admin	137	UDP	This port may not be one administrators want to open, so some discussions with your security administrators may be needed to open this port.
File and Printer Sharing	139	TCP	Depending on the quorum model, the cluster may need to access file shares. Access to file shares may also be needed if you're using replication.
File and Printer Sharing	445	TCP	Depending on the quorum model, the cluster may need to access file shares. Access to file shares may also be needed if you're using replication.
File and Printer Sharing	138	UDP	Depending on the quorum model, the cluster may need to access file shares. Access to file shares may also be needed if you're using replication.
RPC	135	TCP	RPC is used by Cluster Service, MSDTC, and SQL Server Integration Services.
SQL Server	1433	TCP	1433 is the default dynamic port an instance of SQL Server will attempt to use. See Chapter 5 for more information.
SQL Server Browser	1434	UDP	1434 is the port used by the SQL Server Browser.

For a list of other ports you may need to open depending on what other functionality may be in use, consult KB832017 (http://support.microsoft.com/default.aspx/kb/832017), as well as the topic "Configuring the Windows Firewall to Allow SQL Server Access" in SQL Server Books Online (currently at http://msdn.microsoft.com/en-us/library/cc646023.aspx; the latest version can always be found at the Microsoft site).

Choosing a Quorum Model

With Windows Server 2003, there were only two quorum types: Disk and Majority Node Set. For those unfamiliar with those models, here is a quick recap of what those were:

- *Disk*: This is a traditional quorum device placed on a dedicated shared disk attached to the cluster.

- *Majority Node Set (MNS)*: This does not require a dedicated drive and drive letter to maintain quorum. It uses a directory on the local system drive for the quorum and can be found at %SystemRoot%\Cluster\MNS.%ResourceGUID%$\%ResourceGUID%$\MSCS. This directory and its contents should never be modified. For one node to be able to access the quorum to update the cluster database on another node, a share is set up as \\%NodeName%\%ResourceGUID%$. For the cluster to remain up and running, the majority of nodes must be operational.

As noted in Chapter 1, there are four types of quorum models to choose from. The expanded types are now included to provide more protection and availability for the failover cluster, and eliminate single points of failure. The calculation for determining majority is as follows:

Majority (rounded down) = (Total Voters/2) + 1

A voter can be a node, a disk witness, or a file share witness. The witness types are as follows:

- *No Majority*: This is the same as the old disk-based quorum where the quorum disk is a single point of failure. There is no other mechanism; only the disk, which counts as a vote. This type is not the default as it was in all versions of Windows prior to Windows Server 2008, and is not recommended as a configuration by either Microsoft or myself, since it would be a single point of failure.

- *Node Majority*: This is the same as the old Majority Node Set quorum just described. This is best for an odd number of nodes. Not only does SQL Server require the use of shared drives, but a configuration of a clustered SQL Server instance should never be placed in a position where SQL Server will go down if a majority of nodes are lost. Sure, you can force quorum—but again, you may cause an availability problem where there should not have been one.

- *Node and Disk Majority*: This quorum model is a combination of both the witness disk (No Majority) and a majority of nodes (Node Majority), giving your more protection by ostensibly reducing the single point of failure that exists with just No Majority. This is the default witness type when configuring a Windows Server 2008 failover cluster. I agree with this default; there should be no need to change the witness type unless you have a good reason to do so. Consider the following two examples based on a five-node failover cluster:

  - A massive power surge causes two nodes to fail, leaving you with three. The witness disk is still up. Using the first calculation, (5 + 1) / 2 + 1 = 4, but since there are four voters in play (disk witness plus three nodes), the cluster is still up and running. Even if you lost the witness disk, the calculation would be (5 / 2) + 1 = 3.5, which is rounded down to 3. Three nodes are still up, and the majority would still be in play.

  - This is similar to the previous scenario, except all but one node remains up; and this time, the part of the SAN that has the witness disk has failed as well. (6 / 2) + 1 = 4, but only one node is up, so there is no majority. The cluster would go offline and you would have to either force it manually to come online or fix the issues.

- *Node and File Share Majority*: This is similar to the Node and Disk Majority, but uses a file share instead of a witness disk. The calculations are the same, but the witness disk is swapped out for the file share. This witness type is a logical choice for a geographically dispersed cluster.

Using the preceding calculation (majority (rounded down) = (total voters / 2) + 1), assume for a second that you have only two nodes and a No Majority quorum model. You would have three voters: the two nodes and the disk witness. So, the calculation would be (3 / 2) +1, or 2.5, which is rounded down to 2. That means if a node fails, both the disk and other node need to be up. If you suffer a more catastrophic failure such as a node and the disk, you would be out of luck. This is why the new quorum models in Windows Server 2008 protect your availability much better.

Other Configuration Considerations

This section details other Windows-level considerations for deploying SQL Server 2008 failover clusters on Windows Server 2008. Taking these considerations into account will not only simplify work later for the person who is responsible for the SQL Server portion of the installation, but also ensure that things are properly configured well in advance of installing SQL Server 2008.

Number of Nodes

This topic will be explored a bit more in Chapter 5 since the number will ultimately depend on your SQL Server configuration and how many instances will be installed on the Windows failover cluster. The concepts that you need to understand are N and N+X, where X is a number of nodes above the nodes that will host SQL Server instances. Why would you consider more than N nodes? Since SQL Server 2000, there has been the notion of N+1, where a single node would be a dedicated failover node. For example, if you have a three-node cluster with a few instances, you are assuming only one node would fail, so those resources would go to the +1 node and not affect the others. An N+X configuration is the same principle, except there are multiple possible failover nodes, which you can control with preferences. How many failover nodes you may (or may not) want will depend not only on SQL Server factors, but on things like your SLAs.

OR and AND Dependencies

New to Windows Server 2008 failover clustering are the concepts of OR and AND for dependencies for a resource. An example of what this looks like in Failover Cluster Management is shown in Figure 2-8. If you understand set theory, you know what OR and AND bring to the table. SQL Server 2008 does not support OR logic when it comes to resources and dependencies.

Figure 2-8. *OR and AND in Failover Cluster Management*

Geographically Dispersed Failover Cluster Configuration

For both high availability and disaster recovery purposes, you may want to consider deploying a geographically dispersed cluster. This is not something that you can generally configure after the fact, since it involves clustering at the Windows and SQL layers combined with a special low-level configuration from a hardware vendor (specifically, the storage vendor). The same validation requirements apply to a geographically dispersed cluster as they would to a local-only one. A geographically dispersed cluster is not one that you would configure on your own, because it involves both things you would do as an administrator combined with an advanced hardware configuration.

Realize that deploying a geographically dispersed failover cluster has a few requirements and limitations. To deploy the cluster in this configuration, besides the number of nodes you would need, you need two copies of your storage and a specialized piece of software at the storage level from the vendor, which enables replication between the two storage units. This special software is often not included in the base price of the storage. Clearly, this could be much more expensive than you had initially planned on. Most major storage vendors support a variation of storage replication.

When configuring the replication between the storage units, there is a choice of either asynchronous of synchronous. For no data loss, you should always choose synchronous replication. This means you need good performance for replication. The dark fibre that must be laid out between the sites to enable replication is not only very expensive and prone to limitations, but it will arguably be the most costly part of the configuration. When it comes to distance, current technology is still limited to around 100 miles by most vendors to support synchronous replication. Vendors may support longer distances, but ensure that you get written guarantees and that the latency meets failover clustering requirements for networking, since SANs do have networking underneath the covers.

Although Windows Server 2008 failover clustering added support for utilizing multiple subnets, neither SQL Server 2005 nor SQL Server 2008 failover clustering support the OR functionality described in the previous section. All nodes must be configured on the same subnet. If you are planning to deploy a geographically dispersed cluster, you will still need to configure a virtual local area network (VLAN). It is unlikely this will be fixed in a service pack to either SQL Server 2005 or SQL Server 2008, but support for multiple subnets is something that is being considered for inclusion in the next major version of SQL Server.

Environment Variables

Both the tmp and temp environment variables should be set to a path that does not include spaces. The variables need to be configured for both the user doing the installing as well as the overall system variables. Microsoft Support has seen cases (especially on 64-bit) where having a space in the path names for these two environment variables has caused SQL Server's installation to fail. Setting these variables can be done under System in the Control Panel. Select the Advanced tab and click Environment Variables. A sample is shown in Figure 2-9.

Figure 2-9. *Setting the tmp and temp environment variables*

Microsoft Distributed Transaction Coordinator

The configuration (or lack thereof) of the Microsoft Distributed Transaction Coordinator (MSDTC) has been a hotly contested piece of cluster configuration for all SQL Server deployments going back to the Windows NT 4.0 days. It seems like if you ask two people, they will have ten opinions on this matter.

I will be very clear here: it is *not* a requirement to configure MSDTC for SQL Server 2008; SQL Server 2008 setup will check to see if MSDTC is clustered and configured, but will proceed without it, as shown in Figure 2-10. Some functionality of SQL Server does use MSDTC (e.g., transactional replication with updateable subscriptions and immediate updates). So, you will need to do your own homework to figure out which features of SQL Server you are using and if they do or do not use MSDTC.

From a configuration standpoint, one of the sticking points is that MSDTC requires a clustered disk resource as well as an IP address. The disk resource may or may not be a big deal to you if you only have a few disks presented to the failover cluster. If you do require a clustered MSDTC, never configure it to use the disk that is configured as the witness disk. Should MSDTC's log fill up the disk, you may affect the availability of the cluster itself if it can no longer work properly.

One change to the implementation of MSDTC in Windows Server 2008 is that you can create multiple MSDTC resources, including one per resource group if you wish. For more details on the MSDTC implementation in Windows Server 2008 failover clustering, read the topic at http:// technet.microsoft.com/en-us/library/cc730992.aspx.

I recommend to configure a clustered MSDTC nine times out of ten to most customers. Why? If you do not wind up needing MSDTC, it will consume very little in the way of system resources, and the worst thing would be a disk that does not have to be very big to begin with. As I mentioned, *you* have the responsibility of sorting out what does and does not use MSDTC. If you start using SQL Server, get errors, and determine you need MSDTC, you can always configure it later, so it is a correctable offense. I always frontload work rather than do it later. The choice is yours, but why cause yourself potential heartache for something that should not be a big deal?

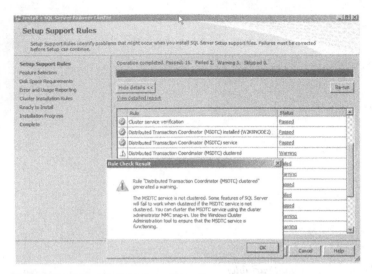

Figure 2-10. *Check in SQL Server 2008's setup for MSDTC*

Prerequisites for SQL Server 2008

SQL Server 2008 requires that a few prerequisites are installed and configured prior to attempting to install a SQL Server instance. The two major components that must be installed are the .NET Framework and an updated Microsoft Installer (MSI). Depending on the version of Windows you are deploying, this may differ slightly. Table 2-5 details the differences. Note that an Itanium-based cluster has a different .NET Framework requirement that is lower than both x86 and x64. You may lose some functionality, such as LINQ (.NET Language Integrated Query), which is a feature that allows developers to build queries using any .NET-based programming language.

Table 2-5. *Prerequisites for SQL Server 2008 Broken Out by Operating System Version*

Operating System	.NET Framework Version	MSI Version
Windows Server 2003	3.5 SP1 (x86, x64), 2.0 SP2 (IA64)	4.5
Windows Server 2008 RTM	3.5 SP1 (x86, x64), 2.0 SP2 (IA64)	4.5
Windows Server 2008 with Service Pack 2 (or later)	3.5 SP1 (x86, x64), 2.0 SP2 (IA64)	4.5 (already installed)
Windows Server 2008 R2	3.5 SP1 (x64—configured if an Application Server role is added; not configured otherwise), 2.0 SP2 (IA64)	4.5 (already installed)

Both the .NET Framework and MSI installations require a reboot, so if other things are running on the server (assuming it is already in use), you will need to schedule an outage to accommodate the reboot. If this is a brand-new deployment of Windows, these prerequisites should become standard components of a Windows build that will ultimately have SQL Server 2008 deployed on it. SQL Server 2008 also requires that a minimum of Microsoft Data Access Components (MDAC) is on the server with a minimum version of 2.8 Service Pack 1 or later. This requirement is most likely already satisfied. Windows Server 2008 RTM ships with MDAC 6.0, and Windows Server 2003's currently supported service packs include MDAC 2.82. To see which version of MDAC is installed, look at the registry key HKEY_LOCAL_MACHINE\SOFTWARE\Microsoft\DataAccess\FullInstallVer.

Also, if you are using Windows Server 2003 as the operating system for your SQL Server 2008 failover cluster, you must install the hotfix for the Filestream feature documented in Knowledge Base article 937444 (http://support.microsoft.com/kb/937444). If this patch is not applied, the Windows Server 2003 FILESTREAM Hotfix check fails during SQL Server setup.

Note A word about .NET Framework 2.0 SP2: Business Intelligence Development Studio (BIDS) has the dependency for updates at the .NET Framework 3.5 SP1 level. All other SQL Server components depend on .NET Framework 2.0 SP2. .NET Framework 2.0 SP2 is not available as a general download, and Microsoft decided to make .NET Framework 3.5 SP1 a preinstallation step in the event you decided to pick BIDS as a feature. The one exception to this rule is on Itanium (IA64) platforms running Windows Server 2003. This is because .NET Framework 3.5 is not supported on IA64 platforms on operating system versions less than Windows Server 2008. Since .NET Framework 2.0 SP2 is still required in these cases for SQL Server 2008, and you cannot run BIDS on IA64, the installation is included on the media source for SQL Server 2008.

Disk Configuration

One of the most difficult things to do when planning a clustered implementation of SQL Server 2008 is the disk configuration. There is not enough space in this book to cover every nuance of a disk configuration since disk configuration for SQL Server is a topic that could be its own book (which I keep threatening to write). This section will highlight the important factors to consider, and give links to other existing information to help you out where possible, and many of those links contain links to other bits of information.

Note Remember that outside of some quorum models that use a share on the local system drive, no storage is considered local. Everything used by a clustered SQL Server instance is on the shared disk subsystem, including any space needed for backups.

Disk Changes in Windows Server 2008

The biggest change that you should be aware of in Windows Server 2008 is that parallel SCSI is no longer supported. This means that the shared storage disk subsystem must use fibre channel, serial attached SCSI (SAS), or iSCSI. The storage must support SCSI-3 SPC-3–compliant SCSI commands.

Windows Server 2008 no longer performs SCSI bus resets, which could potentially be very disruptive, and no longer are there different layers of Windows trying to do similar tasks with different commands, yet no part of the hardware or software knows what to do with that command. For example, prior to Windows Server 2008, you could have ClusDisk.sys issuing a command to reset a Logical Unit (LUN) to the multipath software, which has its own set of instructions. The port driver may not have been able to do the LUN reset, but may have had the ability to just reset the entire bus. The HBA card can't reset everything but tries to do something similar, and finally the storage array throws its proverbial hands up in the air. The bottom line is that there were many players in what should have been a team game, but everyone was out for individual statistics. With Windows Server 2008, persistent reservations are used and must be supported by the storage.

Multipath I/O

To ensure that there is redundancy for your I/O paths, you have to implement Multipath I/O. This is a combination of support in Windows (see the feature noted earlier in the chapter) as well as a configuration done with multiple HBA cards and possibly storage-specific drivers if the storage vendor does not conform to the spec provided by the Multipath I/O feature of Windows Server 2008. Remember to test your Multipath I/O failover capabilities before attempting to install SQL Server since you have the potential of introducing data corruption if it is not configured properly.

iSCSI

You can use iSCSI for connecting to storage. There are some things you should take into consideration if you are going to use iSCSI and a software initiator over NICs vs. a more traditional HBA card. First and foremost, the NIC (or NICs if using Multipath I/O) used for iSCSI traffic must be dedicated; it cannot share either the public or private network. The reason is fairly obvious: since I/O will be transmitted as network packets, the last thing you want to do is clog up your other networks. That dedicated NIC must then be connected to a dedicated switch that is not used for any other cluster communication, and the NIC cannot be teamed. All NICs configured with iSCSI must be on separate subnets. If they are not, cluster validation will fail.

Drive Types

You can only use basic disks with SQL Server 2008 failover clustering. SQL Server 2008 failover clustering does not support the use of dynamic disks. There are two kinds of basic disks you can configure: either a master boot record (MBR) or a GUID partition table (GPT) disk. An MBR disk can support volumes up to 2 TB and four primary partitions. A GPT disk supports volumes bigger than 2 TB and up to 128 primary partitions. GPT also keeps a backup of the partition table at the end of the disk, and some computers use an EFI-based BIOS which uses GPT-style partition tables. For detailed information on GPT disks, you can read the information at http://www.microsoft.com/whdc/device/storage/GPT_FAQ.mspx and http://www.microsoft.com/whdc/device/storage/GPT-on-x64.mspx. MBR disks are historically what most people have been configuring under Windows for years.

By default, a Windows Server 2003 server cluster does not support GPT disks with RTM, Service Pack 1, or Service Pack 2, as documented in Knowledge Base article 284134 (http://support.microsoft.com/kb/284134). There is a hotfix (Knowledge Base article 919117—http://support.microsoft.com/kb/919117/) also linked in Knowledge Base article 284134 that will allow you to use GPT disks with a Windows Server 2003-based server cluster that will use SQL Server 2008.

One thing to take into consideration no matter what type of drive you configure—MBR or GPT—is not to make it too large. In the event that there is a problem and CHKDSK would need to run, the larger the volume is, the longer it will take to run. Manage your volume size to minimize downtime in a bad scenario. Bottom line, if you're not going to have partitions greater than 2 TB, use MBR.

Hardware Settings

Besides the Windows-level considerations, you must also examine the hardware configuration itself and work with your storage administrators to ensure that you will get the right amount of performance and availability from your disk subsystem. Here are two easy tips:

- Check to see that the setting for queue depth on your HBA is set to be optimal to match your system and storage configurations.

- Most storage that will be used by the cluster nodes will generally be configured on a storage unit that is shared with multiple servers. This means that the storage is not dedicated only for SQL Server, so it cannot be completely optimized for use with SQL Server. One of the common challenges in this environment will be the cache. No matter how large (or small) it is, it will be shared with the other servers connected to the storage. Most storage administrators will set the cache to a 50/50 split for reads and writes.

Formatting the Disks

All disks must be formatted with NTFS. For the disks that will be used for SQL Server data and log (or have the potential at some point to be used for SQL Server data or log), the block size must be set to 64KB. Drives that will be used only for backup files can use the operating system defaults if they will not contain any data and log files. It is never recommended to combine backup with data and/or log.

Disk Alignment

One of the biggest changes from Windows Server 2003 to Windows Server 2008 is that Windows Server 2008 automatically accounts for aligning the logical disks in Windows with the corresponding LUN at the disk level. This was a big pain point pre-Windows Server 2008 because you had to know that not only did your SAN vendor require alignment, but you needed their specific offset to configure it properly with the command line tool DISKPART. You can use DISKPART, but it is not necessary. There is an excellent resource for disk alignment and what it means to SQL Server that can be found at http://tinyurl.com/DPADeck. Keep in mind that some vendors may document disk alignment for partitions and their corresponding sizes, and others may say it is not needed. Do your homework; do not necessarily rely on even the vendor's own consultants who may come and set up your storage. Getting this wrong can wind up being an expensive mistake if you need to tear down your configuration and start from scratch.

Drive Letters and Mount Points

SQL Server 2008 failover clustering still requires drive letters to be used for shared cluster drives with Windows Server 2008. As with SQL Server 2005, you can use mount points, but they must be mounted under a drive letter. This is not a limitation of Windows, as mount points have been supported in clusters since Windows Server 2003, but SQL Server has not yet implemented the ability to use mount points in a cluster without requiring them to be mounted under a drive letter first. This may be fixed in the next major release of SQL Server. Check the final feature list to see if it is implemented when that release is available for use.

Sizing and Configuring Disks

Configuring a disk solution for use with SQL Server is about more than just space requirements: you want good performance, so it is also about I/Os as well. Unfortunately, in most IT shops I've worked with over the years, the DBA has little to no control or influence over how the disk subsystem is configured. Generally, all the storage administrators ask is how much space is needed. They then present that space to Windows, and that's the end of any formal discussions. Any choices about how LUNs are carved out or what type of RAID is used is not open for debate. Unfortunately, that is usually where I come in, after things have been configured horribly and I need to assist customers in troubleshooting performance issues related to I/O. Here are a few tips for having better disk configurations for SQL Server deployments:

- The key to proper SQL Server performance is knowing the amount of I/Os needed. The only way to measure how much I/O capacity you need comes through testing. There are two levels of testing: the hardware, and then your application. Both must be done. First, testing the hardware will show you what the configuration can really handle. There are a few tools that you can use: SQLIO, which is a free tool to simulate a SQL Server–like workload (but is *not* SQL Server; it is a good approximation and can be downloaded from http://www.microsoft.com/downloads/details.aspx?displaylang=en&FamilyID=9a8b005b-84e4-4f24-8d65-cb53442d9e19). A good write-up on how to use SQLIO can be found at http://sqlserverpedia.com/wiki/SAN_Performance_Tuning_with_SQLIO. The reality is that the only thing that will determine your I/O needs will be testing your application at its expected full load. This means that prior to purchasing and/or configuring any hardware, you need to simulate your workload in a test environment. You will use a combination of tools like System Monitor/Performance Monitor with the appropriate counters, as well as some of the SQL Server dynamic management views such as sys.dm_io_virtual_file_stats.

- If there was ever a worst configuration, it would be carving up the storage array as one big chunk of disk to maximize storage space using RAID 5 with no eye toward performance. I don't care if you have 20 spindles (disks) or 200—unless some sort of attempt is made to reconcile I/Os and performance, your implementations are destined to be doomed from the start. Even if RAID 1+0 is used, that *still* is not a guarantee of performance. Disk subsystems should not be overly generic and cannot be "one size fits every usage." I/O patterns for an OLTP database will be different in a data warehouse, a DSS system, an Exchange implementation, a file share, and so on. Let me throw in a huge caveat here: properly architected with the right amount of testing, this situation could work. You certainly do not want over-resourcing and wasted capacity (which is why you see a lot of one-chunk carvings of disk), but just be very careful. You can both overthink a disk configuration as well as not think about it at all.

- Carving out multiple LUNs on the same disks may or may not be a good idea; that is an "it depends." The problem is that with modern SANs, the concept of dedicated disks has been lost. By that, I mean in the "old" days with direct attach storage (DAS), when you RAIDed drives together, those drives were dedicated. With more modern storage, the way most are configured is exactly as described in the previous point: one big storage, and the smaller LUNs are created on top of it. The LUNs are spread out across any number of physical disks. You only get a portion of the bandwidth of the underlying disk. The hardware vendors will have you believe that behind the scenes they handle any hotspotting of disks and that there is intelligent management going on to prevent performance problems. That may happen in some cases and not others. I know from firsthand experience that the ability to get dedicated disks and LUNs for SQL Server these days is nearly impossible, and may cause a large row with your storage admins. There is still a place for dedicated disks and LUNs, but it will depend on your requirements and what you can work out with your storage group. Unless you are prepared to buy your own storage, realize it may be shared in all aspects no matter what it looks like in Windows.

- Putting all of the data files on one disk and all of the log files on another disk is not separation or protection. If you lose the data disk, you lose all of your data. Same with the log disk—you lose it, you lose the logs. That is no better than mixing data and log. Combine that practice with LUNs that share the same physical disks, and you can really find yourself in trouble. Even if storage is presented logically in Windows as more than one disk, that storage may all be on one physical disk on the back end (e.g., on the SAN).

- Know how each application uses tempdb. This will hopefully be measured by the testing talked about in the first point. tempdb has both data and log, and as more and more databases get combined under an instance, tempdb must be sized appropriately for I/O in addition to space; otherwise, it will be a very large bottleneck in your SQL Server deployments. Depending on the workload, you may use tempdb data, log, or both. This is also not a "one size fits all" type of sizing exercise. There is some documentation that supports using multiple data files (one per processor, where a core is a different processor) for tempdb to reduce contention, but if your disk subsystem is not optimal at a lower layer and the LUNs are physically sharing the same disks (see the second point in this list), having multiple files may not provide any benefit.

- If you will be using any kind of advanced backups that are hardware based (such as snapshots or clones), you will have to account for that configuration and the disk space they will need up front. This is another feature that is much harder to configure after the solution is already in place.

- Talk to your storage administrators to ensure that the LUNs that are presented to the cluster nodes are properly zoned and masked at the disk level to ensure that they cannot be seen or used by any other servers.

- When calculating the storage needed, remember to account for the largest size the database will grow to. Consider the following example, as shown in Table 2-6. At a growth rate of 10 percent per month where the database starts at 500 GB, the database in question will grow to over triple in size within 12 months. This does not take into account backups; this is pure data growth. If the solution that utilizes the database will be in production for 3 years, the database will grow to be quite large. It will demand a lot of attention and careful planning from a file perspective to make it manageable. Get the sizing right up front or cause downtime later down the road. It is your choice. Up front would also be the time to talk about archival strategies.

Table 2-6. *Projected Database Growth*

Month	Size (in GB)
January	550
February	605
March	665.5
April	732.05
May	805.26
June	885.78
July	974.36
August	1071.79
September	1178.97
October	1296.87
November	1426.56
December	1569.21

- Remember that estimating disk space (as shown in the previous point) and I/O requirements are two completely separate, but equal, components of your disk needs. Having enough storage to just cover the disk space alone may not be enough disks. Size may not matter; you could have a small database with very high I/O requirements and vice versa.

- Always remember to factor backups into any plan, both from an I/O perspective and a space perspective. Retention of said backups also comes into play. If you've got to store 2 weeks of full, differential, and transaction log backups on disk when your main database is multiple terabytes and growing, that's going to be a lot of disk space even if you are utilizing backup compression in SQL Server 2008 Enterprise Edition or one of the third-party tools for backup compression.

- With the growing need and desire for multiple instances and many databases per instance for consolidation, there is no way that you will get complete separation for every data and log file (see the preceding point for some more separation talk). You need to get smarter about what can and cannot be combined. There is no magic formula, and it takes a lot of information to even come close to making the right decisions.

Configuration Example

This section presents a short configuration example. In the example, I show how to translate a basic set of requirements into a reasonable deployment.

Scenario

The disk subsystem will power all databases used by your company's finance department in a consolidation effort. There are 14 databases, two of which are "heavy hitters" when it comes to disk I/O. The other 12 databases have relatively low I/O and are not used as much. One application needs MSDTC to be configured. The following list details the known basic requirements and issues:

- One disk is needed for the witness (assuming the Node and Disk Majority quorum model).

- One disk is needed for a clustered MSDTC.

- You will need 30 days of on-disk retention for making backups to disk.

- One of your applications uses tempdb heavily since it creates temporary tables and does a lot of sorting operations.

- You have no control over the low-level configuration of the shared disks; you can only control size.

Here are your unknowns:

- You do not know the growth patterns of each database.

- When you run out of space on your current drives, you don't know how to size a new environment properly.

- You have intermittent I/O performance issues on your current database servers and do not know the root cause.

- You do not know your I/O requirements.

Planning and Deployment

The previous requirements are not much to go on (but are often all I know when I am brought in to assist customers). The last bullet point in the first list is crucial: you have *no* control over how your disks are configured at the physical level. While this may result in your disks not being able to handle your I/O load (you do not know your I/O requirement anyway), it is not something you will find out until it is too late. In these cases, I always recommend documenting this fact so that if performance problems occur, you have documentation to back up the fact that you were not given the information necessary up front to head off the problems that are currently occurring. If you can't control how disks are configured at a low level, then you shouldn't be held responsible when that low-level configuration is found to be lacking. Just remember to document this fact if disk performance issues arise.

You need a minimum of one drive letter for a clustered instance of SQL Server 2008. You could use mount points under that drive letter, but that may or may not be the right architecture. In this case, if you want to split the data and log for each database, you are looking at 28 drive letters—two more than the alphabet. In my experience, you never really have 26 drives available to you. On your servers, there is always one drive for your program files and operating system (usually C), one for some sort of an optical drive (usually D), and oftentimes one or more drives for mapped drives on your network when a user logs in. In the case of this example, drive X is used for a mapped drive. Take away the disk for MSDTC and the witness disk in this example, and you are down to 21 drive letters already before you even think about SQL Server. What is the best use of those remaining 21 drive letters?

Your goal should not be to use every single drive letter. What happens if you need to deploy another instance of SQL Server on the cluster, or you need some future expansion? Be smart—leave yourself some headroom. Also keep in mind that if you are considering mount points, each is a LUN attached to Windows. A LUN may not have a drive letter, but it still has overhead.

One disk should definitely be your dedicated backup disk (down to 20). This will arguably be your largest disk in size since you will be doing all backups to this drive. Because you have a 30-day retention policy, you will also need to get smart about your backup strategy. Doing full backups every night of every database may not be possible, and to get 30 days worth of backups on a single disk, you may need to look into a way to compress the database backups (such as the feature in SQL Server 2008 Enterprise Edition or a third-party piece of software)—even with compression, it may be a challenge to hold 30 days worth on one drive.

The basic system databases for the instance (master, model, and msdb) can be placed on a single small-size disk with low I/O. You already know that you have high tempdb utilization and you dedicate a single disk for it. The tempdb disk will contain both the data and log files for tempdb since you do not know if there is a performance bottleneck with heavy usage of tempdb's log file; you can always reconfigure tempdb later to split data and log. You also need to size the tempdb disk appropriately since you are now combining the workload of 14 databases onto a single instance of SQL Server.

Since you are combining 14 databases under a single instance of SQL Server, you cannot assume they will all play nicely with each other in terms of disk I/O. It is best to know something about each database's characteristics in determining where it will ultimately be placed. Does the database in question trend toward heavy reads? Heavy writes? Is the database used for reporting? Is the database powering a mission-critical application that must be separated from others at a physical level? Those are just some of the questions you need to ask yourself throughout this configuration process.

Once you know a bit more about the databases to be deployed, you are going to want to spread the I/O load from those databases out somewhat evenly if possible. You know you have two huge databases. Each one of those should get its own dedicated data and log disks, for a total of four drive letters. That leaves the other 12 databases. This is where things get interesting. Each one is of generally low I/O consumption and not very big, so you decide to spread the load—you will put them across three drives (four databases per drive). It really is not feasible nor smart to give each data and log file its own physical drive on the SAN, so combining them across different drives is what will be done.

Each drive will contain both data and log files, but to prevent a single point of failure, none will contain only data or log, and the data and log files for a single database will be split over different drives. While it is technically a "best practice" to separate data from log, besides the impracticality of it in this case, the chances that you would get any performance benefit from doing so with low-volume I/O databases are slim.

I'm avoiding the issue of exact size for each drive in this example, because not only is sizing discussed in the previous example with the 10 percent growth (as shown in Table 2-6), but the exact size is irrelevant for purposes of this discussion. The bottom line is that without growth numbers (as well as performance numbers—even if it is one baseline), no matter what you do, you're just guessing. You already have disk space issues on your current servers. Going to this cluster is supposed to make you more available and give you flexibility. You won't have it if you undersize your disks. If you are maxed out of your current storage, at a minimum you should plan for doubling the size of the disks to accommodate 100 percent growth. Will that be expensive? Most likely, but it is probably better than having an unusable system that does not even come close to meeting your needs. The key is figuring out how long the system is slated to be in production; if you know from day one you are nearly behind the proverbial eight ball, and this system is going to be in play for 3 to 5 years, you are in trouble.

One possible configuration using only drive letters would look like Table 2-7. You are left with 12 drives to use for other purposes or later expansion. Another configuration, shown in Table 2-8, shows the difference if you use mount points instead of all drive letters.

Table 2-7. *Failover Cluster Disk Configuration, All Drive Letters for SQL Server*

Drive Letter	Location	Purpose
C	Internal drive	OS
D	Internal drive	DVD-ROM
E	Shared disk subsystem	System databases (master, model, msdb)
F	Shared disk subsystem	tempdb data and log
G	Shared disk subsystem	Large database 1—data only
H	Shared disk subsystem	Large database 1—log only
I	Shared disk subsystem	Large database 2—data only
J	Shared disk subsystem	Large database 2—log only
K	Shared disk subsystem	Four databases—data and log
L	Shared disk subsystem	Four databases—data and log
M	Shared disk subsystem	MSDTC
N	Shared disk subsystem	Four databases—data and log
Q	Shared disk subsystem	Witness disk
X	Mapped drive	User files

Table 2-8. *Failover Cluster Disk Configuration, One Drive Letter for SQL Server and the Rest Mount Points*

Drive Letter	Location	Purpose
C	Internal drive	OS
D	Internal drive	DVD-ROM
E	Shared disk subsystem	System databases (master, model, msdb)
Mount Point (MP) 1	Shared disk subsystem	tempdb data and log; MP under E:\
MP2	Shared disk subsystem	Large database 1—data only
MP3	Shared disk subsystem	Large database 1—log only
MP4	Shared disk subsystem	Large database 2—data only
MP5	Shared disk subsystem	Large database 2—log only
MP6	Shared disk subsystem	Four databases—data and log
MP7	Shared disk subsystem	Four databases—data and log
M	Shared disk subsystem	MSDTC
MP8	Shared disk subsystem	Four databases—data and log
Q	Shared disk subsystem	Witness disk
X	Mapped drive	User files

Upgrading Existing Clusters to Windows Server 2008

While there have been many improvements that come with the rewrite of failover clustering in Windows Server 2008, there is one possible pain point you may encounter. If you were planning on just upgrading existing Windows Server 2003 cluster nodes in a rolling upgrade like you were able to going from Windows 2000 Advanced Server to Windows Server 2003 Enterprise Edition, then give up now. Such a rolling upgrade is not possible. There is no direct upgrade from Windows Server 2003 to Windows Server 2008 in a clustered configuration. This means that if you need to repurpose existing hardware to deploy Windows Server 2008 failover clustering (assuming it is "Certified for Windows Server 2008," as noted earlier), then you will also need to plan for and incur some downtime.

Windows Server 2008 does provide the Migrate a Cluster Wizard, which you can use to migrate existing server cluster settings, but it cannot be used to migrate clustered SQL Server instances. To be honest, when you are considering using Windows Server 2008 with SQL Server and using existing nodes, it is much easier to start from a completely clean slate. The best way to upgrade existing cluster nodes that will become Windows Server 2008 cluster nodes is to perform the following steps. The steps are high level, and some will be covered in detail in upcoming chapters.

1. Back up and document all SQL Server databases (including the system databases), settings, and so on. The backups of the databases will be used later in the process, but will also provide a failsafe in the event that things need to be rolled back.

2. Uninstall all SQL Server instances. If you are using SQL Server 2005, follow the instructions as shown in the section "Uninstalling a Failover Clustering Instance" in Chapter 9 of *Pro SQL Server 2005 High Availability*. Performing this step will ensure that each SQL Server instance was removed cleanly from the existing cluster.

3. Install a fresh copy of Windows Server 2008 on each node. Installing a new copy of the operating system means that there will be no lingering registry entries or other problems coming over that may have existed with the prior configuration.

4. Cluster the nodes. See Chapter 3 for complete instructions.

5. Install SQL Server (2005 or 2008). For SQL Server 2005, see Chapter 8 of *Pro SQL Server 2005 High Availability*, or for SQL Server 2008, consult Chapter 6 of this book.

6. Restore (or attach) databases, settings, users, and objects. If you've installed SQL Server 2008 in step 5, any 2005 databases will be upgraded during the restoration process.

■**Tip** Available for download is a helpful planning and configuration Excel spreadsheet/Word document that will help you document all of the components and settings needed for your upcoming Windows and SQL Server 2008 failover cluster.

Summary

This chapter covered all of the aspects of planning the Windows-specific considerations for clustering SQL Server 2008 with Windows Server 2008. The SQL Server–specific considerations for clustering SQL Server 2008 are documented in Chapter 5. As noted earlier, it is crucial to take the time and get things right now, because if you don't, you will have problems with SQL Server later on, even if they do not manifest themselves immediately. Having said that, at this point you should be able to proceed to the installation and configuration of the Windows portion of your failover cluster with no problems.

■ ■ ■

CHAPTER 3

Clustering Windows Server 2008
Part 1: Preparing Windows

After putting the plan together for a Windows Server 2008 failover cluster deployment, it must be executed. This chapter will cover all of the steps to prepare for clustering Windows. Where possible, it will describe how to configure using an interface as well as via scripting. In some cases where there are multiple ways to script, I have selected to show what I felt to be the most straightforward.

Check the downloads on the Apress site (http://www.apress.com), as well as on http://www.sqlha.com, for job aids related to planning and deploying a Windows and SQL Server failover cluster (such as checklists and workbooks for entering the configuration).

■ **Tip** SQL Server 2008 can also be deployed as a failover clustering configuration using Windows Server 2003 (RTM or R2) with Windows Server 2003 Service Pack 2 or later. Read Chapters 4 through 6 of *Pro SQL Server 2005 High Availability* to see how to cluster Windows Server 2003. Any differences in planning for SQL Server 2008 failover clustering using the Windows Server 2003 (instead of Windows Server 2008) configuration are detailed in Chapter 2 and Chapter 5.

Step 1: Install and Configure Hardware and Windows Server 2008

The first step is arguably the easiest and one in which most DBAs and Windows administrators will not have a lot of involvement in: get the hardware in-house, and configure what needs to be done outside the Windows and SQL Server aspects. However, it is up to the administrators to communicate their requirements for low-level configurations, such as disk.

Each node's hardware configuration should ideally be the same (see the section "Cluster Validation" in Chapter 2, as well as Chapter 5, for sizing hardware for nodes). Also, you should ensure that all firmware and BIOS levels for each component matches what the respective vendor says is supported with Windows Server 2008 failover clustering. As noted in the section "Cluster Validation" in Chapter 2, Microsoft no longer maintains a list of the valid configurations for a failover cluster (but it does have the Failover Cluster Configuration Program [FCCP], which is slightly different). So you can either consult the FCCP, or even better, check the web site for the vendor of each component (especially any hardware related to the disk subsystem) to see what versions they have tested, recommend, and support for use with Windows Server 2008 failover clustering configurations. Even if you are only the DBA, you should verify that the configuration you will be using will be supportable not only by Microsoft, but by the hardware vendors themselves.

Once that task is complete, you can install Windows Server 2008 on your servers. Remember that the Core variation of Windows Server 2008 is not supported for use with SQL Server 2008 failover clustering.

Step 2: Configure Networking for a Failover Cluster

How to plan the network configuration for a failover cluster was covered in Chapter 2 in the section "Networking." This section will demonstrate how to implement the proper network configuration for a failover cluster.

Configure the Network Cards

There are two sides to configuring your network cards. First, you have the so-called public network side, which allows your cluster to communicate with clients and the outside world. Then there is the private network, which is what your cluster nodes use to communicate among themselves.

Configure the Public Network

The public network will serve as the network used for connectivity to the SQL Server instances in the cluster. To configure the public network, follow the instructions in this section.

1. Log onto one of the servers that will serve as a node in the server cluster with an account that has privileges to configure networking.

2. If you are using the RTM branch of Windows Server 2008, from the Start menu, right-click *Network*, select *Properties*, and finally, select the option *Manage network connections*. If you are using Windows Server 2008 R2, open Control Panel. Under Network and Internet, select *View network status and tasks*, and select *Change adapter settings* from the Network and Sharing Center dialog. The Network Connections dialog will now be displayed.

3. Right-click the network card you want to configure and select *Rename*.

4. Enter a name for the public network that is easy to identify, such as **Public Network**, and press Enter. The new name will now be reflected as shown in Figure 3-1.

Figure 3-1. *Successfully renamed network card*

5. Now it is time to alter the properties of the public-facing network card. Right-click the network card you just renamed and select *Properties*; alternatively, you can double-click it.

6. My recommendation is to deselect any unnecessary protocols or features that will not be used or that are not necessary. On the public network, I always recommend to generally keep everything checked unless you are 100 percent sure you will not use it. For example, if your network is not configured to use Internet Protocol version 6 (IPv6), deselect that option. An example of IPv6 being disabled is shown in Figure 3-2. The rest of this section will show configuring a public network based on an IPv4 address. If you do use IPv6, the configuration steps will be similar to what is shown in this section.

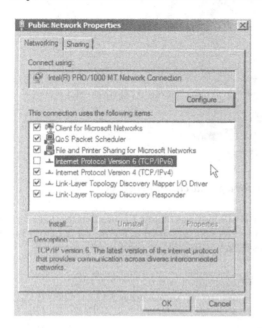

Figure 3-2. *Removing unused options*

7. Select *Internet Protocol Version 4 (TCP/IPv4)*, and either double-click that item or click the Properties button. The Internet Protocol Version 4 (TCP/IPv4) Properties dialog box will now be displayed.

8. While Windows Server 2008 cluster nodes support DHCP functionality, as noted in the section "Networking" in Chapter 2, it is not recommended to use it. It is better to use a static IP address because predictability is a good thing when you want to ensure availability. Click the *Use the following IP address* option, and enter a static IP address, a valid gateway in the *Default gateway* field, and a primary and secondary DNS server in the *Preferred DNS server* and *Alternate DNS server* fields. When finished, your properties dialog should look something like Figure 3-3. Click Advanced.

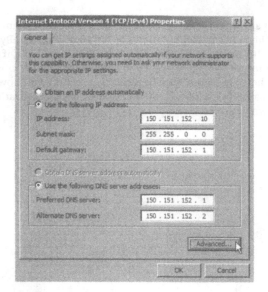

Figure 3-3. *Example TCP/IP properties for a public cluster network*

9. Select the *DNS* tab of the Advanced TCP/IP Settings dialog. Ensure that the *Register this connection's addresses in DNS* option is checked, as shown in Figure 3-4. You may benefit from explicitly configuring the DNS suffixes here, but it is not a requirement.

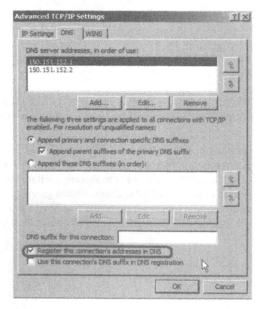

Figure 3-4. *DNS tab*

10. Select the *WINS* tab of the Advanced TCP/IP Settings dialog. Ensure that the *Enable NetBIOS over TCP/IP* option is checked, as shown in Figure 3-5. Click OK. Click OK again on the Internet Protocol Version 4 (TCP/IPv4) Properties dialog. Finally, click OK on the main properties page to save all settings.

Note An interesting point was raised while this chapter was reviewed. There are numerous places in Microsoft's documentation that state NetBIOS is not available from Windows Server 2008 on (e.g., `http://msdn.microsoft.com/en-us/library/bb870913(VS.85).aspx`). Yet others say the complete opposite (e.g., the IPv4 name resolution documentation for Windows Server 2008, at `http://technet.microsoft.com/en-us/library/dd379505.aspx`). So for now, I would configure the NetBIOS settings as described here (and in the next section for the private network). That way, if NetBIOS is relevant, you will have it; if it is not relevant, it won't hurt that you have it. Better to be safe than sorry.

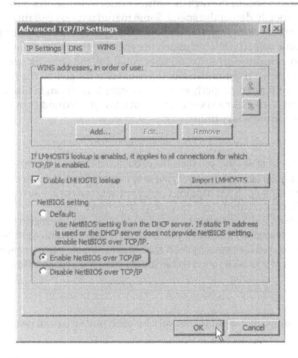

Figure 3-5. *WINS tab*

11. Right-click the network card you just renamed in step 4, and select *Properties*. The properties for the network card will be displayed. Click Configure. Had you tried this before saving the settings that were configured in the prior steps, you would have seen the dialog box in Figure 3-6.

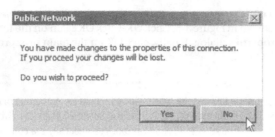

Figure 3-6. *Warning dialog*

12. Select the *Advanced* tab of the network card's properties. Under *Property*, look for a setting such as *External PHY, Link Speed & Duplex*, or *Speed & Duplex*, where you can set the actual speed at which communications will occur through the network card. Never set this parameter to let the network card automatically detect the speed. Some manufacturers call this *Auto Detect*, some *Auto Sense*, and others *Auto Negotiation*. Select the appropriate value for your network, and click OK. The value selected should match the speed of the network switch that the server is connected to, not some arbitrary number you think the network speed is running at. Also check with the network administrator to ensure that the switch the NIC will ultimately be connecting to is configured properly as well. An example is shown in Figure 3-7. It should also be noted that some network card vendors do not allow you to modify the speed and duplex without the use of a proprietary utility.

■**Note** There is a bit of controversy as to whether you should leave the speed/duplex at the default value of auto when you have a gigabit Ethernet network (especially one over copper). Some literature says it is mandatory. I have found both http://www.ethermanage.com/ethernet/pdf/dell-auto-neg.pdf and http://www.dell.com/content/topics/global.aspx/power/en/ps1q01_hernan?c=us&cs=555&l=en&s=biz give good background on some of the considerations. Some of the core argument centers around the idea that if you do not set to automatically negotiate on gigabit Ethernet networks over copper, you are deploying out of spec. Check with your internal networking experts as well as the manufacturers of your hardware to ensure you are deploying a supportable network configuration—clustering or not.

---

13. Repeat steps 1 through 12 to configure the public network for each node that will be used for the failover cluster.

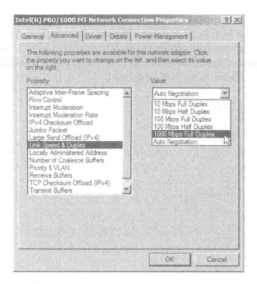

Figure 3-7. *Setting the speed of the public network*

Configure the Private Cluster Network

The private cluster network will serve as the network used exclusively for internal communication for all instances in the failover cluster. To configure the private cluster network, follow the instructions in this section.

1. Log onto one of the servers that will serve as a node in the server cluster with an account that has privileges to configure networking.

2. If you are using the RTM branch of Windows Server 2008, from the Start menu, right-click *Network*, select *Properties*, and finally, select the *Manage network connections* option. If you are using Windows Server 2008 R2, open Control Panel. Under Network and Internet, select *View network status and tasks*, and select *Change adapter settings* from the Network and Sharing Center dialog. The Network Connections dialog will now be displayed.

3. Right-click the network card you want to configure and select *Rename.*

4. Enter a name for the public network that is easy to identify, such as **Private Network**, and press Enter. The new name will now appear similar to the example shown previously in Figure 3-1.

5. Right-click the network card you just renamed and select *Properties.* The properties for the network card will be displayed.

6. With the introduction of the new quorum models in Windows Server 2008, it is possible that the private cluster network may also be used differently since there is the possibility of a file share majority. If you will only be using a disk only–based quorum with no file or node majority, having only TCP/IP selected on the *Networking* tab of the network card's properties dialog will be sufficient. If you will be using any other quorum model, at a minimum also ensure that *File and Printer Sharing for Microsoft Networks* is selected along with *Client for Microsoft Networks.*

7. Select *Internet Protocol Version 4 (TCP/IPv4)*, and either double-click that item or click the Properties button. The Internet Protocol Version 4 (TCP/IPv4) Properties dialog box will now be displayed. If you are going to configure an IPv6 network, the process will be similar to the one that follows.

8. While Windows Server 2008 cluster nodes support DHCP functionality, as noted in Chapter 2, never use it on the private network. Use a static IP address. Click the *Use the following IP address* option, and enter a static IP address and subnet mask. For valid IP ranges for the private network, see the section "Private Cluster Network" in Chapter 2. When finished, the dialog should look something like Figure 3-8. Click Advanced.

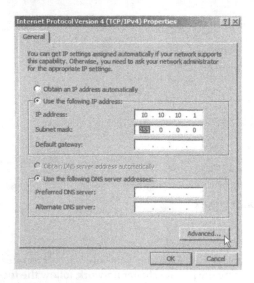

Figure 3-8. *Example TCP/IP properties for a private cluster network*

9. Select the *DNS* tab of the Advanced TCP/IP Settings dialog. Ensure that the option *Register this connection's addresses in DNS* is deselected, as shown in Figure 3-9.

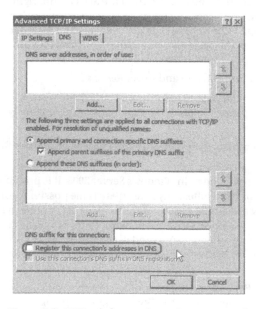

Figure 3-9. *DNS tab for a private cluster network*

10. Select the *WINS* tab of the Advanced TCP/IP Settings dialog. Ensure that the option *Disable NetBIOS over TCP/IP* is selected, as shown in Figure 3-10. Click OK. Click OK again on the Internet Protocol Version 4 (TCP/IPv4) Properties dialog. Finally, click OK on the main properties dialog to save all settings.

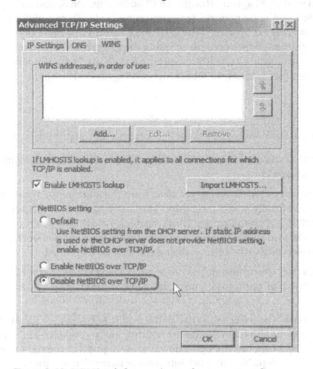

Figure 3-10. *WINS tab for a private cluster network*

11. Right-click the network card you just renamed in step 4, and select *Properties*. The properties for the network card will be displayed. Click Configure. Had you tried this before saving the settings that were configured in the prior steps, you would have seen the dialog box shown earlier in Figure 3-6.

12. Select the *Advanced* tab of the network card's properties. Follow the instructions found in step 12 of the process for configuring the public network. One important difference to note is that if a switch is involved in the physical configuration for the private cluster network (which is going to be the case if you are using more than two nodes), you should verify that the switch's speed setting is also not set to *Automatic*. Again, heed the warnings I mentioned earlier about the supportability of your network to ensure that any change you may make will not make your infrastructure unsupported.

13. Repeat steps 1 through 12 to configure the private network for each node that will be used for the failover cluster.

■**Tip** For each network—public or private—ensure that the network cards are named the same way across all nodes for all networks. You'll avoid confusion by maintaining a consistent naming convention.

Configuring the Public and Private Cluster Networks via Scripting

Unfortunately, outside of doing some "real" coding in WMI or PowerShell, no single (and simple) command line utility I could find can configure all aspects detailed in the preceding sections. NETSH can handle the renaming as well as assigning things like IP addresses, DNS, and so on, but the more advanced stuff would need to be coded. Documentation for NETSH can be found at http://www.microsoft.com/downloads/details.aspx?FamilyID=f41878de-2ee7-4718-8499-2ef336db3df5&displaylang=en. Another good resource on scripting the properties of network cards, even though it is a few years old, is "Automating TCP/IP Networking on Clients," which can be found at http://www.microsoft.com/technet/scriptcenter/topics/networking/default.mspx.

Set Network Priority

For your networking to work properly at the Windows level, the networks need to be prioritized properly:

1. Log onto one of the servers that will serve as a node in the server cluster with an account that has privileges to configure networking.

2. If you are using the RTM branch of Windows Server 2008, from the Start menu, right-click *Network*, select *Properties*, and finally, select the option *Manage network connections*. If you are using Windows Server 2008 R2, open Control Panel. Under Network and Internet, select *View network status and tasks*, and select *Change adapter settings* from the Network and Sharing Center dialog. The Network Connections dialog will now be displayed.

3. From the Advanced menu, select the option *Advanced Settings*. On Windows Server 2008 R2, by default, the menu bar is not displayed, so you must first select *Options*, *Layout*, and finally *Menu Bar*.

4. In the Advanced Settings dialog box, make sure that all the public networks are listed above all the private cluster networks, as shown in Figure 3-11. If they are not, select each network that is misplaced in *Connections*, and use the up or down arrow to put it in the right place in the order. You can prioritize which public network and private network takes precedence over another one.

5. Repeat steps 1 through 4 for every node in the cluster.

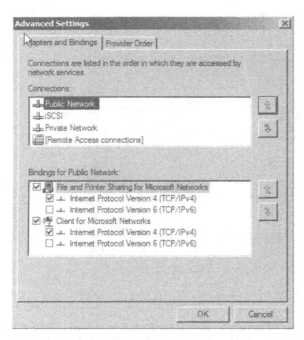

Figure 3-11. *Advanced Settings dialog box*

Step 3: Add Features and Roles

Windows Server 2008 has the concept of features and roles, which are exactly what they sound like—you add features to the server and define roles that it can perform. This section will show how to configure features and roles in Windows Server 2008.

Add Features in Server Manager

For failover clustering to work, the appropriate features must be added to each node. This section will demonstrate how to use Server Manager to add the features needed for failover clustering.

1. From the Start menu, select *Administrative Tools* and then *Server Manager*.

2. In Server Manager, select *Features*, right-click, and select *Add Features*.

3. Select the features to be installed. The recommended list can be found in the section "Server Features and Server Roles" in Chapter 2. The only feature technically required is *Failover Clustering*, but the others that are recommended may prove useful in managing your cluster nodes and deployments. Click Next, as shown in Figure 3-12.

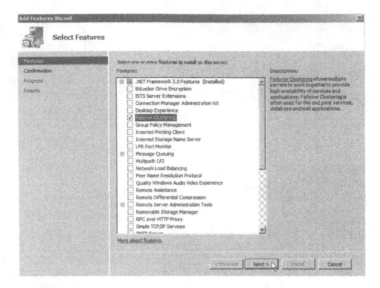

Figure 3-12. *Selecting features*

4. Confirm that the options selected are what you want to install, as shown in Figure 3-13, and click Install. The example shows that both *Windows PowerShell* (which also requires the Windows Internal Database to be installed) and *Windows System Resource Manager* were also selected.

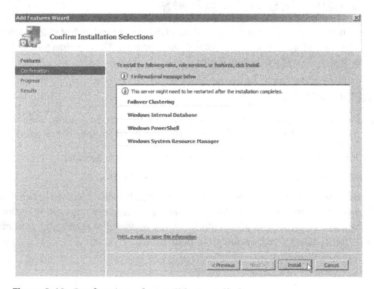

Figure 3-13. *Confirming what will be installed*

5. When the features are installed, you will see the dialog shown in Figure 3-14. Click Close. The roles and role services will be reflected as shown in Figure 3-15.

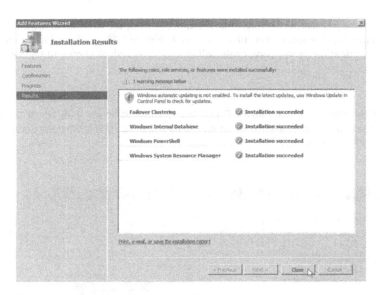

Figure 3-14. *Completed feature installation*

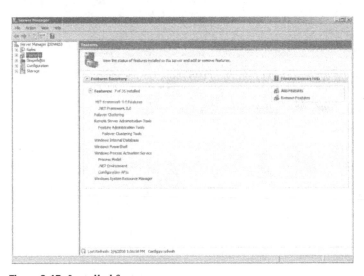

Figure 3-15. *Installed features*

Add Server Roles in Server Manager

If you will be configuring the Microsoft Distributed Transaction Coordinator (MSDTC; see the section "Microsoft Distributed Transaction Coordinator" in Chapter 2), you will need to configure the appropriate server roles on each node. Here are the steps to follow:

1. From the Start menu, select *Administrative Tools* and then *Server Manager*.

2. In Server Manager, select *Roles*, right-click, and select *Add Roles*.

3. When the first dialog of the Add Roles Wizard (Before You Begin) is displayed, click Next.

4. Select the *Application Server* server role. You will then be prompted to confirm the additional subfeatures of the Application Server role, as shown in Figure 3-16. Click Add Required Features. The Application Server server role will then be checked, as shown in Figure 3-17. Click Next.

Note The screenshots were done with the RTM branch of Windows Server 2008, which clearly installs .NET Framework 3.0 as a dependency. In my testing with build 7000 of Windows Server 2008 R2, it installs .NET Framework 3.5.1.

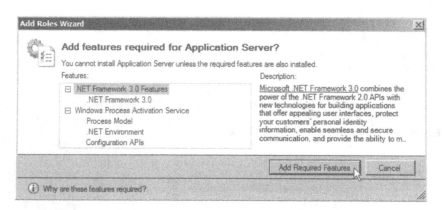

Figure 3-16. *Add Roles Wizard (RTM branch of Windows Server 2008)*

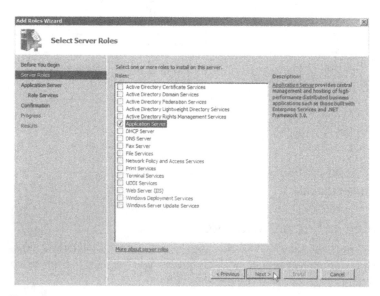

Figure 3-17. *Application Server selected*

5. Click Next on the Application Server informational dialog shown in Figure 3-18.

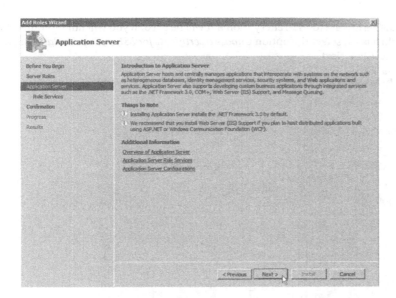

Figure 3-18. *Information about the Application Server server role (RTM branch of Windows Server 2008)*

6. To properly configure the server for MSDTC, select the Application Server Foundation, COM+ Network Access, and Distributed Transactions role services, as shown in Figure 3-19. Click Next. Doing this configures the proper network access. Prior to Windows Server 2008, you had to modify this option after configuring MSDTC.

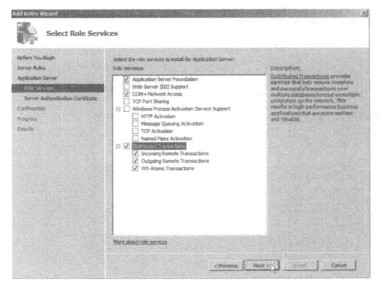

Figure 3-19. *Selecting role services*

7. Configure the certificate for SSL encryption if it will be used. If you will not be configuring SSL or will do it later, select the option *Choose a certificate for SSL encryption later*, as shown in Figure 3-20. Click Next.

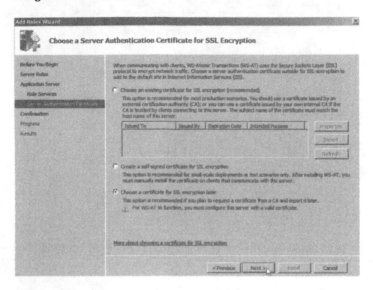

Figure 3-20. *Configuring SSL encryption*

8. Confirm that the options selected are what you want to install, as shown in Figure 3-21, and click Install.

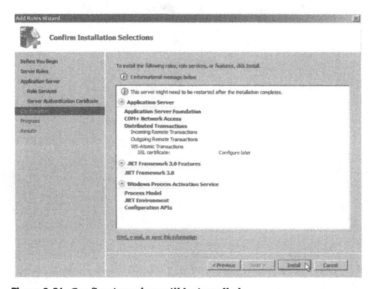

Figure 3-21. *Confirming what will be installed*

9. When the roles and role services are installed, you will see the dialog shown in Figure 3-22. Click Close. The roles and role services will be reflected as shown in Figure 3-23.

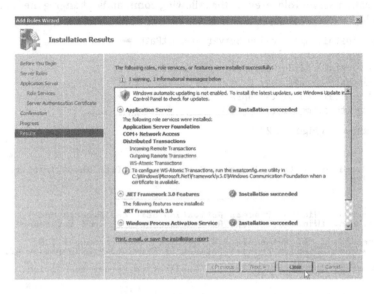

Figure 3-22. *Completed role installation*

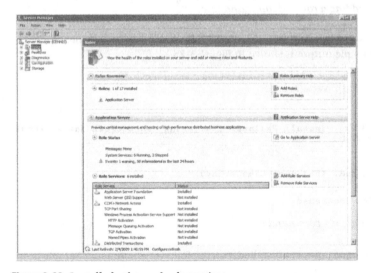

Figure 3-23. *Installed roles and role services*

Add Server Roles and Features via Command Line

Besides using Server Manager to add roles and features, the task can be done using the command line tool ServerManagerCmd.exe. Full documentation can be found at http://technet.microsoft.com/ en-us/library/cc748918.aspx. To add a feature or role, use the -install switch. -resultPath, which denotes an XML file to store the output, should also be used, along with -logPath. By default, the log will be %WINDIR%\Temp\Servermanager.log, but you may want to put the log in an easier-to-find place.

To add the Application Server role, execute the following commands, changing the values for -resultPath and -logPath accordingly:

```
ServerManagerCmd.exe -install Application-Server -resultPath ➡
installresult.xml  -logPath svrmgr.log
ServerManagerCmd.exe -install AS-Ent-Services -resultPath ➡
 installresult.xml -logPath svrmgr.log
ServerManagerCmd.exe -install AS-Dist-Transaction -resultPath ➡
installresult.xml -logPath svrmgr.log
```

Sample output is shown in Figure 3-24.

```
C:\>ServerManagerCmd.exe -install Application-Server -resultPath installresult.x
ml -logPath svrmgr.log
..

Start Installation...
[Installation] Succeeded: [Windows Process Activation Service] Process Model.
[Installation] Succeeded: [Windows Process Activation Service] .NET Environment.

[Installation] Succeeded: [.NET Framework 3.0 Features] .NET Framework 3.0.
[Installation] Succeeded: [Windows Process Activation Service] Configuration API
s.
[Installation] Succeeded: [Application Server] Application Server Foundation.
<100/100>

Success: Installation succeeded.
```

Figure 3-24. *Example of adding a role via command line*

To install the Failover Clustering feature, run the following command. Repeat for any features that you wish to add. Sample output is shown in Figure 3-25.

```
ServerManagerCmd.exe -install Failover-Clustering -resultPath ➡
installresult.xml -logPath svrmgr.log
```

```
C:\>ServerManagerCmd.exe -install Failover-Clustering -resultPath installresult.
xml -logPath svrmgr.log
..

Start Installation...
[Installation] Succeeded: [Failover Clustering].
<100/100>

Success: Installation succeeded.
```

Figure 3-25. *Adding a feature via command line*

To see what features and roles are installed, run the following command. Sample output is shown in Figure 3-26.

```
ServerManagerCmd.exe -query | more
```

```
      [ ] Identity Federation Support
  [X] Application Server  [Application-Server]
      [X] Application Server Foundation  [AS-AppServer-Foundation]
      [ ] Web Server (IIS) Support  [AS-Web-Support]
      [X] COM+ Network Access  [AS-Ent-Services]
      [ ] TCP Port Sharing  [AS-TCP-Port-Sharing]
      [ ] Windows Process Activation Service Support  [AS-WAS-Support]
          [ ] HTTP Activation  [AS-HTTP-Activation]
          [ ] Message Queuing Activation  [AS-MSMQ-Activation]
          [ ] TCP Activation  [AS-TCP-Activation]
          [ ] Named Pipes Activation  [AS-Named-Pipes]
      [X] Distributed Transactions  [AS-Dist-Transaction]
          [X] Incoming Remote Transactions  [AS-Incoming-Trans]
          [X] Outgoing Remote Transactions  [AS-Outgoing-Trans]
          [X] WS-Atomic Transactions  [AS-WS-Atomic]
  [ ] DHCP Server  [DHCP]
  [ ] DNS Server  [DNS]
  [ ] Fax Server  [Fax]
  [ ] File Services
      [ ] File Server  [FS-FileServer]
      [ ] Distributed File System  [FS-DFS]
          [ ] DFS Namespaces  [FS-DFS-Namespace]
          [ ] DFS Replication  [FS-DFS-Replication]
      [ ] File Server Resource Manager  [FS-Resource-Manager]
  -- More  -- _
```

Figure 3-26. *Seeing what is configured*

Step 4: Configure the Shared Disks

This section documents how to configure the disks on your shared disk array. There are two ways that will be shown here to configure the disks: via Computer Management and command line. You can also manage your disks using Storage Manager for SANs (not demonstrated in this chapter), as long as your vendor provides a Virtual Disk Service hardware provider that it can use. Storage Manager for SANs must first be added as a feature (see the previous section), and can be found under Administrative Tools.

One big difference from previous versions of Windows is while you still need to do the proper LUN zoning and masking at the disk level with vendor-provided tools, you do not need to only have one node up at a time to recognize the disks. This will become more apparent when the cluster is validated in Chapter 4.

Prepare and Format the Disks

This section will walk through the configuration of the disks for use with the failover cluster. How to add a disk with a drive letter as well as a mount point will be demonstrated. These steps are only performed on the first node. Adding the already configured disks to the other nodes is covered in the next section.

Tip As noted in Chapter 2, Windows Server 2008 should automatically align the disk sectors. However, if you know of a specific offset from the storage vendor, you can use the command line to do it directly. Controlling disk alignment is an option only available via command line, not via the graphical interface of Computer Management. Aligning your disks must be done prior to formatting them. They cannot be aligned after the disk has been formatted. If the disk was formatted and you want to align them, you must destroy the current configuration.

Create Drives with Letters and Mount Points Using Computer Management

To prepare and format disks with drive letters via Computer Management, follow these steps:

1. From Administrative Tools, start the Computer Management tool.

2. Select *Disk Management*.

3. Select one of the unallocated disks, right-click, and bring it online by selecting the *Online* option. After the disk is online, you will see it listed in Computer Management, similarly to Disk 1 in Figure 3-27, with a status of *Not Initialized*. Repeat for each disk.

Figure 3-27. *Status after bringing the disk online*

4. After bringing a disk online, you must initialize it by right-clicking it and selecting the *Initialize Disk* option. You can either initialize one disk at a time, or multiple disks at once, as shown in Figure 3-28 (if multiple disks were brought online in the previous step). When initializing, you can create a *Master Boot Record* (MBR) or *GUID Partition Table* (GPT) disk. See the section "Disk Configuration" in Chapter 2 for more information. Both are compatible with SQL Server 2008. When complete, the disk will be ready to be formatted, will have a status of online, and will also be a Basic disk, as shown in Figure 3-29.

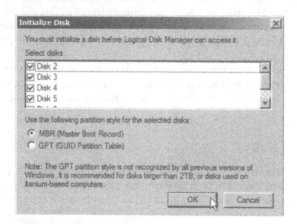

Figure 3-28. *Initializing multiple disks*

Figure 3-29. *Status after initializing a disk*

5. Right-click the disk to format, and select *New Simple Volume*. Depending on whether you have one disk with the status of *Online* or multiple disks, you will see options similar to those in Figure 3-30. Never choose any option other than New Simple Volume for a cluster disk. All RAID or combinations must be done at the hardware level.

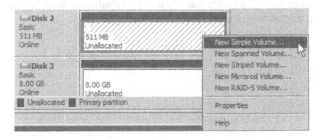

Figure 3-30. *Selecting New Simple Volume with multiple disks online*

6. On the Welcome to the New Simple Volume Wizard dialog, click Next.

7. On the Specify Volume Size dialog, enter the size of the volume to create (in megabytes). For example, to create an 8 GB volume, use a value of **8192**. Click Next.

8. To create a drive with a letter assignment, select the option *Assign the following drive letter*, and in the dropdown, select an appropriate drive letter. When I configure drive letters, if possible, I give them something easy to remember, like *W* for *Witness*. A completed drive letter change is shown in Figure 3-31. Click Next.

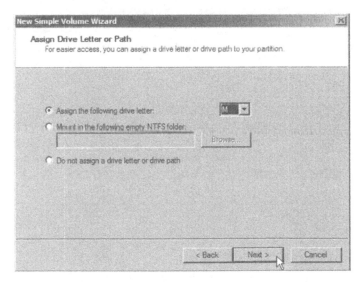

Figure 3-31. *Driver letter successfully changed*

9. To create a mount point, perform the following steps:

   a. Select the option *Mount in the following empty NTFS folder*, and click Browse.

   b. On the Browse for Drive Path dialog, select the drive that contains or will contain the folder to mount the drive. If the folder already exists, expand the drive and select the folder, as shown in Figure 3-32. If a folder has not been created, click New Folder. You will then be prompted to create and name the new folder. Click OK.

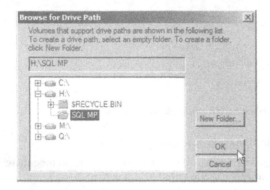

Figure 3-32. *Selecting the folder to mount the drive*

   c. The folder to mount the drive will now be reflected as shown in Figure 3-33. Click Next.

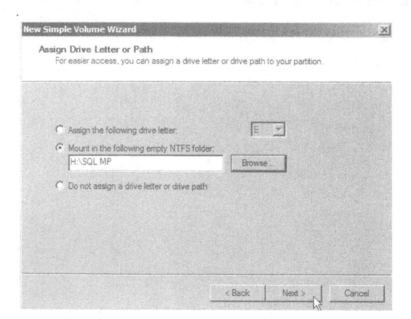

Figure 3-33. *Example of a mount point path*

10. On the Format Partition dialog, select the option *Format this volume with the following settings*. Always select a file system of *NTFS* and name the volume something that makes it easy to identify. Never select the option *Enable file and folder compression*—SQL Server does not support it.

   Your choice for the allocation unit size will depend on the disk usage. If no SQL Server data files will *ever* be placed on the drive, the default value can be left. Good examples of this would be the disks for MSDTC and the witness. All disks that will contain SQL Server data should be formatted with a size of 64 KB since they may contain data. You can technically also use 8192 (the size of a SQL Server write I/O) for data disks, but rarely is a file going to be write-only. Technically, disks that will contain transaction log files and/or backups (but not data files) do not need to be formatted with 8 or 64 KB, but in many environments, data, logs, and backups are intermingled—therefore it is best to format at 64 KB. An example of a non–SQL Server disk can be found in Figure 3-34 and a SQL Server–related disk in Figure 3-35. Never select the *Perform a quick format* option.

   Click Next to continue.

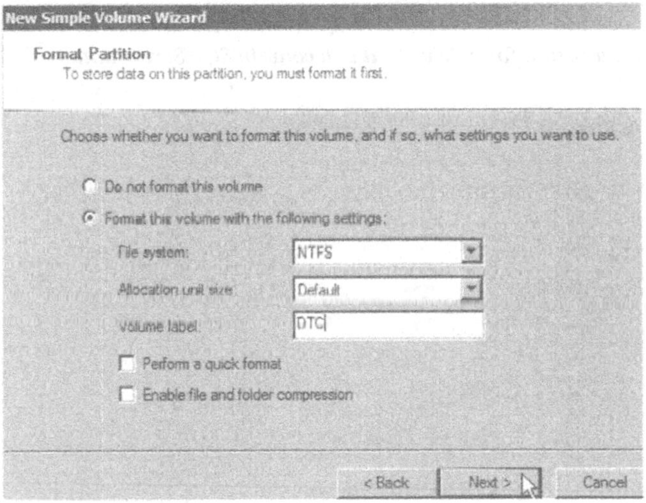

Figure 3-34. *Sample configuration for a drive that will not contain any SQL Server data*

11. At the end of the process, confirm your selections and click Finish, as shown in Figure 3-36. When complete, the disk will appear like Figure 3-37. Note that during the formatting process, the dialog box in Figure 3-38 may appear in the background; click Cancel or just ignore it.

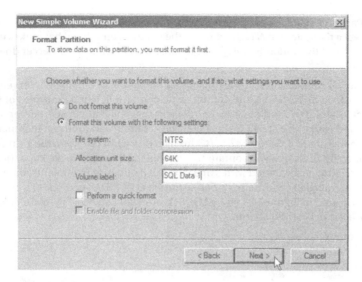

Figure 3-35. *Sample configuration for a drive that will contain SQL Server data*

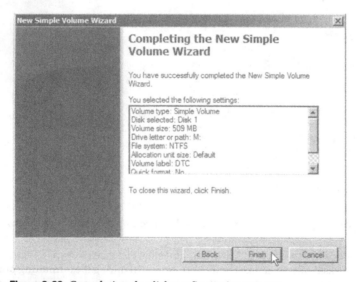

Figure 3-36. *Completing the disk configuration process*

Figure 3-37. *Successfully formatted disk with a drive letter*

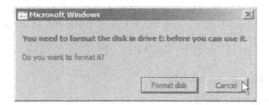

Figure 3-38. *Prompt to ignore while disk is formatting*

12. Repeat until all disks are formatted and ready for use.

Create Drives with Letters and Mount Points via Command Line

To configure drives and mount points via the command line, the DISKPART tool will be used. The steps are slightly different than they were in Windows Server 2003. Full documentation for DISKPART can be found at http://technet.microsoft.com/en-us/library/cc770877.aspx.

■Tip If you do not want to run DISKPART interactively, you can run it using a preconfigured text file as input. For example, diskpart /s myscript.txt > output.txt will run DISKPART with commands in the file myscript.txt, and will put any output in the file output.txt.

---

1. Open a command window and type diskpart.

2. At the DISKPART> prompt, enter the command list disk. This will show the disks that Windows sees and are available for use. Each disk will have a number associated with it, as shown in Figure 3-39. If a disk is already being used by a failover cluster, the status will show a value of Reserved.

```
DISKPART> list disk

  Disk ###  Status       Size     Free     Dyn  Gpt
  --------  ----------  -------  -------    ---  ---
  Disk 0    Online        24 GB      0 B
  Disk 1    Online      1536 MB  1533 MB
  Disk 2    Online      1536 MB  1533 MB
  Disk 3    Online         8 GB  8189 MB
  Disk 4    Online         8 GB  8189 MB
  Disk 5    Online        16 GB    16 GB
  Disk 6    Online        16 GB    16 GB
```

Figure 3-39. *Using the list disk command*

3. At the DISKPART> prompt, enter the command select disk *n*, where *n* is the number of the disk that you want to use. Disk 0 is your system disk. Figure 3-40 shows an example.

```
DISKPART> select disk 1

Disk 1 is now the selected disk.
```

Figure 3-40. *Selecting the disk for configuration*

4. By default, the disk is read-only. To remove that attribute and make it ready to format, at the DISKPART> prompt, enter the command attributes disk clear readonly, as shown in Figure 3-41.

```
DISKPART> attributes disk clear readonly
Disk attributes cleared successfully.
```

Figure 3-41. *Making the disk writeable*

5. At the DISKPART> prompt, enter the command online disk to bring the disk online, as shown in Figure 3-42.

```
DISKPART> online disk
DiskPart successfully onlined the selected disk.
```

Figure 3-42. *Bringing the disk online*

6. Unlike creating disks or mount points in Computer Management, you do not have the explicit option to create either an MBR or a GPT disk at this time. Windows will create an MBR disk at this point. Converting to a GPT disk (if you wish to do so) can be done in a few steps beyond this one. Note that if you convert a disk to GPT and it has data on it, you must copy the data off before destroying the old configuration. In this step, create the volume that will be carved out on the disk. The commands would be create partition primary size=s, where s is the size of the partition in megabytes. This command is where you would include the option for an offset for disk alignment. Consult the documentation linked previously to see the proper syntax. A sample is shown in Figure 3-43 configuring a partition of 512 MB, but it does not show alignment. A partition does not need to consume the entire space available. When complete, if you look in Computer Management, you will see that the disk will say RAW.

```
DISKPART> create partition primary size=512
DiskPart succeeded in creating the specified partition.
```

Figure 3-43. *Creating the partition*

7. Format the volume using the command format fs=*filesystem* label=*description* unit=*block size*, where *filesystem* is the type of file system to be used, *description* is the friendly display name for the disk, and *block size* is the allocation unit size for formatting (see step 8 from the last section for guidance). During the formatting, a percentage will be updated. When complete, the display will look similar to Figure 3-44.

```
DISKPART> format fs=ntfs label="SQL 6" unit=64k
  100 percent completed
DiskPart successfully formatted the volume.
```

Figure 3-44. *Example disk format for a disk to be used with SQL Server*

8. If you want to create a GPT disk, you must destroy the existing volume from the disk. The command to do this task is delete volume. If the volume is in use, execute the command with the additional option of override. An example is shown in Figure 3-45. To convert to a GPT disk, run the command convert gpt, as shown in Figure 3-46. You must now reexecute steps 7 and 8 to create a new volume on the newly created GPT disk.

```
DISKPART> delete volume

The selected volume is in use.
To continue with the delete use the OVERRIDE parameter.

DISKPART> delete volume override

DiskPart successfully deleted the volume.
```

Figure 3-45. *Deleting the volume*

```
DISKPART> convert gpt

DiskPart successfully converted the selected disk to GPT format.
```

Figure 3-46. *Converting the MBR disk to a GPT disk*

9. To assign a drive letter to a volume, execute the command assign letter=l, where l is the letter to use. To check the assignment, run the list volume command. An example is shown in Figure 3-47.

```
DISKPART> assign letter=g

DiskPart successfully assigned the drive letter or mount point.

DISKPART> list volume

  Volume ###  Ltr  Label        Fs     Type        Size     Status     Info
  ----------  ---  -----------  -----  ----------  -------  ---------  --------
  Volume 0     D   KRMSxWOHVOL  UDF    CD-ROM      2512 MB  Healthy
  Volume 1     C                NTFS   Partition     24 GB  Healthy    System
  Volume 2     W   Witness      NTFS   Partition    512 MB  Healthy
* Volume 3     G   SQL 1        NTFS   Partition   4096 MB  Healthy
  Volume 4         SQL 2        NTFS   Partition   8189 MB  Healthy
```

Figure 3-47. *Assigning a drive letter*

To create a mount point, you must first manually create the folder on the source disk. That can be done via command line or in Windows Explorer. An example of doing it via the command line is shown in Figure 3-48. A good rule of thumb is to use an easy-to-identify name for the directory. The following example uses SQL MP as the directory to show that it is a mount point—but use a name that makes sense for this deployment of SQL Server 2008. Next, create the mount point with the command assign mount=mp, where mp is the directory to mount the disk. When complete, run the list volume command to check that it was done properly. An example is shown in Figure 3-49.

```
G:\>mkdir "sql mp"

G:\>dir
 Volume in drive G is SQL 1
 Volume Serial Number is 0C1E-D92A

 Directory of G:\

02/04/2009  12:26 AM    <DIR>          sql mp
               0 File<s>              0 bytes
               1 Dir<s>   8,314,028,032 bytes free
```

Figure 3-48. *Creating the folder for the mount point*

```
DISKPART> select volume 4

Volume 4 is the selected volume.

DISKPART> assign mount="g:\sql mp"

DiskPart successfully assigned the drive letter or mount point.

DISKPART> list volume

  Volume ###  Ltr  Label        Fs     Type        Size     Status     Info
  ----------  ---  -----------  -----  ----------  -------  ---------  --------
  Volume 0     D   KRMSxWOHVOL  UDF    CD-ROM      2512 MB  Healthy
  Volume 1     C                NTFS   Partition     24 GB  Healthy    System
  Volume 2     W   Witness      NTFS   Partition    512 MB  Healthy
  Volume 3     G   SQL 1        NTFS   Partition   4096 MB  Healthy
* Volume 4         SQL 2        NTFS   Partition   8189 MB  Healthy
    G:\sql mp\
```

Figure 3-49. *Creating the mount point*

10. Repeat steps 2 through 9 until all disks and mount points are created.

11. At the DISKPART> prompt, enter the command exit, and then close the command window.

Verify the Disk Configuration

Now that the disks are formatted and added to one node, verify that they are working properly.

Tip At this point, you should also verify that the storage, while not fully configured on each node, is available to each server. If you are using iSCSI, make sure that each server is connected to each LUN at the iSCSI target; otherwise, when validation is run (see Chapter 4), you will get errors.

---

1. Either via command line or in Windows Explorer, select one of the disks that was just created and formatted.

2. Create a file, such as a text document, and open it to verify that you can both read and write to the disk.

3. Repeat steps 2 and 3 until all disks are tested. Test any mount points as well.

4. Repeat steps 1 through 3 until all nodes have a successful disk test.

Step 5: Perform Domain-Based Tasks

This section will cover all of the domain-related tasks for preparing the cluster nodes. You perform these tasks on each node. These include tasks such as renaming the nodes and creating a cluster administration account.

Rename a Node and Join to a Domain

In this section, you will learn how to rename a node and join that node to a domain. Remember that the node needs to have a unique name in the domain. I combine these steps since they require a reboot, and the tasks are performed in a similar fashion.

Rename and Join Using the System Applet

To rename the node and join the domain using from Control Panel's System applet, follow these instructions:

1. From the Start menu, select *Control Panel*. If this is the RTM branch, double-click System (alternatively, right-click it and select *Open*). If this is R2, select *System and Security*, and then on the System and Security dialog, click System.

2. Select *Change settings* in the Computer name, domain, and workgroup settings.

3. Click Change on the *Computer Name* tab of System Properties.

4. Enter a new name for the server in the *Computer name* entry field. Select *Domain*. Enter the fully qualified domain name and click OK, as shown in Figure 3-50.

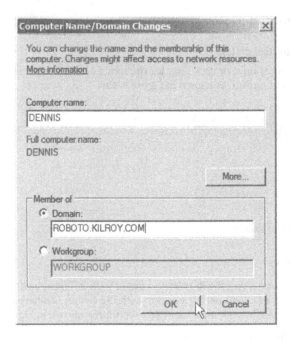

Figure 3-50. *Entering a new computer name and the domain name*

5. You will be prompted to enter an account with its accompanying password that has privileges to add the node to the domain. Click OK. If the operation is successful, you will see a similar dialog to the one shown in Figure 3-51. Click OK. An informational dialog as shown in Figure 3-52 will appear letting you know the server must be rebooted for the change to take effect. Click OK.

Figure 3-51. *Successful operation joining to the domain*

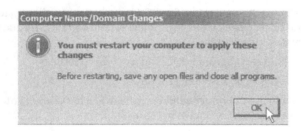

Figure 3-52. *Reboot information dialog*

6. Click Close on the System Properties dialog.

7. You can either restart the computer now, or do it later for the name and domain changes to take effect. Select the appropriate option, as shown in Figure 3-53.

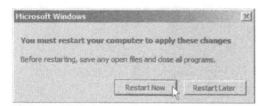

Figure 3-53. *Dialog to restart the computer*

Rename and Join via Command Line

Renaming and joining the domain are done using the NETDOM command with different options and switches. To rename the computer, use the RENAMECOMPUTER option with the switch /NewName to enter the new name for the node. The syntax is as follows, and a sample execution is shown in Figure 3-54:

```
NETDOM RENAMECOMPUTER %COMPUTERNAME% /NewName:NewNameofNode
```

```
C:\>netdom renamecomputer %computername% /NewName:Tommy
This operation will rename the computer WIN-WG60JJY7E4F
to Tommy.

Certain services, such as the Certificate Authority, rely on a fixed machine
name. If any services of this type are running on WIN-WG60JJY7E4F,
then a computer name change would have an adverse impact.

Do you want to proceed (Y or N)?
y
The computer needs to be restarted in order to complete the operation.

The command completed successfully.
```

Figure 3-54. *Renaming the node*

To have the computer join the domain, use the JOIN option with the switches /Domain for the domain to join, /UserD to enter the account that has privileges to add the node to the domain, and /PasswordD to enter the password for the account. The syntax is as follows, and a sample execution is shown in Figure 3-55:

```
NETDOM JOIN %COMPUTERNAME% /Domain:DomainName /UserD:User /PasswordD:Password
```

```
C:\>netdom join %computername% /Domain:roboto.kilroy.com /UserD:administrator /P
asswordD:P@ssword1
The computer needs to be restarted in order to complete the operation.

The command completed successfully.
```

Figure 3-55. *Joining the domain*

Create the Cluster Administration Account in the Domain

To create an account used for administering a failover cluster in Active Directory, follow the steps outlined in the following subsections. The steps were configured using a Windows Server 2008–based domain controller, but should be similar for a Windows Server 2003–based domain controller.

Create the Cluster Administration Account Using Active Directory Users and Computers

This section will show how to add the cluster administrator account using the Active Directory Users and Computers utility.

1. Log onto one of the servers as an administrator who has rights to add or modify accounts to the domain. Unless a server has the right tools, the server that you will have to log onto may be one of the domain controllers.

2. From Administrative Tools, start the Active Directory Users and Computers tool.

3. In the pane on the left, expand the domain, right-click *Users*, select *New*, and then select *User*.

4. In the New Object – User dialog box, you must enter at least a first name or a last name, as well as the user logon name, as shown in Figure 3-56. Click Next.

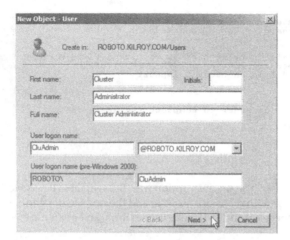

Figure 3-56. *Creating the cluster administration account*

5. When creating a password, it is recommended to set the password to never expire if your security policy allows it. If you choose that option, you will see the warning in Figure 3-57. Enter the password for the account and click Next, as shown in Figure 3-58.

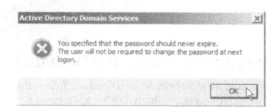

Figure 3-57. *Warning about password expiration*

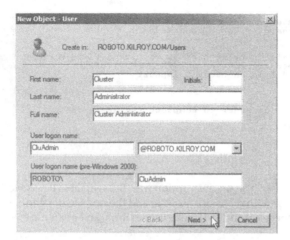

Figure 3-58. *Allowing the password to never expire*

6. Click Finish to complete the account creation process, as shown in Figure 3-59. The new user will now be shown in the right-hand pane, as shown in Figure 3-60.

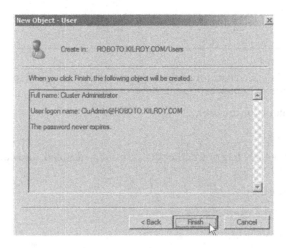

Figure 3-59. *Completing the account creation*

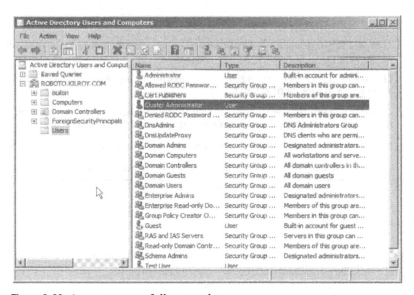

Figure 3-60. *Account successfully created*

Create the Cluster Administration Account via Command Line

For any Windows Server 2008 computer that has the Active Directory Domain Services server role, a command line tool called DSADD allows you to create users in Active Directory. DSADD is very picky about things like spaces. Do not put spaces between the commas; otherwise, you will not be able to run the command successfully.

DSADD has many parameters (as documented at http://technet.microsoft.com/en-us/library/cc731279.aspx), but Table 3-1 shows the ones that will be used to create the cluster administration account.

Table 3-1. *DSADD Parameters*

Parameter	Description
acctexpires	This sets the flag to tell Active Directory if the account will expire, and if so, when. It is either a number, which represents days, or Never.
cn	This is the common name for the user.
dc	This is the domain context.
disabled	This sets the Active Directory flag of whether the account is disabled, and can have a value of Yes or No.
display	This is the display name for the user.
fn	This is the first name of the user.
ln	This is the last name of the user.
mustchpwd	This sets the flag to force the user to change the password, and can be a value of Yes or No.
pwd	This sets the user's password.
pwdneverexpires	This sets the flag to allows the password to never expire, and can have a value of Yes or No.
reversiblepwd	This tells Active Directory to store the password using reversible encryption, and can have a value of Yes or No.
samid	This sets the unique Security Accounts Manager (SAM) name for the user. If this is not stated, the first 20 characters of the value for cn will be used.
u	This is the username, which is used for logging onto the domain or a server.
upn	This sets the user principal name of the Active Directory user.

Here is an example of a fully formed statement:

```
dsadd user cn=CluAdmin,cn=Users,dc=Roboto,dc=Kilroy,dc=com
 -samid CluAdmin -fn Cluster -ln Administrator -display "Cluster Admin"
-upn "cluadmin@roboto.kilroy.com" -disabled No -pwd P@ssword1
 -pwdneverexpires Yes -reversiblepwd No -mustchpwd No
```

Figure 3-61 shows a successful running of that command.

```
C:\>dsadd user CN="Cluster Administrator",CN=Users,DC=Roboto,DC=Kilroy,DC=com -s
amid CluAdmin -pwd P@ssword1 -fn Cluster -ln Administrator -display "Cluster Adm
in" -upn CluAdmin@Roboto.Kilroy.com -disabled No -pwdneverexpires Yes -reversibl
epwd No -mustchpwd No -desc "Windows Server 2008 Failover Cluster Administration
Account"
dsadd succeeded:CN=Cluster Administrator,CN=Users,DC=Roboto,DC=Kilroy,DC=com
```

Figure 3-61. *Adding the domain account via DSADD*

Configure Security for the Cluster Administration Account

When using Windows Server 2008 nodes, the cluster administration account must have the Create Computer Object privilege and also be added to each node's Administrators group.

Configuring Security Using Active Directory Users and Computers

This section will show how to add the Create Computer Object privilege using Active Directory Users and Computers.

1. Log onto one of the servers as an administrator who has rights to add or modify accounts to the domain. Unless a server has the right tools, the server that you will have to log into may be one of the domain controllers.

2. From Administrative Tools, start the Active Directory Users and Computers tool.

3. Under the View menu, ensure that Advanced Features is selected. This will display additional items under the domain name, as shown in Figure 3-62.

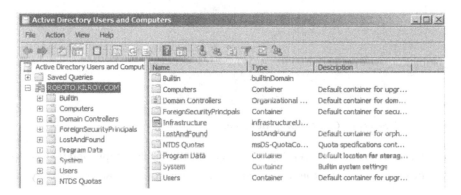

Figure 3-62. *More options in Active Directory Users and Computers*

4. Select *Computers*, right-click, and select *Properties*.

5. On the Computers Properties dialog, select the *Security* tab.

6. Click Advanced.

7. On the *Permissions* tab of the Advanced Security Settings for Computers dialog, click Add.

8. On the Select User, Computer, or Group dialog, enter the name or part of the cluster administration account's name that you configured, and click Check Names. The name will be resolved. Click OK.

9. When the Permission Entry for Computers dialog is displayed, scroll down and check *Create Computer objects*, as shown in Figure 3-63. Click OK.

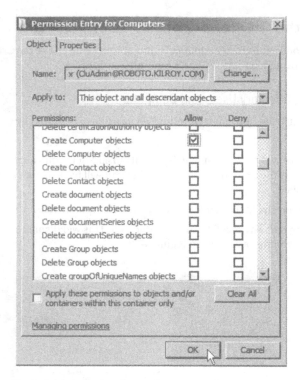

Figure 3-63. *Selecting Create Computer objects*

10. On the Advanced Security Settings for Computers dialog, click Apply, and then click OK.

11. On the Computers Properties dialog, click OK. You can now close Active Directory Users and Computers.

Configuring Security via Command Line

For any Windows Server 2008 computer that has the Active Directory Domain Services server role, a command line tool called DSACLS allows you to add the right permissions to an object in the domain. DSACLS has many parameters (as documented at http://technet.microsoft.com/de-de/library/cc771151.aspx). The relevant switches are /G, which grants permissions, and /I, which controls inheritance. A value of CC for the /G switch corresponds to the ability to create child computer objects. A value of T for the /I switch grants rights for the object and all of its children.

Here is an example of a fully formed statement:

```
dsacls "cn=Computers,dc=Roboto,dc=Kilroy,dc=com"
 /G "ROBOTO\cluadmin":CC;computer /I:T
```

Figure 3-64 shows the result of a successful completion.

To verify the permissions, either check them within Active Directory Users and Computers as shown in the previous section, or run the following command:

```
dsacls "cn=Computers,dc=Roboto,dc=Kilroy,dc=com" | more
```

```
erited from parent>
                                    READ PROPERTY
Inherited to user
Allow BUILTIN\Pre-Windows 2000 Compatible Access
                                    SPECIAL ACCESS for Logon Information    <In
herited from parent>
                                    READ PROPERTY
Inherited to inetOrgPerson
Allow BUILTIN\Pre-Windows 2000 Compatible Access
                                    SPECIAL ACCESS for Logon Information    <In
herited from parent>
                                    READ PROPERTY
Inherited to user
Allow BUILTIN\Pre-Windows 2000 Compatible Access
                                    SPECIAL ACCESS for Account Restrictions
<Inherited from parent>
                                    READ PROPERTY
Inherited to inetOrgPerson
Allow BUILTIN\Pre-Windows 2000 Compatible Access
                                    SPECIAL ACCESS for Account Restrictions
<Inherited from parent>
                                    READ PROPERTY
The command completed successfully
```

Figure 3-64. *Successful run of DSACLS*

As you are stepping through the permissions, you will see the output shown in Figure 3-65.

```
Allow ROBOTO\CluAdmin           SPECIAL ACCESS for computer
                                CREATE CHILD
```

Figure 3-65. *Verifying the privilege*

Add the Cluster Administration Account to Each Node

Once the cluster administration account is created, it must be added locally to each node's Administrators group.

Add the Cluster Administration Account Using Computer Management

To add the cluster administration account to each node, follow these steps:

1. Log onto one of the servers, which will be a node in the cluster with an account that has the administrative access to add and modify users.

2. From Administrative Tools, start Computer Management.

3. Expand Local Users and Groups, and select *Groups*.

4. Select the Administrators group, right-click, and select the *Add to Group* option; alternatively, double-click Administrators.

5. In the Administrators Properties dialog box, click Add.

6. In the Select Users, Computers, or Groups dialog box, verify that the *From This Location* value is set to the proper domain. If is not pointing to the right place, click Locations. You may be prompted for a domain login if you are only logged on as a local administrator. In the Locations dialog box, select the correct domain. Click OK in the Locations dialog box to return to Select Users, Computers, or Groups.

7. Enter the name of the cluster service account you created earlier in the *Enter the Object Names to Select* box. Click Check Names. The account will be validated against the domain. Click OK.

8. The Administrators Properties dialog box will now reflect the addition of the account. Click Apply and then OK.

9. Log off from the node on which you are working.

10. Repeat steps 1 through 9 until you've added the cluster administration account to every node that will participate in the Windows failover cluster.

Add the Cluster Administration Account via Command Line

To add the cluster administration account to each node, use the command NET LOCALGROUP with the /add switch. A sample execution would be

```
NET LOCALGROUP Administrators DOMAIN\UserName /add
```

Verify the user was added by executing the command NET LOCALGROUP <Groupname>. An example is shown in Figure 3-66.

```
C:\>NET LOCALGROUP Administrators SIGNALS\cluadmin /add
The command completed successfully.

C:\>NET LOCALGROUP Administrators
Alias name        Administrators
Comment           Administrators have complete and unrestricted access to the compu
ter/domain

Members

-------------------------------------------------------------------------------
Administrator
SIGNALS\cluadmin
SIGNALS\Domain Admins
The command completed successfully.
```

Figure 3-66. *Results of adding a user to the local Administrators group*

Create the Cluster Name Object

If you are in a networked environment that does not allow dynamic DNS, follow the instructions in this section for creating the cluster name account, which is the name of the Windows failover cluster with a $ added to it. If your environment allows dynamic DNS, skip this section.

1. From the Start menu, select *Administrative Tools* and then *Active Directory Users and Computers*. You will need domain administration privileges, and this tool will most likely only reside on domain controllers.

2. Make sure that the *Advanced Features* option is selected under the View menu.

3. Select *Computers*, right-click, select *New*, and then select *Computer*.

4. On the New Object – Computer dialog, enter the *Computer name* that will be used for the new Windows failover cluster. An example is shown in Figure 3-67. Click Next.

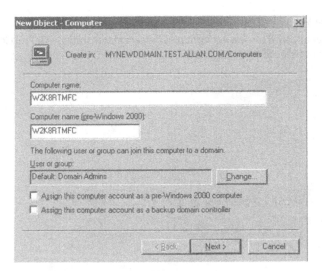

Figure 3-67. *New Object – Computer dialog*

5. To finish the process as shown in Figure 3-68, click Finish.

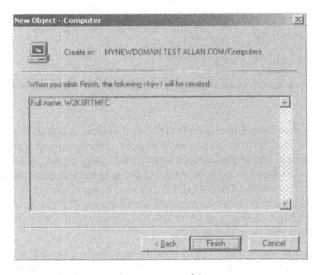

Figure 3-68. *Creating the computer object*

6. Right-click the computer you just created. Select the *Security* tab.

7. Click Add. Add the cluster administration account previously created and give it Full Control rights. A sample is shown in Figure 3-69. Click OK.

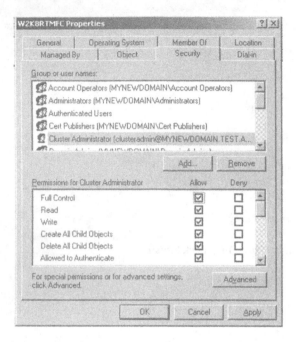

Figure 3-69. *Allowing the cluster administration count to administer full control over the Windows failover cluster*

8. For each SQL Server instance and any clustered MSDTC (or more than one MSDTC), follow steps 3 through 5; however, do not close the dialog window after performing step 5. You must also add the cluster computer account you created with the following rights: Allowed to authenticate, Change password, Read, Read account restrictions, Read DNS host name attributes, Read MS-TS-GatewayAccess, Read personal information, Read public information, Receive as, Reset password, Send as, Validated write account restrictions, Write DNS host name attributes, Write to DNS host name, and Write MS-TS-GatewayAccess validated write to service princ. An example is shown in Figure 3-70.

9. For any computer accounts that were created, right-click them and select *Disable Account*. If the accounts are enabled while the cluster or resources are being created, the creation process will fail.

■**Tip** Remember to enable the accounts after creating the objects in Chapters 4, 6, and 7.

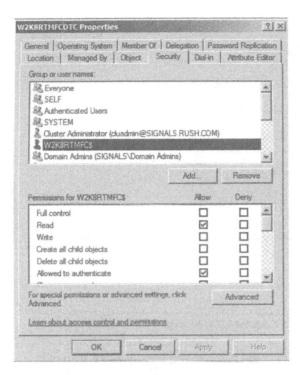

Figure 3-70. *Adding the cluster computer account to a sample MSDTC computer account*

Step 6: Perform Final Configuration Tasks

This section will walk you through the final steps for configuring Windows Server 2008 to be completely ready for clustering the nodes into a failover cluster.

Configure Windows Update

Production severs, especially highly available, mission-critical, clustered ones, should never be set to update automatically. This can lead to pending reboots or forced reboots that will cause availability outages. To configure Windows Update so that administrators have control over how it is patched, follow the directions in this section.

1. From the Start menu, select *Control Panel*. If this is the RTM branch, double-click Windows Update. If this is R2, select *System and Security*, and then on the System and Security dialog, click Windows Update.

2. If this is RTM, select *View advanced options*. If this is R2, select *Let me choose my settings*.

3. Select the option *Never check for updates (not recommended)* as shown in Figure 3-71. It could be debated that the option that will check for updates but let you choose would be fine, but the problem is that an administrator would have to physically log onto the box to see what is available, and it also assumes an Internet connection. Click OK. The change will be reflected as shown in Figure 3-72.

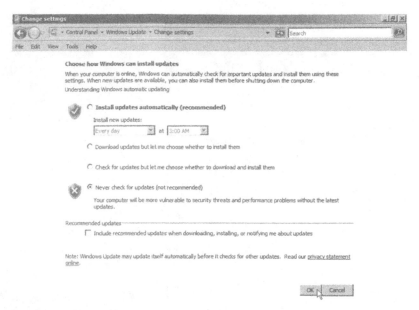

Figure 3-71. *Disabling automatic updates (RTM branch)*

Figure 3-72. *Updated changes to updating preferences*

4. Repeat steps 1 through 3 on each server that will be configured as a node in the failover cluster.

Activate Windows

You must activate Windows Server 2008 with a valid product key within three days. Since you do not enter the product key during the installation process like prior versions of Windows Server, it must be entered after Windows is finished installing. Activation assumes that there is an Internet connection. If not, you will need to validate via phone. This section will show how to validate over the network. Make sure that you perform this task; otherwise, your server may stop functioning.

1. From the Start menu, select *Control Panel*.

2. From Control Panel, select *System*.

3. Select *Change product key* under the Windows Activation section.

4. Enter your valid and licensed product key in the dialog shown in Figure 3-73. Click Next. Windows will then attempt to activate Windows over the Internet. If you are not connected to the Internet, the process will fail and you will need to activate via phone.

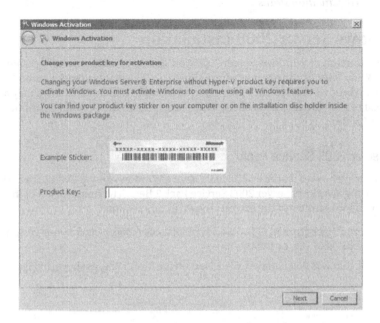

Figure 3-73. *Entering the product key*

5. If activation is successful, you will see the dialog in Figure 3-74. Click Close. The updated status will be reflected as shown in Figure 3-75.

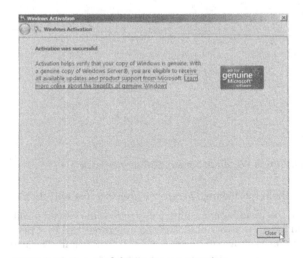

Figure 3-74. *Successful Windows activation*

Figure 3-75. *Updated activation status*

Patch the Windows Server 2008 Installation

If you are using the RTM version of Windows Server 2008, you should consider installing Windows Server 2008 Service Pack 2 or later (if you are not using a slipstreamed version already) immediately. Major updates such as a Windows Service Pack are preferred to individual hotfixes since they are tested in concert instead of individually, and will hopefully keep you on the General Distribution Release (GDR) branch of code.

Install a Windows Server 2008 Service Pack

This section will demonstrate how to install a Service Pack on a Windows Server 2008 server. This example was captured using Windows Server 2008 Service Pack 2 Beta. The final version of the service pack install should look similar to the screens shown in this section.

1. Download the service pack from http://www.microsoft.com/downloads for your version of the operating system (x86, x64, or IA64).

2. Run the executable that was downloaded. Click Next on the first dialog, as shown in Figure 3-76.

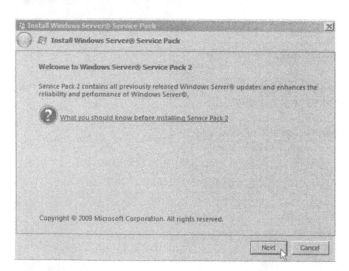

Figure 3-76. *First screen for installing a Windows Server 2008 service pack*

3. Read the license terms, accept them by clicking *I accept the license terms*, and click Next.

4. Select whether or not you want the installer to automatically reboot the server; it will be easier to do this, unless you have a reason not to allow an automatic restart. Check *Automatically restart the computer* as shown in Figure 3-77, and click Install. The status of the install process will be shown, and the server should reboot at least once.

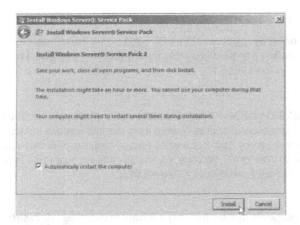

Figure 3-77. *Starting the service pack installation*

5. Upon logging in after the final reboot, a successful service pack install will display the dialog shown in Figure 3-78. Click Close.

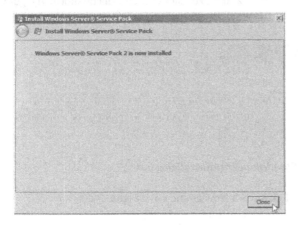

Figure 3-78. *Successful Windows service pack install message*

Install Necessary Windows Hotfixes

To see the latest recommendations and hotfixes for Windows Server 2008–based server clusters, consult Microsoft Knowledge Base article 957311, "Recommended hotfixes for Windows Server 2008–based server clusters" (http://support.microsoft.com/kb/957311). Some of these may be included in the service pack that was installed, so only apply ones that you need and that make sense for installation. The installation process is similar to that of installing Windows Installer 4.5, documented in the following section.

Install Windows Installer 4.5

Installing Windows Installer 4.5 (or later) is a requirement for SQL Server 2008. Installing it while the operating system is being configured makes the most sense because it requires a reboot. This section will show how to install Windows Installer 4.5.

Tip If you are installing Windows Server 2008 with Service Pack 2 slipstreamed or Windows Server 2008 R2, you should be able to skip installing Windows Installer 4.5 separately, since it appears that Windows Installer 4.5 is configured already. I tested this with the beta of Service Pack 2 as well the release candidate of Windows Server 2008 R2, and I did not have to install Windows Installer 4.5. However, you should verify this against the final versions of both Windows Sever 2008 Service Pack 2 and Windows Server 2008 R2.

---

1. You can either download the proper Windows Installer 4.5 from http://www.microsoft.com/ downloads for your version of the operating system, or find it on the SQL Server installation media, in the \<processor type>\redist\Windows Installer folder. There are different versions for Windows Server 2003 and Windows Server 2008.

2. Run the executable. For example, the downloaded 32-bit version for Windows Server 2008 has a file name of Windows6.0-KB942288-v2-x86.exe. Click OK at the dialog shown in Figure 3-79. Windows Installer 4.5 will now be installed.

Figure 3-79. *Windows Update Standalone Installed dialog box*

3. When the install is complete, click Restart Now as shown in Figure 3-80.

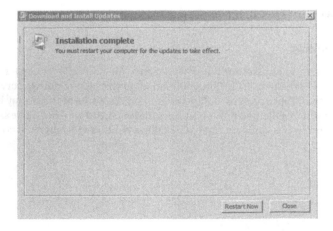

Figure 3-80. *Successful installation of Windows Installer 4.5*

Install .NET Framework

Installing .NET Framework 3.5 Service Pack 1 (or later) is a requirement for SQL Server 2008 on all versions of Windows Server 2008. Installing it while the operating system is being configured makes the most sense because not only does it requires a reboot, but installing it from the SQL Server installation media assumes you have an Internet connection. The executables on the SQL Server media are essentially stubs to go out and download the rest of the package. The reason is simple; at the time the RTM media was finalized, it appears the final .NET Framework 3.5.1 package had not been made available, so they put a link to download it. Remember that if you installed the Application Server role earlier under Windows Server 2008 R2 to configure MSDTC, you should already have .NET Framework 3.5.1.

Note It is worth mentioning that installing .NET Framework 3.5 SP1 will also install side-by-side copies of .NET Framework 2.0 and 3.0. If these exist on your server, they will be patched and updated to later versions.

---

1. Download the proper version of .NET Framework 3.5 SP1 from http://www.microsoft.com/downloads for your operating system. There are different versions for Windows Server 2003 and Windows Server 2008.

2. Run the executable that was downloaded. For example, the 32-bit version has a file name of dotnetfx.exe. You may be prompted for permission to run the package, as shown in Figure 3-81. Click Continue. The installer will then unpack the files and start the installer.

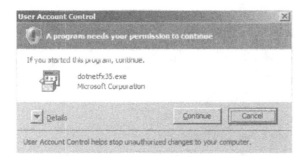

Figure 3-81. *Asking for permission to run .NET Framework 3.5 SP1*

3. Read the license terms, accept them, and click Install. It is optional to send information to Microsoft, so you do not have to select that option. A sample is shown in Figure 3-82. Setup will now install the files to the node and the status will be updated.

4. When the .NET Framework 3.5 SP1 setup is finished, you will see the dialog box in Figure 3-83. Click Exit.

Figure 3-82. *Main installation screen and EULA for .NET Framework 3.5 SP1*

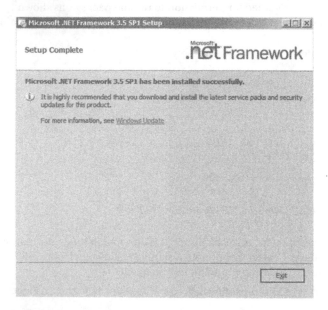

Figure 3-83. *Successful installation of .NET Framework 3.5 SP1*

5. As shown in Figure 3-84, you can choose to reboot now or later. Select Restart Later and continue to the next section to finish the configuration before rebooting.

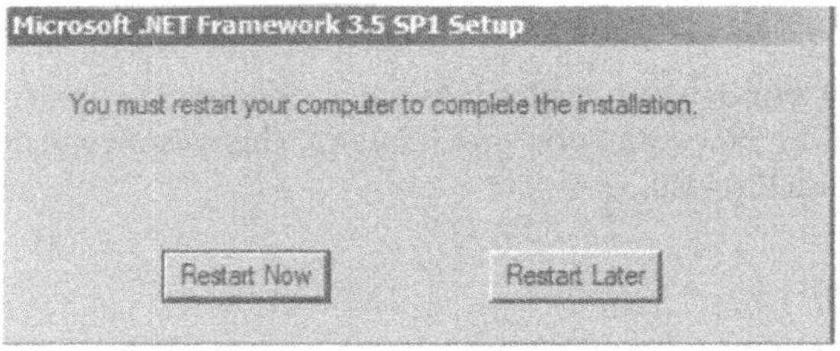

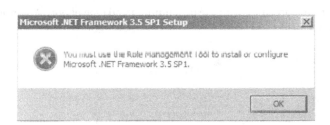

Figure 3-84. *Prompt for rebooting*

■**Caution** As of the release candidate of Windows Server 2008, you can no longer install .NET Framework 3.5 SP1 this way. If you do, you will see the error in Figure 3-85. You must add .NET Framework 3.5 SP1 using Server Manager as a feature. A sample dialog is shown in Figure 3-86.

Figure 3-85. *Error message when trying to install .NET Framework 3.5 SP1 on Windows Server 2008 R2*

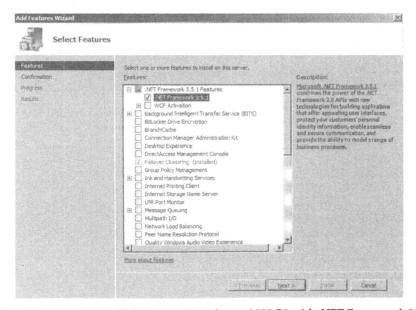

Figure 3-86. *Features dialog in Windows Server 2008 R2 with .NET Framework 3.5.1*

Configure Windows Firewall

For failover clustering to work properly, Windows Firewall needs to be configured to open certain ports. Those ports are listed in the section "Network Ports" in Chapter 2. This section will demonstrate how to add these ports to Windows Firewall.

Windows Server 2008 (RTM Branch)

These instructions will walk you through the process for adding a port exception in the RTM branch of Windows Server 2008. Note that the process changes with R2, and that I describe the R2 process in the next section.

1. From the Start menu, open Control Panel, and double-click Windows Firewall.

2. On the main Windows Firewall dialog, select *Change settings*.

3. On the Windows Firewall Settings dialog, select the *Exceptions* tab.

4. Click Add port.

5. Enter a unique name for the port along with the port number and type of port. A sample is shown in Figure 3-87. Click OK.

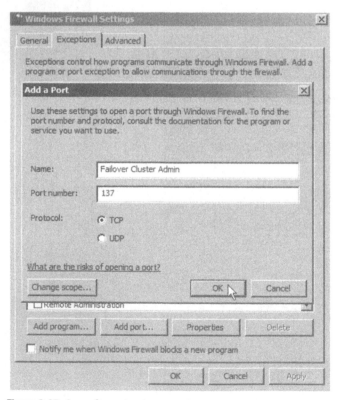

Figure 3-87. *Sample port entry*

6. Repeat steps 4 and 5 until all ports are added.

7. Click OK to close the Windows Firewall Settings dialog when finished.

8. Close the main Windows Firewall dialog.

9. Repeat on all nodes of the cluster.

Windows Server 2008 R2

These instructions will walk you through how to add a port exception on Windows Server 2008 R2.

1. From the Start menu, open Control Panel, and click Check Firewall status.

2. Select *Advanced settings*. The Windows Firewall with Advanced Security tool will be displayed.

3. Select *Inbound Rules*, right-click, and select *New Rule*.

4. On the Rule Type dialog, as shown in Figure 3-88, select *Port*. Click Next.

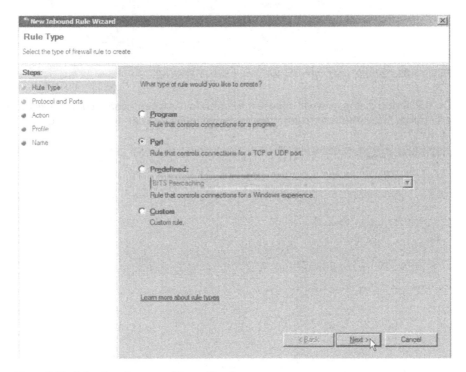

Figure 3-88. *Selecting the type of firewall rule*

5. On the Protocol and Ports dialog, select the type of port (TCP or UDP), and ensure *Specific local ports* is selected. Enter the port number. An example is shown in Figure 3-89. Click Next.

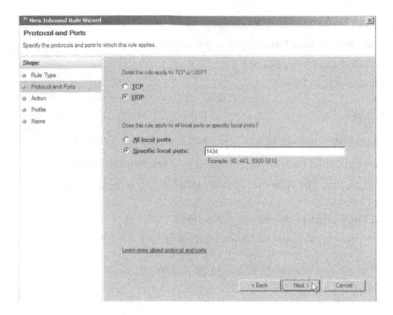

Figure 3-89. *Sample port entry for Windows Server 2008 R2*

6. On the Action dialog, you will choose the action to use when a connection meets the port exception. Select *Allow the connection* as shown in Figure 3-90, and click Next.

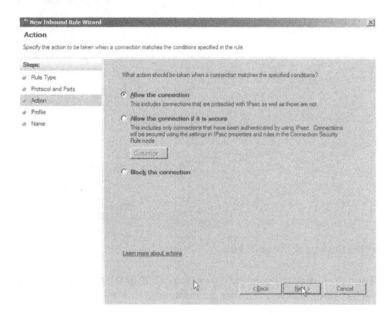

Figure 3-90. *Selecting an action*

7. On the Profile dialog, select the scope that the rule applies to. A sample is shown in Figure 3-91. Click Next.

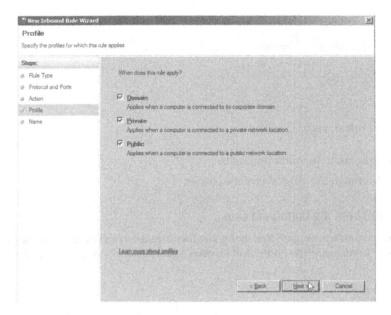

Figure 3-91. *Selecting when the rule applies*

8. On the Name dialog, enter a name for the new port exception. A sample is shown in Figure 3-92. Click Finish. The new rule will appear as shown in Figure 3-93.

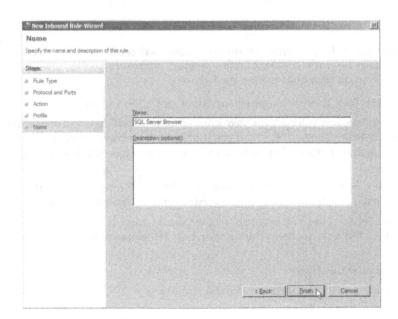

Figure 3-92. *Naming the new rule*

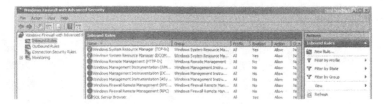

Figure 3-93. *New rule successfully added*

9. Repeat steps 3 through 7 for outbound rules.

10. Repeat steps 1 through 8 on all nodes of the cluster.

Configure the Firewall from the Command Line

NETSH can be used to add port openings. A link to the full documentation can be found earlier in this chapter, in the section "Configuring the Public and Private Cluster Networks via Scripting." A sample is shown in Figure 3-94.

```
C:\>netsh
netsh>firewall
netsh firewall>set portopening udp 3343 "Cluster Service" enable
Ok.
```

Figure 3-94. *Sample port exception added via NETSH*

Configure Anti-Virus

Microsoft's recommendations for placing anti-virus on computers that will run SQL Server are documented in Knowledge Base article 309422 (http://support.microsoft.com/kb/309422). You should configure anti-virus on each node to filter the following:

- All SQL Server data files. These will have extensions of .mdf, .ldf, and .ndf.

- All SQL Server backup files. Full backups have a default extension of .bak, and transaction log backups have a default extension of .trn. If you use other extensions (including ones that may be specific to third-party backup tools) for SQL Server backups, add those exclusions as well.

- All full-text catalog files, although for SQL Server 2008, full-text is integrated with the database. This would only apply if you have mixed versions of SQL Server on your cluster.

- If using Analysis Services, the entire directory on the shared drives containing all Analysis Services data files. If you do not know this location now, remember to set the filter post-installation.

- The entire quorum/witness disk.

- The \MSDTC directory on disks used by an MSDTC resource.

- The \Cluster subdirectory of the Windows installation.

Summary

There is quite a bit of preparation to do before you get to cluster Windows or SQL Server. The tasks and steps outlined in this chapter are essential to creating the foundation of a stable failover cluster. Do not attempt to go on to Chapter 4 to cluster Windows and then subsequently cluster SQL Server on top of Windows if you encounter errors during this chapter's configuration process, or if something does not seem to work as it should based upon the examples in this chapter. Plowing ahead is nearly a guarantee of encountering problems down the road, and poor configuration accounts for a large percentage of the support calls that Microsoft receives from customers for clustered SQL Server configurations. Do not add to the statistics.

■ ■ ■

CHAPTER 4

Clustering Windows Server 2008 Part 2: Clustering Windows

Once the building blocks for a failover clustering implementation are in place, you can embark on clustering the operating system. This chapter will cover both Windows Server 2008 RTM (which would include all Windows Server 2008 Service Packs that apply to RTM) and Windows Server 2008 R2. Where possible, a scripted as well as a GUI-based option is presented.

■**Note** Windows Server 2008 R2 is still prerelease software as I write this chapter, so consider the R2 content in this chapter a preview. When it does release, I'll post any updates affecting this chapter's content to my own site at http://www.sqlha.com and also to the Apress web page for this book (http://www.apress.com/book/view/1430219661).

Step 1: Review the Windows Logs

Before you run any processes, review the various logs in Event Viewer (from the Start menu, select *Administrative Tools* and then *Event Viewer*). At a minimum, review the Application, Security, and System logs, which can be found under the Windows Logs folder, as well as the Hardware Events log under Applications and Services Logs. If something does not look right or is clearly a problem, investigate and fix whatever is wrong. You will have a greater chance of starting off on the right foot and passing cluster validation the first time if you fix any obvious problems now. Scouring the logs early on also will establish a baseline so that you will know that at some point the server was "clean," and you will know approximately when problems started occurring.

Step 2: Validate the Cluster Configuration

You must validate the proposed failover cluster configuration prior to clustering the nodes. As noted in Chapter 2 in the section "Cluster Validation," to have a fully supported failover cluster from Microsoft, you must run every verification test and it must pass. If a test does not pass on a cluster that needs support, the problem must be fixed. Warnings may be acceptable for a nonproduction environment (assuming they are not fatal).

■Tip The validation process can take a considerable amount of time, and it will vary depending on how many nodes you have and what needs to be scanned, tested, and validated. Arguably the longest tests will be the ones related to storage, especially the ones that have to do with disk failovers. This is a very good reason not to have a million disks and/or mount points, because as you will see in Chapter 8, when you make certain configuration changes to the cluster, you must rerun validation. Thus, you will incur possibly quite a considerable outage just to change your configuration, even if the change itself is trivial. Get your configuration right up front and you may not have to worry about running validation again.

Validating the Cluster Configuration Using Failover Cluster Management

This section will show you how to use the new cluster validation wizard that is included as part of the new Failover Cluster Management tool provided in Windows Server 2008. If you are using versions of Windows Server 2008 prior to R2, this is your only option for validating the cluster; there is no way to script the process. The following instructions show how to validate a cluster using Failover Cluster Management.

1. Ensure that all nodes of the cluster are online. This step is fundamentally different from the pre–Windows Server 2008 process, where you created a one-node cluster and then added each node in separately.

2. Log onto one of the nodes of the cluster with the domain-based cluster administration account that you created in Chapter 3. First, select *Switch User*. Then select *Other User* and enter the name of the cluster administration account. Click the right arrow to continue.

3. From the Start menu, select *Administrative Tools* then *Failover Cluster Management*. Even though the cluster administration account is in the local Administrators group, you will be prompted as shown in Figure 4-1 for access. This happens because Windows Server 2008 has a feature called Local User Administrator (LUA) security. By default, nothing will run as an administrator account unless you are logged in as the local administrator, so you must explicitly escalate to run as an administrator. Click Continue.

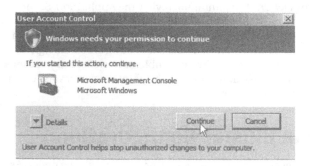

Figure 4-1. *Allowing permission to run with escalated privileges*

4. After Failover Cluster Management is loaded, select *Validate a Configuration*. There are two places on the main window to select it. An example is shown in Figure 4-2.

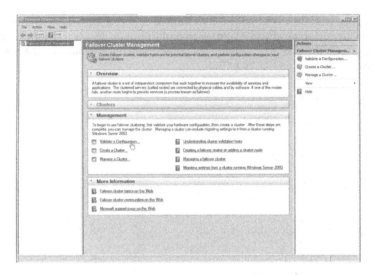

Figure 4-2. *Starting validation*

5. On the Before You Begin dialog, read the information, and when done, click Next.

6. On the Select Servers or a Cluster dialog, you have two options: you can manually enter the names of the nodes if you know them, or you can use the tool to assist you. If you want to manually input the names of the nodes, add them to the *Enter name* field and click Add. You can enter them one by one or all at once if you separate them by semicolons. An example is shown in Figure 4-3.

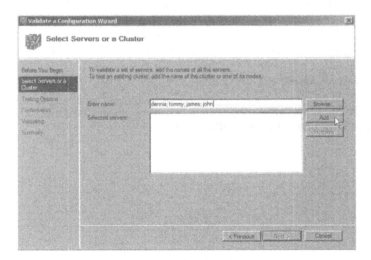

Figure 4-3. *Entering the names of potential cluster nodes for validation*

7. If you want assistance with the node names, click Browse. Input part of what you think a name is and click Check Names. If you are entering multiple node names, separate them by semicolons. An example is shown in Figure 4-4. After resolving, the names will appear similar to the example in Figure 4-5. Click OK.

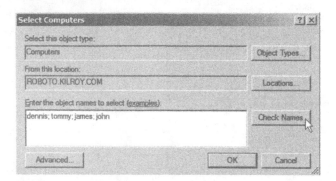

Figure 4-4. *Using the browse functionality*

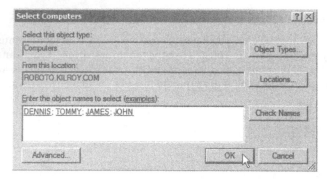

Figure 4-5. *Resolved server names*

8. The servers will then finish the verification process. When the process has finished, you will see a dialog similar to the one in Figure 4-6. Click Next.

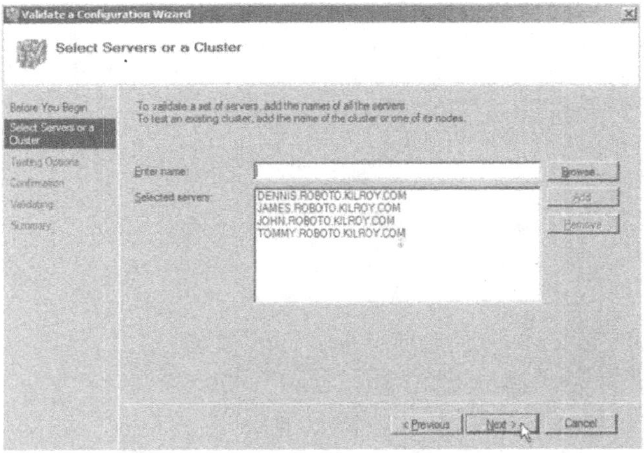

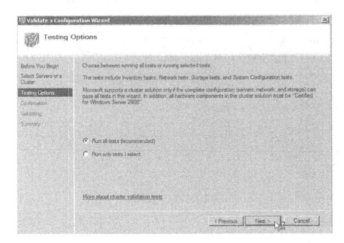

Figure 4-6. *The servers are verified.*

9. On the Testing Options dialog, select *Run all tests* as shown in Figure 4-7. You can also run a subset of tests, but this would not validate a certified cluster in the eyes of Microsoft. A good reason to select that option (a sample of a smaller number of tests is shown in Figure 4-8) is to test an area you know is a problem or to run just one test (or a smaller number of tests) to verify that a problem was fixed before rerunning the entire validation test again. Click Next.

Figure 4-7. *Selecting to run all tests*

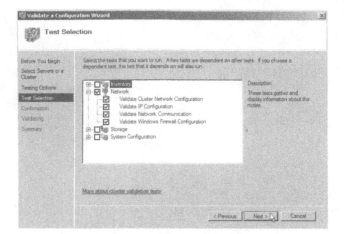

Figure 4-8. *Selecting a subset of tests to run during verification*

10. On the Confirmation dialog shown in Figure 4-9, click Next to start the validation tests. The tests will now run on each proposed node of the cluster. The status for each test will be displayed as it is run.

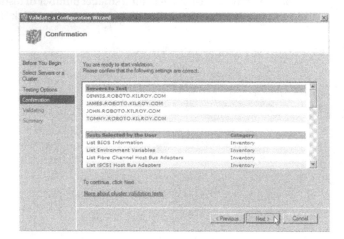

Figure 4-9. *Final step before validation runs*

11. When validation is complete, you will see a dialog similar to Figure 4-10, with the variations of headings shown in Figures 4-11, 4-12, and 4-13, depending on whether validation was a success, a partial run, or a failure, respectively. Note the differences in wording at the top—these are very important since they affect the supportability of the failover cluster. To see the validation report, click View Report. Details on how to interpret the report are in the upcoming section "Reading the Validation Report." Click Finished.

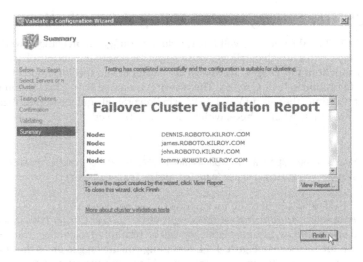

Figure 4-10. *Completely successful verification run*

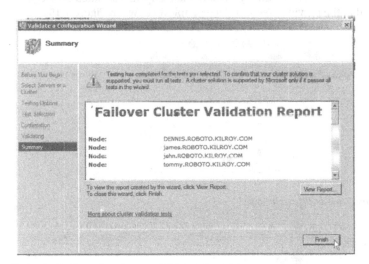

Figure 4-11. *Completed tests with warnings*

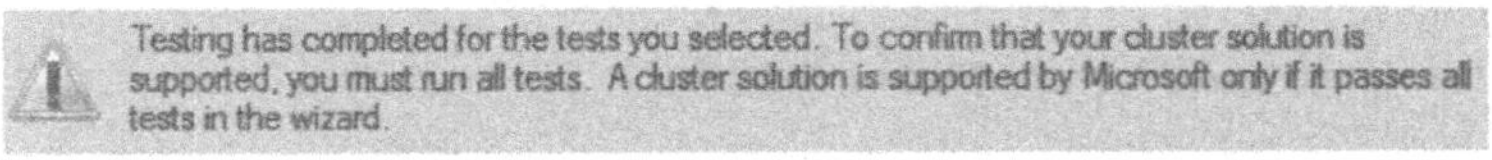

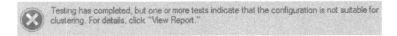

Figure 4-12. *Completed limited set of tests, but the cluster will not be supported by Microsoft*

Testing has completed, but one or more tests indicate that the configuration is not suitable for clustering. For details, click "View Report."

Figure 4-13. *Validation run with failures*

Validating the Cluster Configuration Using PowerShell

New to Windows Server 2008 R2 is the ability to validate the cluster configuration using PowerShell. Windows Server 2008 R2 ships with a bunch of failover cluster–specific commandlets (cmdlets), some of which will be shown throughout this chapter as well as in Chapter 8. The specific cmdlet for validating the cluster configuration is Test-Cluster. The reason it is named Test-Cluster and not Validate-Cluster is that at this time, there is no Validate verb in PowerShell, and for standardization purposes, it is much easier to utilize what is there, which includes a Test verb.

■**Tip** To see the full documentation and help for a PowerShell cmdlet, type Get-Help <cmdlet>, where <cmdlet> is the name of the cmdlet you are trying to use (e.g., Get-Help Test-Cluster).

---

1. From the Start menu, select *Administrative Tools*, right-click *Failover Cluster PowerShell Management*, and select *Run as Administrator.* You will be prompted to confirm the escalated privileges with the message in Figure 4-14. Assuming you are logged on as the cluster administration account you created in Chapter 3, you will see an error relating to privileges when you try to execute a command if you do not launch with escalated privileges due to LUA as described in the previous section. An example is shown in Figure 4-15.

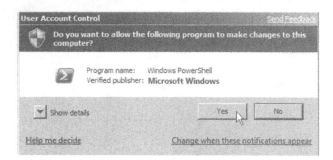

Figure 4-14. *Prompt to escalate privileges*

Figure 4-15. *Error when privileges are not escalated*

2. At the prompt, enter the command Test-Cluster -Node <node list separated by commas> to run all validation tests. An example that would run the driver tests is Test-Cluster -Node Dennis,Tommy,James,John. During the validation process, the status will be updated as shown in Figure 4-16. The "status bar" will appear near the top of whatever command window is open.

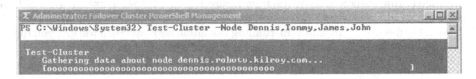

Figure 4-16. *Status while all validation tests are being run*

3. To run a single test, execute Test-Cluster -Node <node list separated by commas> -Include <list of tests separated by commas>. An example that would run the driver tests is Test-Cluster -Node Dennis,Tommy,James,John -Include "List System Drivers", "List Unsigned Drivers". Other examples with their results are shown in Figures 4-18 and 4-19. To see a full list of the validation tests, execute Test-Cluster -Node <node name> -List. Use the value found under the Display Name column. When complete, you will see output similar to one of the following: Figure 4-17 (success), Figure 4-18 (warnings), or Figure 4-19 (failure).

```
PS C:\Windows\System32> Test-Cluster -Node Dennis,Tommy,James,John

Mode             LastWriteTime        Length Name
----             -------------        ------ ----
-a---           3/22/2009  11:53 PM   2176672 Test-Cluster on 2009.02.22 At 23.19.08.mht
```

Figure 4-17. *Successful execution of Test-Cluster with no errors*

```
PS C:\> Test-Cluster -Node Dennis,Tommy,James,John -Include "Validate Cluster Network Configuration", "Validate IP Confi
guration"
WARNING: Networking - Validate IP Configuration: Warning.
WARNING:
Test Result:
HadUnselectedTests, ClusterConditionallyApproved
Testing has completed for the tests you selected. You should review the warnings in the Report. A cluster solution is
supported by Microsoft only if it passes all tests in the wizard.
Test report file path: C:\Users\cluadmin\AppData\Local\Temp\Test-Cluster on 2009.02.22 At 09.08.23.mht

Mode             LastWriteTime        Length Name
----             -------------        ------ ----
-a---           2/22/2009   9:08 AM   133431 Test-Cluster on 2009.02.22 At 09.08.23.mht
```

Figure 4-18. *Successful execution of Test-Cluster with a warning*

```
PS C:\> Test-Cluster -Node Dennis,Tommy,James,John -Include "Validate Cluster Network Configuration", "Validate IP Confi
guration"
WARNING: Networking - Validate IP Configuration: Failed.
WARNING:
Test Result:
ClusterSkippedTestsCompleted, HadFailures
Testing has completed for the tests you selected. One or more tests indicate that the configuration is not suitable for
clustering. A cluster solution is supported by Microsoft only if it passes all tests in the wizard.
Test report file path: C:\Users\cluadmin\AppData\Local\Temp\Test-Cluster on 2009.02.22 At 09.05.53.mht

Mode             LastWriteTime        Length Name
----             -------------        ------ ----
-a---           2/22/2009   9:06 AM   133502 Test-Cluster on 2009.02.22 At 09.05.53.mht
```

Figure 4-19. *Execution of Test-Cluster with errors*

Reading the Validation Report

Whether you run validation from Failover Cluster Management or via PowerShell, the result is the same: a report is generated. The report is an .mht file, which is readable in a web browser. The validation report is created in two places. First, it can be found under X:\Users\<username>\AppData\ Local\Temp, where X is the drive letter where Windows is installed and <username> is the name of the account used to run validation. If you run from Failover Cluster Management, the file will have a name of tmpXXXX.tmp.mht, where XXXX is a unique identifier. A sample of files is shown in Figure 4-20. As shown in Figures 4-17, 4-18, and 4-19, running validation via PowerShell will give you the name of the file created. The second location is found under %windir%\Cluster\Reports.

■Tip If you do not see the report in the %windir%\Cluster\Reports directory, copy it from the temporary location to somewhere more permanent and safe. You may want to consider disabling or not installing tools that will wipe temporary files from the server.

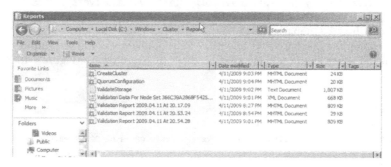

Figure 4-20. *List of report files on a server*

Once you open the validation report, it will appear similar to Figure 4-21. The report is extremely detailed, and in many ways, you can use it as a catalog of each node's configuration. All successful tests are marked with a white check mark in a green circle. A failure is denoted with a white X with a red circle as shown in Figure 4-22. A warning is denoted with a yellow triangle with a black exclamation point as shown in Figure 4-23.

Each top-level category can be clicked, and when you do so, you will see the detailed output for each test process. If you have a completely successful validation, you do not have to look at the details unless you feel the need to. If you have failures or warnings, you must evaluate the report's results. Examples of what the report shows for failures (in red onscreen) and warnings (in yellow onscreen) are shown in Figure 4-24. These items must be cleared up. Once you fix a problem, rerun validation for that specific test to ensure that the problem is fixed. Even if the problem is fixed, at this point Windows will allow you to cluster the nodes, but do not do that. You must rerun the entire validation test for all steps, not only for Microsoft supportability, but also because SQL Server will check to see that there were no failures in the entire run during its installation process.

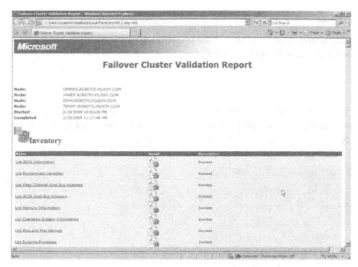

Figure 4-21. *Sample Failover Cluster Validation Report*

Figure 4-22. *Example of a failure*

Figure 4-23. *Example of a warning*

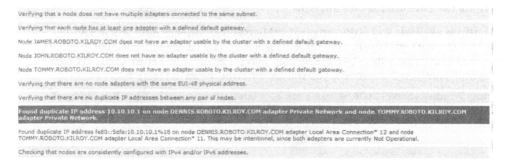

Figure 4-24. *Sample detail failure and warning messages*

Common Cluster Validation Problems

Some validation problems are more common than others. This section will not only show some of the common problems, but also describe how to resolve them.

Invalid Operating System SKU

There is one known problem that you should be aware of if you deploy the RTM version of Windows Server 2008 without Hyper-V. If you run Cluster Validation, the validation process will fail with the error "The operating system SKU is not compatible" as shown in Figure 4-25.

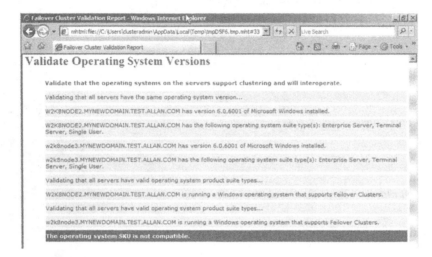

Figure 4-25. *Failed validation due to using Windows Server 2008 without Hyper-V*

There are two potential fixes for this issue:

- A hotfix is available and is documented in Microsoft Knowledge Base article 950179 (http://support.microsoft.com/kb/950179/en-us). This fix can be applied only after the Failover Clustering feature (see the section "Server Features and Server Roles" in Chapter 2) has been configured; otherwise, you will see the error shown in Figure 4-25.

- Apply Windows Server 2008 Service Pack 2 (or later). It contains the fix in Knowledge Base article 950179 (see Figure 4-26). This fix is also in Windows Server 2008 R2.

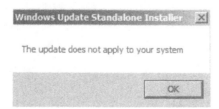

Figure 4-26. *Error applying the Knowledge Base fix if Failover Clustering is not added as a feature*

Teredo

Another known possible validation failure has to do with Teredo, which is an IPv6 tunneling protocol (see the section "Networking" in Chapter 2 for more information on IPv6) as shown in Figure 4-27. The problem is that Teredo assigns the same IPv6 address to each of its interfaces and causes the validation to fail because failover clustering expects unique TCP/IP addresses for each network interface.

Another reason you may see this error is that the servers were built with the same image, and the automatically created Cluster NetFT adapter has the same MAC address as that of another node. This is one of the reasons you need to ensure that there are no problems if you are using imaging to install Windows.

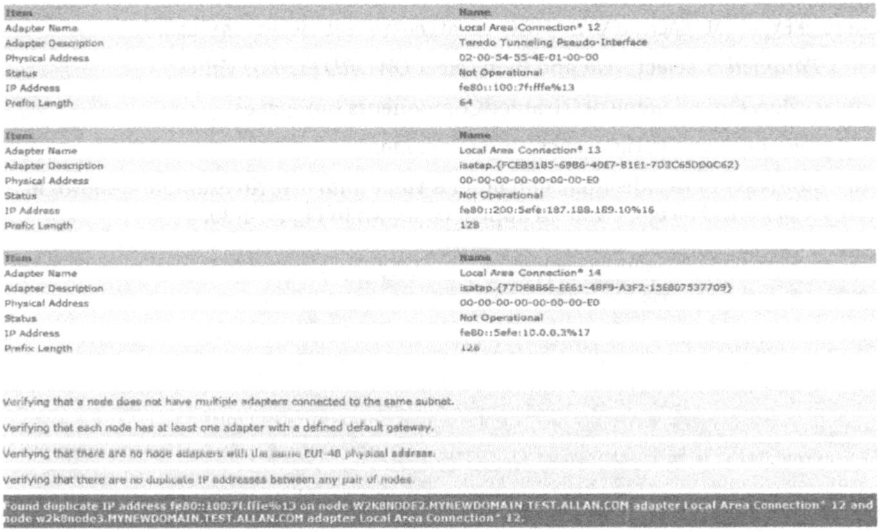

Figure 4-27. *Teredo-related validation error*

There are two ways to resolve this issue: one is via the command line and the other is through the registry.

Fixing Teredo Using the Command Line

This section will show the instructions on how to fix the Teredo validation error via the command line. A sample execution is shown in Figure 4-28.

1. Open a command window.

2. At the command prompt, type netsh.

3. At the netsh> prompt, type interface.

4. At the netsh interface> prompt, type teredo.

5. At the netsh interface teredo> prompt, type set state disabled.

```
C:\>netsh
netsh>interface
netsh interface>teredo
netsh interface teredo>set state disabled
Ok.
```

Figure 4-28. *Disabling Teredo*

Fixing Teredo Using the Registry

The following steps show how to fix the Teredo validation error via the Windows registry.

1. Start regedit.

2. Navigate to HKEY_LOCAL_MACHINE\SYSTEM\CurrentControlSet\Services\Tcpip6.

3. Right-click *Parameters*, select *New*, and then select *DWORD (32-bit) Value*.

4. For the new value, enter a name of **DisabledComponents** (no spaces).

5. Select *DisabledComponents*, right-click, and select *Modify*.

6. Make sure *Base* is set to Hexidecimal, and enter a *Value data* of **8**. An example is shown in Figure 4-29. Click OK. The entry should appear as shown in Figure 4-30.

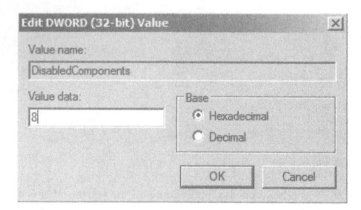

Figure 4-29. *Editing the DWORD for DisabledComponents*

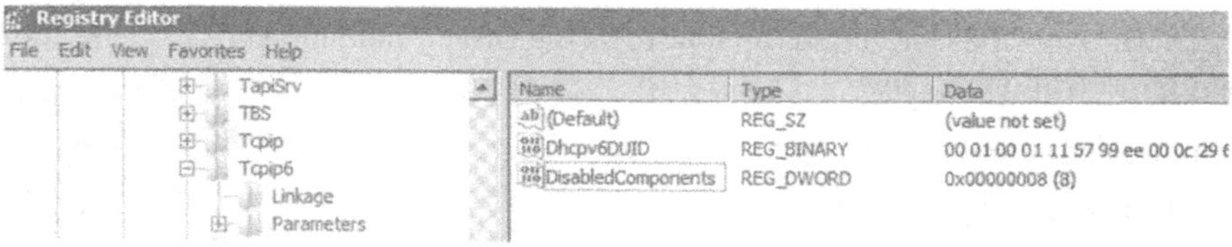

Figure 4-30. *Disabled Teredo in the registry*

Different Networks on the Same Subnet

An explicit check of the validation process is that no two networks are on the same subnet even if they are used for disjoint purposes. For example, if you are using iSCSI to connect to your shared disk subsystem, and you have Multipath I/O enabled, you will have two IP addresses on two different NICs. Even your storage networks must be on different subnets, so you will have to work with your storage administrators to ensure that the storage configuration will not cause validation to fail. This is documented in Knowledge Base article 951434 (http://support.microsoft.com/kb/951434).

Changes Introduced in Windows Server 2008 with Service Pack 2 and Windows Server 2008 R2

As I was writing later chapters, doing some testing, and starting to edit this chapter, the release candidate (RC) for Windows Server 2008 Service Pack 2 hit the Web. I previously tested earlier versions of Windows Server 2008 Service Pack 2 with no issue, but there was a change introduced into the RC build that will be in the final as well as any version of R2 past build 7000. This change broke the ability to install SQL Server 2008 on Windows Server 2008: you can pass the Windows cluster validation with flying colors, but you will see the error shown back in Chapter 2 in Figure 2-5 that SQL Server fails on the MSCS check. With Windows Server 2008 Service Pack 2 or later, there is a change that impacts the location of the validation report that SQL Server must use to pass the tests that SQL Server 2008's Setup executes.

What happened? The problem is related to the Federal Information Processing Standard (FIPS), a U.S. government standard that provides a benchmark for implementing cryptographic software. A new algorithm was implemented if the FIPS policy in Windows is enabled. Due to the different algorithm, SQL Server cannot find the successful Windows cluster validation report. SQL Server 2008 Setup was coded against the Windows Server 2008 RTM algorithm. FIPS may also be a potential validation problem even without Windows Server 2008 Service Pack 2 or R2. A hotfix is documented in Knowledge Base article 960334 (http://support.microsoft.com/kb/960334).

Note You can find more information on FIPS at http://technet.microsoft.com/en-us/library/cc750357.aspx, and for SQL Server, Knowledge Base article 955720 at http://support.microsoft.com/kb/955720.

This problem is fixed in SQL Server 2008 Service Pack 1, which was released as this book was being written. SQL Server allows you to patch the files used during the setup process prior to installing SQL Server. More on that process will be covered in Chapter 6.

Caution If you make a change to the SQL Server FIPS bit as per Knowledge Base article 955720, you must rerun cluster validation.

Step 3: Create the Windows Failover Cluster

Creating the Windows failover cluster in Windows Server 2008 is different than in all previous versions of Windows. Prior to Windows Server 2008, you created a one-node cluster with the first node, and the other nodes were added individually (or all at once) after the creation of the first node of the cluster was complete. With Windows Server 2008, you create the failover cluster with all nodes at the same time. You can do it piecemeal, but that approach will not be covered in this chapter. Adding an individual node will be covered in Chapter 8.

You can configure a cluster in three ways: through a graphical interface with Failover Cluster Management, via the command line with `cluster.exe`, or via PowerShell.

Creating a Failover Cluster Using Failover Cluster Management

The following instructions will show you how to create the new Windows failover cluster with Failover Cluster Management.

1. Log on to the node where the disks were configured in Chapter 3 with the cluster administration account.

2. From Administrative Tools, start Failover Cluster Management.

3. Select the option *Create a Cluster* from the main window shown earlier in Figure 4-2.

4. On the Before You Begin dialog, read the information, and when done, click Next.

5. On the Select Servers or a Cluster dialog, you have two options: you can manually enter the names of the nodes if you know them, or you can use the tool to assist you. If you want to manually input the names of the nodes, add them to Enter name and click Add. You can enter them one by one or all at once if you separate them with a semicolon. An example is shown earlier in Figure 4-3.

6. If you want assistance with the node names, click Browse. Input part of what you think the name is and click Check Names. If multiple node names are being entered, separate them by a semicolon. An example is shown earlier in Figure 4-4. After resolving, the names will appear similar to the example shown earlier in Figure 4-5. Click OK.

7. The servers will then finish the verification process. When finished, you will see a dialog similar to the one shown earlier in Figure 4-6. Click Next.

8. At this point, the Create Cluster Wizard will check to see if you need to run the cluster verification. If you run it, the steps will be the same as those documented earlier. Otherwise, proceed to step 9.

9. On the Access Point for Administering the Cluster dialog, enter the name of the Windows failover cluster in the *Cluster Name* field. Remember that this is a unique name in the domain and must be different from any server name or SQL Server instance name. Use an intuitive name that makes sense in your environment. This particular example uses W2K8SP2FC, which denotes that this is a Windows Server 2008 (W2K8) failover cluster (FC) with Service Pack 2 (SP2). Once you enter a name, check one or more networks to use for the public traffic, and enter a valid IP address in that subnet in the *Address* field. An example is shown in Figure 4-31. Click Next.

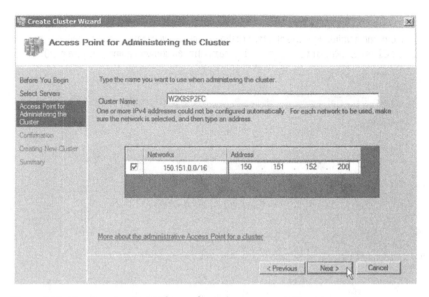

Figure 4-31. *Configuring the failover cluster's name and IP address*

10. On the Confirmation dialog shown in Figure 4-32, verify that the entries are correct and click Next to start the configuration process.

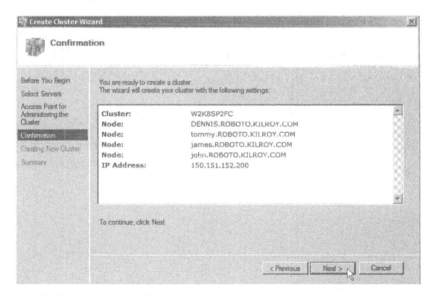

Figure 4-32. *Confirmation dialog*

11. When the cluster configuration is complete and successful, you should see a dialog similar to the one in Figure 4-33. You can view a report of what was configured by clicking View Report. A sample is shown in Figure 4-34. Click Finish to close the dialog and complete the creation process. Figure 4-35 shows the new failover cluster in Failover Cluster Management.

■**Tip** Like running validation, the cluster creation process will create a report which is
`%Windir%\Cluster\Reports\CreateCluster.mht`, as shown earlier in Figure 4-20.

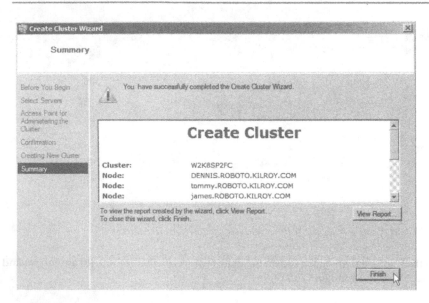

Figure 4-33. *Successful Windows failover cluster configuration*

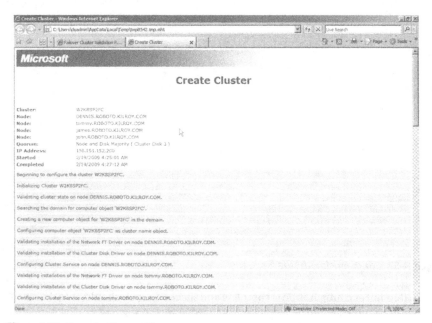

Figure 4-34. *Sample Create Cluster report*

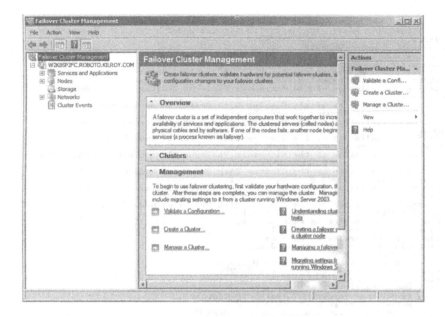

Figure 4-35. *New failover cluster as shown in Failover Cluster Management*

Creating a Failover Cluster Using cluster.exe

You can also create a failover cluster via using cluster.exe. Remember when starting Command Prompt from the Start menu to right-click and select *Run as administrator*. The command you will use is cluster <*cluster name*> /create /ipaddress:x.x.x.x/y.y.y.y /Nodes:"<*node list separated by commas*>", where x.x.x.x is the IP address for the failover cluster, and y.y.y.y is the subnet mask for the public IP address. A sample execution is shown in Figure 4-36.

Note Creating a failover cluster with cluster.exe creates only the base cluster (name, IP address, networking). You will have to add all storage as a poststep. How to add disks is documented in Chapter 8 in the section "Add a Disk to the Failover Cluster."

```
C:\>cluster W2K8R2FC /create /ipaddress:160.161.162.200/255.255.0.0 /Nodes:"Denn
is,Tommy,James,John"
   3% Initializing Cluster W2K8R2FC.
   7% Validating cluster state on node Dennis.
  10% Searching the domain for computer object W2K8R2FC
  14% Creating a new computer object for W2K8R2FC in the domain
  17% Configuring computer object W2K8R2FC as cluster name object
  21% Validating installation of the Microsoft Failover Cluster Virtual Adapter o
n node Dennis.
  25% Validating installation of the Cluster Disk Driver on node Dennis.
  28% Configuring Cluster Service on node Dennis.
  32% Validating installation of the Microsoft Failover Cluster Virtual Adapter o
n node Tommy.
  35% Validating installation of the Cluster Disk Driver on node Tommy.
  39% Configuring Cluster Service on node Tommy.
  42% Validating installation of the Microsoft Failover Cluster Virtual Adapter o
n node James.
  46% Validating installation of the Cluster Disk Driver on node James.
  50% Configuring Cluster Service on node James.
  53% Validating installation of the Microsoft Failover Cluster Virtual Adapter o
n node John.
  57% Validating installation of the Cluster Disk Driver on node John.
  60% Configuring Cluster Service on node John.
  64% Starting Cluster Service on node Dennis.
  64% Starting Cluster Service on node Tommy.
  64% Starting Cluster Service on node James.
  64% Starting Cluster Service on node John.
  67% Forming cluster W2K8R2FC.
  71% Adding cluster common properties to W2K8R2FC.
  75% Creating resource types on cluster W2K8R2FC.
  78% Creating group 'Cluster Group'.
  78% Creating group 'Available Storage'.
  82% Creating IP Address resource 'Cluster IP Address'.
  85% Creating Network Name resource 'W2K8R2FC'.
  89% Searching the domain for computer object W2K8R2FC
  92% Verifying computer object W2K8R2FC in the domain
  96% Configuring computer object W2K8R2FC as cluster name object

 100% Bringing resource group 'Cluster Group' online.
```

Figure 4-36. *Creating a failover cluster via cluster.exe*

Creating a Failover Cluster Using PowerShell

Creating a new Windows failover cluster with Windows Server 2008 R2 and PowerShell is fairly easy. As noted in the chapter introduction, R2 is still prerelease, so not all functionality was implemented in the version I used for testing. To start PowerShell, from Administrative Tools select *PowerShell for Failover Clustering*. The PowerShell cmdlet for creating a failover cluster is New-Cluster. New-Cluster has a few parameters; you can see the full list via the help command, as documented earlier. The example in Figure 4-37 specifies the –Name parameter, which gives the name of the failover cluster; the –Node parameter, which lists all nodes (separated by commas) to use in the creation of the failover cluster; and finally –StaticAddress to enter a valid IP address for the failover cluster. When finished, PowerShell will display the location of the cluster creation report and display the name of the failover cluster.

```
PS C:\Windows\System32> New-Cluster -Name W2K8R2FC -Node Dennis,Tommy,James,John -StaticAddress 160.161.162.224
Report file location: C:\Users\cluadmin\AppData\Local\Temp\tmp9DEA.tmp.mht

Name
----
W2K8R2FC
```

Figure 4-37. *Configuring a Windows failover cluster via PowerShell*

Step 4: Perform Postinstallation Tasks

After performing the initial installation steps for the failover cluster itself, you must complete configuration tasks immediately afterward. This section will walk you through what you need to do and how to achieve it.

Configure the Cluster Networks

This section will show you how to rename and set the purpose of the networks once they have been configured as part of the Windows failover cluster. Prior to Windows Server 2008, you also had to set the priority of the cluster networks in addition to the prioritization of networks done at the Windows level (see Chapter 3).

The goal with the rewrite of failover clustering in Windows Server 2008 was to make it as easy as possible to use and configure. The cluster network driver (netft.sys) is now configured to allow the Windows failover cluster to choose how it communicates and over which network the communication should happen. netft.sys maintains its own routing table. As is shown in the upcoming Figure 4-40, you do have the control to select how the network will be used (or not, as the case may be). By default, all networks are enabled for cluster communications, but only networks with a gateway defined will be allowed for client communication.

Configuring the Cluster Networks Using Failover Cluster Management

The following steps tell how to configure the networks defined as part of the Windows failover cluster using Failover Cluster Management.

1. From Administrative Tools, start Failover Cluster Management.

2. Expand the tree containing Windows failover cluster and then expand Networks as shown in Figure 4-38. Notice that the networks are named Cluster Network N, where N is a number.

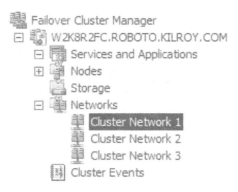

Figure 4-38. *Example tree after configuring a failover cluster*

3. Select one of the networks and look at the center section of Failover Cluster Management—it will be more descriptive and tell you the name of the network on each node. In Figure 4-38, the network selected happens to be the public network. You can now see why it is important to name the networks the same on each node. Now that you know the purpose of the network, right-click the network's name in the tree and select *Rename*. Name the network something more descriptive that matches its purpose and press Enter. The new name will now be reflected in the list. A sample is shown in Figure 4-39.

Figure 4-39. *Renamed cluster network*

4. Right-click the network that was just renamed and select *Properties*. Depending on the use of the network, different options should be selected. For the public network, the options *Allow cluster network communications on this network* and *Allow clients to connect through this network* should be selected. An example is shown in Figure 4-40. As shown in Figure 4-41, for the private cluster network, only select *Allow cluster communication on this network* but do not allow client connections. You also may have other networks that were detected (such as those used by iSCSI). Those should not be used for the cluster, so select the option *Do not allow cluster network communication on this network* as shown in Figure 4-42. Click OK when done.

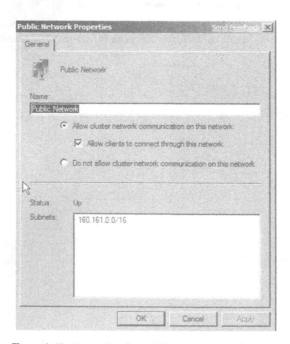

Figure 4-40. *Example of a public network configuration*

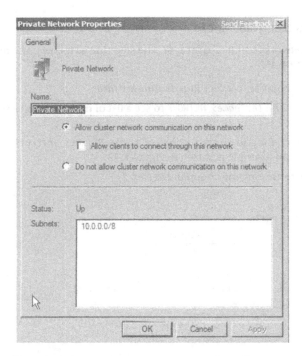

Figure 4-41. *Example of a private network configuration*

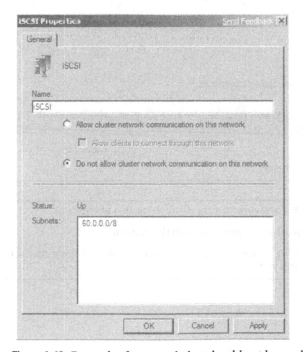

Figure 4-42. *Example of a network that should not be used by the cluster*

Configuring the Cluster Networks Using cluster.exe

You can also configure the cluster networks using cluster.exe. The steps are as follows, and an example execution is shown in Figure 4-43:

1. Start a command prompt. Remember to select *Run as administrator.*

2. Enter the command cluster *<cluster name>* NETWORK to see a list of the networks as shown in Figure 4-43.

3. To rename a network, use the command cluster *<cluster name>* NETWORK *<network name>* /RENAME:*<new network name>*. An example is shown in Figure 4-43.

4. You can verify the change by rerunning the command in step 2.

```
C:\>cluster W2K8RTMFC NETWORK
Listing status for all available networks:

Network                                        Status
------------------------------------------     ------------
Cluster Network 3                              Up
Public Network                                Up
Private Network                               Up

C:\>cluster W2K8RTMFC NETWORK "Cluster Network 3" /RENAME:iSCSI

Renaming network 'Cluster Network 3'...

Network                                        Status
------------------------------------------     ------------
iSCSI                                          Up

C:\>cluster W2K8RTMFC NETWORK
Listing status for all available networks:

Network                                        Status
------------------------------------------     ------------
iSCSI                                          Up
Public Network                                Up
Private Network                               Up
```

Figure 4-43. *Renaming a network using cluster.exe*

5. To change the use of the network, you must set the Role property of the network. The values are as described in Table 4-1.

Table 4-1. *Role Values for cluster.exe*

Role	Description
0	Do not allow cluster network communication on this network.
1	Allow cluster network communication on this network.
3	Allow cluster network communication on this network and allow clients to connect through this network.

6. To set the value, execute the command cluster `<cluster name>` network `<network name>`
    /PROP Role=`<value>`. To verify, use the command cluster `<cluster name>` network `<network
    name>` /PROP. An example of configuring the private network for only cluster communications
    is shown in Figure 4-44.

```
C:\Users\cluadmin>cluster W2K8RTMFC network "Private Network" /PROP Role=1


C:\Users\cluadmin>cluster W2K8RTMFC network "Private Network" /PROP

Listing properties for 'Private Network':

T  Network           Name                      Value
-- ---------------   -----------------------   -------------------
SR Private Network   Name                      Private Network
MR Private Network   IPv6Addresses
MR Private Network   IPv6PrefixLengths
MR Private Network   IPv4Addresses             10.0.0.0
MR Private Network   IPv4PrefixLengths         8
SR Private Network   Address                   10.0.0.0
SR Private Network   AddressMask               255.0.0.0
S  Private Network   Description
D  Private Network   Role                      1 (0x1)
```

Figure 4-44. *Changing and verifying the network use via cluster.exe*

Verify the Quorum Configuration

After configuring the networks, take a look at the quorum's configuration. Depending on what
Windows decided during the configuration of the failover cluster, it may not have put things where
you wanted them to go or selected the quorum model you wanted to use. For example, perhaps
Windows configured the witness disk on a shared cluster disk that you had not intended. This
section will show you how to configure the quorum. For more information on the quorum models
and what to choose, read the section "Choosing a Quorum Model" in Chapter 2.

■Tip When configuring the quorum, a report will be generated, located at %Windir%\Cluster\Reports\
QuorumConfiguration.mht.

Configuring the Quorum Using Failover Cluster Management

The following steps demonstrate how to configure the quorum model for a failover cluster in
Failover Cluster Management.

1. From Administrative Tools, start Failover Cluster Management.

2. Select the failover cluster that was just created, right-click, select *More Actions*, and then
    choose *Configure Cluster Quorum Settings*.

3. On the Before You Begin dialog of the Configure Cluster Quorum Wizard, read the infor-
    mation, and when done, click Next.

4. On the Select Quorum Configuration dialog, notice that Windows makes recommendations
    on what you should use. (Recall that the quorum models were described in Chapter 2 in
    depth.) You will likely wind up configuring a Node and Disk Majority quorum as shown
    in Figure 4-45. Click Next to continue. Note that with some cluster creation methods, storage
    is not added by default, so you may have to add storage to the cluster to successfully con-
    figure the quorum. An example is shown in the next section with cluster.exe. To see how to
    add a disk to the storage pool, refer to Chapter 8.

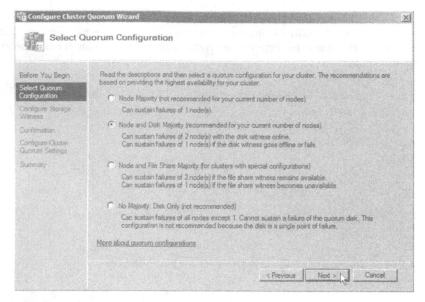

Figure 4-45. *Selecting a quorum model*

5. Assuming you selected a quorum model that uses a shared disk, on the Configure Storage Witness dialog, select the disk that the witness will be configured to use. If a disk-based quorum model is in use, a check mark will appear next to the disk in use. You may have to expand the tree next to the disk (which appears as Cluster Disk *N*, where *N* is a number) to see the drive letter. In Figure 4-46, the disk Q is selected for use. Click Next.

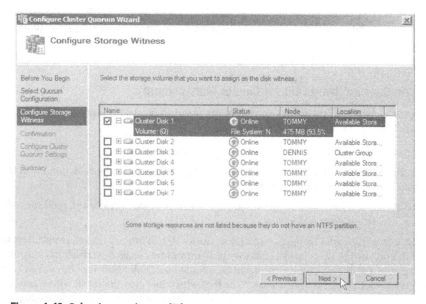

Figure 4-46. *Selecting a witness disk*

6. Ensure that the Confirmation dialog (see Figure 4-47) reflects the configuration you want, and click Next. The quorum model will now be configured.

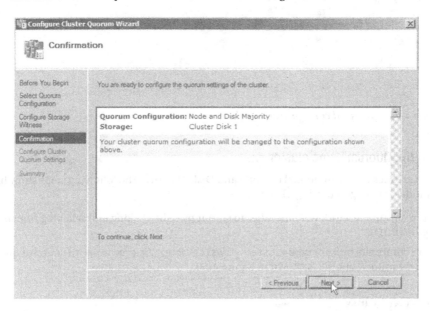

Figure 4-47. *Confirming the configuration*

7. When the configuration is finished, click Finish on the Summary dialog as shown in Figure 4-48. The change will also be reflected on the main summary display. An example is shown in Figure 4-49.

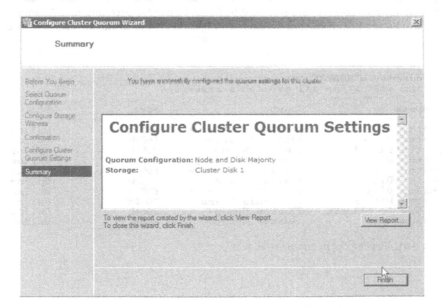

Figure 4-48. *Successful configuration of the quorum*

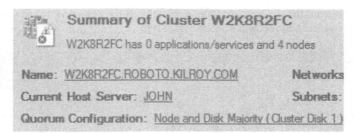

Figure 4-49. *Successful configuration of the quorum*

Configuring the Quorum Using cluster.exe

This section assumes a quorum model of Node and Disk Majority. The following steps show how a quorum model is configured using cluster.exe.

1. Start a command window. Remember to start it by right-clicking and selecting *Run as administrator*.

2. At the command prompt type cluster <*cluster name*> /quorum to see the current quorum configuration. A sample is shown in Figure 4-50.

```
C:\>cluster W2K8R2FC /quorum
Witness Resource Name Path                                                        Type
--------------------- ----------------------------------------------------------- --------
Cluster Disk 3        G:\Cluster\                                                  Majority
```

Figure 4-50. *Viewing the current quorum configuration*

3. Type the command cluster <*cluster name*> res to see a list of all the available cluster disks. res is an abbreviation for resource, and both can be used interchangeably. A sample is shown in Figure 4-51. Note that Available Storage and Cluster Group are owned by two different nodes.

```
C:\>cluster W2K8R2FC res
Listing status for all available resources:

Resource                Group                 Node          Status
--------------------    ------------------    --------      --------
Cluster Disk 1          Available Storage     TOMMY         Online
Cluster Disk 2          Available Storage     TOMMY         Online
Cluster Disk 3          Cluster Group         JOHN          Online
Cluster Disk 4          Available Storage     TOMMY         Online
Cluster Disk 5          Available Storage     TOMMY         Online
Cluster Disk 6          Available Storage     TOMMY         Online
Cluster Disk 7          Available Storage     TOMMY         Online
Cluster Disk 8          Available Storage     TOMMY         Online
Cluster IP Address      Cluster Group         JOHN          Online
Cluster Name            Cluster Group         JOHN          Online
```

Figure 4-51. *Viewing the available resources*

4. To configure a disk as the witness, you must move it into the Cluster Group. As noted in step 3, the Available Storage and Cluster Group resource groups are not owned by the same node. If you try to move the disk you want, and the groups are owned by different nodes, you will see the error shown in Figure 4-52. Move the storage group (or the cluster one; it doesn't matter) with the command cluster <cluster name> group "<group name>" /move:<node name>. An example of this is shown in Figure 4-52 as well. Now you can move the disk resource into the Cluster Group with the command cluster <cluster name> res "<resource name>" /move:<node name>. A sample is shown in Figure 4-53.

```
C:\>cluster W2K8R2FC res "Cluster Disk 1" /move:"Cluster Group"

Moving resource 'Cluster Disk 1' to group 'Cluster Group'...


System error 5019 has occurred (0x0000139b).
The operation could not be completed because the cluster resource is online.
C:\>cluster W2K8R2FC group "Cluster Group" /move:TOMMY

Moving resource group 'Cluster Group'...

Group               Node              Status
------------------- ----------------- -------------
Cluster Group       TOMMY             Online
```

Figure 4-52. *Moving the resource group so everything is on the same node*

```
C:\>cluster W2K8R2FC res "Cluster Disk 1" /move:"Cluster Group"

Moving resource 'Cluster Disk 1' to group 'Cluster Group'...

Resource            Group                 Node              Status
------------------- --------------------- ----------------- --------
Cluster Disk 1      Cluster Group         TOMMY             Online
```

Figure 4-53. *Moving the new witness disk into the Cluster Group*

5. To create a Node and Disk Majority quorum, use the command cluster <cluster name> /quorum:"<disk resource moved>". An example is shown in Figure 4-54.

```
C:\>cluster W2K8R2FC /quorum:"Cluster Disk 1"
Witness Resource Name Path                                               Type
--------------------- ------------------------------------------------- --------
Cluster Disk 1        Q:\Cluster\                                        Majority
```

Figure 4-54. *Confirming the configuration*

6. Unlike Failover Cluster Management, at this point, the command line version did not move the old witness disk into Available Storage, so you must move it manually with a similar command to the one shown earlier in Figure 4-53, except you will use the other disk name and the Available Storage group.

Configuring the Quorum Using PowerShell

In this section, you will configure the quorum using PowerShell in Windows Server 2008 R2, assuming a quorum model of Node and Disk Majority. Creating a new Windows failover cluster with Windows Server 2008 R2 and PowerShell is fairly easy. As noted in the chapter introduction, some functionality was not implemented in build 7000, so this section is more of a preview than anything else. To start PowerShell, from Administrative Tools, right-click *PowerShell for Failover Clustering* and select *Run as administrator*.

First, check to see what the current configuration of the quorum is with the cmdlet Get-ClusterQuorum -Cluster <cluster name>. A sample is shown in Figure 4-55.

```
PS C:\> Get-ClusterQuorum -Cluster W2K8R2FC

Cluster                          QuorumResource                          QuorumType
W2K8R2FC                         Cluster Disk 3                          NodeAndDiskMajority
```

Figure 4-55. *Checking the current quorum configuration*

Next, use the cmdlet Get-ClusterResource -Cluster <cluster name> to see the list of available cluster resources. A sample is shown in Figure 4-56.

```
PS C:\> Get-ClusterResource -Cluster W2K8R2FC

Name                 State         Group                    ResourceType
Cluster Disk 1       Online        Available Storage        Physical Disk
Cluster Disk 2       Online        Available Storage        Physical Disk
Cluster Disk 3       Online        Cluster Group            Physical Disk
Cluster Disk 4       Online        Available Storage        Physical Disk
Cluster Disk 5       Online        Available Storage        Physical Disk
Cluster Disk 6       Online        Available Storage        Physical Disk
Cluster Disk 7       Online        Available Storage        Physical Disk
Cluster Disk 8       Online        Available Storage        Physical Disk
Cluster IP Address   Online        Cluster Group            IP Address
Cluster Name         Online        Cluster Group            Network Name
```

Figure 4-56. *The list of available cluster resources*

Finally, use the cmdlet Set-ClusterQuorum -Cluster <cluster name> -NodeAndDiskMajority "<disk resource>" to create a Node and Disk Majority quorum. An example is shown in Figure 4-57. Note that PowerShell as of build 7000 of R2 acts the same as in Failover Cluster Management: it moves the old disk back to the Available Storage resource group.

```
PS C:\> Set-ClusterQuorum -Cluster W2K8R2FC -NodeAndDiskMajority "Cluster Disk 1"

Cluster                          QuorumResource                          QuorumType
W2K8R2FC                         Cluster Disk 1                          NodeAndDiskMajority
```

Figure 4-57. *Changing the quorum configuration*

Create a Clustered Microsoft Distributed Transaction Coordinator

Before performing any steps in this section, refer to the section "Microsoft Distributed Transaction Coordinator" in Chapter 2 to determine whether you need to configure MSDTC. If you do require a clustered MSDTC, this section will show you how to create it in Failover Cluster Management. Remember that you can configure more than one MSDTC with Windows Server 2008, so in theory you could have one for every SQL Server failover clustering instance. For that to work, each MSDTC would need to be placed into the resource group with the SQL Server resource group (not configured until Chapter 6) and have a dependency on a disk in the SQL Server resource group. This section shows the traditional method of one MSDTC per cluster.

Creating the MSDTC Resources Using Failover Cluster Management

To create the MSDTC resources, follow these steps:

1. From Administrative Tools, start Failover Cluster Management.

2. Expand the tree associated with the failover cluster you are managing, select *Services and Applications*, and then select *Configure a Service or Application*.

3. On the Before You Begin dialog of the High Availability Wizard, read the information, and when done, click Next.

4. On the Select Service or Application dialog, select *Distributed Transaction Coordinator (DTC)* as shown in Figure 4-58.

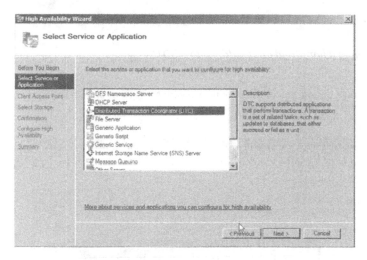

Figure 4-58. *Selecting the DTC to install*

5. On the Client Access Point dialog, enter a name for the DTC (the default name will be the name of the cluster plus DTC). Select the network to use, and enter a valid IP address. An example is shown in Figure 4-59. Click Next.

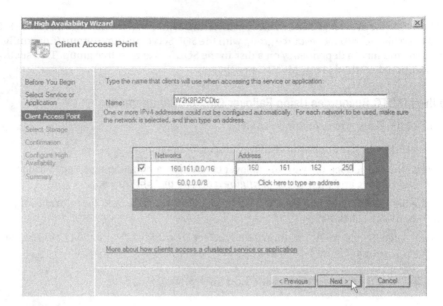

Figure 4-59. *Assigning a name and an IP address to MSDTC*

6. On the Select Storage dialog, select the disk to use with MSDTC as shown in Figure 4-60. Click Next.

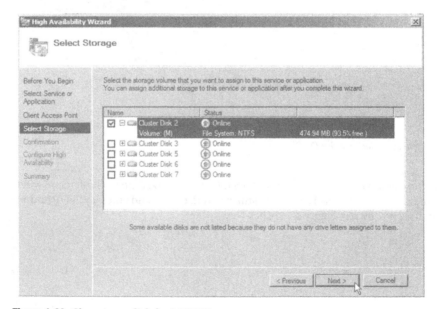

Figure 4-60. *Choosing a disk for MSDTC*

7. On the Confirmation dialog shown in Figure 4-61, verify that the configuration is what you want and click Next to configure MSDTC.

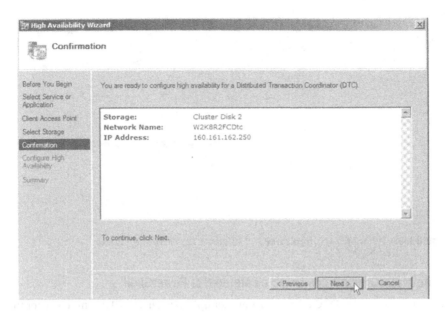

Figure 4-61. *Confirming the MSDTC configuration*

8. On the Summary dialog shown in Figure 4-62, click Finish. Figure 4-63 shows what a successful MSDTC configuration looks like in Failover Cluster Management. If you configured your prerequisites for MSDTC properly in Chapter 3, unlike in prior versions of Windows, you do not have to enable network MSDTC access since that should have been configured when you added the roles.

Figure 4-62. *Completed MSDTC configuration*

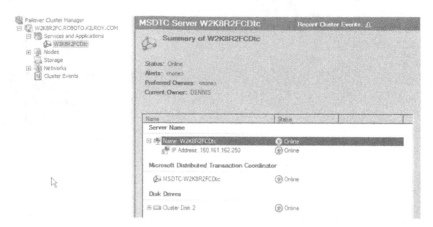

Figure 4-63. *What MSDTC looks like in Failover Cluster Management*

Creating the MSDTC Resources Using cluster.exe or PowerShell

To be blunt, creating the MSDTC resources is an example of when the GUI is much faster than the command line. While it can be done, I do not recommend configuring MSDTC using the various cluster.exe or PowerShell commands. If you really want to see how to configure MSDTC via a script, then view the example code download for this book. You'll find it in the Source Code area of the Apress web site (http://www.apress.com) as well as at http://www.sqlha.com.

Step 5: Verify the Failover Cluster

Once the Windows failover cluster is fully configured, you must ensure that it works properly. If you do not, a failure to test might result in big problems for installing SQL Server and the stability of your production platform.

Review All Logs

One of the easiest things to do to ensure that the cluster is up and running properly is look at the various Windows logs as well as the cluster log. You can also look at any messages or errors in Failover Cluster Management (see the section "Introducing Failover Cluster Management" in Chapter 8 for more information). If there are serious problems, more than likely they will first start appearing in the logs. All the messages that appear in the various logs in Event Viewer should not indicate any problems and should point to the failover cluster working properly.

The traditional cluster log is no longer included with Windows Server 2008. In previous versions of Windows, you could find it in %systemroot%\system32\LogFiles\Cluster. Logging for a Windows Server 2008 failover cluster is now done using event trace logging via Event Tracing for Windows. To see the events outside of using Failover Cluster Management, you can dump the trace log into a file with the command cluster.exe <cluster name> log /generate /copy <file location>. An example would be cluster.exe W2K8R2FC log /generate /copy "C:\temp".

Verify Network Connectivity and Cluster Name Resolution

Before you installed the cluster, Cluster Validation verified intranode communication. Now that the failover cluster is fully configured, you must verify the failover cluster can do the same. The instructions that follow will show you how to verify connectivity and name resolution.

1. Open a command window.

2. Ping the failover cluster IP address as well as the failover cluster name. A successful result looks similar to the one shown in Figure 4-64.

```
C:\>ping 160.161.162.224

Pinging 160.161.162.224 with 32 bytes of data:
Reply from 160.161.162.224: bytes=32 time<1ms TTL=128
Reply from 160.161.162.224: bytes=32 time<1ms TTL=128
Reply from 160.161.162.224: bytes=32 time<1ms TTL=128
Reply from 160.161.162.224: bytes=32 time<1ms TTL=128

Ping statistics for 160.161.162.224:
    Packets: Sent = 4, Received = 4, Lost = 0 (0% loss),
Approximate round trip times in milli-seconds:
    Minimum = 0ms, Maximum = 0ms, Average = 0ms

C:\>ping W2K8R2FC

Pinging W2K8R2FC.ROROTO.KILROY.COM [160.161.162.224] with 32 bytes of data:
Reply from 160.161.162.224: bytes=32 time<1ms TTL=128
Reply from 160.161.162.224: bytes=32 time<1ms TTL=128
Reply from 160.161.162.224: bytes=32 time<1ms TTL=128
Reply from 160.161.162.224: bytes=32 time<1ms TTL=128

Ping statistics for 160.161.162.224:
    Packets: Sent = 4, Received = 4, Lost = 0 (0% loss),
Approximate round trip times in milli-seconds:
    Minimum = 0ms, Maximum = 0ms, Average = 0ms
```

Figure 4-64. *Pinging the cluster IP address successfully*

3. Repeat step 2 from every node in the cluster.

4. From a server or computer outside of the cluster nodes, ping the failover cluster IP address and name to ensure that it can be reached from computers that are not part of the cluster itself.

5. From Failover Cluster Management on every node, connect to the failover cluster you configured.

Validate Resource Failover

All nodes should be able to access the resources in the cluster. The easiest way to verify this is to force a failover of the resources to another node. Because Windows Server 2008 obscures things like the Cluster Group via Failover Cluster Management, using the command line is the only way to perform this task for that resource group. If configured, MSDTC can be failed over to another node either in Failover Cluster Management or via the command line.

Resource Failover in Failover Cluster Management

The following instructions demonstrate how to fail over resources from one node to another using Failover Cluster Management.

1. From Administrative Tools, start Failover Cluster Management.

2. Expand the cluster, select *Services and Applications*, select the application (which is the same as a resource group) to move to another node, select *Move this service or application to another node*, and finally choose where to move it to. The sample shown in Figure 4-65 is a four-node failover cluster. When testing resources, make sure to specifically select a node, and not the option *Best possible*. The purpose of this test is to ensure every node can own the resources.

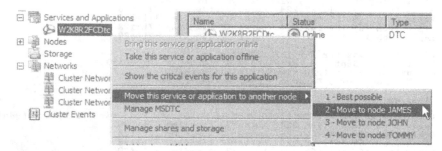

Figure 4-65. *Option to move a resource group*

3. On the Please confirm action dialog shown in Figure 4-66, select the option to move the resource group to another node. If it was successful, it should look similar to Figure 4-67.

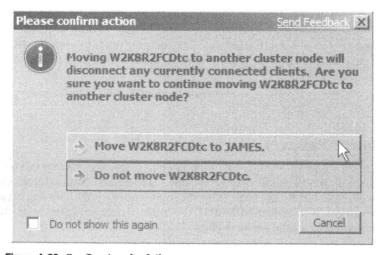

Figure 4-66. *Confirming the failover*

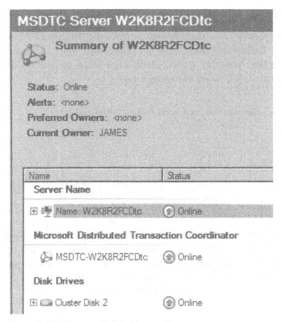

Figure 4-67. *Successful failover of a resource group*

Resource Failover Using cluster.exe

This section will show you how to fail resources over from one node to another using cluster.exe. The instructions that follow will work for all resource groups, including ones like Available Storage and Cluster Group, which are not exposed in Failover Cluster Management. To see a list of all resource groups, enter the command cluster <cluster name> group (e.g., cluster W2K8R2FC group).

1. Start a command prompt. Remember to select *Run as administrator.*

2. To see a list of the configured groups, you can enter the command cluster <cluster name> group. To fail over one of the groups to another node, enter the command cluster <cluster name> group "group name" /MOVE:<node name>. A sample is shown in Figure 4-68.

```
C:\>cluster W2K8R2FC group "Cluster Group" /MOVE:DENNIS
Moving resource group 'Cluster Group'...
Group                    Node             Status
---------------------    -------------    -------
Cluster Group            DENNIS           Online
```

Figure 4-68. *Manually failing over a resource group to another node*

3. Repeat step 2 to move the resource group to all other nodes of the server cluster and back.

4. Repeat steps 2 and 3 for all resource groups.

Resource Failover Using PowerShell

This section will show you how to fail resources from one node to another using PowerShell. The cmdlet to use is Move-ClusterGroup with the parameters -Cluster, -Name, and -Node. An execution would look like Move-ClusterGroup –Cluster *<cluster name>* –Name *<resource group>* –Node *<node to host the resources>*. A sample execution is shown in Figure 4-69.

```
PS C:\Windows\System32> Move-ClusterGroup -Cluster W2K8R2FC -Name "Available Storage" -Node Tommy

Name                              OwnerNode                                                State
----                              ---------                                                -----
Available Storage                 tommy                                                    Online
```

Figure 4-69. *Moving a group using PowerShell*

Summary

You have done a lot of work over the past two chapters to lay a solid foundation for installing SQL Server. If you are unsure if the Windows failover cluster is configured properly, now is the time to correct it. Once SQL Server is installed, some things may not be easy to change. If you are satisfied with your Windows failover cluster, you can proceed to install SQL Server 2008.

■ ■ ■

CHAPTER 5

Preparing to Cluster SQL Server 2008

If clustering Windows represents an appetizer, then clustering SQL Server would be the main course. Although this chapter falls after the three dedicated Windows ones, plan for both the Windows and SQL Server implementations at the same time since the two are coupled together. It is nearly impossible to plan one without any knowledge of the other.

This chapter will cover everything you need to take into account for the SQL Server 2008 portion of the process that is not Windows related (that content is in Chapter 2). Upgrading existing SQL Server 2000 or SQL Server 2005 failover clusters to SQL Server 2008 will be covered in Chapter 7.

Basic Considerations for Clustering SQL Server 2008

Before discussing SQL Server–specific technical considerations for your cluster deployments, there are some basics that you have to understand before diving a bit deeper. This section will go through the things you need to know, which may be different than your understanding of clustering with previous versions of SQL Server.

Clusterable SQL Server Components

Not all SQL Server server-based components are able to be clustered. This section will go through the major components and let you know what can and cannot be clustered.

Database Engine

The core of SQL Server, its database engine, can be clustered. The database engine is the most common cluster configuration that I see at client sites and is arguably the main reason you are reading this book. When I am talking about the database engine, I am not just referring to SQL Server, but SQL Server Agent as well.

Analysis Services

Support for clustering Analysis Services as part of Setup was introduced in SQL Server 2005 and that support continues in SQL Server 2008. If you are going to cluster Analysis Services, you will need to make some design decisions. If the only thing that you are clustering is Analysis Services, your deployment is straightforward.

If you are going to place both the database engine of SQL Server and Analysis Services within the same Windows failover cluster, the recommended configuration for Analysis Services is that it be installed separately from the database engine into its own cluster resource group (which would include its own dedicated disk resource, name, and IP address). As with installing multiple clustered instances of the relational engine, the name and IP address of Analysis Services must be different from anything else in the cluster or the domain.

However, if you want or need to conserve a name and an IP address and some disk space, you can install SQL Server and Analysis Services in the same group. You should be aware of the implications of this configuration. First and foremost, while you can still assign the Analysis Services resource its own dedicated disks, any Analysis Services system databases will be on the same drive as the SQL Server system databases. If you lose that disk, you potentially lose both Analysis Services and SQL Server. Analysis Services and SQL Server will also share a name and an IP address. Whenever possible, you should install Analysis Services into its own resource group for availability purposes. Realistically, if both SQL Server and Analysis Services are on the same Windows failover cluster, you will have to worry about resource utilization (much as you would with multiple SQL Server instances), but the planning is not a completely different exercise.

Another issue with putting both in the same cluster group is that you may be forced to upgrade your Analysis Services installation at the same time as your SQL Server installation, even if you don't want to. Ultimately, the goal in your installation should be flexibility, and combining the two in a single cluster group reduces that.

■**Tip** Instead of using failover clustering to make Analysis Services available, consider using Network Load Balancing (NLB) if the Analysis Services databases are read-only and have no MOLAP writeback. Remember that you cannot configure an NLB cluster on the same hardware as a failover cluster, so if NLB is your strategy for making Analysis Services available, you need separate hardware.

Full-Text Search and SQL Server Broker

Prior to SQL Server 2008, full-text search (FTS) was a separate service and had its own cluster resource. With SQL Server 2008, FTS is now integrated into the SQL Server database engine. SQL Server Broker is also built into the engine, and anything using that functionality should function normally after a failover (assuming the application is coded to handle the failover condition).

Reporting Services and SQL Server Integration Services

Other than clustering the database engine and Analysis Services, most of the other major SQL Server functionality (which includes, but is not limited to, Reporting Services and SQL Server Integration Services [SSIS]) is not cluster-aware and cannot be clustered via SQL Server Setup. Technically the functionality can be clustered by creating a generic resource (or application) in the cluster. A generic clustered application is one where you create a resource group, create an IP address and name, install the software in the same way on the cluster nodes, and then create a generic resource that points to the executable on a node. This is a bit convoluted and a lot of work for little reward. Yes, it can make certain applications available to fail over, but the application was not coded to be cluster-aware like SQL Server's database engine or Analysis Services.

One of the items most requested by customers to be made cluster-aware is SSIS. SSIS is interesting not only because many use it, but also because it creates a conundrum postfailover. If you need SSIS along with a clustered instance of SQL Server, you could certainly install SSIS on each node because it would be a local installation, and you could place the SSIS packages on one of the shared cluster drives. But postfailover, connecting to SSIS is local, so you would have to know which node is hosting the shared drive (and SQL Server) so that you could connect to the right server with SSIS. You can certainly put SSIS on another server in your environment outside the cluster, but if that server goes down, what do you do? There is no easy answer to make SSIS highly available at the moment.

Note If you would like to see SSIS made cluster-aware, my only suggestion is to go to Microsoft Connect (http://connect.microsoft.com) and make your request.

Reporting Services can be made available by splitting it into a front end and a back end deployment. The front end, or the web servers with the Reporting Services functionality, can be deployed in a farm-method using a technology like NLB, and you can deploy the Reporting Services database on a clustered SQL Server.

Note In SQL Server 2008, Notification Services no longer exists.

SQL Writer and Failover Clustering

The SQL Writer Service provides functionality for backup and restore of SQL Server 2008 through the Volume Shadow Copy Service (VSS) framework. The SQL Writer Service is installed on each node of the cluster during the installation process, but it is disabled by default. If you will be using advanced backup strategies such as SAN-based backups, you will most likely need to enable the SQL Writer Service on a node when it owns the SQL Server resources.

SQL Server Browser Service

The SQL Server Browser Service directs connection attempts that use instance names to the proper instance on the server. It is installed on each node in the cluster and is not cluster-aware. Unlike a standalone install of SQL Server 2008, the SQL Server Browser Service is started automatically for a clustered instance of SQL Server. Using fixed port numbers and connecting to the known port will enhance your implementations.

Changes to Setup in SQL Server 2008

Feature-wise, failover clustering is failover clustering; that hasn't changed in SQL Server 2008. The biggest change to failover clustering comes by way of Setup. As you may be aware, with both SQL Server 2000 and SQL Server 2005, when you installed a SQL Server instance in a cluster, it would configure all nodes at the same time (in 2005, the tools were only installed on the node initiating the install, but all nodes got SQL Server and all related services). The way Setup works with regard to deploying a failover cluster has changed in SQL Server 2008.

SQL Server 2008 Setup no longer configures every node as part of the installation process—you install one node at a time. There is one install for the instance itself and every other installation is an operation that adds that node to an instance. That is not bad if you are installing only one instance of SQL Server in your cluster, and the cluster has a small number of nodes. However, this must be done *per instance*. If you are installing multiple instances in your cluster, all of a sudden you are doing a lot of installs. Patching SQL Server 2008 will also work in the same manner. Despite the additional installations, realize that the process for adding a node to an instance is a much quicker install process than installing the instance itself. While the number of installations is what it is, it is nowhere near as painful as it sounds.

Note There is one exception to some degree for the per instance/per node rule. Using the prepare/complete Setup option (see Chapter 6), you can do all nodes somewhat at the same time.

When I first saw the installation process during the beta phase of SQL Server 2008, I was quite taken aback. Table 5-1 shows how many installs you will be doing if you have up to eight nodes and up to four instances of SQL Server. You can do the math beyond what is shown. The formula is simple:

```
Number of installations = number of nodes X number of instances
```

The horizontal axis in Table 5-1 is the number of instances and the vertical axis is the number of nodes. Of course, you will feel the most pain if you do every installation using the graphical setup interface. As with SQL Server 2005, you can script the installations. The various installation methods and how they work are covered in Chapter 6.

Table 5-1. *Number of Installations Depending on the Number of Nodes and Instances*

	1 Instance	2 Instances	3 Instances	4 Instances
2 Nodes	2	4	6	8
3 Nodes	3	6	9	12
4 Nodes	4	8	12	16
5 Nodes	5	10	15	20
6 Nodes	6	12	18	24
7 Nodes	7	14	21	28
8 Nodes	8	16	24	32

This change to the installation process was done for the right reason. Prior to SQL Server 2008, some of you may have had an occasional failed installation on a cluster where Setup would not properly populate each node with every needed file. An incomplete installation (of which missing files are a part) is not a good thing for obvious reasons and was hard to troubleshoot. With SQL Server 2008, the SQL Server Product Team decided to revamp the installation approach to ensure all nodes get each file.

There are other reasons for the way the new Setup process works, namely the following:

- Windows Server is locking down remote execution with each subsequent release, so SQL Server's Setup cannot afford to take any risks that Setup will break if Windows introduces a new release in the middle of supporting the current version of SQL Server.

- With Windows Server 2008 R2 and PowerShell, technically you should be able to code custom deployment solutions that will configure every node. The way SQL Server 2008's Setup works now provides the building blocks.

- The ultimate goal for Setup is to guarantee a reliable, stable install of SQL Server. The Product Team made a decision to make Setup easier and more robust (which in turn drove up the number of installs for a clustered instance) to ensure a better cluster experience, which in turn increases, not decreases, availability.

One positive aspect of this new installation process is that you can do a rolling upgrade from a previously clustered SQL Server 2000 or 2005 instance (see Chapter 7 for how to upgrade existing clusters to SQL Server 2008) and updates to a clustered SQL Server 2008 instance instead of taking the entire instance out at once. Also, the ability to troubleshoot failed installations will now be more localized. For example, instead of trying to troubleshoot where Setup failed on an eight-node cluster, you will absolutely know the problem is isolated. Even if the install fails on the fifth node, you already have four nodes up and running—you have a highly available SQL Server instance.

Another change in Setup worth mentioning is this: if you are familiar with older versions of a clustered SQL Server instance, you know that you could select only a single drive for use with that instance you were installing during Setup. Postinstallation, you would need to manually add in the other drive letters (or mount points, since they were supported in SQL Server 2005). With SQL Server 2008, as long as they are available and configured within the Windows failover cluster, you can select multiple drive letters during Setup. This is a huge improvement I've been talking about since SQL Server 2000; it's nice to see it finally implemented.

You can also add other administrators during Setup. For example, if you have a domain-level group that contains all of the individual logins for the DBAs, this group can be added in at installation time, not only saving you a configuration step post-Setup, but also granting all DBAs immediate access to the instance.

Mixing Local and Clustered Instances on Cluster Nodes

Installation of local, nonclustered instances of SQL Server on servers that are participating as nodes in a cluster is fully supported. Some exceptions may exist, such as applications that will install a local copy of SQL Server to the node. The whole purpose of implementing clusters is to make your SQL Servers highly available. It makes no sense to mix and match clustered and nonclustered instances of SQL Server on the same hardware. A good rule to institute is that if you are implementing clusters, all instances must be clustered, as it will make administration easier and reduce confusion.

Combining SQL Server 2008 with Other Clustered Applications

When companies want to maximize their IT budgets, and they already have a cluster or are planning a Windows failover cluster deployment, they often want to put multiple applications (such as Exchange) on the cluster along with SQL Server. Technically it may be possible to run other applications along with SQL Server, but it may not be the best idea—and more often than not it is a bad idea. You're putting competing (and sometimes disparate) workloads on the same cluster. It's bad enough to try to get multiple SQL Server instances to play nicely, let alone different applications.

Also, I cannot comprehend why anyone would put two mission-critical, resource-intensive applications on the same cluster, knowing that they really may not play well in the sandbox together. I have seen this done, and then when a problem occurs, people were taken aback. It shouldn't be a surprise. Let's say Exchange goes down and subsequently brings SQL Server down for whatever reason. That makes no sense—in the zeal to make these available, you've actually affected availability in an unintended way.

Would you combine SQL Server and an application like Exchange on a regular, standalone server in production? Nine times out of ten, the answer would be no. The one exception may be for a very small business that purchases something like Small Business Server and its deployments of SQL Server and Exchange are so lightweight that there is no contention. There is always an exception to the rule, but the rule is there for a reason. The security risks alone should be a red flag. Do you want both fighting for system resources such as memory, processor, and disk I/O? What will you do if SQL Server needs more memory and you need to mix memory models—how will Exchange fare? What about worrying about potential incompatibilities with prerequisites? Combining these two major server applications is definitely one case where the risks outweigh the advantages. If you are looking to standardize how your availability is achieved, and you like what clustering has to offer, whether it is Exchange or SQL Server where you started, you may want to mandate that clustering is your "gold standard" for a base platform and then modify the template to suit your SQL Server or Exchange needs.

FAILOVER CLUSTERING TERMINOLOGY HELL

I made this plea in the last book, and it bears repeating here. Two terms have become synonymous with failover clustering: *Active/Passive* and *Active/Active*. Those terms are at best loosely accurate, and with SQL Server 2000 (as well as in the book *SQL Server 2000 High Availability* published by Microsoft Press in 2003 and various whitepapers I have written since 2001), I have fought the good fight to get people away from those terms and standardize on terms that actually make sense. I still haven't won the battle, but I am going to state my case yet again.

The history of Active/Passive and Active/Active stems from about 1998, when with a clustered SQL Server 7.0 installation, you could have at most two installs of SQL Server on a single Windows failover cluster. In that context, Active/Passive and Active/Active both make perfect sense. SQL Server then adopted the instance model in SQL Server 2000, allowing you to break the barrier of two installs per single Windows server cluster with a maximum of 16 instances on a single Windows server cluster. If you install only a single clustered instance of SQL Server in your cluster, Active/Passive is technically still valid because only one node may be active at any given time. But if you have eight instances spread out over four nodes, are you going to call this Active/Active/Active/Active or Active/Active/Active/Active/Active/Active, depending on whether you are addressing the number of SQL Server instances or the number of nodes? If you configure all of your SQL Server instances in one way, this makes sense, but since you are not bound to do it one way, it can become confusing. With SQL Server 2000, the terms *single instance failover cluster* and *multiple instance failover cluster* were introduced. Because people seem to be stuck on the whole "Active" thing, you may hear the terms *single active instance failover cluster* and *multiple active instance failover cluster*.

The next time you are tempted to use the ever-popular Active/Passive or Active/Active terms, put some thought into what you actually are trying to say, because Active/Active can also be applied to Exchange clusters or even Windows itself. When you are referring to SQL Server in a clustered environment, it is always better to include enough information to describe how your cluster is actually configured, because Active/Active can mean different things to different people—especially when you now can also go beyond two nodes in a Windows server cluster.

Technical Considerations for SQL Server 2008 Failover Clustering

Besides some of the high-level planning aspects, you will need to take into account more technical ones as well. This section will discuss the various technical considerations specific to deploying SQL Server 2008 failover clustering. Of course, this entire chapter has been about "technical considerations," but in this section we look at some nitty-gritty points that administrators often overlook or don't think about until it's too late.

Note As I was wrapping up the book, the release candidate of Windows Server 2008 R2 hit the Web. Since Chapter 2 was already completed, I felt I had to put this information in the book somewhere and this seemed like the most logical place. If you are going to be deploying SQL Server 2008 on Windows Server 2008 R2, it will only be supported if it is deployed with SQL Server 2008 Service Pack 1 or later. The dialog shown in Figure 5-1 is what you will see.

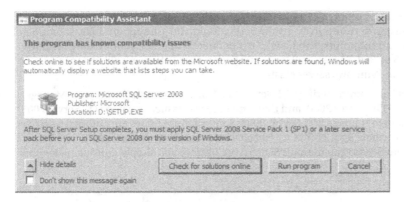

Figure 5-1. *Warning to install SQL Server 2008 Service Pack 1*

Side-by-Side Deployments

As long as the operating system supports the version of SQL Server (e.g., Windows Server 2003 supports SQL Server 2000, 2005, and 2008, but Windows Server 2008 supports only SQL Server 2005 and 2008), you can mix and match instances of different versions (or the same version) on the same Windows failover cluster. This condition is known as a *side-by-side deployment*. All of the basic planning rules apply as they are laid out in this chapter, but you would be fully supported by Microsoft. Side-by-side deployment is generally used only in upgrade scenarios (failover clustering upgrades will be covered in Chapter 7). However, you still may choose to deploy SQL Server 2008 in a side-by-side configuration in certain scenarios. The following are some caveats to take into account when considering a side-by-side architecture:

- If you are going to have a side-by-side cluster implementation, you must install all previous versions in order before installing SQL Server 2008. That means the order of install would be SQL Server 2000, then 2005, and finally 2008. Once you install the later versions of SQL Server, changing the configuration (such as adding a node) as well as maintenance of the older version is not really possible, so you have to ensure that you are completely patched to where you want to be before installing the newer version.

- You are still bound by the standard rules for named and default instances, so if any existing SQL Server instance in the cluster is already a default instance, any SQL Server 2008 instance cannot be a default instance unless you decide at some point to uninstall the instance that is the current default instance.

- Since SQL Server 2000 is not supported with Windows Server 2008, you can have a side-by-side configuration only with both SQL Server 2000 and SQL Server 2008 using Windows Server 2003.

- Once you install SQL Server 2008, you will never have a "pure" environment for the older versions of SQL Server. Some common components will be shared. While this is fully supported, you should test such a configuration prior to using it in production to make sure your applications function properly.

- Do not reuse the same domain service accounts for your prior SQL Server deployments with SQL Server 2008. If you do, you will bypass all of the new security enhancements in SQL Server 2008. You must use new domain-based service accounts.

- Using mount points with your SQL Server 2008 instances where you already have a clustered SQL Server 2000 instance results in an invalid configuration from a supportability standpoint. If you want to use mount points, you have to either directly upgrade your existing instance to SQL Server 2005 or SQL Server 2008, or install your new SQL Server 2008 instance on a completely different Windows server cluster.

- Know how you will be administering SQL Server 2008. SQL Server 2000 Enterprise Manager cannot administer SQL Server 2008, and there are potential issues in using SQL Server 2005 Management Studio to manage SQL Server 2008. Some of those issues are outlined with fixes in Knowledge Base article 946127 (http://support.microsoft.com/kb/946127/). SQL Server 2008's Management Studio can manage SQL Server 2005, so you should consider using that version.

Note As you can probably tell, planning and implementing a side-by-side configuration must be completely thought through. In general, this is not a configuration I would lead with as a consultant unless a customer had a specific need. In a development or test environment, it may be better since hardware is scarcer, but think about the ramifications of such a configuration in production.

Determining the Number of Instances and Nodes

This section will discuss the considerations for determining how many instances and nodes will be deployed as part of your SQL Server 2008 failover cluster. The planning process is not straightforward.

Number of Instances

One of the most difficult aspects of planning a SQL Server failover cluster is deciding on the number of instances to deploy, since that decision is based on a few factors. For some reason, I still find many people still believe or are in the mindset that you can have only a single instance of SQL Server in a given Windows failover cluster. Support for multiple instances was introduced in SQL Server 2000 and rightly or wrongly got a bad reputation mainly due to Windows and 32-bit limitations at the time along with poor deployment and planning. This soured many people's experiences with multiple instances.

However, the one instance, one cluster mentality led to another unfortunate situation: the perception of wasted resources. IT often saw a clustered SQL Server deployment as wasteful because most people have historically deployed only two-node clusters with a single instance of SQL Server. Since only one node was in use, the other was sitting there idle. The conversation is generally much like the following:

Customer: So what you are telling me is I am spending all this money to buy two identical N processor servers with M gigabytes of memory, and one of them is going to sit there completely unused, just waiting for the SQL Server to fail?

Me: Yes, that is the case. In the event of a failover of your SQL Server instance, everything will perform at the same level as it did previously.

Customer: Are you serious? That is a waste. I want my servers utilized to their maximum capabilities. I have only so much in the budget available to me, and it needs to stretch as far as it can go.

Now, I do not completely disagree with the customer in this scenario, and in our current economy where every ounce of server needs to be maximized, the customer's request to fully utilize their equipment is not a completely unreasonable request, but one that should be considered with extreme caution. Just because the capacity is there, is it the right thing to do? That is where multiple instances come in, but their deployment needs to be planned very carefully. Think of it another way: would you take the spare tire out of the trunk of your car just to make more room? The answer is probably no; you would want the ability to change a flat tire if you were in the middle of nowhere.

Having said that, not every situation is one where multiple instances is recommended, and even if you have multiple instances, you still cannot use every resource, because other items on the nodes (such as Windows itself) also require some resources. This all ties back to the reason you are deploying a failover cluster: for *availability*, not to *cram in as much as you can*. For example, if I was deploying a mission-critical application such as SAP, I would not be loading up the cluster with other applications or instances.

There is a lot of risk and reward that can come out of deploying multiple instances. Besides the budget crunches everyone is experiencing (which are pushing people to consolidate), a few things are turning the tide toward multiple instance deployments.

First and foremost, 64-bit deployments change the playing field. From a performance perspective, in arguably 8 or 9 times out of 10, a 64-bit deployment should perform faster than its 32-bit counterpart. As well, 64-bit allows all memory to be dynamic (should you want it to be) with no special switches (more on memory in a bit). Other changes, such as the advent of multiple cores in a processor, have allowed IT to do more with much less. A four-processor, multi-core server is not the same as a four (or more)-processor server from even 5 years ago. SQL Server scales better than it used to; with SQL Server 2000, there was clearly a point at which adding processors was not going to gain you much. The bottom line is that these days it is much easier to deploy multiple instances and still get reasonable performance, whereas with Windows 2000 Advanced Server and SQL Server 2000 Enterprise Edition, you were often lucky to get above two instances (if you could even do that). A reviewer did point out that one customer of his configured 13 SQL Server 2000 clustered instances on a two-node cluster, but I can tell you from my experience that scenario is the exception. They would have had to achieve that through very careful planning.

To put it bluntly, achieving success in a multiple instance failover cluster configuration is based on all of the planning you do taking into account everything in this chapter as well as what was presented back in Chapter 2. If you think you are actually going to deploy 25 instances with SQL Server 2008 Enterprise Edition (16 for Standard Edition) on your cluster, I would suggest you rethink your implementation. Just because you technically can do it or are allowed to do it does not mean you should. Use your common sense.

One big caveat to multiple instances is maintenance, which includes patching of the operating system and SQL Server instances. If you have to perform maintenance to a node or instance in the cluster, it may affect more than just one of the SQL Server instances (which may be used by multiple applications . . . and so on). There is a chain reaction effect that could possibly happen. For example, if you have a four-node, five-instance failover cluster, you will have 20 separate installs to patch to a service pack (one install per instance per node). If a reboot is required for one of those installs, that will affect any instance running on that particular node where the install was initiated. Another example is that an update (hotfix, cumulative update, or service pack) may change some of the common files used by all SQL Server instances. While Microsoft supports multiple patch levels of SQL Server on the same server, these are scenarios you need to test to ensure that this configuration will not affect the applications themselves, and if using third-party applications, that the vendors support your configuration. Think about these types of scenarios when you are coming up with your multiple instance architecture and balancing it with your SLAs.

Remember that a SQL Server update may update some shared components so an update to a particular instance of SQL Server via a service pack may affect other instances. For example, the connectivity layer (and its associated files) is shared among all of the instances configured on the cluster. If an update affects the connectivity layer, it will affect every instance. This is a fully supported scenario and nothing to worry about, but you should be aware of how things work behind the scenes.

Last, but certainly not least, you need to think about anything done to an instance or a node that that may ultimately affect another. I am not just referring to a problem occurring on one node causing a failure, which then causes multiple SQL Server instances to fail over to another node. If your Windows administrators need to patch a driver, you should be notified ahead of time to plan accordingly since that driver update may cause a reboot. It will also alert you to watch for any potential other problems that will crop up post–driver install.

Number of Nodes

The number of nodes is somewhat based on the number of instances as well as other factors such as SLAs, performance guarantees, and so on. When the ability to cluster more than two nodes was introduced with Windows 2000 Datacenter, some interesting options became possible. Assume a configuration where you would previously have two nodes and two instances of SQL Server (one on each node prefailover). If you just have two nodes, you will have to always worry about more major contention after a failover; I discuss this in more detail later in the "Memory and Processor" section. If you set up a "dedicated" failover node and change the preferred failover order (see Chapter 6 on how to do that for an instance when you have more than two nodes), either instance could now fail over to that dedicated failover node first and not affect the other node unless you had multiple failures. This configuration is known as N+i, where i is the number of additional nodes you add to the cluster for this failover purpose. N+1 is the most common configuration.

An N+i cluster is beneficial in the sense that statistically, the chance of all of your instances and their respective nodes failing at once is pretty small. You may lose a single server at any given time, but more than that indicates a bigger problem in your ecosystem, such as a full disk subsystem failure. That is then something you need to mitigate and plan for whether or not you have multiple instances. You can configure the dedicated failover node(s) with additional memory and processor capacity to ensure that in the worst-case scenario, all instances, or at least most of them, will run smoothly on that one node. For example, you could give a single, dedicated failover node (making your cluster N+1) double the amount of processors and triple the amount of memory found on any other node.

If you decide to change the preferred failover node for an instance, ensure that no single node will become overburdened by being able to own multiple SQL Server instances at any one time since you are taking the decision-making control away from Windows.

Disk Considerations

Introduced in Chapter 2 was the notion that configuring disks for a SQL Server failover cluster was not straightforward. This section will complete that picture. The comment regarding the inability to configure 25 instances made earlier in the chapter was not meant to be flippant; it's reality. SQL Server has no hard-coded limit of how many instances can be deployed, but there are some limitations and considerations that will affect how things are ultimately deployed when it comes to your disk configuration.

■**Tip** If you did not get the hint from Chapter 2, your disk configuration will control most of the performance of your SQL Server instances. The disk will most likely be the first place you notice bottlenecks.

Drive Letters

You already know that you need drive letters and that a single cluster resource group should contain only a single clustered instance of SQL Server or Analysis Services. This means that any of the drive letters used for one clustered instance of SQL Server cannot be used with another. At the Windows level, even if two logical drives (say, I and J) are configured on a single LUN, to clustering, those look like one drive, so you would be out of luck if you tried to make that work for multiple instances.

At a minimum, three drive letters are most likely already taken: one each for the witness disk, your local system drive, and some sort of optical drive like a CD or a DVD drive. There may be a fourth drive letter unavailable, since some servers might still have a floppy drive in them. If you are configuring a clustered MSDTC, make that a potential fifth, and if you have any mapped drives, make it a sixth drive letter unavailable to you. That means before you even start SQL Server 2008 Setup, you may only have somewhere between 20 and 22 possible drive letters. Technically, you shouldn't use A or B since I've been told there are some BIOS dependencies there, so that knocks you down further to between 18 and 20 drives. Having that few drive letters available will obviously limit the number of instances that can be deployed. Many clustered installations will use more than one physical drive, and historically, most customers use drive letters. The more drive letters you use for a single instance of SQL Server, the fewer are available to other ones. With SQL Server 2008, you can use a mount point, but it must be mounted under at least one drive letter (just like SQL Server 2005). Mount points will save drive letters, but you are still going to have a hard time deploying 25 instances for the reasons just stated. You also want to leave some drive letters free just in case you want to add an instance to the cluster at some later point; maxing out your configuration from day one leaves you virtually nowhere to go in the future.

Drives for Data, Log, and Backups

Over the years, it's been beaten into our heads to separate data from log, and never place backups where you have either data or log. This best practice is still completely valid and increases availability since it prevents a single point of failure, and it may increase performance depending on the low-level disk configuration. However, as talked about in Chapter 2, if you as the DBA cannot influence or control the low-level disk configuration, you do not have any idea whether drive H may physically sit next to drive I on your storage unit. In Windows they may appear as completely separate disks, but is that reality? From a performance perspective, two drives that share the same underlying disks may or may not be bad. If you've got enough physical spindles powering your deployments to ensure you have no I/O contention, all may be well. The problem is that in the modern world, SANs are more often than not shared with everything from file shares to the HR system and everything in between. The days of dedicated storage for SQL Server are pretty much over.

For some deployments, there may not be a strong case to separate out all aspects of your SQL Server disk deployment (data, log, and backup) for any reason other than administrative purposes to make them easier to discern. The storage unit should be smart enough that if a physical drive fails and multiple LUNs were configured on it, that would not break every drive since the LUN is spread out over other disks as well. You should talk to your storage administrators to understand how a problem they may have will affect your SQL Server deployments. Different LUNs may also translate into better performance, but again, there is no guarantee with shared drives.

Think of the transaction log and how it works. It is not unlike a record: you want the needle (in this case, the disk head) to go down, write data to it, and never have that stylus lift up (except for going back and doing reads to back up the transaction log). If you stick data, log, and backup on the same drive, and then compound that with multiple LUNs sharing the same physical drives, that disk head will be bouncing all over the place. On a heavily used database with lots of operations that will write to the transaction log, you could very easily become what is known as *log bound* if you do not have the I/O horsepower as well as the isolation it needs. As noted in Chapter 2, if you see the need to combine data and log, try to stagger data and log to eliminate a single point of failure and to stagger I/O patterns.

Performance considerations aside, there is a practical reason that separating things to the nth degree is not possible: it can limit how many instances you can deploy. For example, if you are going to deploy a consolidated SQL Server where you want a 50:1 ratio of databases to instance, how are you going to do that with approximately 20 drives available to you? It's just not going to happen, even with mount points, since at some point you don't want to attach so many physical drives to Windows. I've never tested the limits of Windows, but there is definitely going to be a tipping point when it comes to the number of drives that Windows can manage. And do your Windows or storage administrators really want to manage a server with 50 or more drives?

To build on the previous paragraph, you also want to manage the size of the drives presented. You do not want to have 150 50 GB drives attached to the system; the amount of work to create and maintain databases that need to be spread over that many drives will be hard for the DBA. Work with your storage administrators to come up with drive sizes that make sense for your environment and that balance manageability with all other aspects of disk configuration. This problem is something I see fairly often.

Deciding on a Disk Configuration

You need to get "smart" about how you architect SQL Server databases and instances. Combine where it's applicable. Yes, you do need availability, and clustering gives you some of that, but you're not going to necessarily sacrifice complete availability by putting your data and log on the same LUN or drive letter in all cases. What you need to do is test prior to going into production to ensure that you will have no issues (this would be no different than a standalone deployment).

You have to be realistic about what you are trying to achieve in terms of both performance and availability. You will have to share some drives with other databases, so you have to know each database's I/O characteristics to make intelligent decisions. Do not forget about the system databases, in particular tempdb, which may need to be on its own drive for performance reasons. Size is also a problem as described in Chapter 2—you will be limited by how big you can make the disks in Windows depending on what type of drive is configured (GPT or MBR).

If you are having trouble, use the 80/20 rule—figure out where 80 percent of your I/O is going in terms of data and logs. Remember that reads do not hit the log file (reads occur only when doing a transaction log backup and for transaction rollbacks; they represent minimal to no overhead unless the rollback is extensive). It is better to isolate those data and log files that represent 80 percent of your total I/O requirements on their own disks. Then place the remaining 20 percent of the rest of the data and log files on staggered but combined disks. If you put all of your data files on one disk, and all of your transaction logs on another, that may not be preferable because if you lost one of those drives, it may be harder to recover than if you had staggered the data and log files. As time goes on in production, you may need to perform further optimizations and tuning to your disk configuration.

The easiest way to show the design considerations for a clustered instance of SQL Server is by example. Consider a BizTalk implementation. Depending on how BizTalk is used by the application, you will be using different BizTalk databases. Some of those databases can be I/O heavy, which logically dictates that they be split out from other databases (or placed with ones that have low I/O), assuming that your storage is configured properly and there will be no I/O contention whether the LUNs created are completely isolated or share the same underlying disks. For the purposes of this example, assume the BizTalk installation will be using primarily the MessageBox database (BizTalkMsgBoxDb) and the tracking database (BizTalkDTADb). From an overall BizTalk implementation standpoint, the Single Sign-On (SSO) database is important because without it BizTalk cannot run. It has very low I/O, but if it is not available, you are in trouble.

Knowing these parameters, you need to consider sizing as well: how big will the drives be? If you are creating a 30 TB warehouse, you may need to get a little creative due to the size limitations imposed by Windows for the type of disk you are using. Your drive sizes should be manageable, and in the event that chkdsk needs to run, it will not take forever to do so. If chkdsk needs to run after, say, a failover and a reboot, you may potentially be waiting hours and blow your SLAs out of the water.

You should also keep in mind that a drive or two may go to storing backups. These drives need to be dependencies (like all data and log drives) of the SQL Server resource, and they will arguably provide the best storage for your backups for a clustered instance of SQL Server since they will at least logically be separated from data and log, so you will not have a single point of failure. Losing data, log, and backups is not a scenario I would want to face as a DBA.

■**Tip** Please review the I/O considerations outlined in Chapter 2.

Memory and Processor

After thinking about your disk configuration, you need to consider what the processor and memory configuration will look like. As noted earlier, it is easier to deal with memory and processors now than it ever has been with the addition of cores. Even blade servers can handle large amounts of memory. So many of the historical bottlenecks can be overcome out of the gate—to a point.

Before you go and configure anything, you have to test each application's database(s) under the maximum workload you plan on it supporting not just today, but well into the future. This is different from doing something like SQLIO, which was mentioned in Chapter 2; I am talking about devising some tests, most likely using a load generation tool and/or with some automated testing, to stress your disk subsystem. The only way to completely ensure that your servers from a performance stand-point (disk, memory, and processor) will support the workloads you need for the number of years the application will be in production is to do this kind of testing. Throwing some random workload or a TPC-like test is *not* necessarily a valid test, because while it will generate some information, is it the right information? That application's footprint is what you will be managing as a DBA. Work with the application owners to ensure that you can do this testing before going live in production. Once the application is in production, your ability to fix problems may be limited.

This testing comes even more into focus when you have multiple instances deployed. You do not want any kind of contention in the event that two or more of the instances would need to be owned by a single node in the failover cluster. I/O factors in a bit since the underlying hardware (such as HBA cards) will be shared, but the biggest problems in this scenario for performance will most likely be memory and/or processor contention. The last thing you want to encounter is the failover of an instance to another node, and it starts to underperform, or even worse, it may be starved for resources to the point it will not even start. The analogy I have used for years is this: think of a glass of your favorite beverage. The glass has a maximum capacity. Once you exceed that capacity, the excess liquid will spill over the sides. The failover scenario is very much the same.

Memory

With SQL Server 2008, you have a few options to configure your memory to ensure that there will be very little or no contention in a failover condition. Again, the whole point of clustering SQL Server is that in the event of a problem, SQL Server fails over to another node, is up and running, and you do not have to worry about it. For a 32-bit SQL Server 2008 installation, to access more than 4 GB of memory, you must put /PAE in boot.ini and enable Address Windowing Extensions (AWE) in SQL Server. All 64-bit versions of SQL Server 2008 can access all system memory with no special switches. All memory can be either dynamic or fixed. Keep in mind that memory management is a pretty complex topic that can fill up many pages, but the key concept I want you to understand here is that there are a lot of objects besides data that consume memory in SQL Server: connections, the non-buffer pool (used to be known as Mem-to-Leave), threads, and so on. For example, assume for a second that you are using an IA64 server. Each thread SQL Server uses in this case consumes 4 MB of memory. If your instance requires 2,000 threads, before you even issue a SELECT statement, SQL Server is consuming 8 GB of memory just for threads.

Always remember to leave room for Windows, too. The assumption for years was that if you leave 1 GB of memory you should be fine, but this is not always the case. You may actually need more memory for Windows, and my general rule of thumb is that the larger the system, the more memory you need for Windows. Starving Windows for memory will have a direct effect on SQL Server.

So how do you deal with ensuring multiple instances play nicely in the failover condition? You have three main options:

- Set a fixed maximum amount of memory for each instance.
- Set a fixed minimum amount of memory for each instance.
- Allow all memory to be dynamic.

Fixed Maximum Amount of Memory

My recommendation more often than not over the years has been to set a fixed maximum amount of memory for each instance. The problem is that the perception of those outside of the SQL Server DBAs is that you were "wasting" resources. Consider this example: if you have a two-node, single-instance failover cluster as shown in Figure 5-2, your maximum average utilization is 50 percent because nothing is installed on the second node, and you can have a maximum of 100 percent utilization on the first node, so 100 – (100 + 0) / 2 = 50. If the each node has 8 GB of memory and you want to reserve 1 GB for Windows, you will have 7 GB of memory available for that one instance. SQL Server will use the full complement of 7 GB, and there will be no contention in a failover. To the IT guys, one node is just sitting there idle. But isn't the whole point to ensure that the instance works postfailover? That argument unfortunately does not fly with some.

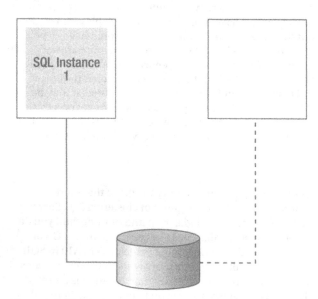

Figure 5-2. *Single-instance failover cluster with a maximum of 50 percent utilization*

If you want to better utilize your two nodes and add another instance of SQL Server, you can do that. However, you will discover that if you set a fixed maximum amount of memory per instance, you may not be getting any more utilization. If you are planning properly, at most you will use 50 percent of each node, taking into account the failover situation for each instance, so (50 + 50) / 2 = 50 (see Figure 5-3). If you translate that into a physical implementation, use the same two-node, 8 GB configuration with 1 GB for Windows. To configure two instances of SQL Server that will not starve each other in a failover, you have only 7 GB available to you, so any combination of the two that adds up to 7 GB would work. If you configured them equally, that equates to 3.5 GB per instance. If your tested memory requirements are more than 3.5 GB of memory for the instance, you start playing Russian roulette if you do not take into account the failover condition. Ultimately, you are balancing and making tradeoffs between availability and performance/capacity management. Would you rather have functioning systems with reduced performance, or ones that at one point were highly performing but now no longer process anything?

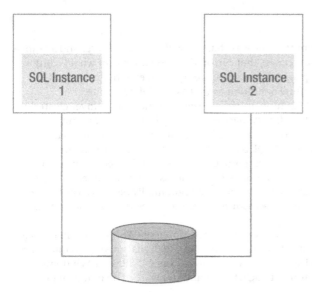

Figure 5-3. *Multiple-instance failover cluster with a maximum of 50 percent utilization*

Fixed Minimum Amount of Memory

In a perfect world, everyone would deploy servers with large amounts of memory (32 GB, 64 GB, 128 GB) so that if you set a fixed amount of memory per instance, it would be no big deal. Since not everyone can afford such large servers, a possible middle ground would be to configure your SQL Server instances with a fixed minimum amount of memory in the hope that in a failover, the multiple instances will not dip below a certain point, in turn guaranteeing you a minimum level of performance. In theory, that should work. Remember that after failover, any instances of SQL Server on a particular node will be fighting for memory, so it may take time to adjust. Also, if for whatever reason the instance cannot get that minimum amount of memory, there is a chance it could fail to start, since it is expecting to use that amount of memory. Obviously, this is a condition you would test before going live in production and with load being generated against each instance. Do not learn for the first time when there is a problem how your memory will adjust.

All Memory Dynamic

Finally, there is the simplest configuration: do not configure any settings, and let each instance fight for the amount of memory it wants to use. This is the default configuration in SQL Server. I do not recommend this approach, since you want both performance and availability from your clustered instances. While you may get what you want if you have fairly low resource-intensive SQL Server instances, chances are not all of your instances are "low maintenance."

■ **Tip**   Although it is a bit old, there is a great write-up on consolidation with 64-bit SQL Server at http:// technet.microsoft.com/en-us/library/cc917532.aspx, which talks about memory contention and the effects of it in Appendix A of that whitepaper. There are charts that compare the number of transactions per second depending on what type of memory configuration you employ.

Processor

Processor capacity is similar to that of memory in the way that you will approach server and instance configuration. Besides accounting for all processes that run on the node no matter what (Windows itself, any programs like anti-virus, backup agents, etc.), you are trying to ensure that your SQL Server instances have enough CPU in a normal condition as well as in a failover state.

There are only a few "knobs" available to tune processor usage for multiple failover clustering instances. Within SQL Server, you can set the affinity mask and affinity I/O mask (or affinity64 mask or affinity64 I/O mask options for 33 to 64 processors) configuration options. Affinity mask (or affinity64 mask) tells that particular instance of SQL Server to use only certain processors. Affinity I/O mask (or affinity64 I/O mask) binds I/O to certain processors. I do not see people using these very often, but they do get used. You need to remember which processors you assigned to what instance to ensure no contention. Again, like memory, this could potentially be seen as not utilizing your resources because you are limiting which processor resources a SQL Server instance can use in the nonfailover condition.

You can also consider the use of Windows System Resource Manager (WSRM) to help manage CPU usage for multiple instances of SQL Server. For Windows Server 2008, as noted in Chapter 2 and shown in Chapter 3, you would add WSRM as a feature of Windows. Since WSRM is a Windows-level option for dealing with CPU usage, it is external to SQL Server and unaware of instances; it just manages processes.

WSRM allows you to set a percentage of CPU use to a particular SQL Server instance, and you will be shown how to use it in Chapter 8. WSRM allows you to configure up to 99 percent of the available processor usage on any given server. Consider this example: if you have that same two-node, two-instance failover cluster mentioned in the "Memory" section, you want to ensure both will run after a failover. Leaving overhead for Windows and any other processes (let's assume 20 percent for this example), you now have 80 percent left for the two SQL Server instances. You could create a WSRM policy that would constrain the two processes (in whatever percentage you desire) as long as the two numbers added up to 80. You may run at reduced CPU usage if both instances prefailover were running closer to 100 percent, but things will work (albeit more slowly). That is ultimately the key: your SQL Server instances are up and running even if it means slightly reduced performance.

It is important to note that while WSRM can technically manage other items like memory, only use it to constrain processor utilization with SQL Server. Use SQL Server's built-in memory to handle memory configuration.

■**Tip** Another feature you can potentially use to reduce processor and memory contention is the new Resource Governor feature in SQL Server 2008. This will be discussed in Chapter 8.

Example

This section will show a more detailed example for processor and memory configuration. Consider the following five-instance, four-node configuration where memory is hard-capped with the max server memory configuration option in SQL Server:

- Instance 1 requires 4 GB of memory and averages 40 percent CPU utilization on a four-processor server.

- Instance 2 requires 2 GB of memory and averages 23 percent CPU utilization on a four-processor server.

- Instance 3 requires 6 GB of memory and averages 25 percent CPU utilization on a four-processor server.

- Instance 4 requires 3 GB of memory and averages 35 percent CPU utilization on a four-processor server.

- Instance 5 requires 5 GB of memory and averages 43 percent CPU utilization on a four-processor server.

Do the simple math. The total amount of memory needed just for all these SQL Server instances in the single-server failover cases is 20 GB of memory. The CPU usage adds up to 166 percent. Clearly, money can solve the memory contention as both Windows Server 2003 and Windows Server 2008 can handle large amounts of memory. Resolving the CPU contention is partially a money problem—you could certainly buy more processors, but is that the right thing to do? There are no real ways around the physics here.

You can take these five instances, put them on four nodes smartly, and minimize your risk in several ways. First, decide how you want to lay the nodes out. Each node will have 8 GB of memory. Figure 5-4 shows one valid configuration permutation.

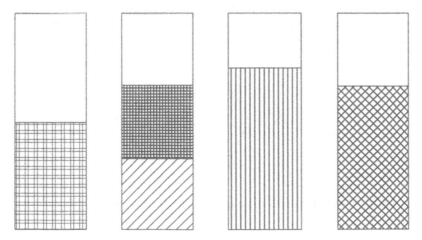

Figure 5-4. *Five SQL Server instances balanced on four cluster nodes; each instance is shown using a different pattern to distinguish between them*

In a perfect world where no failovers occur, all of these instances would work on their respective nodes because they utilized under 100 percent of CPU and memory. If you are not going to buy another node, you can decide in what order you want an instance to fail over to the other nodes by setting the failover preferences for that instance. For example, for instance 1, you could set node 3 as the primary failover node, and then order the others.

Realistically, for the most part you are still not going to escape the laws of implementing hardware. At some point, you will exceed capacity on a single node during a failover event, especially when out of your five instances, one consumes 6 GB of memory and each node has a total of only 8 GB of memory. However, there is a way to get around this problem. You can configure an N+i failover cluster as mentioned earlier. Figure 5-5 shows the same cluster from Figure 5-4 with a very large failover node that has more memory (24 GB) but not more processors and is shown in approximate scale due to the increased memory. It shows the worst-case failover state where all instances would be owned by a single node, but in this case, there should be enough resources to handle everything.

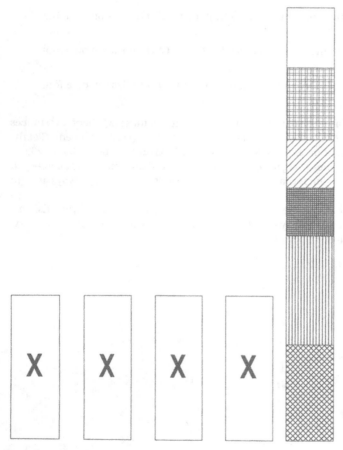

Figure 5-5. *The cluster from Figure 5-4, but after all nodes have failed over to the spare*

■**Tip** Test your worst-case failover condition (and especially under load). Even if what you observe is ugly, at least you know what it will look like.

Security Considerations

Assuming you have read Chapters 2, 3, and 4, you have planned for and possibly have already implemented the domain-level service account for the Windows server cluster. SQL Server has similar, but different, requirements. Other than configuring domain accounts to be used on the nodes, no local accounts can be used for a clustered SQL Server instance.

Service SID vs. Domain Groups for Instance Management

If you are deploying SQL Server 2008 on Windows Server 2003, you need to do what was done with SQL Server 2005: configure domain groups and place the proper accounts in them, and then subsequently add the domain groups to each node in the proper places (to be detailed shortly). While SQL Server 2008's install process should assign these rights, I always configure security manually prior to installation to ensure that everything is properly configured prior to the actual install, leaving nothing to chance.

If you are going to deploy on Windows Server 2008, things are much better and different. While you can use the domain cluster groups, there is no need to do so. With the combination of SQL Server 2008 and Windows Server 2008, you can deploy using what is known as a *Service SID*. The only exception is that if you are upgrading an instance from SQL Server 2005, it will use the existing domain groups during the upgrade. Note that utilizing a Service SID applies only to a SQL Server 2008 deployment, not any other version of SQL Server. Therefore, if you are going to deploy with SQL Server 2005 in a side-by-side configuration, SQL Server 2005 will still require domain groups.

A Service SID on Windows Server 2008 is a more secure way of deploying a service under Windows at the time of installation than using the older, domain group approach required by SQL Server 2005 (and SQL Server 2008 on Windows Server 2003). It basically creates a unique identity for the service enabling access control using the existing Windows model for access control. The SQL Server install will apply an explicit access control list (ACL) to resources that are private to the service. That means other services and users will be restricted from or have limited access to the service. Clearly you can see the benefit in a more secure SQL Server deployment that would limit who has access and what can be done at the service level.

To see what Service SID is associated with a service, use the utility sc.exe and the option showsid. If you want to know how the Service SID is set, use the switch qsidtype. Examples of both options are shown in Figure 5-6. The first example shows the Service SID for a default instance of SQL Server, and the second shows the type of Service SID associated with a named instance of SQL Server.

```
C:\>sc.exe showsid MSSQLSERVER

NAME: MSSQLSERVER
SERVICE SID: S-1-5-80-3880718306-3832830129-1677859214-2598158968-1052248003

C:\>sc.exe qsidtype MSSQL$PICTURES
[SC] QueryServiceConfig2 SUCCESS

SERVICE_NAME: MSSQL$PICTURES
SERVICE_SID_TYPE:  UNRESTRICTED
```

Figure 5-6. *sc.exe examples*

Service Accounts, Domain Groups, and Rights

When creating the service accounts for use with the SQL Server services, you should use separate accounts for each major service (SQL Server, SQL Server Agent, Analysis Services). You should also use separate service accounts from what you are using to deploy other SQL Server versions and deployments where possible. When creating the accounts in Active Directory, use names that are easy to remember, like sql2k8svcaccount, and if possible, do not allow the password to expire. If your accounts have a security policy that makes them expire, it means that every N days you will have to reset the password. To change this in SQL Server will require stopping and starting the SQL Server services, so please factor that into your planning and availability SLAs. If you do not stop and restart, objects that use those service accounts (such as SQL Server Agent jobs) may not function because they will be using the old account information until you restart SQL Server.

Similar to service accounts, if you are using domain groups for your clustered SQL Server instance, you should use separate domain groups (although you need a minimum of one) for SQL Server, SQL Server Agent, and Analysis Services. These groups will contain the domain users that you created.

Only the service account or domain group used for SQL Server Agent needs to be placed in the local Administrators group on every node if you are using the auto restart feature, otherwise nothing needs to be placed there. You will need to assign different local rights depending on the account (or group), as listed in Table 5-2.

Notice that the requirement for assigning *Act as part of the operating system* no longer exists as it did in previous versions of SQL Server. The only time anything would need to be assigned to that privilege would be for the SQL Server service account (or group that contains the SQL Server service account) if xp_cmdshell is going to be used by someone other than a SQL Server administrator. Also consider that SQL Server 2008 has the concept of proxies for SQL Server Agent (see "Implementing SQL Server Agent Security" in Books Online).

Table 5-2. *Rights Needed for SQL Server 2008 Accounts*

Local Security Policy	SQL Server	SQL Server Agent	Analysis Services
Adjust memory quotas for a process (SeIncreaseQuotaPrivilege)	Yes	Yes	No
Bypass traverse checking (SeChangeNotifyPrivilege)	Yes	Yes	No
Log on as a batch job (SeBatchLogonRight)	Yes	Yes	No
Log on as a service (SeServiceLogonRight)	Yes	Yes	Yes
Replace a process-level token (SeAssignPrimaryTokenPrivilege)	Yes	Yes	No

If you use cluster domain groups, the reality is that to have isolated security for each instance, you must use separate domain accounts and groups for each instance. In my experience, it is hard enough to get one dedicated service account, let alone more than that. You must work with your security administrators to implement security that both protects your server and data, and fits into your corporate security standards.

For configuring service accounts for SQL Browser and SQL Full-text Filter Daemon Launcher, while you can use a domain account for these services, the recommendation is that a least-privileged account should be used that is different from the SQL Server or SQL Server Agent service account. The account for these can run as LOCAL SERVICE. If you are upgrading from SQL Server 2005, you will notice that the SQL Browser account will default to the same account used for the SQL Server 2005 installation. You should change the SQL Browser postinstallation to be specific to SQL Server 2008.

The Windows failover cluster must have access to your clustered SQL Server instance to run the LooksAlive and IsAlive checks. For Windows Server 2003–based deployments, you must add the domain cluster administrator service account to the SQL Server 2008 instance. For Windows Server 2008, see the following Caution.

■**Caution** Since Windows Server 2008 failover clustering no longer uses a domain account as its service account, by default it is running under the Local System account (NT AUTHORITY\SYSTEM). This account is added to SQL Server 2008 automatically during installation. Do not remove this account post-Setup, otherwise your clustered instance will stop working.

Clustered SQL Server Instance Names

When clustering SQL Server, you are still bound by the same rules as a standalone installation: you can have one default instance per cluster, and then every other instance must be a named instance of SQL Server.

A default instance has a single name and is different than naming a standalone install of SQL Server. For a standalone default instance of SQL Server 2008, the default instance will assume the name of its underlying server. For a failover clustering implementation, the name must be completely different from the name of any of the nodes themselves or of the Windows failover cluster. In addition, the name must be completely unique within the domain. This is not unlike the requirement presented in Chapter 3 in which you need unique IP addresses for various entities in the cluster. For example, if you have a Windows failover cluster named CORNERSTONE and nodes with the names BABE, LIGHTS, and WHYME, you could not install a SQL Server 2008 failover clustering instance using any of those names. The instance name that will be installed would need to be something unique, like EDDIE. The default instance is also what becomes the name value associated with the Network Name resource at the Windows failover cluster level.

A named instance has two portions to it, and they are separated by a backslash (\). The first portion functions like the default instance name, and the part after the slash is what makes it unique. An example is PIECES\OFEIGHT, where OFEIGHT is the named portion. The part of the named instance before the slash follows the same rules as the default instance, and the part after the slash differs in that it must be unique on that particular Windows failover cluster, but the named portion can be reused on another Windows failover cluster.

This unique name requirement can potentially cause problems within companies that use some sort of naming scheme for their servers that assumes SQL Server itself takes on the same name as the server. For example, say your naming scheme is something like BOSSQLPRD1, where BOS denotes the server location of Boston, SQL denotes the type of server, PRD denotes the category of server such as production or test, and 1 is the sequential number assigned and is incremented for every server. You may need to extend your naming convention or change it slightly to work with names for clustered entities such as the Windows server cluster, the nodes, and SQL Server itself.

When creating instances, adhere to the following rules:

- Instance names are not case sensitive, so there is no difference between allan, Allan, and ALLAN.

- The words *default*, *MSSQLServer*, or any other SQL Server reserved keyword as defined in the Books Online topic "Instance Name" cannot be used; otherwise, an error will occur during setup.

- An instance name can have a maximum of 16 characters due to a NetBIOS restriction; otherwise, a setup error will occur. For example, MYNAMEDINSTANCE is valid because it does not exceed 16 characters, but MYSECONDNAMEDINSTANCE is not.

- The first character of an instance name must be a letter, the number/pound sign (#), or an underscore (_). The letter must conform to the Unicode Standard version 2.0, which includes the standard Latin-based characters of A to Z and its lowercase equivalents, and some language-specific characters from various international character sets.

- The instance name must conform to the Windows code page used on the nodes. If a Unicode character that is unsupported is used, the installation will fail.

- All characters after the first can be any of the characters in Unicode Standard version 2.0, numerals, the dollar sign ($), or an underscore.

- Spaces are not allowed; the named instance must be one contiguous string of characters. Other characters disallowed are the backslash (\), the comma (,), the colon (:), the semicolon (;), the single quote ('), the ampersand (&), and the at symbol (@).

Table 5-3 lists examples of both valid and invalid instance names on the same Windows failover cluster.

Table 5-3. *Example Clustered SQL Server Instance Names on a Single Windows Failover Cluster*

Instance Name	Valid	Reason
SQLINS	Yes	This name for a default instance is not used for any other entity in the domain.
SQLINS\NI	No	SQLINS is already used in the domain for a default instance, but the named instance of NI would be fine if SQLINS were valid. To make this valid, SQLINS would need to be altered to be unique such as SQLINS1\NI.
SQLINS2\MY INSTANCE	No	A named instance cannot contain spaces.
SQLINS2\NI	Yes	Both SQLINS2 and NI are unique and conform to the named instance naming conventions.
SQLINS3\NI	No	While SQLINS3 is unique in the domain, NI is not unique on this particular Windows failover cluster.
SQLINS3\NI2	Yes	Both SQLINS3 and NI2 are unique and conform to the named instance naming conventions.

Instance ID and Program File Location

New to SQL Server 2008 is the concept of an *Instance ID*. Technically, it has been around since SQL Server 2000, but SQL Server 2008 is the first time you get to configure it yourself. The Instance ID is configured during the installation process and is used to uniquely identify the instance that is being installed. The Instance ID is mainly used in the pathname as well as the registry hive for the SQL

Server 2008 program files (which has also changed in this version of SQL Server). The default path-name for SQL Server files in 2008 is X:\Program Files\Microsoft SQL Server\MSSQL10.*InstanceID*, where X is your system drive such as C. For Analysis Services, it is X:\Program Files\Microsoft SQL Server\MSAS10.*InstanceID*, and for Reporting Services, it is X:\Program Files\Microsoft SQL Server\MSRS10.*InstanceID*. Consult the Books Online topic "File Locations for Default and Named Instances of SQL Server" for more information.

If you are installing a default instance of SQL Server 2008, the value of the Instance ID defaults to MSSQLSERVER. Do not use that as your Instance ID. Remember from the previous section that you must give each failover clustering instance a unique name in the domain. If you need to go administer an instance and look at your file system, is the name MSSQLSERVER going to make sense? No, not really, because you'll have to remember that represents a default instance. A senior DBA may know this but a junior may not. Why leave that to chance? For all clustered deployments, the Instance ID that you use should parallel the names you use for the instance itself during config-uration to make it easy to identify when you need to do tasks at the operating system level. Consider the following two examples:

- You are going to install a default instance of SQL Server 2008 with the name of TOMMY. In this case, use TOMMY as the Instance ID.

- You are going to install a named instance of SQL Server 2008 with the name of PARADISE\ THEATER. My recommendation now would be to use PARADISE_THEATER as the Instance ID.

The path for the SQL Server program files must be the same on each node. This requires each node to have the same basic configuration, such as a C drive for Windows and any programs. SQL Server Setup enforces the rule that all nodes must be configured the same by checking the installa-tion parameters from the initial node via remote registry, and those parameters are used during Setup. If the node is configured differently, the add node operation will fail. Check prior to beginning your SQL Server 2008 installation that all nodes are configured exactly the same.

Caution Instance IDs cannot begin with an underscore (_), a number/pound sign (#), or a dollar sign ($).

Resource Dependencies

As you learned back in Chapter 1, SQL Server in a clustered configuration will have resources contained in a single cluster resource group. Some of those resources have dependencies on others. If the parent resource cannot start, the child will not either. Figure 5-7 details the dependencies for a failover clustering implementation of SQL Server 2008. The dependency tree was captured from Failover Cluster Management.

Caution It is very important that unless directed to by Microsoft support, you do not change how the depen-dencies are set up for a clustered SQL Server instance. You could potentially break your clustered implementation.

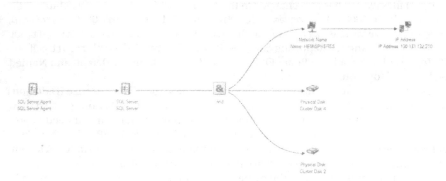

Figure 5-7. *SQL Server 2008 failover clustering resource dependency tree*

Summary

Along with the more Windows-specific information presented in Chapter 2, this chapter has given you the rest of the considerations to go ahead and start planning your SQL Server 2008 failover clustering deployments. There are enough subtle differences from standalone deployments that you should spend the proper amount of time planning. The devil is always in the details. A few years back, I spent 3 months planning a clustered SQL Server for a client, yet the actual installation and configuration of both Windows and SQL Server once the hardware was received was fairly quick (probably a day if you added the time together). The reason it went smoothly was that we covered every angle and got things right the first time. There are definitely some challenges when it comes to deploying a cluster, not the least of which are using drive letters, deploying multiple instances, and geographically dispersed clusters. Once you sort out your configuration and ensure it will be a supportable architecture (both in terms of Microsoft supportability as well as one your administrators can handle), you can then schedule your installation of SQL Server.

CHAPTER 6

■ ■ ■

Installing a New SQL Server 2008 Failover Clustering Instance

Once Windows is clustered and verified, it is time to get on with the business of deploying a clustered SQL Server 2008 instance. This chapter will cover how to install a SQL Server 2008 failover clustering instance both using SQL Server's GUI-based installer and via the command line. This chapter will cover only the installation of a new SQL Server instance; upgrading from previous versions of SQL Server failover clustering will be discussed in Chapter 7.

Pre–SQL Server Installation Tasks

Although you have already worked through a series of prerequisites and clustered Windows, the process starts over again when you have to cluster SQL Server. The tasks outlined in this section will ensure that prior to attempting to install a clustered instance of SQL Server, you have eliminated virtually everything that can cause a problem during the setup process.

Configure SQL Server–Related Service Accounts and Service Account Security

In addition to the Windows domain–based administration accounts, SQL Server requires its own domain-based service accounts. The accounts needed and their rights are covered in Chapter 5 in the "Security" section under "Service Accounts, Domain Groups, and Rights." If you already have existing domain-based SQL Server service accounts, technically you can choose to reuse them, but as noted in Chapter 5, you should consider new service accounts to minimize any unauthorized access from other administrators who deal with other versions of SQL Server in your environment. It is up to you if you want different accounts for every instance, especially in a side-by-side configuration, but the more isolated each instance is, the higher your security will be. Even if you are not going to be using the domain security groups for SQL Server 2008 security and Security SIDs, it is generally better to create groups with the users who will be administrators in your SQL Server instances.

Here are the steps to follow:

1. Create each necessary domain-based service account for SQL Server by following the instructions in Chapter 3 under the section "Create the Cluster Administration Account in the Domain," but use names like sql2k8svcaccount, sql2k8agtsvcaccount, and as2k8svcaccount for the respective SQL Server–based service accounts. Such names are intuitive and easy to remember. Do not do anything other than create the accounts.

2. Once the accounts are created, you have two options: you can leave them "as is" and add them to every node of the cluster in the subsequent steps, or you can create groups at the domain level that will contain the service accounts. These groups will be easier to manage. Consider this example: besides the service account, each DBA in your environment needs administrative access to SQL Server. It makes no sense to add each user to every node, stand-alone server, and SQL Server instance in your environment, because if the user quits or is fired, it is a lot of cleanup to have to go to every node and remove that person as a user. By putting users in groups, you can effectively add and remove users easily. Also, if there is some sort of security breach tied to an account, you can deal with it more effectively for the same reason. Creating a group in the domain requires the same access outlined in Chapter 3 when creating accounts. If you do not have this ability or it is not in the scope of your job, work with your security administrators to get the task completed.

The following are the steps to create a group using Active Directory Users and Computers.

a. In the left pane of Active Directory Users and Computers, expand the domain, right-click *Users*, and select *New* and then *Group*.

b. In the New Object – Group dialog box, enter a name for the group. Ensure the name makes sense, such as **SQL Server 2008 Admins**. Make sure the scope of the group is *Global* and the group type is *Security*. (See Figure 6-1 for an example.) Click OK.

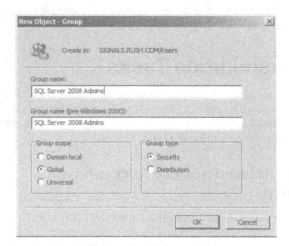

Figure 6-1. *Creating a domain group*

c. Repeat steps a and b for SQL Server Agent and Analysis Services (if needed).

It's also possible to create a group from the command line. To create a group in Active Directory via the command line, on the domain controller, use the command dsadd with the options -secgrp with a value of yes and -scope with a value of G to indicate a global domain group. The statement would look like this:

```
dsadd group "CN=<Group Name>,CN=Users, DC=<enter the fully qualified domain context>"
  -secgrp yes -scope G
```

A successful execution is shown in Figure 6-2.

```
C:\>dsadd group "CN=SQL Server 2008 Admins,CN=Users,DC=SIGNALS,DC=RUSH,DC=COM" -
secgrp yes -scope G
dsadd succeeded:CN=SQL Server 2008 Admins,CN=Users,DC=SIGNALS,DC=RUSH,DC=COM
```

Figure 6-2. *Example dsadd execution*

Once you create a group, you can add an account to that group. To add an account to an Active Directory group, execute these steps:

a. In the right pane of Active Directory Users and Computers, select the group you want to add an account to, right-click, and select *Properties*; alternatively, double-click the group name. You will see the Properties dialog box for the group.

b. Select the *Members* tab.

c. Click Add. In the Select Users, Contacts, Computers, or Groups dialog box, enter the name (or partial name) of the domain user you want to add to the domain group. Click Check Names, and the name will be resolved. Click OK. The user will now be part of the domain group, as shown in Figure 6-3. Repeat this process to add other users to the same group.

Figure 6-3. *Member added to the domain group*

d. Repeat steps a–c for the other resource groups you created.

To add an account to an Active Directory group using the command line, use the command dsmod with the option -addmbr. The statement would look like this:

```
dsmod group "CN=<Group Name>,CN=Users,DC=<enter the fully qualified domain context>"
-addmbr "CN=<Domain User Name>,CN=Users,
DC=<enter the fully qualified domain context>".
```

A sample execution is shown in Figure 6-4.

```
C:\>dsmod group "CN=SQL Server 2008 Admins,CN=Users,DC=SIGNALS,DC=RUSH,DC=COM" -
addmbr "CN=SQL Server 2008 Service Account,CN=Users,DC=SIGNALS,DC=RUSH,DC=COM"
dsmod succeeded:CN=SQL Server 2008 Admins,CN=Users,DC=SIGNALS,DC=RUSH,DC=COM
```

Figure 6-4. *Member added to the group using the command line*

To verify the account was added to the group, issue the command dsget with the option -members. The statement will look like this:

```
dsget group "CN=<Group Name>,CN=Users,
DC=<enter the fully qualified domain context>" -members
```

A sample execution is shown in Figure 6-5.

```
C:\>dsget group "CN=SQL Server 2008 Admins,CN=Users,DC=SIGNALS,DC=RUSH,DC=COM" -
members
"CN=SQL Server 2008 Service Account,CN=Users,DC=SIGNALS,DC=RUSH,DC=COM"
```

Figure 6-5. *Member added to the group*

3. See Chapter 5 to determine if you need to add the service account for SQL Server Agent or a domain-based group that has the SQL Server Agent service account to the local Administrators group on every node of the cluster. Follow the instructions in Chapter 4 under the section "Add the Cluster Service Account to Each Node."

4. Finally, the SQL Server–related service accounts must be assigned the proper rights. Refer to the section "Service Accounts, Domain Groups, and Rights" in Chapter 5 to see which policies need to be assigned to each domain account or user group. If a policy is already granted to the Administrators group, and that policy is also needed for SQL Server Agent, you do not need to explicitly add it to the domain groups since the account or group for SQL Server Agent is already part of the local Administrators group.

Here are the steps to follow to assign local rights to SQL Server service accounts or groups:

   a. On the node, from the Start menu, select *Administrative Tools* and then *Local Security Policy*.

   b. Expand Local Policies, and select *User Rights Assignment*.

   c. Right-click the required security policy in the right pane and select *Properties*; alternatively, double-click it. The Properties dialog box for the specific policy will be shown.

   d. Click Add User or Group.

   e. Click Add. In the Select Users, Contacts, Computers, or Groups dialog box, enter the name (or partial name) of the domain user(s) or group(s) you want to add to the security policy. Click Check Names, and the name will be resolved. Click OK. The user will now be added to the local security policy, as shown in Figure 6-6. Click OK.

   f. Repeat steps c–e until all security policies are assigned the proper user(s) or group(s).

   g. Exit Local Security Policy when finished.

5. Repeat steps 3 and 4 for each node of the cluster.

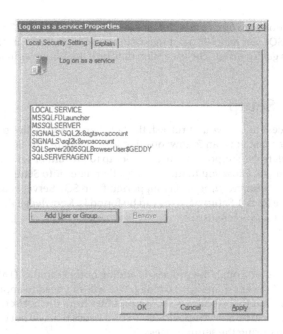

Figure 6-6. *Member added to the local security policy*

Stop Unnecessary Processes or Services

Prior to installing SQL Server 2008, you should stop or temporarily disable items that are not required for setting up a clustered SQL Server. The two big things you should disable are anti-virus and anything having to do with monitoring. Never disable any services or processes needed, such as the ones related to your disk subsystem.

Check for Pending Reboots

One of the things that can cause a SQL Server installation to fail early is that the server has files pending and is waiting for a reboot. While SQL Server Setup does check for this condition, you can save yourself some time by checking this prior to executing Setup. To check for files that may be causing a reboot, look at the registry key HKEY_LOCAL_MACHINE\SYSTEM\CurrentControlSet\Control\Session Manager. If you see PendingFileRenameOperations, you need to reboot.

Install SQL Server Setup Support Files

Since you are creating a new installation and this is not an upgrade, unless you have specific Setup issues, there should be no reason to install the SQL Server Setup Support Files prior to installing the clustered instance of SQL Server. You will see quite a few documents out there that refer to prein- stalling those files (in addition to .NET Framework 3.51 SP1 and MSI 4.5, which were covered during the Windows portion of the configuration) as an absolute prerequisite before launching Setup. While it is true that the Setup Support Files must be installed, they can be installed when you launch Setup itself.

I am basing this recommendation also on the fact that in most environments, the DBAs will most likely run the installation of SQL Server 2008, so it makes no sense to perform any SQL Server–related tasks until the DBAs get involved. The exception may be if the Windows folks are also knowledgeable about SQL Server.

Patch SQL Server 2008 Setup

SQL Server 2008's installation process allows you to refresh the SQL Server Setup files prior to installation. There are two processes that you can follow: one that is targeted for pre–Service Pack 1 deployments that allows you to update the support files used by Setup to prevent or solve any issues with SQL Server Setup, and one that will allow you to incorporate all updates into Setup (not just ones to fix Setup), which is known as *slipstreaming* and is supported from SQL Server 2008 Service Pack 1 and later. A list of pre–Service Pack 1 Setup hotfixes can be found in Knowledge Base article 955392 at http://support.microsoft.com/kb/955392.

Hotfix-Only Patching

The following instructions will take you through the process of adding hotfixes to the RTM installation media. The process detailed is different than slipstreaming. You will still need to apply a full hotfix after installation. The process that follows allows the support files from the hotfix to be used during the install. The whole purpose is to be able to apply fixes to solve issues that will not completely patch a SQL Server 2008 installation during the setup process.

1. From your original installation media, copy the root as well as the correct subdirectory for your processor (x86, x64, IA64) to a known location. For example, copy to C:\SQL Server 2008\x86.

2. Download the update (individual hotfix or Cumulative Update) to a known location.

3. Extract the files to a directory you create, such as C:\SQL Server 2008\KB955949, using the /x command line switch. For example, issue the command SQLServer2008-KB955949-x86-ENU.exe /x:"C:\SQL Server 2008\KB955949".

4. Copy the file sqlsupport.msi from the updated setup to the original installation. A sample command is robocopy "C:\SQL Server 2008\KB955949\x86\setup" "C:\SQL Server 2008\x86\Setup" sqlsupport.msi.

5. Copy setup.exe and setup.rll from the root of the updated setup to the original installation. Sample commands are as follows:

   ```
   robocopy "C:\SQL Server 2008\KB955949\x86" "C:\SQL Server 2008\" setup.exe
   robocopy "C:\SQL Server 2008\KB955949\x86" "C:\SQL Server 2008\" setup.rll
   ```

6. Copy all files except Microsoft.SQL.Chainer.PackageData.dll in the specific architecture directory in the update to the architecture folder from the installation media. A sample is robocopy "C:\SQL Server 2008\KB955949\x86\setup" "C:\SQL Server 2008\x86" /XF Microsoft.SQL.Chainer.PackageData.dll.

7. Repeat steps 1–6 for each version of the installer that you will use.

8. Setup will now run with the updated support files.

Slipstreaming a SQL Server Service Pack

Starting with SQL Server 2008 Service Pack 1, Microsoft supports slipstreaming of updated files into Setup. Slipstreaming has been an ability of Windows for years, but SQL Server has not supported this in any other version until now. The advantage of slipstreaming is that you can install the latest and greatest—in this case, SQL Server 2008 with SQL Server 2008 Service Pack 1—all in one shot. The following steps show how to slipstream a Service Pack 1 (or later) update into SQL Server 2008's Setup:

1. From your original installation media, copy the root as well as the correct subdirectory for your processor (x86, x64, IA64) to a known location. For example, copy to C:\SQL Server 2008\x86.

2. Download the update (e.g., SQL Server 2008 Service Pack 1) to a location you know.

3. Extract the files to a directory you create, such as C:\SQL Server 2008\SP1, using the /x command line switch. For example, issue the command SQLServer2008SP1-KB968369-x86-ENU.exe /x:"C:\SQL Server 2008\SP1".

4. Copy the file sqlsupport.msi from the updated setup to the original installation. A sample command would be robocopy "C:\SQL Server 2008\SP1\x86\setup\1033" "C:\SQL Server 2008\x86\Setup" sqlsupport.msi.

5. Copy setup.exe and setup.rll from the root of the updated setup to the original installation. Sample commands are as follows:

   robocopy "C:\SQL Server 2008\SP1\" "C:\SQL Server 2008\" setup.exe
   robocopy "C:\SQL Server 2008\SP1\" "C:\SQL Server 2008\" setup.rll

6. Copy all files except Microsoft.SQL.Chainer.PackageData.dll in the specific architecture directory in the update to the architecture folder from the installation media. A sample command is robocopy "C:\SQL Server 2008\SP1\x86" "C:\SQL Server 2008\x86" /XF Microsoft.SQL.Chainer.PackageData.dll.

7. Create a file called defaultsetup.ini in the original installation location for the processor (e.g., C:\SQL Server 2008\x86). Remember to include your license key (PID). The file should contain the following lines:

   ;SQLSERVER2008 Configuration File
   [SQLSERVER2008]
   PID=
   PCUSOURCE=".\SP1"

8. Repeat steps 1–7 for each version of the installer that you will use.

Setup will now run with the updated files slipstreamed. You can confirm that you are using a slipstreamed install by looking at your Installation Rules Check dialog, where you should see a result for a rule called Update Setup Media Language Compatibility. Figure 6-7 shows a passing result for that rule. You will also see mention of the rule in the confirmation of setup, as shown in Figure 6-8. If you look at the setup log postinstallation, it will also be reflected there.

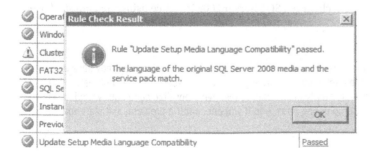

Figure 6-7. *Update Setup Media Language Compatibility check*

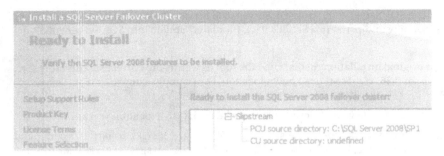

Figure 6-8. *Slipstream showing up during the confirmation of the installation options*

Method 1: Installing Using Setup, the Command Line, or an INI File

As noted in Chapter 5, SQL Server 2008's installation process for a failover cluster is completely different from that in previous releases since you need to install each node for every instance individually. There are three distinct methods of installing a clustered SQL Server 2008 instance: through the Setup interface, via the command line or an INI file, or using the new cluster preparation feature. This section covers the most traditional methods: using SQL Server Setup and a command line/INI file–based setup. The next major section will cover the new approach: cluster preparation.

■**Tip** If you are going to be executing the SQL Server 2008 installation remotely via Terminal Services, start your session with the following command: `mstsc /v:<server or cluster node name> /console`. If you are using Terminal Services from Windows Vista, substitute `/admin` for `/console`.

Install the First Node

The first official task in installing a brand-new clustered SQL Server instance is to configure one node as a single-node SQL Server 2008 failover cluster. This can be done one of two ways: either via the Setup user interface or via the command line. And the command line approach can be further subdivided: you can specify options on the command line or via an INI file.

Using the SQL Server Setup User Interface

This section will show how to install a clustered SQL Server 2008 instance using the graphical user interface of Setup.

■**Tip** Setup provides you the ability to return to previous screens and correct anything you may have entered or selected incorrectly via the use of the Back button. In my experience, this works just fine, but realize that in a complex product such as SQL Server, it is nearly impossible to test every possible code path variation. My suggestion is to always walk though Setup in one pass, and if you encounter a problem, just start again.

The following is the process to install a clustered instance using Setup:

1. Start setup.exe from your installation point for SQL Server 2008. After it is loaded, you will see the SQL Server Installation Center as shown in Figure 6-9.

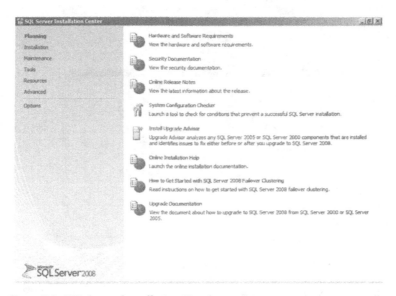

Figure 6-9. *SQL Server Installation Center*

2. Select *Installation*. You will then see a new set of options as shown in Figure 6-10. Select *New SQL Server failover cluster installation*. The installation will fail at this point if .NET Framework 3.51 SP1 or MSI 4.5 is not installed.

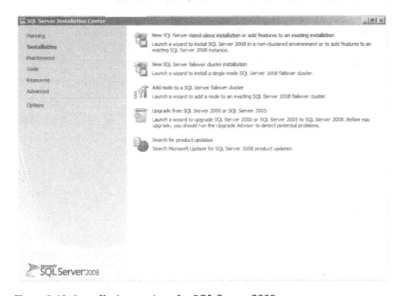

Figure 6-10. *Installation options for SQL Server 2008*

3. The first thing Setup will do is check any common issues that may affect the installation of SQL Server 2008. A sample of a successful check is shown in Figure 6-11. Click OK to continue.

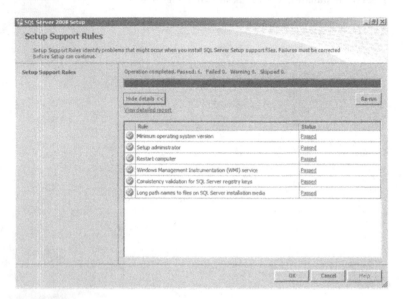

Figure 6-11. *Successful check of the support rules*

4. On the Setup Support Files dialog, click Install as shown in Figure 6-12. If you are using a slipstream copy of SQL Server 2008 Setup, the updated Setup support files will be installed. Clicking Install will update the common files if there are any other instances of SQL Server on the cluster. Once the installation of the files is complete, click Next.

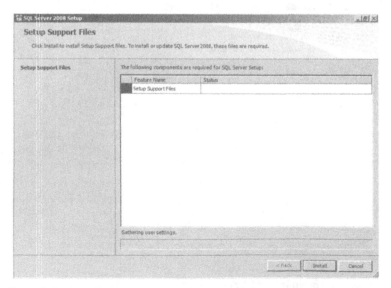

Figure 6-12. *Installation*

5. Setup will then do another check to ensure that other aspects of the cluster are configured properly to have a supported SQL Server configuration. Warnings are acceptable if they are nonfatal, but they should be investigated before accepting that the warning is not indicative of an actual problem. A sample is shown in Figure 6-13. Click Next.

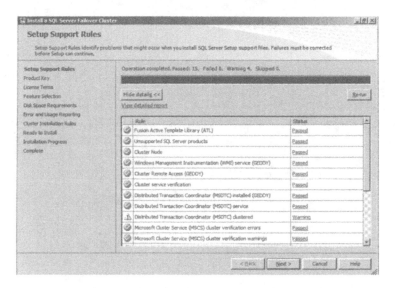

Figure 6-13. *Further Setup Support Rules validations*

6. On the Product Key dialog, enter your valid product key for SQL Server 2008 and click Next. A sample is shown in Figure 6-14.

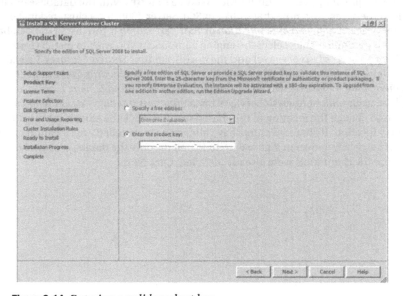

Figure 6-14. *Entering a valid product key*

7. On the License Terms dialog, read the license terms for SQL Server 2008 and click the check box next to *I accept the license terms*. A sample is shown in Figure 6-15. Click Next.

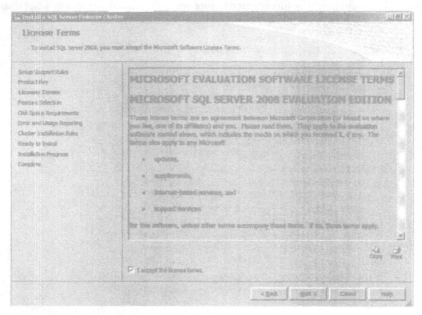

Figure 6-15. *Accepting SQL Server's license agreement*

8. On the Feature Selection dialog, select the components of SQL Server you want to install. Although it is mentioned in Chapter 5, I want to reiterate that Reporting Services is not clusterable despite it appearing under the Instance Features with the database engine and Analysis Services. Also note that unlike in SQL Server 2005, for a clustered installation, you cannot deselect *SQL Server Replication* or *Full-Text Search* if you install the database engine. For a minimal install, select the engine component you wish to install (*Database Engine Services* or *Analysis Services*) and the corresponding *Shared Features*. I always recommend to install *Client Tools Connectivity*, *Client Tools Backwards Compatibility*, and *Management Tools – Basic* (which will automatically select *Management Tools – Complete*). If you will be using SSIS or Analysis Services, install *Business Intelligence Development Studio*. If you want to change the location of the shared features, click the ellipsis button and enter/select a new location. If shared features have already been installed, this location cannot be changed. A sample is shown in Figure 6-16 to install the only the database engine of SQL Server where the client tools were already installed. Click Next.

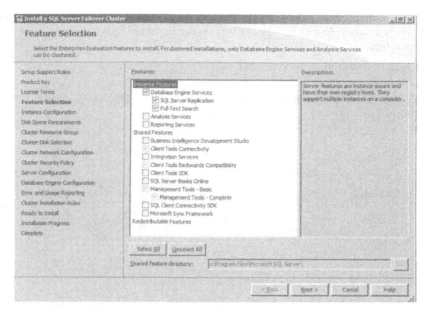

Figure 6-16. *Sample Feature Selection dialog*

9. The Instance Configuration dialog is one of the most important—if not *the* most important—dialogs in Setup. Fill in the fields carefully, and think through your choices. The job aids available for download from the Apress web site (http://www.apress.com) and http://www.sqlha.com should help you. The value entered for *SQL Server Network Name* is the name by which users and computers will access the clustered SQL Server instance from the network. This is the part before the slash if your instance is a named instance. The name used must adhere to the rules documented in Chapter 5 in the section "Clustered SQL Server Instance Names."

Once you enter a network name, choose whether to install a default or named instance of SQL Server. Remember that you can only have one default instance per cluster. The bottom of Figure 6-17 shows other instances already installed; a default instance will show up as MSSQLSERVER. If you have selected a named instance, enter the named part of the instance.

Next, enter a name for the *Instance ID*, which was discussed in Chapter 5. If you are installing a default instance of SQL Server, the default value will be MSSQLSERVER. You should change this value to be the same as the SQL Server network name for a default instance or a combination of the network name and named instance name for a named instance to avoid any confusion should you have to administer SQL Server and look at the directories on the server itself. In the example shown in Figure 6-17, I use the value POWER_WINDOWS for a named instance of POWER\WINDOWS.

Finally, if desired, change the value for *Instance root directory*, which is the location for the SQL Server program files. Make a note if you change this since each node must have the same configuration.

Click Next to continue.

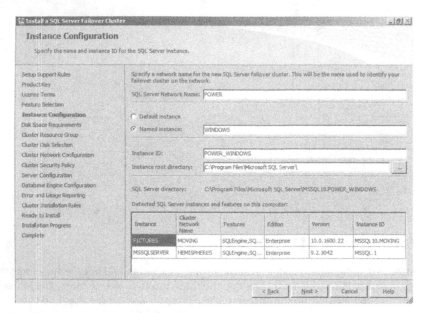

Figure 6-17. *Sample Instance Configuration dialog*

10. Click Next on the Disk Space Requirements dialog, which you see in Figure 6-18.

11. On the Cluster Resource Group dialog, enter a value in *SQL Server cluster resource group name* for the name of the cluster resource group that will contain the SQL Server 2008 resources. There will be a default name already configured. For example, a named instance will have a default name of SQL Server (*NamedInstanceName*). In the case of the installation from the previous step, it would default to SQL Server (Windows). I suggest naming the resource group something that makes more sense to your environment and is easy to identify. For both a default and a named instance, I recommend incorporating the name of the instance into the value for the group. I often incorporate the version into the name to make it easy to identify when viewing in Failover Cluster Management. An example is shown in Figure 6-19.

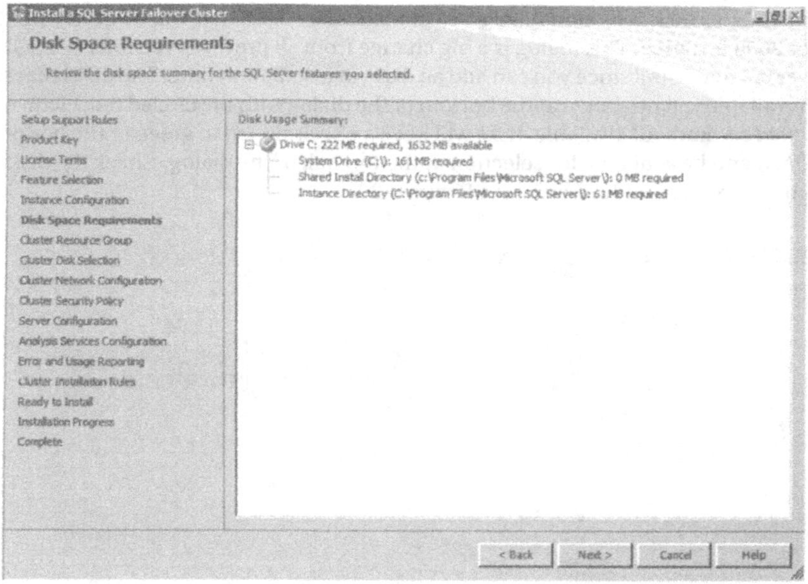

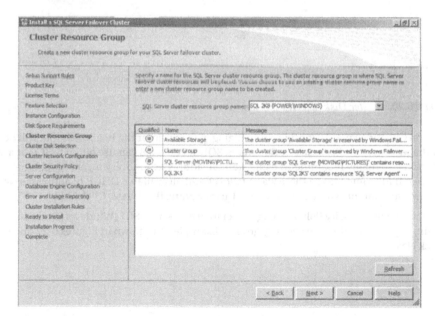

Figure 6-18. *Disk Space Requirements dialog*

Figure 6-19. *Entering a cluster resource group name*

12. On the Cluster Disk Selection dialog, select the disk or disks that will be used with this SQL Server 2008 instance. This dialog is a big change from all previous versions of a SQL Server failover cluster install since you can add all disks at installation time. The disks that are in use or unavailable will be shown at the bottom of the dialog with the circled red *X* icon under the *Qualified* column. All available disks will have a check circled in green at the bottom under *Qualified* and be available for selection at the top half of the dialog. Check the disks to use, and click Next. A sample is shown in Figure 6-20.

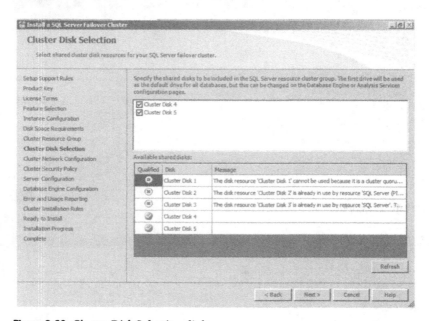

Figure 6-20. *Cluster Disk Selection dialog*

13. On the Cluster Network Configuration dialog, you will enter the IP address that will be used by the instance. As discussed in Chapter 5, SQL Server 2008 can use either DHCP or a static IP address. I highly recommend using static IP addresses for every installation. What would happen if for some reason there was a failover and all available DHCP IP addresses were taken? The example shown in Figure 6-21 uses a static IP address. Click Next.

14. On the Cluster Security Policy dialog, select to use a Service SID (Windows Server 2008 only) or the appropriate domain security groups. Examples are shown in Figures 6-22 and 6-23. Click Next.

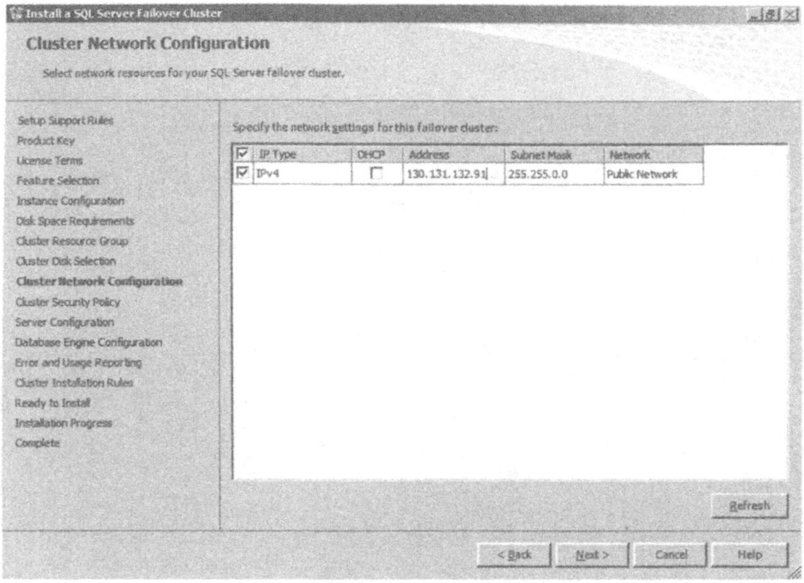

Figure 6-21. *Cluster Network Configuration dialog*

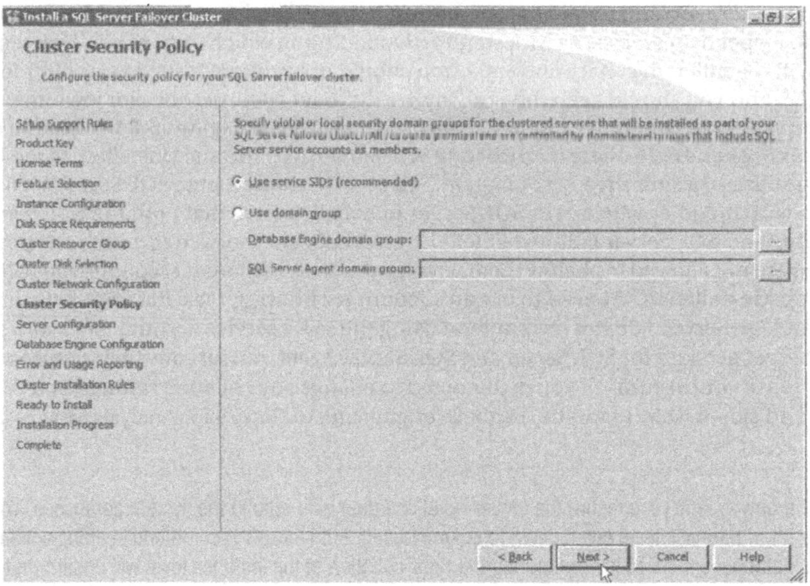

Figure 6-22. *Cluster Security Policy dialog for the database engine*

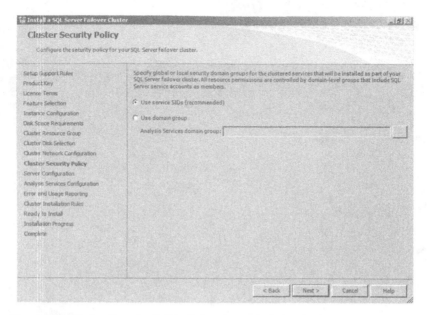

Figure 6-23. *Cluster Security Policy dialog for Analysis Services*

15. On the *Service Accounts* tab of the Server Configuration dialog, enter the domain accounts for the respective services. As with step 14, depending on which options you selected earlier, you will see different service accounts. You should use a different service account for each service, and you should keep those accounts different from the ones for any other SQL Server version in your environment. Samples are shown in Figures 6-24, 6-25, and 6-26. In Figures 6-24 and 6-26, there is an existing SQL Server 2005 instance installed, so the Browser account uses the one already configured. Figure 6-25 shows a pure SQL Server 2008 installation with no other versions of SQL Server installed. Notice that both the SQL Server Browser and SQL Server Full-text Filter Daemon Launcher service accounts are grayed out, so you are not allowed to change them. If you want to use different accounts, you will have to do it postinstallation. If I need to use an account for Browser, I use the same account as the one for SQL Server. I do not recommend using the same service account (such as a single SQL Server account for SQL Server and SQL Server Agent, not just one über service account) to increase your security. If you do not need to change any collation settings, you can click Next and skip to step 18 for the database engine and to step 19 for Analysis Services.

▓Caution   The only way to reconfigure the server-level collation is to rebuild the system databases. You can change collation at a database level (even down to column level), but I always recommend keeping collations the same across all databases if possible. Configuring the right collation at the instance level will ensure that all user databases created inherit that collation. If you are unsure of what to use, ask the owners of the applications whose databases will be housed in the instance.

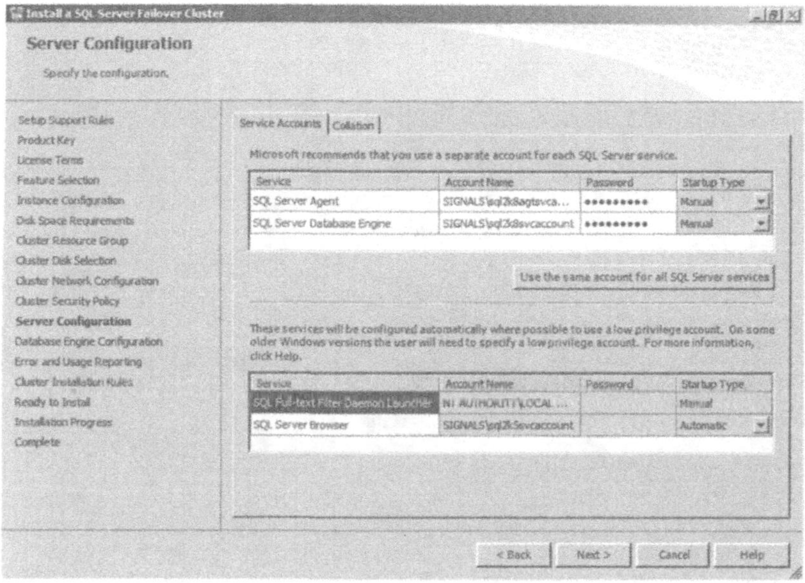

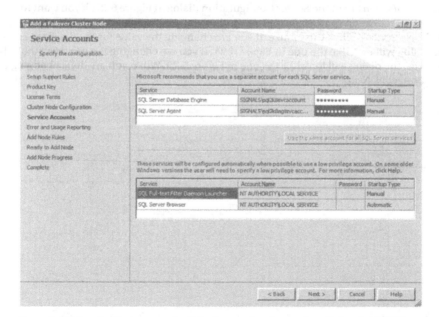

Figure 6-24. *Service Accounts tab of the Server Configuration dialog for the database engine with an existing SQL Server 2005 installation*

Figure 6-25. *Service Accounts tab of the Server Configuration dialog for SQL Server with no existing SQL Server 2005 installations*

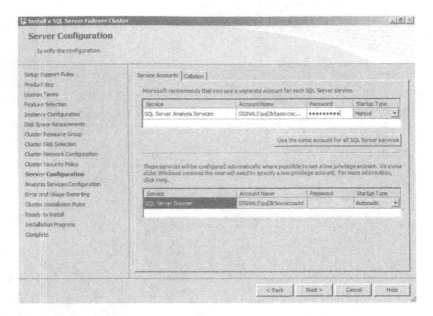

Figure 6-26. *Service Accounts tab of the Server Configuration dialog for Analysis Services*

16. On the *Collation* tab of the Server Configuration dialog in Figure 6-27, if you want to change the default collation for the appropriate option you are installing (the database engine or Analysis Services), click Customize. If you are changing the value for the database engine, the dialog will look like the one in Figure 6-28. If you are changing the value for Analysis Services, the dialog will look like the one in Figure 6-29. When you are done changing the collation, click Next.

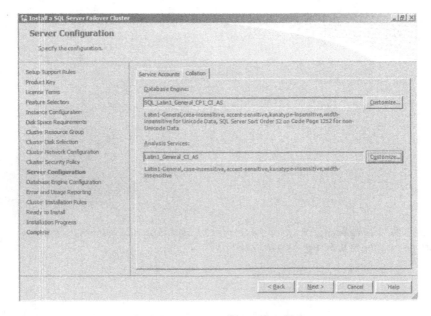

Figure 6-27. *Collation tab of the Server Configuration dialog*

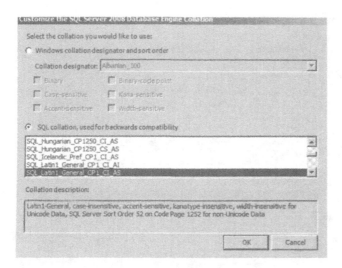

Figure 6-28. *Collation dialog for the database engine*

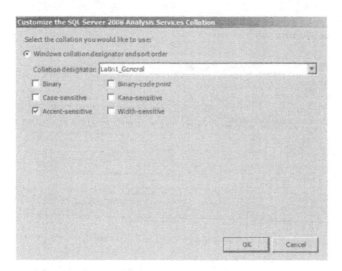

Figure 6-29. *Collation dialog for Analysis Services*

17. The Database Engine Configuration dialog has three different tabs: *Account Provisioning*, *Data Directories*, and *FILESTREAM*. On the *Account Provisioning* tab as shown in Figure 6-30, select the type of authentication for SQL Server to use, and if you want to add any accounts or groups (local or domain) as administrators, you can do so here. On the *Data Directories* tab in Figure 6-31, you can modify where the various files on the shared drive will be stored. The paths will default to the first drive selected in step 12. The *FILESTREAM* tab in Figure 6-32 is where you would enable Filestream and configure its settings. If you are going to be using Filestream, this is the best time to have it installed and configured. When finished, click Next and skip to step 20.

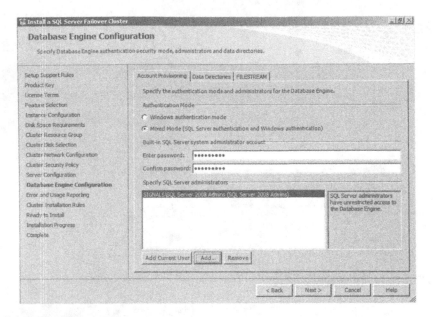

Figure 6-30. *Account Provisioning tab*

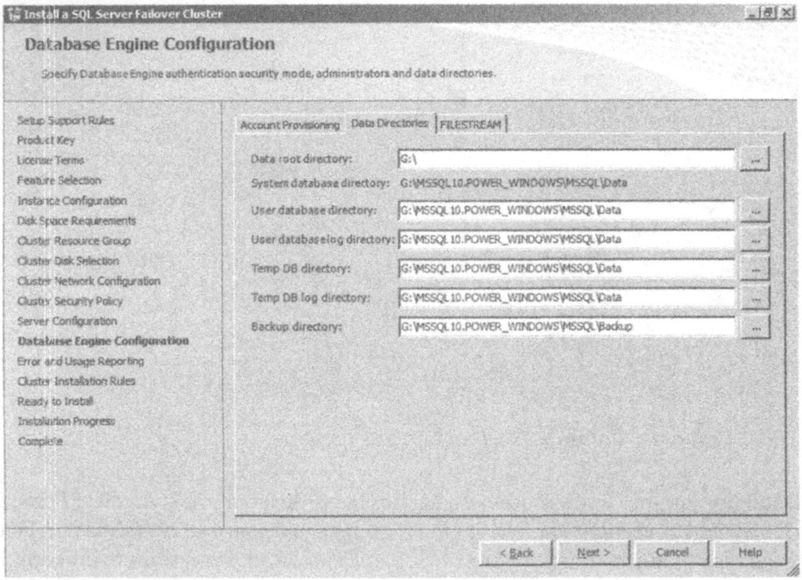

Figure 6-31. *Data Directories tab*

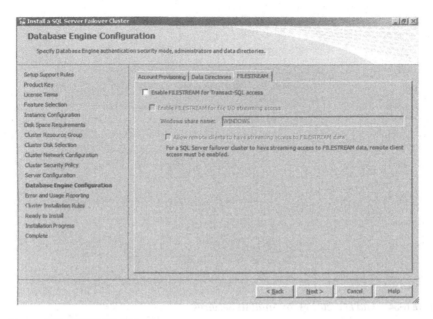

Figure 6-32. *FILESTREAM tab*

18. On the Analysis Services Configuration dialog, there are two different tabs: *Account Provisioning* and *Data Directories*. On the *Account Provisioning* tab as shown in Figure 6-33, you can add any accounts or groups (local or domain) as administrators. On the *Data Directories* tab in Figure 6-34, you can modify where the various files on the shared drive will be stored. The paths will default to the first drive selected in step 12. When finished, click Next.

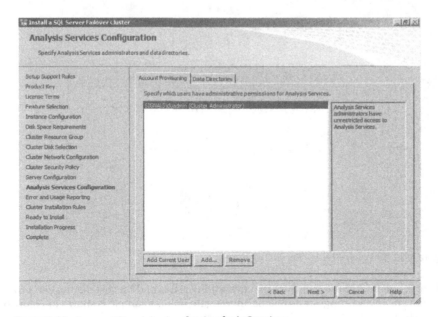

Figure 6-33. *Account Provisioning for Analysis Services*

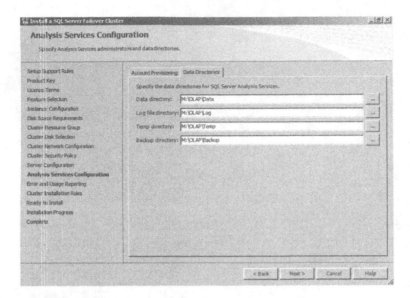

Figure 6-34. *Data Directories for Analysis Services*

19. On the Error and Usage Reporting dialog in Figure 6-35, the default is for nothing to be selected. If you want to send information to Microsoft, check the appropriate boxes and click Next to continue.

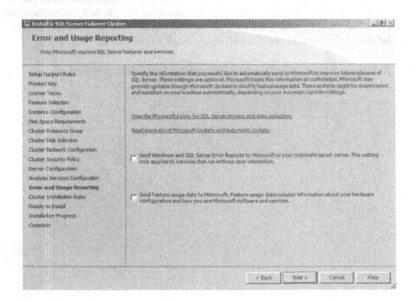

Figure 6-35. *Error and Usage Reporting dialog*

20. There is one final check to ensure that everything is fine and the installation can proceed. If there are any warnings or problems, investigate them. A sample is shown in Figure 6-36. Click Next.

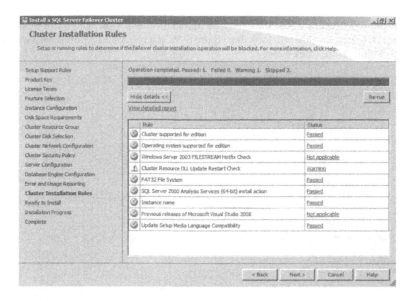

Figure 6-36. *Cluster Installation Rules dialog*

21. On the Ready to Install dialog in Figure 6-37, verify your settings. Click Install. Again, as noted in the last step, if you encountered any warnings, do not click Install unless you are sure there are no problems. One thing that should be mentioned is that the *Configuration file path* area at the bottom of the Ready to Install dialog explicitly points out the location of the INI file that will be used during installation. If you want to see examples of INI files to use to install via the method described later, this is a good place to get started.

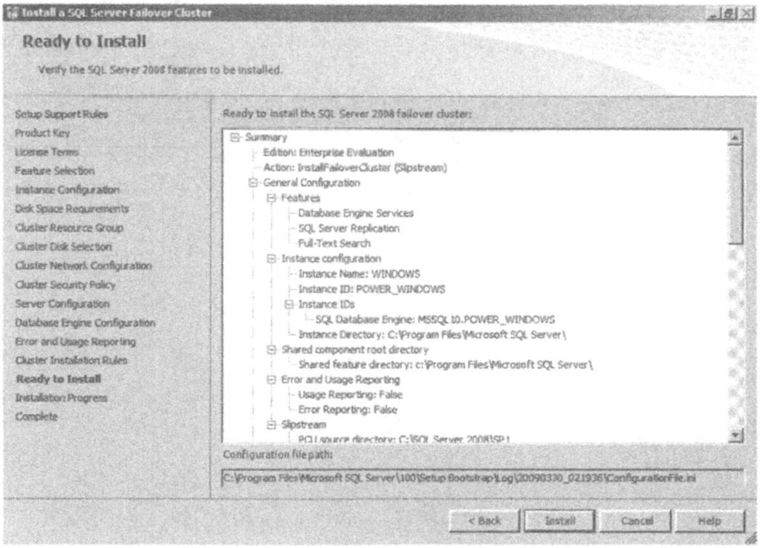

Figure 6-37. *Ready to Install dialog*

22. When complete, a successful database engine installation will look like Figure 6-38 and an Analysis Services installation will look like Figure 6-39. If a reboot is required, you will see the message in Figure 6-40. Click Next.

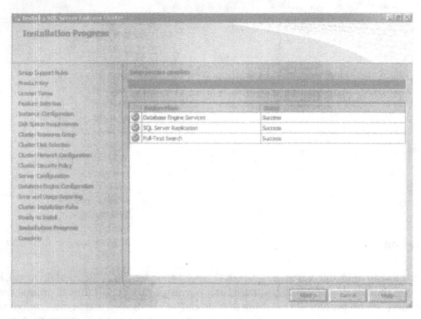

Figure 6-38. *Completed database engine installation*

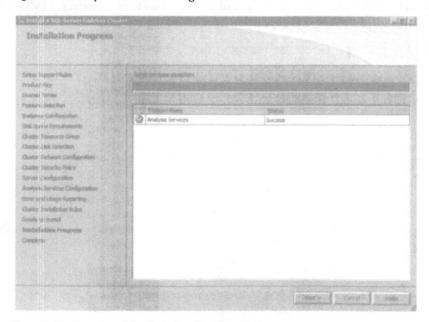

Figure 6-39. *Completed Analysis Services installation*

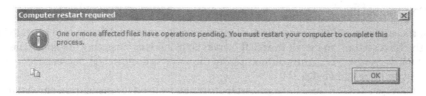

Figure 6-40. *Setup notifying you of a reboot*

23. Click Close on the dialog shown in Figure 6-41. Note the location of the log files for this installation. You can click the link shown and review the summary. If a reboot is required, the message in Figure 6-42 will be shown; click OK.

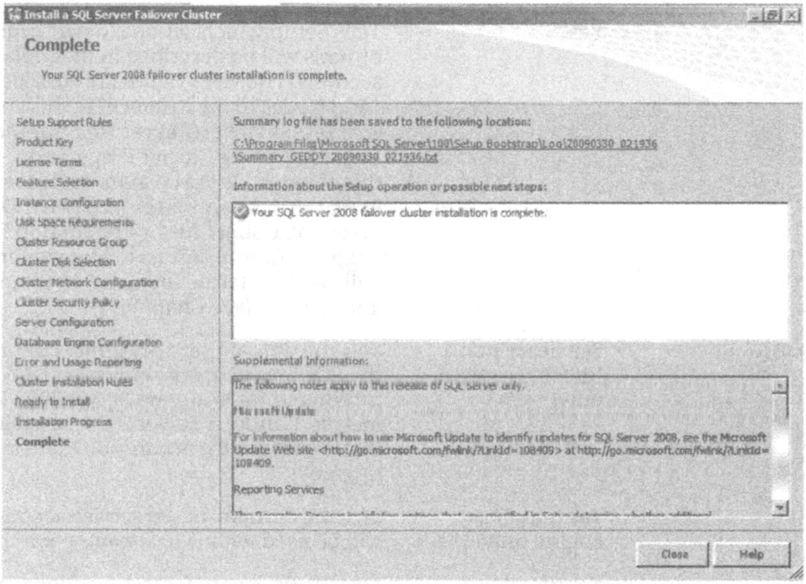

![Install a SQL Server Failover Cluster — Complete dialog]

Figure 6-41. *Completed installation*

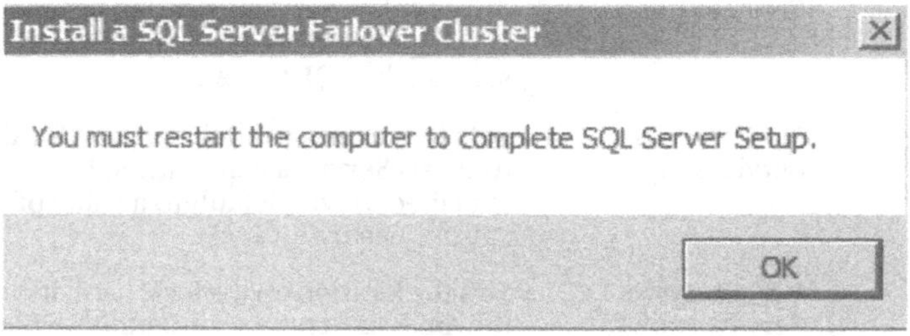

![Install a SQL Server Failover Cluster reboot dialog: "You must restart the computer to complete SQL Server Setup." with OK button]

Figure 6-42. *Another reboot notification*

Using the Command Line

Following in the tradition of SQL Server 2005, you can use the command line as well as an INI file (covered in the next section) to install your SQL Server 2008 failover clustering instance. The way it was done in SQL Server 2005 is slightly different from the way it is done in SQL Server 2008, so do not necessarily rely on prior knowledge.

Table 6-1 shows all of the possible parameters that can be used for installing a clustered SQL Server 2008 instance and indicates whether or not they are required. Not all parameters apply for a new installation, but the table lists them all for your convenience.

Table 6-1. *Command Line and INI Parameters for a SQL Server 2008 Failover Clustering Installation or Upgrade*

Parameter	Required	Description
ACTION	Yes	Tells Setup which actions to perform; exact options will be described in their related sections. The valid values are AddNode (see "Add Nodes to the Instance" in this chapter), CompleteFailoverCluster (see "Method 2: Installing Using Cluster Preparation" in this chapter), InstallFailoverCluster, PrepareFailoverCluster (see "Method 2: Installing Using Cluster Preparation" in this chapter), RemoveNode (see "Uninstalling a Failover Clustering Instance" in Chapter 8), and Upgrade (see Chapter 7).
AGTDOMAINGROUP	See description (database engine only)	Sets the domain security group containing the SQL Server Agent service account. This is required for Windows Server 2003–based installs, Windows Server 2008–based installs that do not use the Security SID, and in-place upgrades.
AGTSVCACCOUNT	Yes (database engine only)	Sets the domain-based service account that will be used with SQL Server Agent.
AGTSVCPASSWORD	Yes (database engine only)	Sets the password for the account specified by AGTSVCACCOUNT.
ASBACKUPDIR	No (Analysis Services only)	Sets the default directory on the shared drive for Analysis Services database backups. If not specified, it will default to a drive selected by SQL Server.
ASCOLLATION	No (Analysis Services only)	Sets the instance-level collation for the Analysis Services installation. If not specified, it will default to a value of Latin1_General_CI_AS.
ASCONFIGDIR	No (Analysis Services only)	Sets the location on the local hard drive for the Analysis Services configuration files. If not specified, it will default to %Program Files%\Microsoft SQL Server\<instance directory>\<AS Instance ID>\OLAP\Config.

Table 6-1. *Command Line and INI Parameters for a SQL Server 2008 Failover Clustering Installation or Upgrade (Continued)*

Parameter	Required	Description
ASDATADIR	No (Analysis Services only)	Sets the location on a shared drive for the Analysis Services data files. If not specified, it will default to a drive selected by SQL Server.
ASDOMAINGROUP	See description (Analysis Services only)	Sets the domain security group containing the Analysis Services service account. This is required for Windows Server 2003–based installs, Windows Server 2008–based installs that do not use the Security SID, and in-place upgrades. It is not required for Windows Server 2008 installs that will use the Security SID.
ASLANGUAGE	Yes (Analysis Services only)	Sets the instance-level language for an Analysis Services installation.
ASLOGDIR	No (Analysis Services only)	Sets the location on a shared drive for the Analysis Services log files. If not specified, it will default to a drive selected by SQL Server.
ASPROVIDERMSOLAP	No (Analysis Services only)	Sets whether the MSOLAP provider runs in-process: 0 = disabled, 1 = enabled.
ASSVCACCOUNT	Yes (Analysis Services only)	Sets the domain-based service account that will be used with Analysis Services.
ASSVCPASSWORD	Yes (Analysis Services only)	Sets the password for the account specified by ASSVCACCOUNT.
ASSYSADMINACCOUNTS	Yes (Analysis Services only)	Specifies the accounts that will serve as the system administrators for an instance of Analysis Services.
ASTEMPDIR	Yes (Analysis Services only)	Sets the location on a shared drive for the Analysis Services temporary files. If not specified, it will default to a drive selected by SQL Server.
CONFIGURATIONFILE	No	If you will be installing using a configuration file (see the section "Method 2: Installing Using Cluster Preparation" for more information), this specifies the file to use.
ERRORREPORTING	No	Sets whether automatic error reporting back to Microsoft is enabled or disabled: 0 = disabled, 1 = enabled.
FAILOVERCLUSTERDISKS	Yes	Sets the available disks in the Windows failover cluster that the instance will use.

Continued

Table 6-1. *Command Line and INI Parameters for a SQL Server 2008 Failover Clustering Installation or Upgrade (Continued)*

Parameter	Required	Description
FAILOVERCLUSTERGROUP	Yes	Sets the name of the resource group within the Windows failover cluster that will be used to house the SQL Server (or Analysis Services) resources. This can be either an empty, existing resource group or a new one that will get created as part of the installation process. If this parameter is not explicitly specified, a default value of SQLServer(*<instance name>*) will be used.
FAILOVERCLUSTERIPADDRESSES	Yes	Sets the network and IP address that the instance will use.
FAILOVERCLUSTERNETWORKNAME	Yes	Sets the name that will be used to access the SQL Server instance; for a named instance, this would be the portion before the slash.
FAILOVERCLUSTERROLLOWNERSHIP	No (upgrade only)	See the section "Upgrading Using the Command Line" in Chapter 7 for detailed information on how to use this parameter. There are three valid values: 0, 1, and 2.
FEATURES	Yes	Specifies which components to install during the setup process. Multiple components are listed using commas. Valid values are AS (Analysis Services); IS (Integration Services); RS (Reporting Services); SQL (database engine); TOOLS (all of the SQL Server client tools including SQL Server Books Online); BC (backward compatibility components); BOL (SQL Server Books Online); BIDS (Business Intelligence Development Studio); Conn (Connectivity components); SSMS (SQL Server Management Studio with support for the database engine and SQL Server Express, sqlcmd, and the SQL Server PowerShell provider); ADV_SSMS (everything that is installed with SSMS plus SQL Server Management Studio support for Analysis Services, Integration Services, and Reporting Services; SQL Server Profiler; and the Database Engine Tuning Advisor); and SDK (SQL Server software development kit).
FILESTREAMLEVEL	No (database engine only)	Sets whether Filestream will be used by the instance of SQL Server. Valid values are as follows: 0 = disabled (default), 1 = enabled (Transact-SQL only), 2 = enabled (Transact-SQL and file I/O; *invalid on cluster configurations*), and 3 = allow remote clients to have streaming access to Filestream data.
FILESTREAMSHARENAME	No (database engine only)	Sets the Windows share that contains the Filestream data. It must be set if FILESTREAMLEVEL is set to anything other than the default of 0.

Table 6-1. *Command Line and INI Parameters for a SQL Server 2008 Failover Clustering Installation or Upgrade (Continued)*

Parameter	Required	Description
FTSVCACCOUNT	No	Sets the password for the SQL Full-text Filter Daemon Launcher; used by Windows Server 2003–based installations only. If not specified, it will default to the Local Service Account and the service will be disabled.
FTSVCPASSWORD	No	Sets the password for the account specified in FTSVCACCOUNT.
FTUPGRADEOPTION	Yes (upgrade only)	Tells setup.exe how to upgrade existing full-text indexes. The valid values are Rebuild, Reset, or Import. If you are upgrading to SQL Server 2008 from SQL Server 2000, even if Import is specified, Rebuild will be used.
HIDECONSOLE	No	Tells setup.exe to hide or close the console window: 0 = disabled, 1 = enabled.
INDICATEPROCESS	No	Tells setup.exe to display the output of what will also be in the setup log file to the screen: 0 = disabled, 1 = enabled.
INSTALLSHAREDDIR	No	Sets a nonstandard location on the local drive where the shared SQL Server files are placed. It must be the same on each node.
INSTALLSHAREDWOWDIR	No (64-bit installs only)	Sets a nonstandard location on the local drive where the 32-bit shared SQL Server files are placed. It must be the same on each node.
INSTALLSQLDATADIR	Yes (database engine only)	Sets the location on one of the shared disks specified by FAILOVERCLUSTERDISKS where the data files will be placed.
INSTANCEDIR	No	Sets the top-level location on the local drive where the SQL Server files are installed. It must be the same on each node.
INSTANCEID	No	Sets the value for the Instance ID (see the section "Instance ID and Program File Location" in Chapter 5 for more information). If not specified, it will set the value to either MSSQLSERVER for a default instance or X for a named instance.
INSTANCENAME	Yes	Sets whether this is a default or a named instance of SQL Server. For a default instance, use MSSQLSERVER. For a named instance, this is the part after the slash.
ISSVCACCOUNT	Yes (Integration Services only)	Sets the domain-based service account that will be used with Integration Services.

Continued

Table 6-1. *Command Line and INI Parameters for a SQL Server 2008 Failover Clustering Installation or Upgrade (Continued)*

Parameter	Required	Description
ISSVCPASSWORD	Yes (Integration Services only)	Sets the password for the account specified by ISSVCACCOUNT.
ISSVCSTARTUPTYPE	No (Integration Services only)	Sets the startup mode for the local Integration Services installation. Valid values are Automatic, Disabled, and Manual.
PCUSOURCE	No	Specifies the directory for the extended service pack files used to update the install media if a service pack or an update is slipstreamed.
PID	Yes	Specifies the valid, licensed product key for the installation. It will install an Evaluation Edition if this is not included.
QUIET	No	Tells setup.exe to run completely "silent." It can be shortened to Q.
QUIETSIMPLE	No	Tells setup.exe to run unattended, but progress will be shown via the normal install dialog windows with no ability to see errors or input anything. It can be shortened to QS.
RSINSTALLMODE	No (Reporting Services only)	Specifies the install mode for Reporting Services.
RSSVCACCOUNT	Yes (Reporting Services only)	Sets the domain-based service account that will be used with Reporting Services.
RSSVCPASSWORD	Yes (Reporting Services only)	Sets the password for the account specified by RSSVCACCOUNT.
RSSVCSTARTUPTYPE	No (Reporting Services only)	Sets the startup mode for the local Reporting Services installation. Valid values are Automatic, Disabled, and Manual.
SECURITYMODE	No (database engine only)	Sets whether to use Windows Authentication or Mixed Mode (both SQL Server and Windows authentication). No value indicates Windows Authentication and a value of SQL will configure Mixed Mode.
SAPWD	See description (database engine only)	Sets the password for the sa user when SQLDOMAINGROUP=SQL.
SQLBACKUPDIR	No (database engine only)	Sets the default directory on the shared drive for SQL Server database backups. If not specified, it will default to a drive selected by SQL Server.

Table 6-1. *Command Line and INI Parameters for a SQL Server 2008 Failover Clustering Installation or Upgrade (Continued)*

Parameter	Required	Description
SQLCOLLATION	No (database engine only)	Sets the instance-level collation for the SQL Server install. If not specified, it will default to a value of Latin1_General_CI_AS.
SQLDOMAINGROUP	See description (database engine only)	Sets the domain security group containing the SQL Server service account. This is required for Windows Server 2003–based installs, Windows Server 2008–based installs that do not use the Security SID, and in-place upgrades.
SQLSVCACCOUNT	Yes (database engine only)	Sets the domain-based service account that will be used with SQL Server.
SQLSVCPASSWORD	Yes (database engine only)	Sets the password for the account specified by SQLSVCACCOUNT.
SQLSYSADMINACCOUNTS	Yes (database engine only)	Specifies the accounts that will serve as the system administrators for the instance of SQL Server.
SQLTEMPDBDIR	No (database engine only)	Sets the location on a shared drive for tempdb data files. If not specified, it will default to the value used by INSTALLSQLDATADIR.
SQLTEMPDBLOGDIR	No (database engine only)	Sets the location on a shared drive for tempdb log files. If not specified, it will default to the value used by INSTALLSQLDATADIR.
SQLUSERDBDIR	No (database engine only)	Sets the location on a shared drive for the user-created database files. If not specified, it will default to the value used by INSTALLSQLDATADIR.
SQLUSERDBLOGDIR	No (database engine only)	Sets the location on a shared drive for the user-created log files. If not specified, it will default to the value used by INSTALLSQLDATADIR.
SQMREPORTING	No	Sets the flag whether or not to send error reports automatically back to Microsoft: 0 = disabled, 1 = enabled.
USESYSDB	No (database engine only)	Sets the location on a shared drive for the system databases. It cannot use a path with \Data at the end.

The following example installs a default instance of SQL Server 2008 with two disks and adds one domain account and one domain group as administrators. This example also installs the connectivity components and management tools.

```
setup.exe /ACTION=InstallFailoverCluster
/AGTSVCACCOUNT="SIGNALS\sql2k8agtsvccaccount" /AGTSVCPASSWORD="P@ssword1"
/ERRORREPORTING=0 /FAILOVERCLUSTERDISKS="Cluster Disk 3" "Cluster Disk 4"
/FAILOVERCLUSTERGROUP="SQL2K8 - HEMISPHERES"
/FAILOVERCLUSTERIPADDRESSES="IPv4;130.131.132.68;Public Network;255.255.0.0"
/FAILOVERCLUSTERNETWORKNAME="HEMISPHERES"
/FEATURES=SQL,BC,Conn,ADV_SSMS
/FILESTREAMLEVEL=0
/INSTALLSQLDATADIR="F:\SQL Data" /INSTANCEID="HEMISPHERES" /INSTANCENAME=MSSQLSERVER
/SECURITYMODE=SQL /SAPWD="P@ssword1" /SQLBACKUPDIR="F:\SQL Backups"
/SQLCOLLATION="SQL_Latin1_General_CP1_CI_AS"
/SQLSVCACCOUNT="SIGNALS\sql2k8svccaccount"
/SQLSVCPASSWORD="P@ssword1"
/SQLSYSADMINACCOUNTS="SIGNALS\cluadmin" "SIGNALS\SQL Server 2008 Admins"
/Q /INDICATEPROGRESS
```

This next example creates a named failover clustering instance of Analysis Services 2008 with Integration Services (which is not clustered), Business Intelligence Development Studio, connectivity, and SQL Server Management Studio.

```
setup.exe /ACTION=InstallFailoverCluster
/ASSVCACCOUNT="SIGNALS\sql2k8assvccaccount" /ASSVCPASSWORD="P@ssword1"
/ASSYSADMINACCOUNTS="SIGNALS\cluadmin"  /ERRORREPORTING=0
/FAILOVERCLUSTERDISKS="Cluster Disk 5"
/FAILOVERCLUSTERGROUP="AS2K8 - POWER\WINDOWS"
/FAILOVERCLUSTERIPADDRESSES="IPv4;130.131.132.69;Public Network;255.255.0.0"
/FAILOVERCLUSTERNETWORKNAME="GRAND"
/FEATURES=AS,BIDS,Conn,ADV_SSMS /FILESTREAMLEVEL=0
/INSTALLSQLDATADIR="F:\SQL Data" /INSTANCEID="GRAND_ILLUSION"
/INSTANCENAME=ILLUSION /Q /INDICATEPROGRESS
```

A successful run will look like Figure 6-43. In fact, all command line and INI examples will have output similar to Figure 6-43.

```
Sco: Attempting to get registry value HiddenDisplayName
Completed Action: CreateARPRegKeyAction, returned True
-----------------------------------------------------------------
Running Action: NotifyProgressComplete
Completed Action: NotifyProgressComplete, returned True
-----------------------------------------------------------------
Running Action: ProduceStatusLogsBeforeFinishPage
Completed Action: ProduceStatusLogsBeforeFinishPage, returned True
-----------------------------------------------------------------
Running Action: FinalizeProgressStatus
Completed Action: FinalizeProgressStatus, returned True
-----------------------------------------------------------------
Running Action: RebootMessageAction
Completed Action: RebootMessageAction, returned True
-----------------------------------------------------------------
Running Action: CloseUI
Stop action skipped in UI Mode Quiet
Completed Action: CloseUI, returned True


-----------------------------------------------------------------
Setup result: 0
```

Figure 6-43. *Successful instance creation via the command line*

Using an INI File

A variation on using the command line is using an INI file to specify all of the appropriate options, and then invoking setup.exe utilizing that INI file. There are two ways to approach the INI file: you can put the passwords in the file (which may represent a security risk), or you can specify them at runtime. If you have run the GUI and have some issues coming up with your own INI files, navigate to the %Program Files%\Microsoft SQL Server\100\SetupBootstrap\Log directory, find a successful run, and locate the file named ConfigurationFile.ini. As mentioned earlier in the section showing how to use the Setup interface, you can use that file as a template for creating your own INI files.

This first example is the same as the one shown in the preceding section on using the command line. You would place the following lines in the file. Technically, the options can be placed in any order; I find it easier to place them alphabetically. The parser is pretty fussy about spaces and things like quotes. Be careful about the types of quotes you use around values. If you create an INI file in something other than a pure text editor, you may get Word-style beginning and/or ending quotes, which the parser seems to have an issue with.

```
[SQLSERVER2008]
ACTION="InstallFailoverCluster"
AGTSVCACCOUNT="SIGNALS\sql2k8agtsvcaccount"
ERRORREPORTING=0
FAILOVERCLUSTERDISKS="Cluster Disk 3" "Cluster Disk 4"
FAILOVERCLUSTERGROUP="SQL2K8 - HEMISPHERES"
FAILOVERCLUSTERIPADDRESSES="IPv4;130.131.132.68;Public Network;255.255.0.0"
FAILOVERCLUSTERNETWORKNAME="HEMISPHERES"
FEATURES=SQL,BC,Conn,ADV_SSMS
FILESTREAMLEVEL=0
INSTALLSQLDATADIR="F:\SQL Data"
INSTANCEID="HEMISPHERES"
INSTANCENAME="MSSQLSERVER"
PCUSOURCE="C:\SQL Server 2008\SP1"
SECURITYMODE="SQL"
SAPWD="P@ssword1"
SQLBACKUPDIR="F:\SQL Backups"
SQLCOLLATION="SQL_Latin1_General_CP1_CI_AS"
SQLSVCACCOUNT="SIGNALS\sql2k8svcaccount"
SQLSYSADMINACCOUNTS="SIGNALS\cluadmin" "SIGNALS\SQL Server 2008 Admins"
QUIET="TRUE"
INDICATEPROGRESS="TRUE"
```

Say that you have saved this file on your file system with the name InstallSQL.ini. You can then install a clustered instance of SQL Server 2008 by running the following command:

```
Setup.exe /ConfigurationFile="InstallSQL.ini"
```

If you stripped out AGTSVCPASSWORD and SQLSVCPASSWORD from the INI file for security reasons, you can add those values at runtime. The following is a sample command to initiate an installation with passwords:

```
Setup.exe /ConfigurationFile="InstallSQL.ini"
/AGTSVCPASSWORD="P@ssword1" /SQLSVCPASSWORD="P@ssword1"
```

Add Nodes to the Instance

Once the first node is installed, you have to add the other nodes to the clustered instance. The process and overall approach (command line, INI, or Setup interface) are similar to adding the first node.

Using the SQL Server Setup Interface

This section will show how to add a node to a clustered SQL Server 2008 instance using the graphical user interface of Setup. Here are the steps to follow:

1. Log onto the node that you wish to add into the new SQL Server failover clustering instance you created, and start setup.exe from your installation point for SQL Server 2008. You will see the SQL Server Installation Center as shown earlier in Figure 6-8.

2. Select *Installation*. You will then see a new set of options as shown earlier in Figure 6-10. Select *Add node to a SQL Server failover cluster installation*. The installation will fail at this point if .NET Framework 3.51 SP1 or MSI 4.5 is not installed.

3. The first thing Setup will do is check any common issues that may affect the installation of SQL Server 2008. A sample of a successful check is shown earlier in Figure 6-11. Click OK to continue.

4. On the Setup Support Files dialog, click Install as shown earlier in Figure 6-12. If you are using a slipstream copy of SQL Server 2008 Setup, the updated Setup Support Files will be installed. This installation will update the common files if there are any other instances of SQL Server on the cluster. Once the installation of the files is complete, click Next.

5. Setup will then do another check to ensure that other aspects of the cluster are configured properly to have a supported SQL Server configuration. Warnings are acceptable if they are nonfatal, but they should be investigated. A sample is shown earlier in Figure 6-13. Click Next.

6. On the Product Key dialog, enter your valid product key for SQL Server 2008 and click Next. A sample is shown earlier in Figure 6-14.

7. On the License Terms dialog, read the license terms for SQL Server 2008 and click *I accept the license terms*. A sample is shown earlier in Figure 6-15. Click Next.

8. On the Cluster Node Configuration dialog, in the dropdown, select the instance of SQL Server the node will join. You can only select one instance at a time for installing; you cannot add this node to multiple instances at the same time. The example in Figure 6-44 uses the POWER\WINDOWS named instance. Click Next.

9. On the Service Accounts dialog, enter the passwords for the services associated with the instance you are joining. These would be the passwords associated with the accounts already used for the first node; you cannot change the account that can be used. A sample for the database engine is shown in Figure 6-45 and one for Analysis Services is shown in Figure 6-46. Click Next.

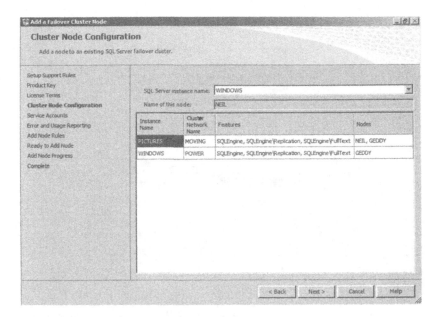

Figure 6-44. *Cluster Node Configuration dialog*

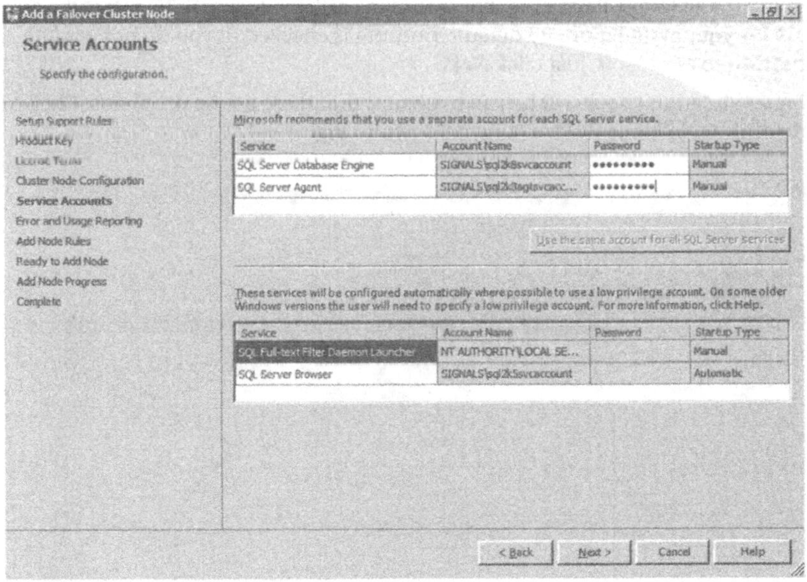

Figure 6-45. *Service Accounts dialog for the database engine*

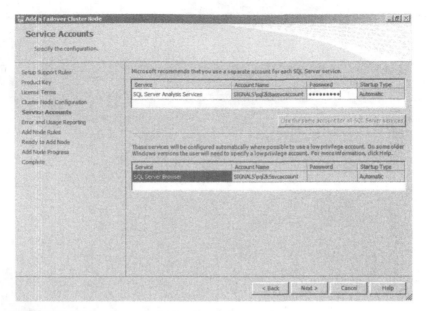

Figure 6-46. *Service Accounts dialog for Analysis Services*

10. On the Error and Usage Reporting dialog shown earlier in Figure 6-35, select the appropriate options for your installation. By default, nothing is checked. If you do not want to send any information to Microsoft, just click Next.

11. One final validation check will be run to ensure that there are no problems. Click Next. A sample of the Add Node Rules dialog is shown in Figure 6-47.

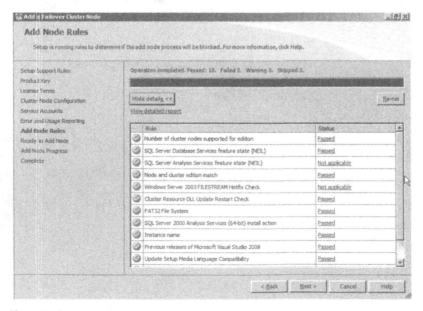

Figure 6-47. *Add Node Rules dialog*

12. On the Ready to Add Node dialog, which you see in Figure 6-48, click Install.

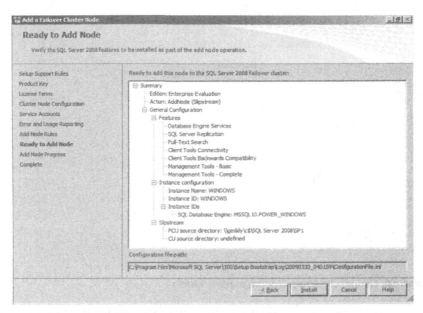

Figure 6-48. *Ready to Add Node dialog*

13. When complete, a successful database engine installation will look like Figure 6-49 and an Analysis Services installation will look like Figure 6-50. If a reboot is required, you will see the message shown earlier in Figure 6-40. Click Next.

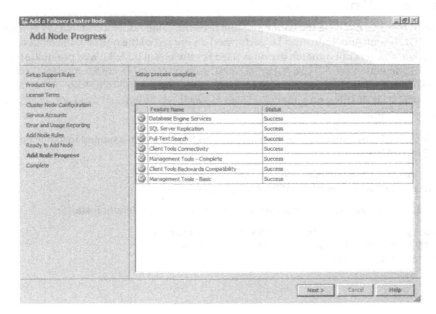

Figure 6-49. *Completed database engine installation*

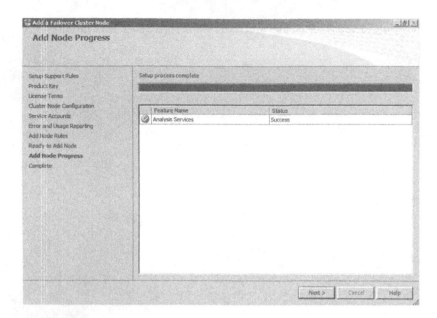

Figure 6-50. *Completed Analysis Services installation*

14. Click Close on the dialog shown earlier in Figure 6-41. Note the location of the log files for this installation. You can click the link shown and review the summary. If a reboot is required, the message shown earlier in Figure 6-42 will be shown; click OK.

15. Repeat steps 1–14 for each additional node that will be added to the instance.

Using the Command Line

The command to add a node via the command line uses the value AddNode for ACTION as indicated in Table 6-1. The action AddNode must be performed on the rest of the nodes of the failover cluster. All values for parameters must match the ones used for the initial install. Valid parameters for use with the AddNode action are ACTION, AGTSVCACCOUNT, AGTSVCACCOUNTPASSWORD, ASSVCACCOUNT, ASSVCPASSWORD, CONFIGURATIONFILE, HIDECONSOLE, INDICATEPROCESS, INSTANCENAME, ISSVCPASSWORD, PID, Q, QS, RSINSTALLMODE (files-only mode), RSSVCPASSWORD, SQLSVCACCOUNT, and SQLSVCPASSWORD.

Here are two samples:

- Adding a node to a clustered instance of Analysis Services with a named instance name of VAPOR\TRAILS:

```
setup.exe /ACTION=AddNode /INSTANCENAME="TRAILS"
/ASSVCPASSWORD="P@ssword1" /INDICATEPROGRESS /Q
```

- Adding a node to a clustered instance of SQL Server that is a default instance:

```
setup.exe /ACTION=AddNode /INSTANCENAME="MSSQLSERVER"
 /AGTSVCPASSWORD="P@ssword1" /SQLSVCPASSWORD="P@ssword1"
/INDICATEPROGRESS /Q
```

Using an INI File

The INI file uses the same options as the command line for the AddNode operation. This example adds a node to the default instance created earlier:

```
[SQLSERVER2008]
ACTION="AddNode"
AGTSVCPASSWORD="P@ssword1"
INDICATEPROGRESS="TRUE"
INSTANCENAME="MSSQLSERVER"
QUIET="TRUE"
SQLSVCPASSWORD="P@ssword1"
```

If you saved these lines as a file named AddNode.ini, on the node that you wish to add, you can then add that node by executing the following command:

```
Setup.exe /ConfigurationFile="AddNode.ini"
```

If you stripped out AGTSVCPASSWORD and SQLSVCPASSWORD for security reasons, execute the command by passing the username and password as parameters, for example:

```
Setup.exe /ConfigurationFile="AddNode.ini"
/AGTSVCPASSWORD="P@ssword1" /SQLSVCPASSWORD="P@ssword1"
```

Method 2: Installing Using Cluster Preparation

A new method for installing a clustered instance of SQL Server 2008 is known as *cluster preparation*. It allows you to configure each node, and then whenever you want to complete the configuration, it is ready and done with one final step. This section will show how to install a new failover clustering instance of SQL Server 2008 using cluster preparation.

Using the SQL Server Setup User Interface, Step 1: Prepare the Nodes

First the cluster nodes must be prepared. Follow the instructions in this section to prepare the nodes for the installation of the failover clustering instance. Here is what you need to do:

1. Start setup.exe from your installation point for SQL Server 2008. After it is loaded, you will see the SQL Server Installation Center as shown earlier in Figure 6-9.

2. Select *Advanced*. You will then see a new set of options as shown in Figure 6-51. Select *Advanced cluster preparation*. The installation will fail at this point if .NET Framework 3.51 SP1 or MSI 4.5 is not installed.

3. Follow steps 3–11 from the "Using the SQL Server Setup User Interface" in the "Install the First Node" section.

4. Follow steps 15–17 from the "Using the SQL Server Setup User Interface" in the "Install the First Node" section.

5. On the Error and Usage Reporting dialog shown earlier in Figure 6-35, by default, nothing is selected. If you want to send information to Microsoft, check the appropriate boxes and click Next to continue.

6. There will be one final check to ensure that everything is fine and the installation can proceed. If there are any warnings or problems, investigate them. A sample is shown in Figure 6-52. Click Next.

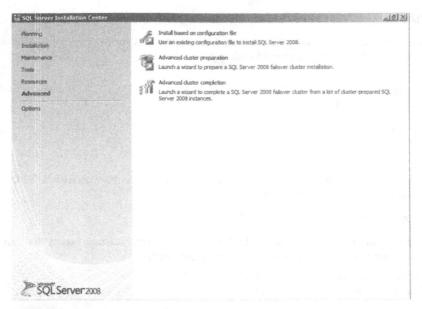

Figure 6-51. *Advanced installation options for SQL Server 2008*

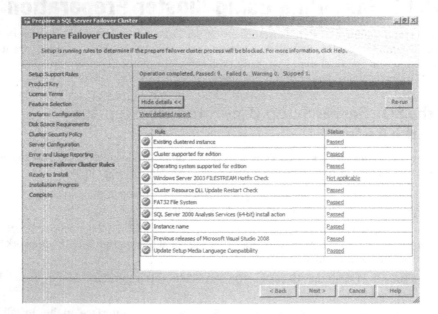

Figure 6-52. *Prepare Failover Cluster Rules dialog*

7. On the Ready to Install dialog shown in Figure 6-53, verify your settings. Click Install.

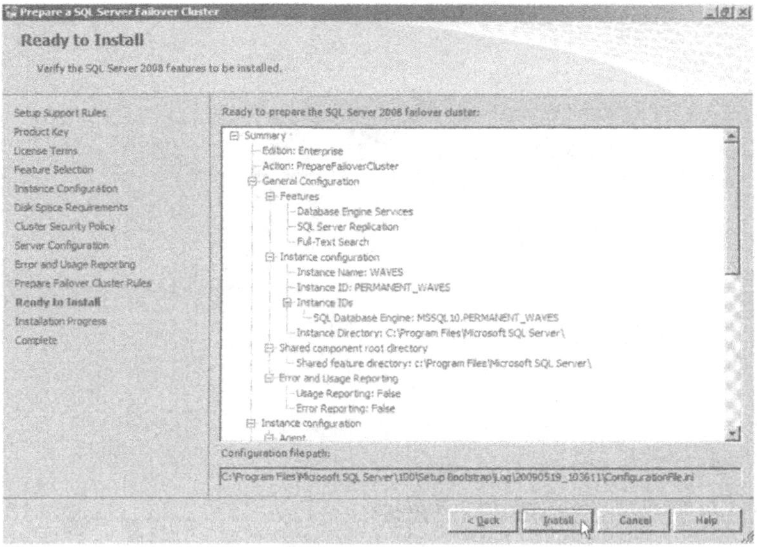

Figure 6-53. *Ready to Install dialog*

8. When complete, a successful database engine installation will look like Figure 6-38 shown earlier and an Analysis Services installation will look like Figure 6-39 shown earlier. If a reboot is required, you will see the message shown earlier in Figure 6-40. Click Next.

9. Click Close on the dialog shown earlier in Figure 6-41. Note the location of the log files for this installation. You can click the link shown and review the summary. If a reboot is required, the message shown earlier in Figure 6-42 will display; click OK.

10. Repeat all steps for every node that will be part of the clustered SQL Server instance.

Using the SQL Server Setup User Interface, Step 2: Complete Nodes

After preparing the nodes, the preparation process must be completed. Follow the instructions in this section to finish the configuration of the clustered instance.

1. Start setup.exe from your installation point for SQL Server 2008. After the file is loaded, you will see the SQL Server Installation Center as shown earlier in Figure 6-9.

2. Select *Advanced*. You will then see a new set of options as shown earlier in Figure 6-51. Select *Advanced cluster completion*. The installation will fail at this point if .NET Framework 3.51 SP1 or MSI 4.5 is not installed.

3. Follow steps 3–8 of the "Using the SQL Server Setup User Interface" in the "Install the First Node" section.

4. On the Cluster Node Configuration dialog, in the dropdown, select the instance of SQL Server that will be completed. Enter the network name that will be used by the instance. You can add only one instance at a time. The example in Figure 6-54 uses the PERMANENT\WAVES named instance. Click Next.

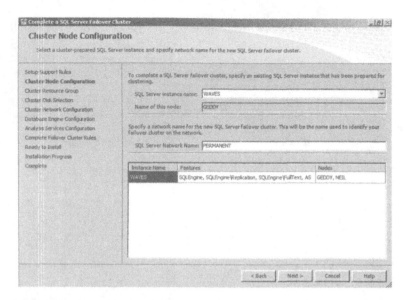

Figure 6-54. *Cluster Node Configuration dialog*

5. Follow steps 12–14 of the "Using the SQL Server Setup User Interface" in the "Install the First Node" section.

6. Follow steps 18 and 19 of the "Using the SQL Server Setup User Interface" in the "Install the First Node" section.

7. There will be one final check to ensure that everything is fine and the installation can proceed. If there are any warnings or problems, investigate them. A sample is shown earlier in Figure 6-36. Click Next.

8. On the Ready to Install dialog in Figure 6-55, verify your settings. Click Install.

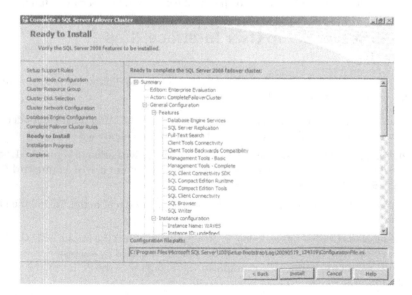

Figure 6-55. *Ready to Install dialog*

9. When complete, a successful database engine installation will look like Figure 6-38 shown earlier and an Analysis Services installation will look like Figure 6-39 shown earlier. If a reboot is required, you will see the message shown earlier in Figure 6-40. Click Next.

10. Click Close on the dialog shown earlier in Figure 6-41. Note the location of the log files for this installation. You can click the link shown and review the summary. If a reboot is required, the message shown earlier in Figure 6-42 will be shown; click OK.

Using the Command Line

There are two different actions associated with this advanced cluster installation technique: PrepareFailoverCluster and CompleteFailoverCluster.

The following example prepares an instance of SQL Server 2008 to have a named instance. Remember that this command must be executed on every node of the cluster.

```
setup.exe /ACTION=PrepareFailoverCluster
/AGTSVCACCOUNT="SIGNALS\sql2k8agtsvcaccount" /AGTSVCPASSWORD="P@ssword1"
/ERRORREPORTING=0 /FEATURES=SQL,BC,Conn,ADV_SSMS /FILESTREAMLEVEL=0
/INSTANCEID="HEMISPHERES" /INSTANCENAME=WAVES
/SQLSVCACCOUNT="SIGNALS\sql2k8svcaccount" /SQLSVCPASSWORD="P@ssword1"
/Q /INDICATEPROGRESS
```

The next example completes the configuration, and has to be run only once:

```
setup.exe /ACTION=CompleteFailoverCluster
/FAILOVERCLUSTERDISKS="Cluster Disk 4" "Cluster Disk 5"
/FAILOVERCLUSTERGROUP="PERMANENT\WAVES"
/FAILOVERCLUSTERIPADDRESSES="IPv4;130.131.132.68;Public Network;255.255.0.0"
/FAILOVERCLUSTERNETWORKNAME="PERMANENT" /FILESTREAMLEVEL=0
/INSTALLSQLDATADIR="G:\SQL Data" /INSTANCENAME=WAVES
/SECURITYMODE=SQL /SAPWD="P@ssword1" /SQLBACKUPDIR="G:\SQL Backups"
/SQLCOLLATION="SQL_Latin1_General_CP1_CI_AS"
/SQLSYSADMINACCOUNTS="SIGNALS\cluadmin" "SIGNALS\SQL Server 2008 Admins"
/Q /INDICATEPROGRESS
```

Using an INI File

You have the option of placing your command line parameters into an INI file. The following is an example of an INI file to prepare an installation:

```
[SQLSERVER2008]
ACTION="PrepareFailoverCluster"
AGTSVCACCOUNT="SIGNALS\sql2k8agtsvcaccount"
AGTSVCPASSWORD="P@ssword1"
ERRORREPORTING=0
FEATURES=SQL,BC,Conn,ADV_SSMS
FILESTREAMLEVEL=0
INSTANCEID="HEMISPHERES"
INSTANCENAME="MSSQLSERVER"
PCUSOURCE="C:\SQL Server 2008\SP1"
SQLSVCACCOUNT="SIGNALS\sql2k8svcaccount"
SQLSVCPASSWORD="P@ssword1 "
QUIET="TRUE"
INDICATEPROGRESS="TRUE"
```

You will also need an INI file for the completion step. Here's an example of such a file:

```
[SQLSERVER2008]
ACTION="CompleteFailoverCluster"
FAILOVERCLUSTERDISKS="Cluster Disk 3" "Cluster Disk 4"
FAILOVERCLUSTERGROUP="SQL2K8 - HEMISPHERES"
FAILOVERCLUSTERIPADDRESSES="IPv4;130.131.132.68;Public Network;255.255.0.0"
FAILOVERCLUSTERNETWORKNAME="HEMISPHERES"
INSTALLSQLDATADIR="F:\SQL Data"
INSTANCENAME="MSSQLSERVER"
PCUSOURCE="C:\SQL Server 2008\SP1"
SECURITYMODE="SQL"
SAPWD="P@ssword1"
SQLBACKUPDIR="F:\SQL Backups"
SQLCOLLATION="SQL_Latin1_General_CP1_CI_AS"
SQLSYSADMINACCOUNTS="SIGNALS\cluadmin" "SIGNALS\SQL Server 2008 Admins"
QUIET="TRUE"
INDICATEPROGRESS="TRUE"
```

Say that you have the preceding two files, and that you have named them PrepareSQL.ini and CompleteSQL.ini. You can then prepare and install a clustered instance of SQL Server 2008 using just two commands:

```
Setup.exe /ConfigurationFile="PrepareSQL.ini"
Setup.exe /ConfigurationFile="CompleteSQL.ini"
```

Remember that the preparation step must be run on each node prior to completing the configuration.

If you stripped out AGTSVCPASSWORD and SQLSVCPASSWORD from the INI files for security reasons, then pass in your passwords on the command line, for example:

```
Setup.exe /ConfigurationFile="PrepareSQL.ini"
/AGTSVCPASSWORD="P@ssword1" /SQLSVCPASSWORD="P@ssword1"
Setup.exe /ConfigurationFile="CompleteSQL.ini" /SAPWD="P@ssword1"
```

GUI, COMMAND LINE, PREPARATION, AND INI FILES . . . OH MY!

As you can tell, you have a plethora of options to install a new clustered instance of SQL Server 2008. That is both good and bad. Sometimes too many choices is not a good thing, especially in the end when the approaches are all pretty close.

Which approach is the best for you? It is going to depend on your needs and the way you like to work. I would argue that most will stick to the GUI. That is fine, but the GUI becomes cumbersome if you have more than a handful of installations to perform. At some point, clicking, typing, and waiting becomes counterproductive. In my experience, SQL Server 2008 is slow to install if you use the GUI. I've used it on various systems of all sizes. I know the Microsoft guys who are reading this may not like me saying it, but I've had a long history with the product. The GUI is just not the most efficient way to get an installation completed quickly. Do not confuse being a bit slow with unusable; the GUI is quite usable and works every time for me. My hope is that the GUI improves in the future.

The Cluster Preparation option is a nice idea. But in my opinion, it does not buy you anything over doing a standard installation. The initial part takes nearly as long if not just as long as doing a regular first node and then all additional node installation. Maybe if I was not deploying for awhile but wanted to get as much work done up front as possible, and then all I had to do was to do the final steps, maybe I would use the Cluster Preparation option. I would have preferred Microsoft implement a true cluster configuration preparation that would allow you to store templates for various SQL Server configurations. That to me is a true preparation type of task. Maybe when and if an alternate method outside of SQL Server (such as sysprep) is supported, cluster preparation will be a much more useful feature when you are deploying large, multinode (four or more nodes) failover clusters. For a two-node failover cluster, cluster preparation does not make a lot of sense.

The straight `setup.exe` command line approach is a bit of a pain for obvious reasons. Sure, you could create a batch file and parameterize it, but at that point the effort seems a bit wasted. To me, the easiest way to install a SQL Server 2008 failover cluster is to create your own INI file and then modify it with the specific parameters you need for each installation, or have some tool that will make the modifications for you. SQL Server Setup has that technically built in—you can get to the end of the Setup GUI, click Cancel, and get the INI file, but at least for me, that is not optimal. I'd rather have a much quicker, streamlined utility to create the INI file.

Method 3: Perform Postinstallation Tasks

After performing the initial installation steps, you must execute some tasks to finish the configuration of your SQL Server or Analysis Services failover cluster. You may want to use the postinstallation checklist included with the downloads when you execute each task.

Verify the Configuration

Once the SQL Server 2008 failover clustering instance is fully configured, you must ensure that it works properly. If you do not, a failure to test might result in big problems for installing SQL Server and the stability of your production platform.

Review All Logs

One of the easiest things to do to ensure that the cluster is up and running properly is to look at the various logs (Cluster, all of the Windows ones, and the SQL Server installation logs). If there are serious problems, more than likely they will first start appearing in the log files. The SQL Server installation logs are found under `X:\Program Files\Microsoft SQL Server\100\SetupBootstrap\Log`, where X is your installation for the programs. There will be dated directories for each installation attempt.

Verify Failover, Network Connectivity, and Cluster Name Resolution

All nodes should be able to access the SQL Server resources in the cluster. The easiest way to verify this is to force a failover of the SQL Server failover clustering instance to another node. The process for testing failover is the same as the one documented in Chapter 4 in the section "Validate Resource Failover." To test the failover, you would use the application/resource group name for the SQL Server instance that you configured using your preferred method of failover (Failover Cluster Management, `cluster.exe`, or PowerShell).

You also must check that you can access the name and IP address of the newly installed SQL Server 2008 instance. This must be done not only on the node that currently owns the SQL Server resources, but all nodes that are potential owners. The steps to test IP address and name resolution are the same as the ones documented in the section "Verify Network Connectivity and Name Resolution" in Chapter 4, except you would substitute the IP address for the newly installed SQL Server instance as well as the network name (in the case of a named instance, the part before the slash). Remember to do this from every node in the cluster as well as from outside the cluster.

Finally, try connecting to the instance using SQL Server Management Studio. Since that will be the main tool that you will be using to manage your instance, ensuring that you can connect to the instance using Management Studio is essential.

If you are having name or IP resolution issues, you may have to do one of three things:

1. Check to see if the TCP/IP port used by the SQL Server instance is defined as an exception in Windows Firewall on all nodes of the cluster.

2. If the TCP/IP port is defined as an exception, troubleshoot the physical network.

3. When pinging the IP address or name, or connecting using SQL Server Management Studio, if you customized the port number, you may have to add it to the connection string. Consider this example: an instance named ROBOTO has a TCP/IP address of 130.131.132.133 with a port of 59000. To add the port to the connection string, use a comma and add the port. So it would look like either ROBOTO,59000 or 130.131.132.133,59000.

Verify the Disk Configuration

Use the dynamic management view (DMV) sys.dm_io_cluster_shared_drives to be able to see what drives are associated with the clustered SQL Server. You must have VIEW SERVER STATE permissions to query the view. Figure 6-56 shows an example of querying sys.dm_io_cluster_shared_drives.

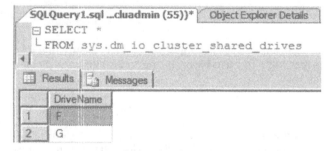

Figure 6-56. *Output of sys.dm_io_cluster_shared_drives*

Verify the Node Configuration

After checking the drive configuration, execute a similar query using the DMV sys.dm_os_cluster_nodes to be able to see what nodes are associated with the clustered SQL Server. You must have VIEW SERVER STATE permissions to query the view. Figure 6-57 shows an example of querying sys.dm_os_cluster_nodes.

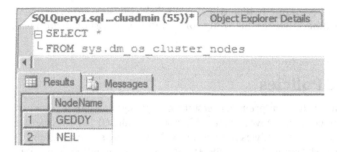

Figure 6-57. *Output of sys.dm_os_cluster_nodes for a two-node cluster*

Install SQL Server Service Packs, Patches, and Hotfixes

If you have not already slipstreamed the updates you need, now is the time to apply any SQL Server service packs, security updates, and/or hotfixes to the newly installed SQL Server 2008 instance as deemed necessary or required by the application or your corporate IT group and its standards. Remember to do the installations on each node of the cluster. Chapter 8 shows how to update a SQL Server 2008 instance in the section "Patching a SQL Server 2008 Failover Clustering Instance."

Remove Empty Cluster Disk Resource Groups

Assuming that you added multiple disks during the installation, the SQL Server 2008 installation moves those disk resources from the resource group where each disk resource was located into the resource group containing the SQL Server 2008 resources. For a Windows Server 2008–based failover cluster, there is nothing that needs to be done since the disks come out of the centralized Available Storage resource group.

Under Windows Server 2003, it is a different story. The SQL Server 2008 installer does not clean up after itself and leaves the empty groups that once housed the disk resources now in use by the SQL Server 2008 instance. To delete the empty groups on a Windows Server 2003–based failover cluster, use the steps in one of the following subsections.

Using Cluster Administrator

Execute the following steps to delete a group using the GUI-based Windows Server 2003 Cluster Administrator tool:

1. Start Cluster Administrator.

2. Expand Groups in the left-hand pane.

3. Select one of the resource groups that is currently empty.

4. Right-click the group and select Delete.

Using cluster.exe

Use the following command to delete a group from the command line:

```
cluster <cluster name> group <group name> /DELETE
```

If you are unsure of the empty group's name (which will most likely be Physical Disk *N* if it was left the default name, where *N* is a number), use the following command to see a list of all groups:

```
cluster <cluster name> group
```

Set the Resource Failure Policies

SQL Server 2008 behaves slightly differently from previous versions of SQL Server when it comes to installing SQL Server and Analysis Services in a failover cluster. When you install SQL Server, whether or not it is combined in the same group with Analysis Services, it will always be set to attempt to restart and then fail to another node as shown in Figure 6-58. Analysis Services, whether or not it is in the same group with SQL Server, is always set to not restart as shown in Figure 6-59. Now, you shouldn't combine both SQL Server (the database engine) and Analysis Services in the same installation as talked about in Chapter 5, and setting the Analysis Services cluster resource to not restart makes sense only if both SQL Server and Analysis Services were combined in the same group because you don't want Analysis Services taking out SQL Server or vice versa. However, if you are clustering only Analysis Services, you would want Analysis Services to automatically fail over to another node if a problem is encountered. Do not change the default settings for SQL Server unless you have to.

To change failure policies, follow these instructions:

1. Start Failover Cluster Management.

2. Expand the cluster, select *Services and Applications*, and select the SQL Server instance.

3. Double-click the SQL Server or Analysis Services resource, select the *Policies* tab, and set the appropriate settings. Figures 6-58 and 6-59 show the *Policies* tab for SQL Server and for Analysis Services, respectively.

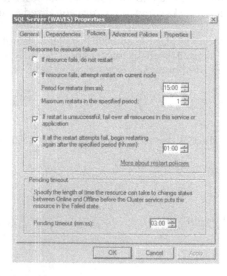

Figure 6-58. *SQL Server resource failure policy*

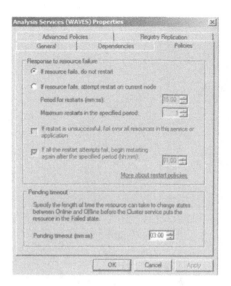

Figure 6-59. *Analysis Services resource failure policy*

Set the Preferred Node Order for Failover

If your cluster has more than two nodes and your clustered SQL Server instance also uses more than two of the nodes, you can alter the order in which the resource group containing SQL Server or Analysis Services will fail over to other nodes. With Windows Server 2008, how the preferred node functionality of a Windows Server 2008 failover cluster works is a bit different than in previous versions of Windows. In previous versions of Windows, once you set the order, that was the order it always tried to work in—no ifs, ands, or buts. However, with Windows Server 2008, there are two levels at play. First, you set the order as you did in the past. However, next to each node name there is also a check box. If the check box is checked, those are truly the nodes you want as preferred nodes; however, even if a node is not checked, as long as the node was added to the SQL Server instance, the group will be able to fail over to that node. The bottom line is that checked nodes come first, and everything else comes afterward.

Here's the procedure to follow:

1. Start Failover Cluster Management.

2. Expand the cluster, select *Services and Applications*, and select the application/resource group containing the resources associated with the clustered SQL Server instance.

3. Right-click and select *Properties*.

4. On the *General* tab, select the preferred owner order by checking the box next to the nodes and moving them up and down in the order using the Up and Down buttons. In the example shown in Figure 6-60, there are three nodes (GEDDY, ALEX2, and NEIL) that can own the SQL Server resources. GEDDY and ALEX are the preferred owners in that order, but if either of those is unavailable, they will fail over to NEIL even though it is not selected as a preferred owner.

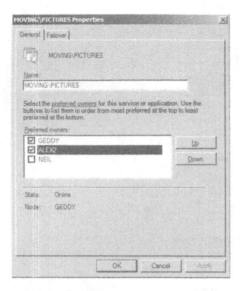

Figure 6-60. *Modified preferred failover order*

Configure a Static TCP/IP Port for the SQL Server Instance

To further secure the newly installed instance of SQL Server, pick a static—not a dynamic or known—port. Think of a port this way: a password is like a lock that is hard to pick. A custom IP address is like hiding the entry. Changing the port associated with the TCP/IP address is like moving the lock so that even if a potential intruder could find the entry and pick the lock, the security system should still trip the alarm bells. Here's how to change the TCP/IP port:

1. From the Start menu, select *All Programs*, then *Microsoft SQL Server 2008, Configuration Tools*, and finally *SQL Server Configuration Manager.*

2. Select *Protocols* for the instance you are altering, and then double-click *TCP/IP.*

3. Select the *IP Addresses* tab of the TCP/IP properties and scroll down to the *IPAll* section. A single instance of SQL Server will by default look like Figure 6-61 with a default port of 1433. Figure 6-62 shows a second instance on a cluster where the dynamic port has been set (*TCP Dynamic Ports* value). If a value has been set for *TCP Dynamic Ports*, delete it. Enter a manual port other than 1433 for the specified instance in *TCP Port*. Click OK.

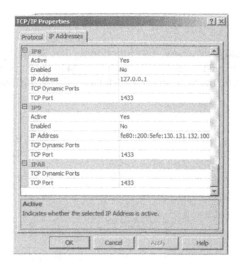

Figure 6-61. *Default port setting of 1433 for a first instance of SQL Server*

■**Caution** Ensure that the firewall configuration both on the nodes and on the network is opened for that TCP port that was just set (in addition to the other TCP and UDP ports mentioned back in Chapter 2). If not, you will be able to administer only the SQL Server instance. To add the port to the firewall exception rules, follow the instructions in the section "Configure Windows Firewall" at the end of Chapter 3.

Figure 6-62. *Dynamic port settings for a second instance of SQL Server*

Summary

It's taken a while to get here, but now you should have a new, fully functioning SQL Server 2008 failover clustering instance. To learn how to administer your new installation, skip to Chapter 8. If you need to upgrade some existing SQL Server 2000 or SQL Server 2005 failover clustering instances to SQL Server 2008, continue to Chapter 7.

■ ■ ■

Upgrading to SQL Server 2008 Failover Clustering

Not everyone will be installing only new instances of SQL Server 2008. Some of you may just want to upgrade existing clustered instances of SQL Server to SQL Server 2008. This chapter will discuss some of the foundations of performing an upgrade, the technical considerations for upgrading to SQL Server 2008 failover clustering, and finally, how to upgrade to SQL Server 2008 failover clustering.

■**Tip** There are many more aspects to upgrading to SQL Server 2008 than I can ever cover in a single chapter. Microsoft has published an excellent and free resource (which I also authored a portion of) that you can use in conjunction with this chapter. It is called the SQL Server 2008 Upgrade Technical Reference Guide, and can be found at http://www.microsoft.com/downloads/details.aspx?FamilyID=66d3e6f5-6902-4fdd-af75-9975aea5bea7&displaylang=en.

Upgrade Basics

Before discussing technical considerations, I want to first address some general issues that will affect any upgrade you would attempt to perform. My intention here is to lay a solid foundation so that even if you do not use the additional information contained in the SQL Server 2008 Upgrade Technical Reference Guide, you will still be able to perform an upgrade and think about more than the technical issues.

Taking Into Account the Application

This chapter is really about SQL Server instances and databases, but when have you ever just had to deal with a database (or an instance) and not worry about the application? The application is arguably the most important, and ignored, aspect of a back end upgrade. Never assume that because you want or need to move to SQL Server 2008 from an IT perspective that the application can go along for the ride automatically. There are two types of applications: ones developed in-house and ones that are purchased from vendors such as Microsoft.

In-house applications are both easier and in some cases, harder to deal with. While some applications have had constant development or bug fixes over the years, others may have been untouched for years. The problem you will face in both cases is having the right development expertise to be able to address any issues that may come up during testing or post-migration. Many applications were either developed by consultants who are no longer assisting you, or by former full-time employees who may not have been in the employ of your company for quite a few years. An even bigger issue is this: do you even have the source code to update and fix as well as the right development environment to do it in?

Applications that were purchased (or inherited via company acquisitions) are a bit more straightforward. The vendor will either support or not support SQL Server 2008. They may dictate a certain patch level of SQL Server 2008. Here is the problem though: the version of the application that supports SQL Server 2008 may not be the version that is currently deployed. The reasons why this is a problem can be boiled down to two main bullet points:

- There may be a cost involved in acquiring the version of the application that does support SQL Server 2008. That means this cost must be factored into the overall cost of upgrading to SQL Server 2008. If there is no budget to acquire the version of the application that supports SQL Server 2008, do not upgrade to SQL Server 2008. You may put yourself at risk when it comes to supportability of the application (assuming you have support), and if you do upgrade, you do not know if it will work properly.

- Assuming you can get the version of the application for SQL Server 2008, are there any changes in functionality, in the user interface, and so on? Not only are you looking at a back end upgrade, but an upgrade of the application itself that must also be planned for. This would also include any training and support that end users would need to be able to use the new version of the application. End user pain is never a good thing.

The one thing that must be done, whether the application is one you purchased or developed in-house, is to discover what application-related steps and considerations must be taken into account in the overall upgrade process. Chances are there are some specific things that must be done prior to the SQL Server upgrade, as well as after the upgrade. I am not talking about just testing; I'm talking about things that will prevent the application from functioning properly post–SQL Server upgrade if they're not done. The tasks I am referring to are ones that the DBA would not perform, nor would they know if they did not ask the right questions of the application owner. For example, there is a custom program or script supplied by the application vendor that must be run after SQL Server and the database is upgraded that manipulates the schema and data. The DBA is not the application expert, so there is virtually no chance that he or she will know this needs to be run. Also, in the case of having no application expertise in-house (such as when it is an old application that no one has touched in years), try and find the vendor (or consultant you hired who wrote it). If you can't do that, it might be worth leaving that application alone until the right resources are found, or you may want to consider virtualizing it for fear of messing up its configuration.

Here's the bottom line when it comes to applications and upgrading your back end: do not upgrade your back end if it will put supportability of the application at risk, or if it will potentially destabilize the application itself. After the upgrade, the end users are expecting the same experience (or possibly even better in terms of performance); they are not expecting it to be worse. Upgrading for the sake of upgrading is never the right thing to do.

DATABASE COMPATIBILITY LEVEL

One very useful feature that was introduced in SQL Server 2000 was the compatibility level you can configure for each database. The problem is that compatibility level is not only a misunderstood feature, but it has also become a crutch for many applications and DBAs. The whole premise of compatibility level is that if it is set for anything other than the version of SQL Server that is deployed (100, or 10.0 for SQL Server 2008), when the database engine goes to execute a query and certain behaviors are different than the currently deployed version, it will try its best to emulate those behaviors if possible. Setting compatibility level of a database to an earlier version of SQL Server (such as 2000) than the version deployed does not mean that all of a sudden your SQL Server 2008 failover clustering instance will become SQL Server 2000. The reason this has become a crutch is that I have seen where may people use compatibility level to avoid properly testing and fixing issues their application may have with newer behaviors. This avoidance may save some time in the short term, but will come back and bite you in the end. For example, the only compatibility levels in SQL Server 2008 are for SQL Server 2000, 2005, and 2008. A lot of people in their upgrades to either SQL Server 2000 or 2005 from SQL Server 6.5 or 7.0 used their respective compatibility levels of 65 or 70. So all of that work that was avoided for 10 years or more now has to be dealt with. My recommendation is to always ensure that in the testing of a database to be upgraded, you set the compatibility level to the version you have deployed, and only change it if absolutely necessary.

Mitigate Risk

While the goal is to always upgrade an existing SQL Server failover cluster successfully, getting there is the result of careful planning, which is ultimately about risk mitigation. This section will talk about the factors that go into mitigating risk during an upgrade.

Devise the Right Upgrade Plan

An upgrade plan is more than a series of technical steps, just like a new implementation is more than a series of technical steps. As much as a plan is important for a new failover cluster, when it comes to an upgrade, it is arguably more important because you are affecting something already in production. Many applications have time constraints. For example, you may not be able to touch the accounting department's databases or instances for their applications for 1 week prior to and after month end close and quarterly close, and for the entire month before and after year end close. That timeframe will certainly narrow down when the upgrade can occur. Even if you figure out the appropriate time, depending on your SLAs, your window for the upgrade will still be fairly small. If you are bound to guarantee only a certain amount of downtime, you need to ensure that the plan meets or exceeds expectations. If you cannot meet the SLA, have frank and open discussions about the implications of that with the application owner and the business. They may be upset, and there may be other repercussions, but it is better to know ahead of time than be surprised afterward that things took longer than expected.

Remember that the timeline may cross groups and steps need to be performed in order. Chances are there are some steps that need to be done by others as well.

When choosing your upgrade method, also make sure that it is one that can be managed and performed by your staff. As I always say to my clients when I work with them, many solutions look great on paper—no matter how much they cost—but if the solution is not one that is workable, it is the wrong solution. Never be pressured into doing something you know will cause more harm than good.

Staff Appropriately

An upgrade touches every group in one way or another. Even if the plan only encompasses SQL Server (assuming the application or other aspects of the infrastructure are not touched), the other groups will either need to be on call or involved in some way. For example, once SQL Server is upgraded, you will want testers for all applications affected by the back end upgrade to test the applications. From a DBA perspective, staff in appropriate shifts where there is a balance of senior and junior DBAs. Realize that the upgrade may take quite a bit of time and if something does happen to go awry, you will need people who are refreshed and not tired. Working a 24-hour shift (or more) is not a good thing. You may want to consider hiring temporary experienced workers to assist if you do not have the expertise in-house.

Upgrades are also about setting expectations with application owners and the end users. Besides clear and effective communication all throughout the process such as e-mails detailing what they need to do, when things will happen, and so on, realize that there will be some nervous folks on the Monday morning after a major change. It has the potential to be chaotic. This means that you should probably have extra staff on hand to deal with any issues that come up, whether they are major or minor. In fact, you should probably have extra staff on hand for at least a week and scale back or gear up accordingly depending on how the week progresses.

Test . . . and Test Some More

Extended downtime is a symptom of being unprepared, missing steps, or not knowing what is going to happen. This generally only happens when testing does not occur. Lack of testing is the barrier to success. Testing is a serious commitment from the entire organization, and is the first thing that is generally cut in the timeline, but the one item that is crucial for success. When the users come in to log onto their computers at 9 a.m., they are expecting everything to work. That does not happen by osmosis.

The only way to mitigate that risk is to do a complete "dry run" of the plan from step A to step Z. As problems are encountered, workarounds can be devised and documented, as well as major problems completely resolved. Testing the plan is only one level of testing. Each application that will be upgraded must be tested against the target platform before the upgrade, as well as after the upgrade or cutover. The test after is often based on a top N list of the functionality that is most used in the application, and must be done by the normal testers. You should not rely on DBAs or anyone else to do that testing, as they are arguably the least familiar with it.

You should strive to have test environments that mirror your production environment, or virtual environments that approximate the end state. The closer you are to what production looks like, the higher your chance of success. This is true of an upgrade and anything else in IT. If you will be using new hardware for the target environment, until it "goes live," it is the best sandbox you have. Testing against the actual servers and configuration that will be used is the perfect scenario. However, never use your current production environment as the first place you run anything. That will decrease your chances of success immensely.

Update Administration Skills

One thing that is sometimes lost in the drive to upgrade is that those who will be administering the target platform need to have their skills updated. I am not just talking about upgrading a DBA's skills for SQL Server 2008. If you are going to deploy a new version of Windows or the application, those administrators will also need to update their skills as well. Budget must be earmarked for sending administrators to training, or if you have consultants onsite, have knowledge transfer be part of their mission. Your chances of success post-upgrade are slim if no one knows what to do to administer the environment, even if the upgrade to SQL Server 2008 was successful.

Technical Considerations for Upgrading

This section will introduce the items besides the planning items introduced in Chapters 2 and 5 that are specific to upgrading to a SQL Server 2008 failover cluster.

Types of Upgrades

There are three types of upgrades you can perform when it comes to SQL Server 2008: an in-place upgrade, a side-by-side upgrade, and a migration to new hardware. This section will define each of the upgrade types and introduce various upgrade methods that can be used by both a side-by-side upgrade and a migration to new hardware.

In-Place Upgrade

An in-place upgrade is when you take an existing failover clustering instance on a Windows failover cluster and upgrade it. The one big risk with an in-place upgrade is that if anything goes wrong, you may be left with a broken SQL Server instance. This risk for the most part has been mitigated with changes to the process in SQL Server 2008 (see "Overview of the Upgrade Process" later in this section).

Side-By-Side Upgrade

A side-by-side upgrade is one where you install a new SQL Server 2008 failover clustering instance on the same Windows failover cluster, and then migrate the databases using another technique (see the section "Methods for Upgrading Databases Using Side-by-Side and New Hardware Migrations"). As noted back in Chapter 5, side-by-side installations of SQL Server 2008 and other versions of SQL Server are allowed as long as the version of Windows supports the particular version(s) of SQL Server you are deploying (with some caveats, of course). Side-by-side configurations pose very little risk, but have the following considerations:

- Applications will need to be redirected to the new instance. If they cannot tolerate a new instance name, something will need to be done to mitigate that problem. The right thing to do is fix the application.

- There is no way to ever have a "pure" system again. By that I mean if you decide to uninstall SQL Server 2008, the shared components have been upgraded to SQL Server 2008 and can never be removed, and will be your connectivity layer for any older version of SQL Server.

- Consider this example: Windows Server 2003 will support SQL Server 2000, 2005, and 2008 clustered. If you install a clustered 2000 instance and then a 2008 instance, you cannot run the 2000 install again to configure another 2000 clustered instance after installing the SQL Server 2008 failover clustering instance. That also you means you cannot patch 2000 after 2008 is installed. So your installation order has to be carefully planned, and older versions of SQL Server should be patched and complete prior to 2008 even being installed.

- You may not be able to shut down, disable, decommission, or uninstall the old instance if all databases have not yet been moved and upgraded. If this is the case, you will have to double- and triple-check that no one is connecting to the old database or instance for a given application. This task is tougher if you are using fat clients where the configuration file is stored on each desktop.

- If you need to add a disk under Windows Server 2003 to the server cluster to support the new SQL Server 2008 instance, that may cause some downtime. With Windows Server 2003, adding a disk to a Windows server cluster requires SQL Server to be taken offline to add the disk as a dependency. As is seen in Windows Server 2008 (and documented in Chapter 8), downtime is no longer required for adding a disk unless it is at the Windows or hardware layer.

- Ensure that you do proper capacity planning when adding an instance to a cluster already in production.

You will seriously want to think about and carefully plan for mixed-version SQL Server failover clusters. On paper it may seem like a good idea, but know what it does and does not give you so that you do not get into trouble later.

Migration to New Hardware

Migration to hardware is not unlike a side-by-side upgrade, except you are installing a new failover clustering instance on different hardware instead of on the same Windows failover cluster. All of the same basic considerations apply. However, migrating and ultimately upgrading databases on new hardware has the least amount of risk associated with it since you would have your fallback plan: the original, untouched environment.

Overview of the Upgrade Process

Like Setup has changed for a new installation, upgrading an existing failover clustering instance has also changed with SQL Server 2008. An in-place upgrade is also a per-instance, per-node affair, so Table 5-1 back in Chapter 5 is completely applicable to an upgrade as well. How many upgrade processes you run will depend on the number of instances and the number of nodes.

What is also different is that you essentially perform an in-place upgrade in reverse of what you would think you should do: first you have to upgrade the nodes associated with a particular instance that do not currently own the instance. As each node is upgraded, that node can no longer be used as a failover node until the instance itself is upgraded. So if you have a two-node cluster, you have no failover options, and for all intents and purposes are left with a temporary one-node failover clustering instance. This is demonstrated later, in Figure 7-26 in the section "Step 2: Upgrade the Nodes That Do Not Own the SQL Server Instance (SQL Server Setup User Interface)."

Depending on the number of nodes, the instance itself (and subsequently its databases) is upgraded when one of the following two conditions is met:

- For a two-node cluster, once the upgrade is initiated on the node owning the resources, the SQL Server instance is immediately failed over to the other node. After the failover, the upgrade scripts are run.

- If you have more than two nodes, once more than half (50 percent) of the nodes are upgraded, the failover will occur just as it would with a two-node cluster and the instance itself will be upgraded.

Like installing a new SQL Server instance, upgrading in this manner means more executions of Setup to upgrade an instance. However, you gain increased reliability and shorter downtime, which to me is a decent tradeoff.

Methods for Upgrading Databases Using Side-by-Side and New Hardware Migrations

There are a finite amount of ways to move databases and objects from instance A to instance B. Depending on how you like to work and your overall preferences, you may wind up using some or all of the following techniques.

Backup and Restore

Backing up the source database and then restoring it is the most tried-and-true method of getting a database from instance A to instance B. However, it may not be the most efficient if you have a limited window for performing the upgrade. First and foremost, depending on the size of the database, it may take a while to perform the backup itself. If you have an 8-hour window, and the backup alone takes 3 of those 8 hours, that may put the upgrade operation in jeopardy. Then there is the copy process. VLDBs with sizes in the hundreds of gigabytes or even the terabyte range can take a long time to copy (up to 24 hours or more no matter how good your disk subsystem is, unless you are using advanced techniques like snapshots at a hardware level). Finally, there is the actual restore of the database, which I find on average takes about 50 percent longer than performing the backup. While backup and restore is a tried-and-true method of migrating and upgrading, it is a process that can be time consuming. Also consider how many databases you have: if you have a lot of databases in a given instance, even if they are small, it may not be a trivial amount of work. Make sure that if multiple DBAs are assisting in the upgrade operation, they are assigned their own databases so there is no confusion as to what is being moved; otherwise, work that is complete may be redone and extend the upgrade process.

Log Shipping

Log shipping is my favorite method of moving databases from instance A to instance B. While you cannot use the built-in feature of SQL Server unless you are log shipping to the same major version (you can download the custom log shipping scripts I wrote for the book *Pro SQL Server 2005 High Availability* from the Apress web site or http://www.sqlha.com to log ship from a lower to a higher version of SQL Server), it provides the best way to minimize downtime. You can do your full, point-in-time backup, copy it, and restore it using WITH NORECOVERY or WITH STANDBY long before the time the actual upgrade process begins. You can then set up the automatic backup of transaction logs (which you should already be doing in production to begin with), as well as the automated copy and restore of the transaction log backups. When it comes time to start the upgrade, you only need to worry about any transaction log backups that have not been applied, and grab the tail of the log on the primary database. You should incur minutes, not hours, of downtime. Log shipping is also very easy for DBAs to manage since it is just based on backup and restore.

Database Mirroring

You can use database mirroring to upgrade from SQL Server 2005 to SQL Server 2008, and while it has many of the same qualities as log shipping and has the potential of being even quicker with downtime measured in seconds, database mirroring is an advanced configuration that may not be the right choice for an upgrade.

Detach and Attach

Contrary to what some may think, detach and attach is not analogous to backup and restore. When you detach a database in SQL Server, you then copy all MDF, NDF, and LDF files to the target location, and finally attach the files in the new instance of SQL Server 2008. While the database is detached from the source instance and the files are being copied, the database is completely unavailable. While the risk is low, there is always a small chance that something is wrong and you will not be able to reattach the database files to the original instance. That would not be a desirable situation. From a time perspective, this would be more like backup and restore, where this could not be done until the cutover time, and depending on the size of your files, could take quite some time to copy to the destination.

BCP

BCP is an ancient utility that dates back to the old SQL Server 4.21a and Sybase days of Microsoft SQL Server. If you have to do something radical like recreate the schema and then bulk insert data, BCP will help you with that task. BCP is a command line utility for generating scripts of your data contained in a table. It can either be "dumb," meaning a straight dump of data, or you can specify a query. This would be helpful in the instance where you may want to prune some unused data out of a table on the way into a new SQL Server 2008 deployment by using a query.

Scripting

Scripting is one of the easiest methods for recreating objects in another instance. Scripts are very portable and one of the most powerful tools in a DBA's arsenal. Even if you do not know how to write your own Transact-SQL scripts, many objects can be scripted out by right-clicking an object in either Enterprise Manager (2000) or SQL Server Management Studio (2005). One thing you definitely want to do is script any replication configuration that may need to be recreated.

DTS/SSIS

There are two things to consider when it comes to DTS/SSIS. First, like scripting, it can be a good way to get objects from instance A to instance B if you use the transfer objects tasks that DTS or SSIS provides. Some DBAs may be uncomfortable creating advanced DTS or SSIS packages. The other thing you need to consider with DTS/SSIS is where you are going to put it. As talked about in Chapter 5, SSIS is not cluster-aware, so you will have to figure out where SSIS for SQL Server 2008 will be installed and where the packages will have to be moved to.

Note You may be asking yourself, "What about the system databases?" Well, if you are going to new hardware, you don't do anything with your existing ones. The instance you are going to use has its own master and msdb. Also, you cannot use options like log shipping, database mirroring, and detach/attach for system databases. This is why it is so important to script and do tasks such as synchronizing objects to be able to use the user databases after the move.

Planning for Downtime

Although Setup has been redesigned to minimize downtime during an upgrade, there are times when the instance and databases will be unavailable. There will be some differences in downtime depending on your upgrade method. All nodes will be affected by the installation of .NET Framework 3.51 SP1 or MSI 4.5 if they are not already installed or part of the operating system (see Table 2-5 in Chapter 2). If there are other applications or SQL Server instances, those outages related to installing the prerequisites should be planned for and coordinated with anyone who will be affected by the reboot. While both .NET Framework 3.51 SP1 and MSI 4.5 can be installed at the same time and the node rebooted once, any instance owned by that node will be failed over to another node in the process.

Planning for Downtime During an In-Place Upgrade

Outside of the prerequisite installs that cause downtime, for the nodes that do not own the instance that is being upgraded, the only issue that may cause a reboot is if some of the shared components (such as underlying DLLs) are in use and locked. This is why you should also consider upgrading the shared components at the same time as installing .NET Framework 3.51 SP1 and MSI 4.5. However, during the noninstance upgrades, the instance will be up and running with no downtime.

When it comes to upgrading the instance itself, there is a bit of a gray area. My recommendation is always to stop all traffic to the instance prior to running Setup to ensure that no one is accidentally connecting during the upgrade process. Having said that, the instance can technically be used until Upgrade is clicked. At that point, the instance will immediately be failed over to another node by Setup, as shown later in Figure 7-31. If you are executing a command line–based upgrade (either all command line switches or via an INI file), you really will have no warning. From a high-level perspective, this failover may mean you only have minutes of downtime. Once the instance fails over, all of the databases (system and user) will be upgraded to SQL Server 2008. Depending on how large your databases are and if you use other features such as full-text, this may take a matter of minutes or hours. This is one of the main reasons you need to test the upgrade in an environment other than production so you actually know how long you should estimate for the entire upgrade process to take to complete. If your user databases only take 10 minutes to upgrade, after doing whatever application testing is necessary, you can then allow the end users to access the application again.

This marked improvement in upgrade despite the number of operations means that instead of waiting until all nodes and databases complete the upgrade process, the only thing you should be waiting for is the upgrade of the databases themselves. The change in upgrade should also minimize failures because any failure would be localized to a node or a database.

Planning for Downtime During All Other Upgrades

Side-by-side upgrades and migration to new hardware are completely different beasts when it comes to downtime and unavailability to end users. How much downtime will occur really only depends on the method you choose to move databases and objects from instance A to instance B. As long as you fully test your upgrade process, you should know how long your outage will be.

Figuring Out the Upgrade Order for an In-Place Upgrade with Multiple Instances

Upgrading a cluster that has multiple instances is more challenging because it will involve a bit of timing. Each instance will be affected by an outage at some point even if it is not being upgraded and will be left alone in a side-by-side configuration with SQL Server 2008. This section will walk through an example of a cluster with multiple instances of SQL Server using the SQL Server 2008 interface as the method for upgrading.

The cluster in this example has three Windows Server 2003 nodes (A, B, C, and D), one instance of SQL Server 2000 (SQL 1), and three instances of SQL Server 2005 (2, 3, and 4). Node D is a dedicated failover node. The current state of the cluster is shown in Figure 7-1.

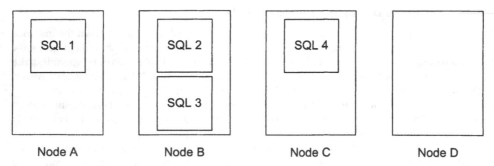

Figure 7-1. *Initial state of the failover cluster pre-upgrade*

With 4 instances of SQL Server over 4 nodes, there will be 16 different executions of Setup to perform the upgrade. Whether you upgrade the lone SQL Server 2000 instance or any of the three SQL Server 2005 instances really does not matter for the sake of this example, but the order of the instance upgrades in your environment will matter depending on factors that would be discovered during your investigation prior to any upgrade.

The first thing to do in this case would be to upgrade the shared components, as well as install .NET Framework 3.5 SP1, MSI 4.5, and the Filestream hotfix (all mentioned in Chapter 2) on Node D, which is the dedicated failover node. In theory, this could even be done during the day, since currently no instances are owned by that node. Node D can be rebooted with no effect on any of the instances or the rest of the cluster, and there are still places for the SQL Server instances to fail over to even if Node D is still finishing the reboot process.

Next, find the appropriate timeframe to also install .NET Framework 3.5 SP1, MSI 4.5, the Filestream hotfix, and the SQL Server 2008 shared files. Assume that every Friday night from midnight to 2 a.m. there is a scheduled maintenance window for the entire production environment. That would be an opportune time to install these components without affecting availability. If there is no maintenance window, work with the appropriate groups (business, application, and IT) to schedule an outage. The installations are all fairly quick and only require a single reboot if done properly. At this point, all nodes are still available for failover for all instances of SQL Server. However, if you cannot schedule an outage to install the prerequisites for SQL Server 2008, they can be done at the time of the first upgrade on that node; it may just extend the outage slightly.

For this example, assume that SQL 1 will be the initial instance to be upgraded. Run the upgrade process on Node D first for SQL 1. Once that upgrade is completed, SQL 1 temporarily will no longer be able to fail over to Node D. Nodes B and C are still options for failing over. Next, upgrade SQL 1 on Node C. Here is where things get a bit more tricky: SQL 4 is currently owned by Node C. Whether a reboot is required or not, coordinate the upgrade of SQL 1 on Node C with the owner of SQL 4's databases to ensure that they are aware of what is going on. Node B would be next, and is similar to Node C's situation: coordinate with the proper groups to let them know a reboot may be required. At this point, there is no failover situation for SQL 1, and the state of the nodes would look something like Figure 7-2. Since this is a GUI-based upgrade, as soon as the upgrade is initiated on Node B, it will trigger the automatic failover since 50 percent (or more) of the nodes have been upgraded. That means that the instance will fail over to C or D and the databases will begin the upgrade process. It should be noted that had a command line–based installation been performed, the parameter FAILOVERCLUSTERROLLOWNERSHIP could have been used to control the failover of the instance (see the section "Upgrading Using the Command Line" later in this chapter for more information on this parameter).

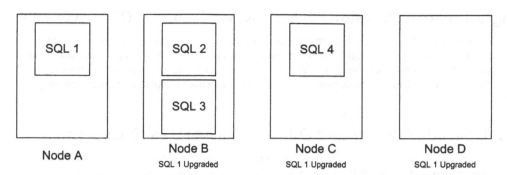

Figure 7-2. *After upgrading the nodes that do not own SQL 1*

At this point, you need to schedule a proper outage to upgrade the actual instance of SQL 1 that is currently owned by Node A. As noted earlier, once the actual upgrade occurs, the SQL Server instance will fail over to another node. Assuming you set the failover preferences for SQL 1 to fail over to Node D first, Node D will now own SQL 1 and the cluster will look like Figure 7-3 when finished. If you want to, you can fail SQL 1 back to Node A if you are still in the outage window, but it is not required.

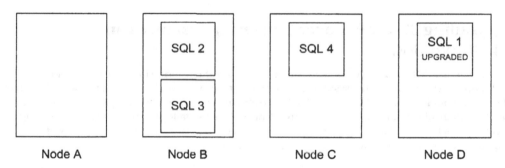

Figure 7-3. *SQL 1 upgrade completed*

SQL 2, 3, and 4 now need to be upgraded. The considerations and process would be similar to that of SQL 1. What your end game should be is to minimize the interruption to all of the other instances configured in the cluster. By that logic, you would think that upgrading all four instances at once would be the way to go, but doing a "big bang" upgrade is more often than not more trouble than it is worth. Trying to figure out what went wrong when you upgrade everything at once is much harder than if you break down the work into more manageable, and logical, chunks. In this example, assuming it is possible, I would upgrade SQL 2 and SQL 3 at the same time, and SQL 4 separately. Again, order is relative and would be based on information that is gathered prior to upgrade. The reason I say to consider upgrading SQL 2 and SQL 3 at the same time is that they are ultimately supposed to coexist on the same node most of the time, so it makes sense to lump the work together.

Upgrading from Versions of SQL Server Prior to SQL Server 2000

With SQL Server 2008, you can only perform upgrades for instances and databases that are SQL Server 2000 or greater. Compatibility level does not matter here. That means that if you are going to upgrade a database from any version of SQL Server prior to SQL Server 2000, the database needs to somehow get into a SQL Server 2000 instance, and then you can use your preferred method to upgrade it to SQL Server 2008.

Run Upgrade Advisor and Other Database Health Checks

Microsoft provides a utility named Upgrade Advisor, which you can either download or use from the SQL Server 2008 installation media. The tool is designed to check your databases to see if there are any potential problems that may ultimately cause the upgrade to fail. By detecting possible problems before the upgrade and then fixing them, you will increase your chances of success greatly. Since testing time may wind up being a premium, using Upgrade Advisor as the first line of defense for an upgrade gives the DBA some power to go back to developers and alert them to problems that need to be addressed, or in a worst-case scenario, provides a document of things to fix post-upgrade if no one wants to do the work ahead of time.

Besides Upgrade Advisor, you should run other checks such as DBCC CHECKDB to ensure that prior to any upgrade, the databases themselves are healthy. Some of those checks may mean you incur downtime and could take quite some time to run, but the old adage "garbage in, garbage out" applies here. Would you prefer a good, stable post-upgrade experience, or nothing but problems?

Upgrading 32-Bit Failover Clustering Instances on 64-Bit Windows

If your existing SQL Server 2000 or SQL Server 2005 failover clustering instance was deployed as 32-bit under a 64-bit operating system, this means that it is using WOW64 to run properly. However, you cannot deploy a 32-bit SQL Server 2008 failover clustering instance using WOW64, nor can you perform an in-place upgrade for an existing 32-bit SQL Server failover clustering instance using WOW64 to SQL Server 2008 (32- or 64-bit). You will need to perform a side-by-side upgrade or a migration to new hardware to upgrade to SQL Server 2008.

Upgrading from a Standalone Instance to a Failover Clustering Instance

You cannot upgrade a SQL Server 2000 or SQL Server 2005 standalone instance to a SQL Server 2008 failover clustering instance. If you wish to deploy SQL Server 2008 in a clustered configuration, you must deploy it as you would a new instance of SQL Server and migrate the databases, objects, and settings to the new SQL Server 2008 failover clustering instance.

Simultaneously Upgrading to Windows Server 2008

As mentioned in Chapter 2, Windows Server 2008 is a complete rewrite of failover clustering in the operating system. An unfortunate but necessary side effect of this is that unlike previous versions of Windows, there is no longer the concept of a rolling upgrade. That means that you cannot upgrade the operating system node by node, and then upgrade SQL Server. To upgrade existing clusters to both SQL Server 2008 and Windows Server 2008, you will need to tear down your existing configurations. So if you want to reuse your existing hardware, following are the steps for one method to go from Windows Server 2003 to Windows Server 2008 during a SQL Server cluster upgrade:

1. For each instance in the cluster, back up all databases, script all SQL Server configurations and settings, and so on. Ensure the backups and scripts are easily available and copied off of the cluster.

2. Cleanly shut down SQL Server when complete. At this point, the MDF (data), LDF (log), and NDF (additional data) files will still be on the shared drives and in a good, consistent state.

3. Install Windows Server 2008 on the cluster nodes. Reformat the system drives to remove any remnants of the old configuration.

4. Cluster the Windows Server 2008 nodes using the same shared drives (which should not need reformatting).

5. Install and cluster SQL Server 2008.

6. If there are no issues, attach the database files from the shared drives. If that does not work, use the backups that were made.

7. Run all scripts and recreate any objects.

8. Redirect applications to the new cluster and test.

This method does incur downtime, but it easily allows you to reconfigure the nodes, the Windows failover cluster, and any SQL Server instances to the same names and IP addresses they were before. If you want to minimize downtime and do not have to worry about names and IP addresses, there is another method, described in the following steps. A quick note: yes, you can change IP addresses and names (limited name-changing ability—see Chapter 8) post-configuration, but in my experience, I would rather get it right up front than get something up and running and have to change its configuration. At the end of the day, it's your choice as to which method is best for you.

1. For each instance in the cluster, back up all databases, script all SQL Server configurations and settings, and so on. Ensure the backups and scripts are easily available and copied off of the cluster.

2. Properly remove one (or more) of the other nodes from SQL Server's definition of the failover cluster. This process will be different depending on whether it is SQL Server 2000 or 2005.

3. Now evict the node (or nodes) just removed from the SQL Server failover cluster in step 2 from the Windows failover/server cluster. At this point, your existing instance of SQL Server is still up and running. If you are doing this on a two-node cluster, you will have no options for failover if a problem happens on the node that is up and running.

4. Install Windows Server 2008 on the evicted node(s).

5. Cluster Windows Server 2008. You may only have a one-node cluster at this point, depending on the number of potential nodes available. Remember that the Windows failover cluster must have a different name than the existing cluster.

6. Cluster a new instance of SQL Server 2008. Like the Windows failover cluster, the instance must have a completely new name.

7. Stop all traffic to the applications whose databases are served by the original instance.

8. Migrate the database from the old instance to the new SQL Server 2008 instance using your preferred method. Remember to move all objects, including jobs, logins, and so on.

9. Redirect applications to the new cluster and test. If everything is acceptable, allow all end users to use the new cluster.

10. Perform a final state backup of the original SQL Server instance, including all system databases.

11. Install Windows Server 2008 on the node with the original instance.

12. Run cluster validation, and if it passes, add it to the Windows failover cluster.

13. Add the node to the SQL Server 2008 failover clustering instance.

Security Considerations

If you perform an in-place upgrade, you will either be using the existing security scheme (domain-based cluster groups as well as service accounts) if upgrading from SQL Server 2005, or you will have to specify the cluster groups during the upgrade as well as use the same service accounts for SQL Server 2000. The only way to take advantage of a Service SID on Windows Server 2008 with a SQL Server 2008 failover clustering instance is to install a new failover clustering instance (either on new hardware or side by side). You should, however, consider changing the service accounts post-upgrade to ones specifically used with SQL Server 2008 instances. Check to see that NT AUTHORITY\System is a sysadmin in an upgraded SQL Server 2005 instance where Windows Server 2008 is the operating system. The reason for this is that the underlying Windows failover cluster in Windows Server 2008 no longer uses the cluster administration account for the IsAlive and LooksAlive tests, and uses NT AUTHORITY\System instead.

In-Place Upgrades to SQL Server 2008

This section will show you how to upgrade to a SQL Server 2008 failover cluster by doing an in-place upgrade. A side-by-side upgrade is really just a new installation followed by a move of all your databases and objects. Thus, I don't cover side-by-side upgrades here. Consult Chapter 6 for information on installing a new failover clustering instance of SQL Server 2008.

Step 1: Install Prerequisites

If it is possible, at some point before the "go live," install the prerequisites for SQL Server 2008 failover clustering (namely, .NET Framework 3.51 SP1, MSI 4.5, and the Filestream hotfix). Follow the instructions shown in Chapter 3. These will require a reboot. You should also consider upgrading the SQL Server 2008 shared files, which should most likely not cause a reboot. However, realize that some of the shared components may include connectivity, so you may want to wait until you've read the following instructions, which show how to upgrade only the shared components. The only way to upgrade the shared components is to use the Setup interface; there is no command line equivalent. Here is the process to follow:

1. Start setup.exe from your installation point for SQL Server 2008 on the node (or nodes) that are being targeted for upgrading first. You may be prompted for permission, as shown in Figure 7-4. After it is loaded, you will see the SQL Server Installation Center, as shown in Figure 7-5.

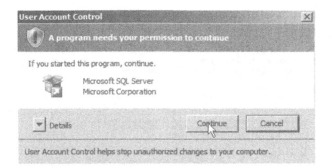

Figure 7-4. *Permission dialog*

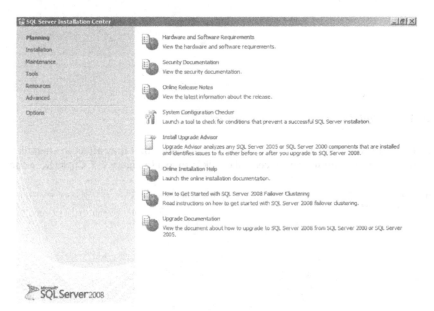

Figure 7-5. *SQL Server Installation Center*

2. Select *Installation*. You will then see a new set of options, as shown in Figure 7-6. Select *Upgrade from SQL Server 2000 or SQL Server 2005*. The installation will fail at this point if .NET Framework 3.51 SP1 or MSI 4.5 are not installed.

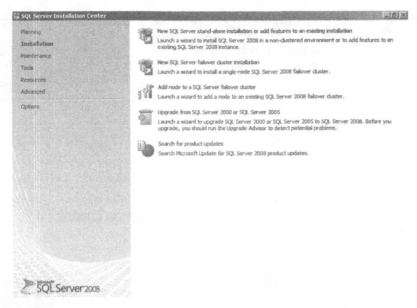

Figure 7-6. *Installation options for SQL Server 2008*

3. The first thing Setup will do is check any common issues that may affect the installation of SQL Server 2008. A sample of a successful check is shown in Figure 7-7. Click OK to continue.

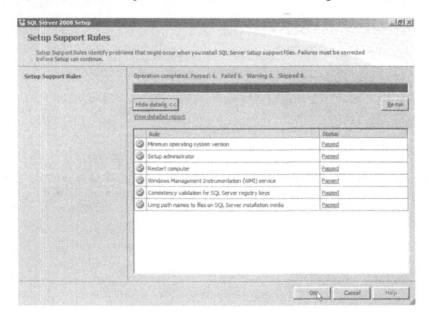

Figure 7-7. *Successful check of the support rules*

4. On the Product Key dialog, enter your valid product key for SQL Server 2008 and click Next. A sample is shown in Figure 7-8.

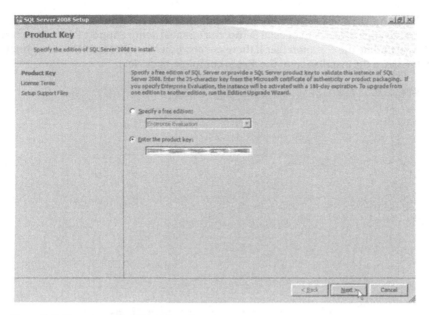

Figure 7-8. *Entering a valid product key*

5. On the License Terms dialog, read the license terms for SQL Server 2008 and click the check box next to *I accept the license terms*. A sample is shown in Figure 7-9. Click Next.

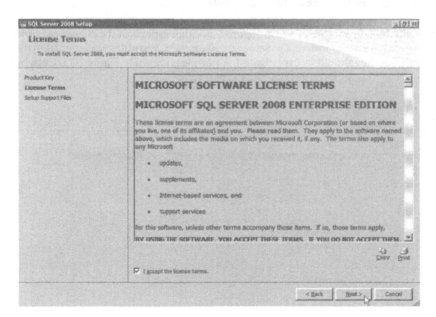

Figure 7-9. *Accepting SQL Server's license agreement*

6. On the Setup Support Files dialog, click Install, as shown in Figure 7-10. If you are using a slipstream copy of SQL Server 2008 Setup, the updated Setup Support Files will be installed. This will update the common files if there are any other instances of SQL Server on the cluster. Once the installation of the files is complete, click Next.

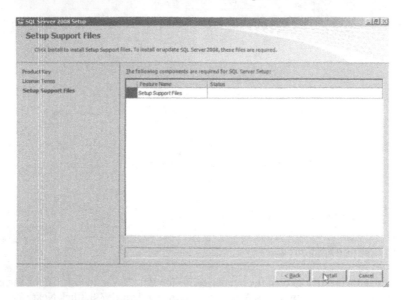

Figure 7-10. *Successful check of the support rules*

7. Setup will then do another check to ensure that other aspects of the cluster are configured properly to have a supported SQL Server configuration. Warnings are acceptable if they are not fatal, but they should be investigated. A sample is shown in Figure 7-11. Click Next.

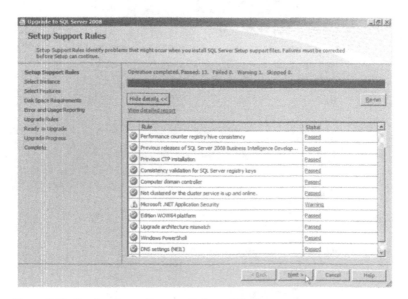

Figure 7-11. *Further Setup Support Rules validations*

8. On the Select Instance dialog, in the *Instance to upgrade* dropdown, select the option *<<Upgrade shared features only>>*. A sample is shown in Figure 7-12. Click Next.

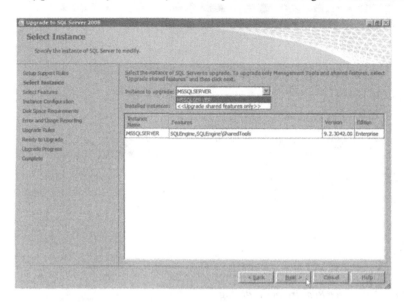

Figure 7-12. *Select Instance dialog*

9. On the Select Features dialog (shown in Figure 7-13), click Next.

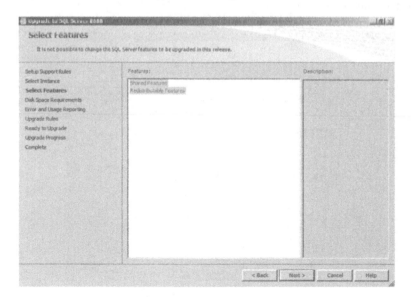

Figure 7-13. *Select Features dialog*

10. Click Next on the Disk Space Requirements dialog (shown in Figure 7-14).

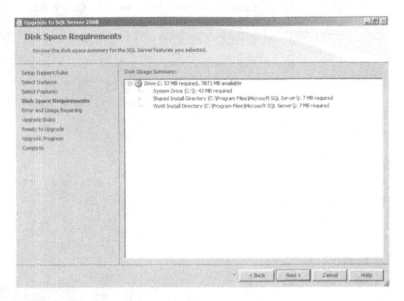

Figure 7-14. *Disk Space Requirements dialog*

11. On the Error and Usage Reporting dialog (shown in Figure 7-15), by default, nothing is selected. If you want to send information to Microsoft, check the appropriate boxes and click Next to continue.

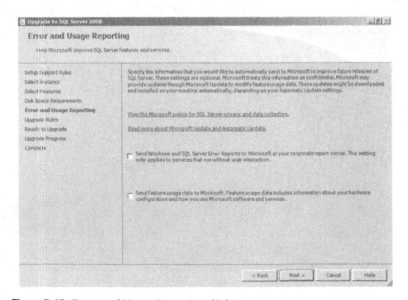

Figure 7-15. *Error and Usage Reporting dialog*

12. There will be one final check to ensure that everything is fine and the installation can proceed. If there are any warnings or problems, investigate them. A sample is shown in Figure 7-16. Click Next.

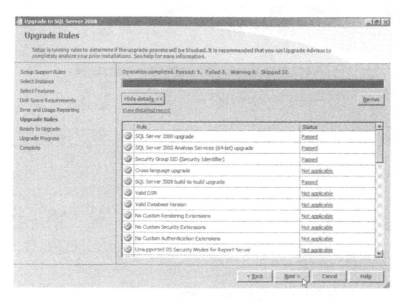

Figure 7-16. *Upgrade Rules dialog*

13. On the Ready to Upgrade dialog (shown in Figure 7-17), verify your settings. Click Install.

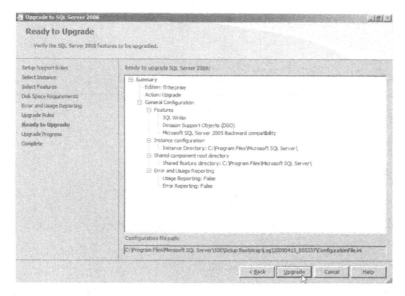

Figure 7-17. *Ready to Upgrade dialog*

14. When complete, a successful shared components upgrade will look like Figure 7-18.
    Click Next.

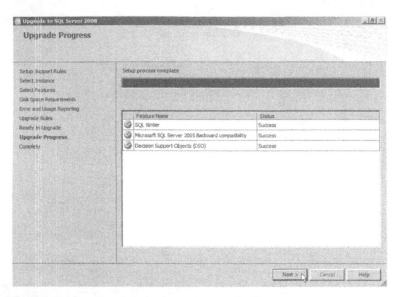

Figure 7-18. *Completed database engine installation*

15. Click Close on the dialog shown in Figure 7-19. Note the location of the log files for this
    installation. You can click the link shown and review the summary.

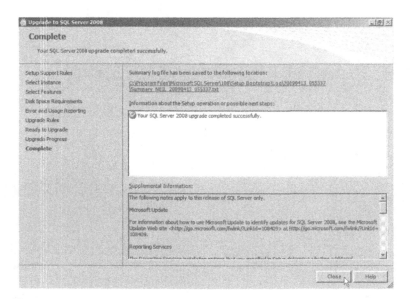

Figure 7-19. *Completed installation*

Step 2: Upgrade the Nodes That Do Not Own the SQL Server Instance (SQL Server Setup User Interface)

This section will show how to upgrade a node of a particular failover clustering instance that does not own the instance itself. The example cluster used as the one to upgrade in this chapter is a two-node failover cluster with a single instance of SQL Server, which is arguably the most common configuration. The cluster has two nodes: GEDDY and NEIL. The following process makes use of the graphical user interface of Setup:

1. Start setup.exe from your installation point for SQL Server 2008. You may be prompted for permission, as shown earlier in Figure 7-4. After it is loaded, you will see the SQL Server Installation Center, as shown earlier in Figure 7-5.

2. Select *Installation*. You will then see a new set of options, as shown earlier in Figure 7-6. Select *Upgrade from SQL Server 2000 or SQL Server 2005*. The installation will fail at this point if .NET Framework 3.51 SP1 or MSI 4.5 are not installed.

3. The first thing Setup will do is check any common issues that may affect the installation of SQL Server 2008. A sample of a successful check is shown earlier in Figure 7-7. Click OK to continue.

4. On the Product Key dialog, enter your valid product key for SQL Server 2008 and click Next. A sample is shown earlier in Figure 7-8.

5. On the License Terms dialog, read the license terms for SQL Server 2008 and click *I accept the license terms*. A sample is shown earlier in Figure 7-9. Click Next.

6. On the Setup Support Files dialog, click Install, as shown earlier in Figure 7-10. If you are using a slipstream copy of SQL Server 2008 Setup, the updated Setup Support Files will be installed. This will update the common files if there are any other instances of SQL Server on the cluster. Once the installation of the files is complete, click Next.

7. Setup will then do another check to ensure that other aspects of the cluster are configured properly to have a supported SQL Server configuration. Warnings are acceptable if they are nonfatal, but they should be investigated. A sample is shown earlier in Figure 7-11. Click Next.

8. On the Select Instance dialog (similar to the one shown earlier in Figure 7-12), select the instance to be upgraded. Click Next.

9. On the Select Features dialog (similar to the one shown in Figure 7-20), click Next.

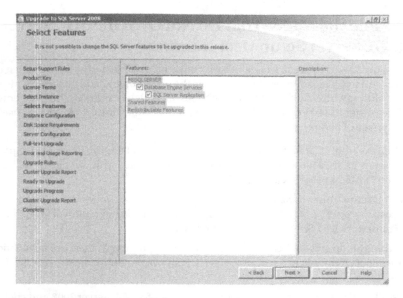

Figure 7-20. *Select Features dialog*

10. On the Instance Configuration dialog, shown in Figure 7-21, you will need to configure the instance ID for the instance to be upgraded. A default instance will have a default value of MSSQLSERVER. As if you were performing a new install, my recommendation is to make a default instance's *Instance ID* the same as the network name, and for a named instance such as CRYSTAL\BALL, set the instance ID to be CRYSTAL_BALL. Make a note of the value used here for use when you upgrade the instance itself. Click Next to continue.

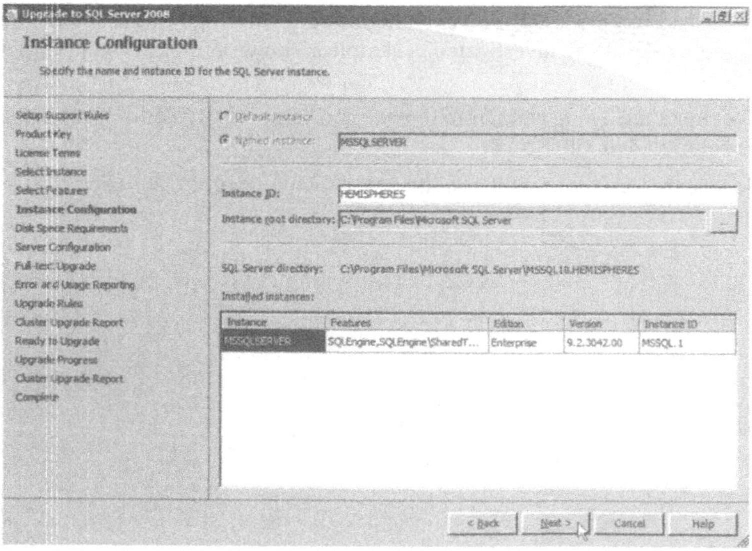

Figure 7-21. *Instance Configuration dialog*

11. Click Next on the Disk Space Requirements dialog (similar to the one shown earlier in Figure 7-14).

12. On the Server Configuration dialog, as shown in Figure 7-22, click Next.

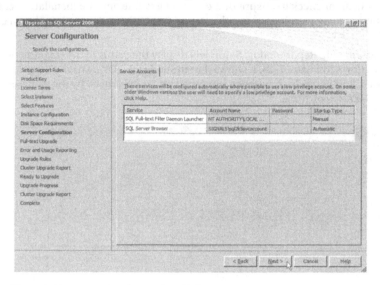

Figure 7-22. *Server Configuration dialog*

13. On the Full-text Upgrade dialog, as shown in Figure 7-23, select *Import, Rebuild,* or *Reset.* If you do not have any full-text catalogs, it does not matter which option is selected. If you are upgrading from SQL Server 2000 and the Import option is selected, underneath the covers SQL Server 2008's Setup will still do a complete rebuild; there is no import process from SQL Server 2000. For more information, see Knowledge Base article 955507 (http://support.microsoft.com/kb/955507). Click Next to continue.

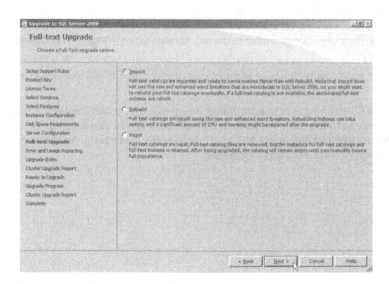

Figure 7-23. *Full-text Upgrade dialog*

14. On the Error and Usage Reporting dialog (shown earlier in Figure 7-15), by default, nothing is selected. If you want to send information to Microsoft, check the appropriate boxes and click Next to continue.

15. There will be one final check to ensure that everything is fine and the installation can proceed. If there are any warnings or problems, investigate them. A sample is shown earlier in Figure 7-16. Click Next.

16. On the Cluster Upgrade Report dialog, Setup will display the status of the upgrade process. In the sample shown in Figure 7-24, it shows that the node GEDDY owns the instance that is being upgraded, and no nodes have been upgraded yet, as evidenced by the values for SQL Version. Click Next to continue.

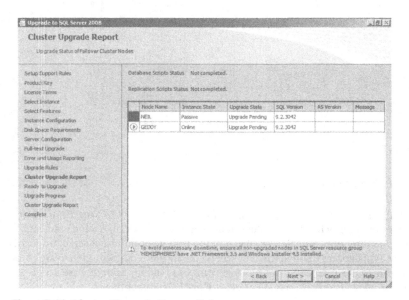

Figure 7-24. *Cluster Upgrade Report dialog*

17. On the Ready to Upgrade dialog (similar to the one shown earlier in Figure 7-17), verify your settings. Click Upgrade.

18. When complete, a successful database engine components upgrade will look like Figure 7-25. Click Next.

19. On the updated Cluster Upgrade Report dialog, Setup will once again display the status of the upgrade process. In the sample shown in Figure 7-26, it shows that the node GEDDY still owns the instance that is being upgraded, but the one node where Setup was just run (NEIL) is successfully upgraded. Click Next to continue.

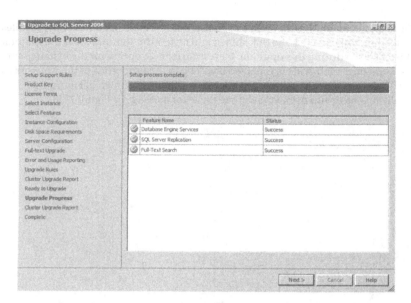

Figure 7-25. *Completed database engine upgrade of the node that does not own the SQL Server resource*

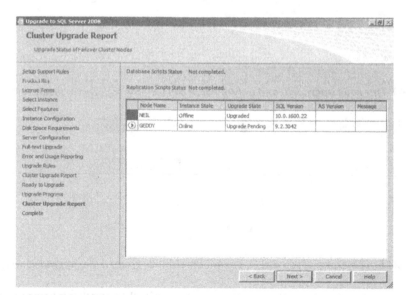

Figure 7-26. *Cluster Upgrade Report dialog*

20. Click Close on the dialog shown earlier in Figure 7-19. Note the location of the log files for this installation. You can click the link shown and review the summary. For the example two-node cluster shown during this upgrade, there is no failover option for the instance since one node has been upgraded. This is reflected if you open the properties of the Network Name resource for the instance in Failover Cluster Management, as shown in Figure 7-27. If you try to manually fail the group over, you will see the error message in Figure 7-28.

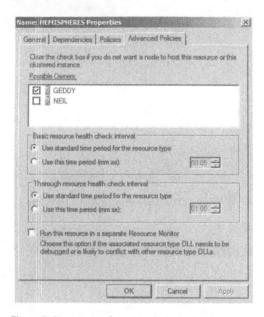

Figure 7-27. *One node upgraded, and only one that can own the SQL Server instance*

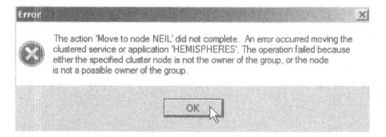

Figure 7-28. *Error message if you attempt to fail the resource group to the upgraded node*

21. Repeat for all other nodes that do not own the instance of SQL Server that is being upgraded.

Step 3: Upgrade the Node Owning the SQL Server Instance (SQL Server Setup User Interface)

This section will show how to upgrade the node of the failover clustering instance that owns the database. The following process uses the graphical user interface of Setup:

1. Start setup.exe from your installation point for SQL Server 2008. You may be prompted for permission, as shown earlier in Figure 7-4. After it is loaded, you will see the SQL Server Installation Center, as shown earlier in Figure 7-5.

2. Select *Installation*. You will then see a new set of options, as shown earlier in Figure 7-6. Select *Upgrade from SQL Server 2000 or SQL Server 2005*. The installation will fail at this point if .NET Framework 3.51 SP1 or MSI 4.5 are not installed.

3. The first thing Setup will do is check any common issues that may affect the installation of SQL Server 2008. A sample of a successful check is shown earlier in Figure 7-7. Click OK to continue.

4. On the Product Key dialog, enter your valid product key for SQL Server 2008 and click Next. A sample is shown earlier in Figure 7-8.

5. On the License Terms dialog, read the license terms for SQL Server 2008 and click *I accept the license terms*. A sample is shown earlier in Figure 7-9. Click Next.

6. On the Setup Support Files dialog, click Install, as shown earlier in Figure 7-10. If you are using a slipstream copy of SQL Server 2008 Setup, the updated Setup Support Files will be installed. This will update the common files if there are any other instances of SQL Server on the cluster. Once the installation of the files is complete, click Next.

7. Setup will then do another check to ensure that other aspects of the cluster are configured properly to have a supported SQL Server configuration. Warnings are acceptable if they are nonfatal, but they should be investigated. A sample is shown earlier in Figure 7-11. Click Next.

8. On the Select Instance dialog (similar to the one shown earlier in Figure 7-12), select the instance to be upgraded. Click Next.

9. On the Select Features dialog (similar to the one shown in Figure 7-29), click Next.

10. On the Instance Configuration dialog (similar to the one shown earlier in Figure 7-21), you will need to configure the instance ID for the instance to be upgraded the same as the one set during the upgrades of the other nodes. Click Next to continue.

11. Click Next on the Disk Space Requirements dialog (similar to the one shown earlier in Figure 7-14).

12. On the Server Configuration dialog, as shown earlier in Figure 7-22, click Next.

13. On the Full-text Upgrade dialog, as shown earlier in Figure 7-23, select *Import*, *Rebuild*, or *Reset*. If you do not have any full-text catalogs, it does not matter which option is selected. Click Next to continue.

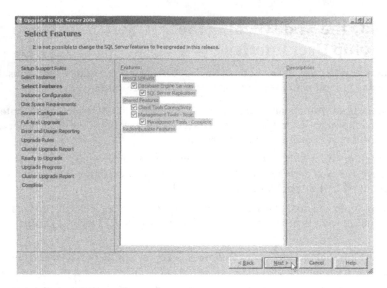

Figure 7-29. *Select Features dialog*

14. On the Error and Usage Reporting dialog (shown earlier in Figure 7-15), by default, nothing is selected. If you want to send information to Microsoft, check the appropriate boxes and click Next to continue.

15. There will be one final check to ensure that everything is fine and the installation can proceed. If there are any warnings or problems, investigate them. A sample is shown earlier in Figure 7-16. Click Next.

16. On the Cluster Upgrade Report dialog, Setup will display the status of the upgrade process. In the sample shown in Figure 7-30, it shows that the node GEDDY owns the instance that is being upgraded, and NEIL has been upgraded. Click Next to continue.

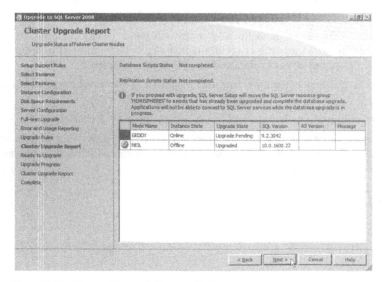

Figure 7-30. *Cluster Upgrade Report dialog*

17. On the Ready to Upgrade dialog (similar to the one shown earlier in Figure 7-17), verify your settings. Click Upgrade. As soon as you click the button, the instance will fail over to an available node in the cluster, as shown in Figure 7-31. Until the upgrade is complete, the node being upgraded cannot own the SQL Server resources. The properties of the network name are changed (a sample is shown in Figure 7-32).

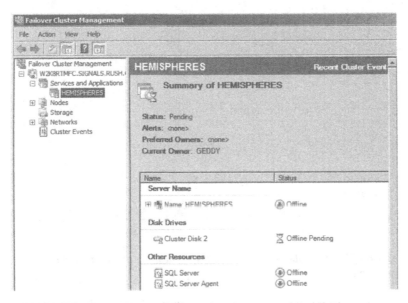

Figure 7-31. *Failover after the upgrade of the instance is initiated*

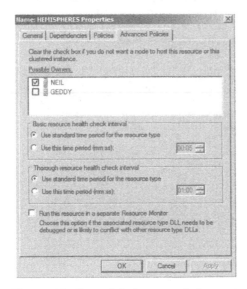

Figure 7-32. *The node being upgraded cannot own the resource*

18. When complete, a successful shared components upgrade will look like Figure 7-33. Click Next.

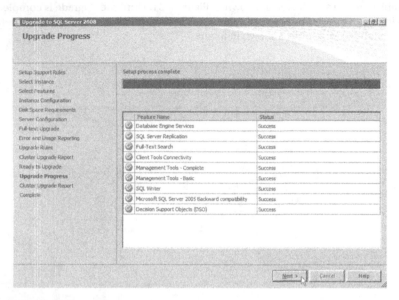

Figure 7-33. *Completed database engine upgrade of the node that owned the SQL Server resources*

19. On the updated Cluster Upgrade Report dialog, Setup will once again display the status of the upgrade process. In the sample shown in Figure 7-34, it shows that both nodes are now upgraded. Click Next to continue.

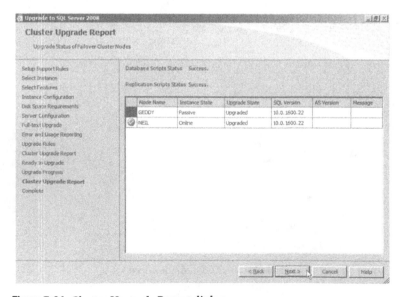

Figure 7-34. *Cluster Upgrade Report dialog*

20. Click Close on the dialog shown in Figure 7-19. Note the location of the log files for this installation. You can click the link shown and review the summary. For the example two-node cluster shown during this upgrade, both nodes can now own the resources. This is reflected if you open the properties of the Network Name resource for the instance in Failover Cluster Management, as shown in Figure 7-35.

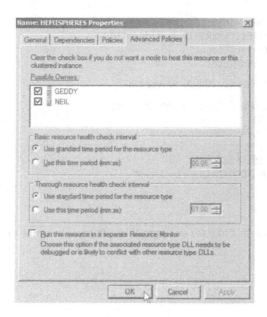

Figure 7-35. *Upgrade complete; both nodes can own the resource*

Upgrading Using the Command Line

You can upgrade the nodes with the command line just like you can install from the command line. Most of the parameters from Table 6-1 are valid for an upgrade, and two are specific to upgrade (other than specifying *Upgrade* for the ACTION parameter): FTUPGRADEOPTION and FAILOVERCLUSTERROLLOWNERSHIP. FTUPGRADEOPTION has three potential values (Rebuild, Reset, and Import) and maps to what is shown earlier using the Setup interface. FAILOVERCLUSTERROLLOWNERSHIP is completely unique to a command line–based upgrade and may be the reason you do a command line–based install. That parameter allows you to control the failover behavior during the upgrade process. As has been documented in a few places, if you're upgrading, once you hit 50 percent or more of the nodes of a clustered instance as upgraded, the instance will fail over to another node. You have no control over that. There are three values for FAILOVERCLUSTERROLLOWNERSHIP:

- 0: This tells the upgrade process not to fail the instance over to one of the upgraded nodes when the conditions are met, and the node is not added to the list of possible owners at the end of the upgrade.

- 1: This tells the upgrade process to automatically fail the instance over to one of the available nodes, and adds the node to the list of the possible owners. The failover will occur at this execution, which would most likely be scheduled and managed.

- 2: This tells Setup to manage the failover and behaves just like the Setup interface. This is the default setting.

My recommendation is to leave the default setting in most upgrade scenarios. If you want to do the automatic failover but control its timing, select a value of 1 for FAILOVERCLUSTERROLLOWNERSHIP. A value of 0 gives you total control, but I do not think many will use it since it assumes a lot of knowledge of what is going on.

The following example upgrades a named instance of SQL Server 2005 that had full-text configured:

```
setup.exe /q /ACTION=Upgrade /INSTANCENAME=INS1
/INDICATEPROGRESS=True /FAILOVERCLUSTERROLLOWNERSHIP=2 /INSTANCEID=
SQLUPGRADE /FTSVCACCOUNT="domainname\ftssvcaccount"
/FTSVCPASSWORD="password" /FTUPGRADEOPTION=Reset
```

This next example upgrades a default instance of SQL Server 2000:

```
setup.exe /q /ACTION=Upgrade /AGTDOMAINGROUP="DOMAIN\Domain Group"
/INSTANCEID=UPGRADEME /INSTANCENAME=INS1
 /FAILOVERCLUSTERROLLOWNERSHIP=2  /FTSVCPASSWORD="password"
/FTSVCACCOUNT="domainname\ftssvcaccount"
/FTUPGRADEOPTION=Import /INDICATEPROGRESS=True
 /INSTANCEID=SQLUPGRADE /SQLDOMAINGROUP="DOMAIN\Domain Group"
```

Using an INI File

Following is an example INI file with parameters in it for an upgrade of a failover instance to SQL Server 2008:

```
[SQLSERVER2008]
ACTION="Upgrade"
AGTDOMAINGROUP="EQUINOX\Agent Admins"
FAILOVERCLUSTERROLLOWNERSHIP=1
FTSVCACCOUNT="EQUINOX\ftssvcaccount"
FTSVCPASSWORD="P@ssword1"
FTUPGRADEOPTION="Rebuild"
INSTANCEID="UPGRADEME"
INSTANCENAME="INS1"
SQLDOMAINGROUP="EQUINOX\SQL Admins"
INDICATEPROGRESS="TRUE"
```

If you saved this INI file as UpgradeSQL.ini, you could run the upgrade by issuing the following command:

```
Setup.exe /ConfigurationFile="UpgradeSQL.ini"
```

If you strip out AGTSVCPASSWORD and SQLSVCPASSWORD for security reasons, then pass those values on the command line as follows:

```
Setup.exe /ConfigurationFile="UpgradeSQL.ini" /FTSVCPASSWORD="P@ssword1"
```

Post-Upgrade Tasks

Once the failover clustering instance is fully upgraded, you should perform all of the validation tests (pinging the name and IP address of the instance, as well as failing the newly upgraded instance to all nodes) documented at the end of Chapter 6 to ensure it is working properly. Since this involves failing the instance over to other nodes, the validation will require a brief scheduled outage. In addition to validating the clustered instance, there are some tasks that you will need to do to ensure that the databases are functioning properly post-upgrade, no matter which method you used to upgrade the database and instances. Depending on what options you use within SQL Server (as well as other factors), what you need to do may vary. Definitely consult the SQL Server 2008 Upgrade Technical Reference Guide referenced at the beginning of the chapter for a complete list of what you will need to do. Some common tasks are as follows:

- Register the instance in SQL Server Management Studio. During the upgrade, the process removes registry settings for the previous SQL Server instance.

- Update the statistics with the UPDATE STATISTICS command for each table in the databases that were upgraded. To ensure that everything is optimal post-upgrade, updating the query optimization statistics when switching versions is recommended.

- Update the usage counters with DBCC UPDATEUSAGE. The command will report and correct any problems to ensure that all row and page counts are accurate post-upgrade.

- If you are upgrading from SQL Server 2000, you should run the DBCC CHECKDB...WITH DATA_PURITY command. The DATA_PURITY option checks the database for column values that may not be valid and/or may be out of range. The reason you need to run it with pre–SQL Server 2005 databases is that column-value checks were not enabled by default, and this command enables them.

- Remember to configure the SQL Server 2008 instance properly. Some of the settings you used for earlier versions may not be appropriate. Also remember that SQL Server 2008 is more secure by default, so some functionality that you may have used before may be disabled by default or no longer there.

Summary

Upgrading is similar to installing a new instance of SQL Server 2008, yet it's different enough that it needed its own chapter in this book. You should now understand all of the considerations for upgrading existing failover clustering instances to SQL Server 2008 if that is your plan. However, there is one final piece of the puzzle, which will be covered in the next chapter: administering SQL Server 2008 failover clusters.

■■■

CHAPTER 8

Administering a SQL Server 2008 Failover Cluster

After you've deployed or upgraded to a SQL Server 2008 failover cluster, there is only one thing left to do: administer it. This chapter will focus on the common administrative tasks that you may need to perform in the course of the instance's lifetime, or ones that are distinctly different from their standalone counterparts. Where possible, both graphic and command line–based versions of the instructions will be presented. Keep in mind that this chapter is only going to present topics that are unique to failover clustering; outside of what is presented here, you should administer a clustered SQL Server 2008 instance and its databases the same way you would administer a standalone instance of SQL Server 2008.

Introducing Failover Cluster Management

The utility named *Failover Cluster Management* in Windows Server 2008 is the replacement for Cluster Administrator. If you have already configured your Windows failover cluster using Failover Cluster Management, you should be somewhat familiar with it, but I want to highlight a few features that may prove useful for administration of your cluster. You may also notice if you have used either the beta or release candidate of Windows Server 2008 R2 that the management tool is called Failover Cluster Manager, not Failover Cluster Management. This change in name to Failover Cluster Manager appears to be a permanent one, and I'm just making you aware of it. The look of Failover Cluster Manager in R2 has changed slightly, but all of the functionality is in the same place.

Note Another change I noticed in the release candidate of Windows Server 2008 R2 is that to access PowerShell, you no longer use Failover Cluster PowerShell Management. Microsoft has moved all PowerShell functionality (including the cluster stuff) to be launched from Windows PowerShell Modules, which is also found under Administrative Tools.

The first thing you should notice about Failover Cluster Management is that once you select the Windows failover cluster in the left pane, you'll see its status displayed at the top of the middle pane. One of the best things is that it will show if there were any recently logged problems. A sample is shown in Figure 8-1. Similarly, when you select a subfolder or a specific object (such as a service or an application), you will also see the middle pane reflect the status of that object, as well as what specific resources are making up that object. This part of the interface is much more intuitive than the old Cluster Administrator in Windows Server 2003 and earlier.

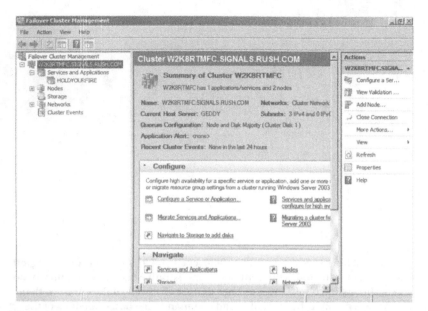

Figure 8-1. *Main screen of Failover Cluster Management with a Windows failover cluster selected*

One feature that I also really love about Failover Cluster Management is that you can see all cluster-related events if you click *Cluster Events*. A sample is shown in Figure 8-2.

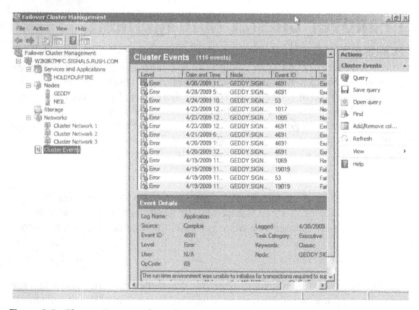

Figure 8-2. *Cluster Events selected*

What is even better about this feature is that you can create your own queries, so if there are different types of items you want to see showing up in Cluster Events, it is completely customizable. Note the *Save query* and *Open query* options. Figure 8-3 is a sample of the Cluster Events Filter dialog showing you some of the various query options. You can show as much or as little as you want, choose which of the event logs to look at, specifically look for certain errors (i.e., event IDs), and set a date range. Prior to Windows Server 2008, a lot of this stuff was not easy to get to, but Microsoft has made it much easier for you to access.

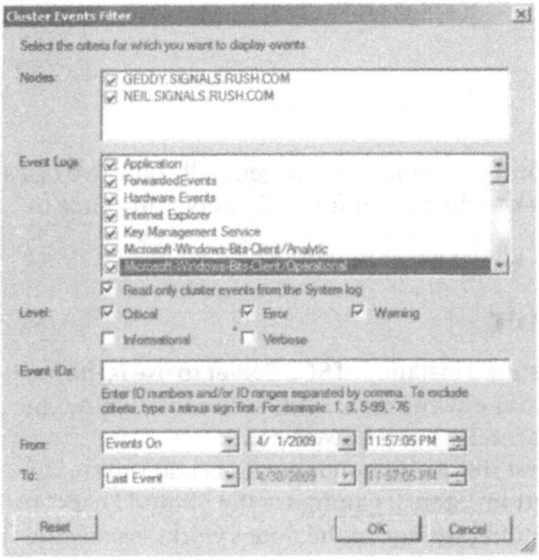

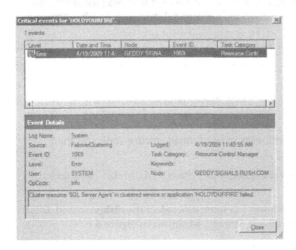

Figure 8-3. *Cluster Events Filter dialog*

Similarly, if you right-click one of the major sub-items such as an application, a node, or a network, and select the option *Show the critical events for <specific item>*, you get a very filtered view of only critical events related to that specific object. Again, if you're looking quickly to see if anything is wrong or has been wrong recently, this is an easy way to do things. Sample output is shown in Figure 8-4.

Figure 8-4. *Critical events for a SQL Server instance named HOLDYOURFIRE*

Tip Many of the tasks, while SQL Server–related, will involve using a Windows-based tool such as Failover Cluster Management, which DBAs may not have proper access to use. If you are in that situation and cannot get the proper privileges to run Failover Cluster Management, `cluster.exe`, or PowerShell, you will need to get someone else in your organization with the proper rights to perform those tasks.

Disk Maintenance

When it comes to administering disks in a clustered configuration, there are generally only two tasks that occur over the cluster's lifetime: adding a new disk to the cluster for a SQL Server instance to use, and putting a disk into maintenance mode.

Adding a Disk to the Failover Cluster

Adding a disk to the Windows failover cluster for a clustered instance of SQL Server to use is the most common disk-related task that will be performed in your environment. This section will show you how to do that via Failover Cluster Management, `cluster.exe`, and PowerShell.

Before doing anything at the cluster level, the first thing that you must do is add the storage to the nodes. Follow all of the instructions in the section "Step 4: Configure the Shared Disks" in Chapter 3 to configure the storage—the process for adding storage to the nodes works exactly the same. Assuming that your storage unit does not require any outages to add the disks to Windows, you can do the work while the nodes are online. Once a disk has been added to all of the nodes and formatted on one of them, you can then add the disk to the Windows failover cluster and then make it a dependency of SQL Server.

Note In Windows Server 2008, adding a dependency to a resource does not require the resource to be taken offline as in previous versions of Windows; it is an online operation. In all versions of Windows prior to Windows Server 2008, you had to take the SQL Server resource offline to add a disk as a dependency, thereby affecting its availability.

Using Failover Cluster Management

To use Failover Cluster Management to add a disk to a SQL Server failover clustering instance, perform the following steps:

1. On any node of the cluster, from the Start menu, select *Administrative Tools* and then *Failover Cluster Management*.

2. Expand the tree with the Windows failover cluster, select *Storage*, right-click, and select *Add a disk*.

3. On the Add Disks to a Cluster dialog, as shown in Figure 8-5, select the disk(s) to add. Click OK. The disk will now show up under Available Storage, as shown in Figure 8-6.

Figure 8-5. *Add Disks to a Cluster dialog*

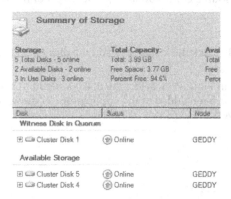

Figure 8-6. *Disk added successfully to the Windows failover cluster*

4. You must now rerun cluster validation with all tests, as was shown in Chapter 3. One difference if you already have a working SQL Server failover clustering instance is that you will see the Review Storage Status dialog, similar to the one in Figure 8-7. Leave the default option selected, which allows you to leave the instance(s) configured up and running. Click Next. When finished, the test should indicate that you have a valid cluster configuration.

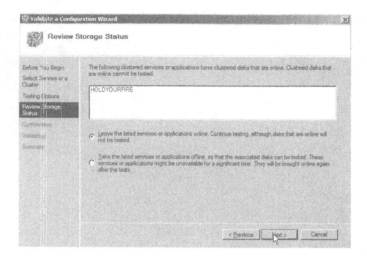

Figure 8-7. *Review Storage Status dialog*

5. You have two ways to add a disk to the resource group containing SQL Server or Analysis Services.

Option 1:

a. Expand *Services and Applications*, right-click the instance to add the disk to, and select the option *Add storage*.

b. On the Add Storage dialog, as shown in Figure 8-8, select the disk(s) to add to the SQL Server instance. Click OK. The disk has been added to the application, as shown in Figure 8-9, but it is not ready for use yet.

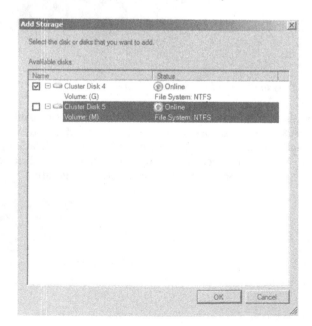

Figure 8-8. *Add Storage dialog*

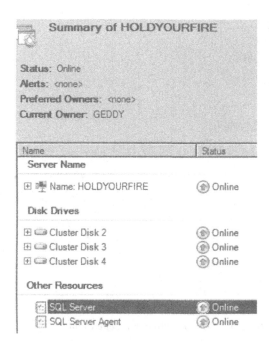

Figure 8-9. *Disk added to the SQL Server resource group*

Option 2:

a. Select the disk in Storage, right-click, select *More Actions*, and then *Move this resource to another service or application*.

b. On the Select A Service or Application dialog, as shown in Figure 8-10, select the instance to add the disk to. Click OK. The disk has been added to the application, as shown earlier in Figure 8-9.

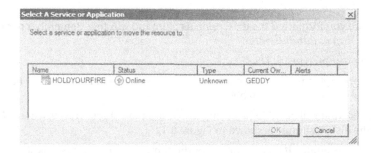

Figure 8-10. *Select A Service or Application dialog*

6. Right-click the SQL Server (or Analysis Services) resource, select *Properties*, and choose the *Dependencies* tab. Click in the entry box that says *Click here to add a dependency*. In the *AND/OR* dropdown, select *AND*. In the *Resource* dropdown, select the newly added disk. A sample is shown in Figure 8-11. Repeat until all disks are added. Click OK.

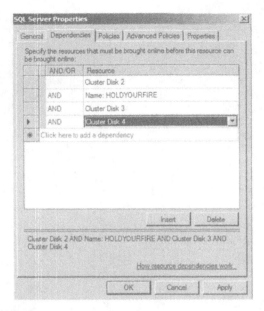

Figure 8-11. *Cluster Disk 4 added to the SQL Server resource as a dependency*

7. Use the dynamic management view (DMV) sys.dm_io_cluster_shared_drives to verify that the disks(s) were added properly to the SQL Server or Analysis Services resource. If you need to see the steps and example output, refer back to the section "Verify the Disk Configuration" in Chapter 6.

Using cluster.exe

Adding a disk via cluster.exe is the most involved of all of the methods for adding a disk to the Windows failover cluster and then SQL Server. The following steps show how to use cluster.exe to add a disk:

1. On the node where you formatted the disk, open a command window. Remember to open it with the option *Run as administrator*.

2. At the command prompt, type DISKPART.

3. At the DISKPART> prompt, type the command list disk, as shown in Figure 8-12. This will show you all of the disks that are available.

4. Next, select the disk that will be added by using the command select disk *N*, where *N* is the number of the disk. A sample is shown in Figure 8-12.

5. Ensure that the disk is online. If it is offline, enter the command online disk, as shown in Figure 8-12.

6. Type the command detail disk, and note the value for *Disk ID*. An example is shown in Figure 8-12.

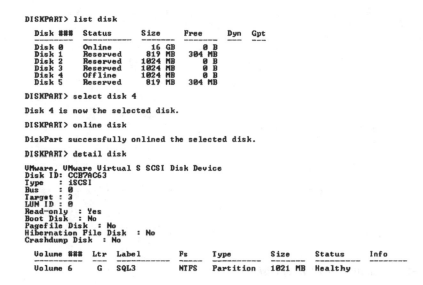

```
DISKPART> list disk

  Disk ###  Status      Size     Free      Dyn  Gpt
  --------  ----------  -------  --------   ---  ---
  Disk 0    Online        16 GB     0 B
  Disk 1    Reserved     819 MB   304 MB
  Disk 2    Reserved    1024 MB     0 B
  Disk 3    Reserved    1024 MB     0 B
  Disk 4    Offline     1024 MB     0 B
  Disk 5    Reserved     819 MB   304 MB

DISKPART> select disk 4

Disk 4 is now the selected disk.

DISKPART> online disk

DiskPart successfully onlined the selected disk.

DISKPART> detail disk

VMware, VMware Virtual S SCSI Disk Device
Disk ID: CCB7AC63
Type  : iSCSI
Bus   : 0
Target : 3
LUN ID : 0
Read-only  : Yes
Boot Disk  : No
Pagefile Disk  : No
Hibernation File Disk  : No
Crashdump Disk  : No

  Volume ###  Ltr  Label      Fs     Type       Size      Status    Info
  ---------   ---  --------   ----   --------    ------    -------   ------
  Volume 6    G    SQL3       NTFS   Partition   1021 MB   Healthy
```

Figure 8-12. *Sample execution of steps 2 through 6*

7. Type exit. You will be placed back at the normal command prompt.

8. Start the calculator found in Windows (the look may vary depending on which version of Windows you are using). Under the *View* menu, select *Scientific*, and then select *Hex*. Enter the value from Disk ID from step 6, as shown in Figure 8-13. Then select *Dec*, and you will see the decimal equivalent of the Disk ID, as shown in Figure 8-14. You will be using this value when adding the disk to the Windows failover cluster.

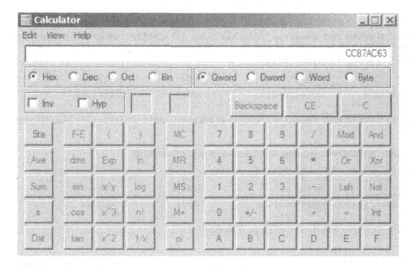

Figure 8-13. *Entering Disk ID from step 6*

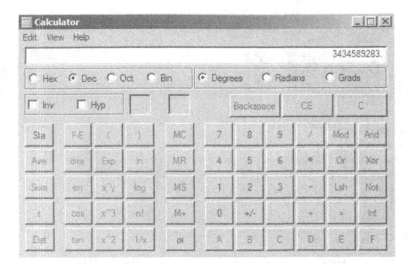

Figure 8-14. *Decimal equivalent of Disk ID*

9. At the command prompt, enter the command cluster *<cluster name>* resource "*<name of disk resource>*" /CREATE /GROUP:*<resource group to add new disk>* /TYPE:"Physical Disk". A sample is shown in Figure 8-15.

10. Add the decimal equivalent of Disk ID from step 8, which is also known as the disk signature, using the following command: cluster *<cluster name>* resource "*<name of disk resource>*" /PRIV DiskSignature=*<decimal value for Disk ID>*. An example is shown in Figure 8-15.

11. Bring the disk resource online with the command cluster *<cluster name>* resource "*<name of disk resource>*" /ONLINE, as shown in Figure 8-15.

```
C:\>cluster W2K8RTMFC resource "Cluster Disk 4" /CREATE /GROUP:HOLDYOURFIRE /TYP
E:"Physical Disk"
Creating resource 'Cluster Disk 4'...

Resource                    Group                    Node              Status
------------------------    --------------------     --------------    -------
Cluster Disk 4              HOLDYOURFIRE             GEDDY             Offline

C:\>cluster W2K8RTMFC resource "Cluster Disk 4" /PRIV DiskSignature=3434589283

C:\>cluster W2K8RTMFC resource "Cluster Disk 4" /ONLINE
Bringing resource 'Cluster Disk 4' online...

Resource                    Group                    Node              Status
------------------------    --------------------     --------------    -------
Cluster Disk 4              HOLDYOURFIRE             GEDDY             Online
```

Figure 8-15. *Example execution of steps 9 through 12*

12. Add the disk as a dependency to the SQL Server (or Analysis Services) resource with the following command: cluster *<cluster name>* resource "*<name of SQL Server or Analysis Services resource>*" /ADDDEPENDENCY:"*<name of disk resource>*", as shown in Figure 8-16.

13. To verify that the dependency was added correctly, use the command cluster *<cluster name>* resource "*<name of SQL Server or Analysis Services resource>*" /LISTDEPENDENCIES.

```
C:\Windows\system32>cluster W2K8RTMFC resource "SQL Server" /ADDDEPENDENCY:"Clus
ter Disk 4"

Making resource 'SQL Server' depend on resource 'Cluster Disk 4'...


C:\Windows\system32>cluster W2K8RTMFC resource "SQL Server" /LISTDEPENDENCIES
Listing resource dependency expression for 'SQL Server':
------------------------------------------------------------
<[Cluster Disk 2]> and <[Cluster Disk 4]> and <[HOLDYOURFIRE]> and <[Cluster Dis
k 3]>

Listing resource dependencies for 'SQL Server':

Resource            Group               Node            Status
------------        ------------        -------         --------
Cluster Disk 2      HOLDYOURFIRE        GEDDY           Online
Cluster Disk 4      HOLDYOURFIRE        GEDDY           Online
HOLDYOURFIRE        HOLDYOURFIRE        GEDDY           Online
Cluster Disk 3      HOLDYOURFIRE        GEDDY           Online
```

Figure 8-16. *Example execution of steps 13 and 14*

14. Use the DMV sys.dm_io_cluster_shared_drives to verify that the disks(s) were added properly to the SQL Server or Analysis Services resource. If you need to see the steps and example output, refer back to the section "Verify the Disk Configuration" in Chapter 6.

Using PowerShell

Adding a disk in PowerShell is infinitely easier than using cluster.exe. The steps in this section show how to add a disk to a failover cluster via PowerShell.

First, to see if there are any disks that can be used with the cluster, use the cmdlet Get-ClusterAvailableDisk with the parameter -Cluster <cluster name>. A sample would be Get-ClusterAvailableDisk -Cluster W2K8R2FC. If any disks are available, they will be shown at this time. To then add the disk (or all the disks if there is more than one available), you would type what you did to see the disk(s) piped through Add-ClusterDisk. An example is shown in Figure 8-17. To validate that the new disk resource was added properly, enter Get-ClusterResource <resource name> -Cluster <cluster name>. If more than one disk was added, omit the specific resource name and use Get-ClusterResource -Cluster <cluster name>. Once the disk has been added, verify the cluster configuration according to Chapter 3.

As with the other methods, you must now add the disk as a dependency to the specific SQL Server resource. The disk resource must first be moved into the resource group with the SQL Server resource with the cmdlet Move-ClusterResource <disk resource name> -Group <resource group> -Cluster <cluster name>. Next, add the resource as a dependency with Add-ClusterResourceDependency <SQL Server resource name> <disk resource name> -Cluster <cluster name>. Finally, verify that the resource was added properly as a dependency with Get-ClusterResourceDependency <SQL Server resource name> -Cluster <cluster name>, as shown in Figure 8-17.

```
PS C:\Windows\system32> Get-ClusterAvailableDisk -Cluster W2K8RTMPC ! Add-ClusterDisk
Name                        State                        Group                        ResourceType
----                        -----                        -----                        ------------
Cluster Disk 5              OnlinePending                Available Storage            Physical Disk

PS C:\Windows\system32> Get-ClusterResource "Cluster Disk 5" -Cluster W2K8RTMPC
Name                        State                        Group                        ResourceType
----                        -----                        -----                        ------------
Cluster Disk 5              Online                       Available Storage            Physical Disk

PS C:\> Move-ClusterResource "Cluster Disk 5" -Group "MOVING\PICTURES" -Cluster W2K8RTMPC
Name                  State          Group               ResourceType
----                  -----          -----               ------------
Cluster Disk 5        Online         MOVING\PICTURES     Physical Disk

PS C:\> Add-ClusterResourceDependency "SQL Server (PICTURES)" "Cluster Disk 5" -Cluster W2K8RTMPC
Name                  State          Group               ResourceType
----                  -----          -----               ------------
SQL Server (PICTURES) Online         MOVING\PICTURES     SQL Server

PS C:\> Get-ClusterResourceDependency "SQL Server (PICTURES)" -Cluster W2K8RTMPC
Resource                                DependencyExpression
--------                                --------------------
SQL Server (PICTURES)                   ([Cluster Disk 3] and ([Cluster Disk 5]) and ...
```

Figure 8-17. *Adding a disk via PowerShell*

Putting a Clustered Disk into Maintenance Mode

Maintenance mode is a setting for a clustered disk resource that was introduced in Windows Server 2003 Service Pack 1. You will put a disk into maintenance mode if you want to perform some type of disk-related task (such as defragmentation or chkdsk) to that clustered disk and not have it affect the other resources that may be dependent on it. When you put a disk resource into maintenance mode, it effectively removes the persistent reservation for that disk. This means that the disk could potentially be picked up by a non-clustered server and could possibly cause corruption. So be very careful about when and how you use maintenance mode; it is a very powerful and important feature of failover clustering, but as with anything else, there are some potential risks you need to take into account.

■ **Note** There is a good writeup found in Knowledge Base article 903650 (http://support.microsoft.com/kb/903650) that talks about maintenance mode in more depth. Although it says it is for Windows Server 2003, the information is completely valid for Windows Server 2008.

Using Failover Cluster Management

Select a disk resource, right-click, select *More Actions*, and then select the option *Turn On Maintenance Mode for this disk*. The disk will appear like the one in Figure 8-18.

Figure 8-18. *Maintenance mode set for a disk*

To remove the disk from maintenance mode, perform the same steps, but choose the option *Turn Off Maintenance Mode for this disk*.

Using cluster.exe

To turn on maintenance mode for a disk resource, at a command prompt, enter the following:

```
cluster <cluster name> resource "<name of disk resource>" /MAINT:on
```

To turn off maintenance mode for a disk resource, at a command prompt, enter the following:

```
cluster <cluster name> resource "<name of disk resource>" /MAINT:off
```

An example showing both turning maintenance mode on and off is shown in Figure 8-19.

```
C:\>cluster W2K8RTMFC resource "Cluster Disk 4" /MAINT:on

Setting maintenance mode for resource 'Cluster Disk 4'
Resource             Group                Node                 Status
-------------------- -------------------- -------------------- -------
Cluster Disk 4       HOLDYOURFIRE         GEDDY                Online(Maintenance)

C:\>cluster W2K8RTMFC resource "Cluster Disk 4" /MAINT:off

Clearing maintenance mode for resource 'Cluster Disk 4'
Resource             Group                Node                 Status
-------------------- -------------------- -------------------- -------
Cluster Disk 4       HOLDYOURFIRE         GEDDY                Online
```

Figure 8-19. *Setting maintenance mode for a disk using cluster.exe*

Using PowerShell

You can also set maintenance mode for a disk resource using PowerShell. The command is not as straightforward as it is with cluster.exe. To turn on maintenance mode for a disk resource, enter the following:

```
Get-ClusterResource "<name of disk resource>"
-Cluster <cluster name> | Suspend-ClusterResource
```

To turn off maintenance mode for a disk resource, at a command prompt, enter the following:

```
Get-ClusterResource "<name of disk resource>"
-Cluster <cluster name> | Resume-ClusterResource
```

An example showing both turning maintenance mode on and off using PowerShell is shown in Figure 8-20.

```
PS C:\Windows\system32> Get-ClusterResource "Cluster Disk 5" -Cluster W2K8RTMFC | Suspend-ClusterRes
ource

Name                 State                Group                ResourceType
----                 -----                -----                ------------
Cluster Disk 5       Online(Maintenance)  Available Storage    Physical Disk

PS C:\Windows\system32> Get-ClusterResource "Cluster Disk 5" -Cluster W2K8RTMFC | Resume-ClusterReso
urce

Name                 State                Group                ResourceType
----                 -----                -----                ------------
Cluster Disk 5       Online               Available Storage    Physical Disk
```

Figure 8-20. *Setting maintenance mode for a disk resource in PowerShell*

General Node and Failover Cluster Maintenance

There are various tasks that you may have to perform at the node level in a failover cluster. Those operations would be adding a node to the failover cluster, changing the domain for the failover cluster, and doing an emergency node repair in the event of a failure.

Monitoring the Cluster Nodes

You need to monitor both Windows and SQL Server for the normal things such as general health and performance; those will not be covered in this section or in this book. What you need to worry about when it comes to monitoring failover clusters is that the services related to clustering are up and running on their respective nodes, and that if a problem does occur and failover happens, those events are properly captured and the right people are notified. Whether you are using a monitoring program such as Microsoft's System Center Operations Manager (SCOM) or a third-party vendor's monitoring solution, what you need to look at is the same. Some vendors provide templates or plug-ins that are focused on clustering (and will make your life easier); others do not. For example, SCOM released the updated Windows Server Cluster Management Pack just before this book was completed, and it works with both Windows Server 2003 and Windows Server 2008. As shown earlier in the section "Introducing Failover Cluster Management," you can view the cluster-specific events in Failover Cluster Management easily, but it may be cumbersome to have to keep checking there (or places like Event Viewer) for cluster-related events. This is why having a utility or tool to do this automatically is crucial for maintaining a highly available environment.

To ensure that the cluster itself is up and running, monitor that the services Cluster Service, Remote Procedure Call (RPC), and Remote Registry are always running on the nodes. A failure to those, especially Cluster Service, will most likely cause problems. For the node that owns the SQL Server instance, the SQL Server and SQL Server Agent services will be started, and the nodes that do not own the resource will not be running the resource.

Note This is one of the reasons why the startup type for clustered SQL Server resources is set to Manual: they are only started on a given node when necessary. Do not alter the settings for the SQL Server services.

You can detect which underlying cluster node owns the SQL Server resource using Transact-SQL. This method may be the only one available to DBAs if they do not have access to the operating system–level tools. To see which node owns the instance, enter the following query: SELECT SERVER-PROPERTY('ComputerNamePhysicalNetBIOS'). An example with its output is shown in Figure 8-21.

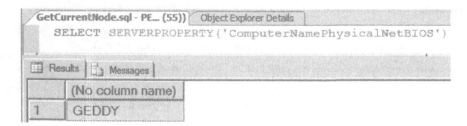

Figure 8-21. *Querying SQL Server to see what node owns the instance*

New to Window Server 2008 R2 are counters specifically for Windows failover clustering. There are a few categories of counters; all begin with WSFC. Unfortunately, I did not have enough time toward the end of writing the book to evaluate each counter to see which would be most useful, and there was no documentation, so I will update any of my recommendations for counters once Windows Server 2008 is released on my blog at http://www.sqlha.com.

Even if you are not using a proper monitoring tool, or the one you are using does not have any functionality specific to monitoring clustering, you still have a way of getting the information you need. Besides checking to see if the services are up and running, you can periodically ping the IP address or name of both the Windows failover cluster as well as SQL Server and/or Analysis Services. You can also set the tool to look at the various Windows logs as well as SQL Server logs to look for problems or failovers. Many programs allow you to trap Simple Network Management Protocol (SNMP) messages generated by applications (such as SQL Server) or operating systems. Most tools also allow you to monitor counters, too.

■**Tip** Remember that not only the system administrators, but the DBAs and any application owners should be notified when a failover happens, since there may be specific steps that must happen for an application to reconnect to SQL Server. The DBAs will most likely not have anything to do with those steps, but they can check the errors to see what caused the failover and if it needs any attention to fix.

Adding a Node to the Failover Cluster

Adding a node is a straightforward task under Windows Server 2008. From a high-level standpoint, no matter what method you choose to add the node to the cluster, these steps need to be performed:

1. Validate the proposed cluster configuration with the new node as shown in Chapter 4.

2. Add the node to the Windows failover cluster.

3. Add the node via SQL Server Setup.

The rest of this section will demonstrate how to add the node using Failover Cluster Management, cluster.exe, and PowerShell.

Using Failover Cluster Management

To add a node from Failover Cluster Management, perform the following steps:

1. Start Failover Cluster Management.

2. Validate the cluster configuration as shown in Chapter 4. If the validation comes back as a supported configuration, proceed to step 3.

3. Expand the Windows failover cluster tree, right-click *Nodes*, and select *Add Node*.

4. On the Before You Begin dialog of the Add Node Wizard, select Next.

5. On the Select Servers dialog, as shown in Figure 8-22, enter the name of the node to be added. Click Next.

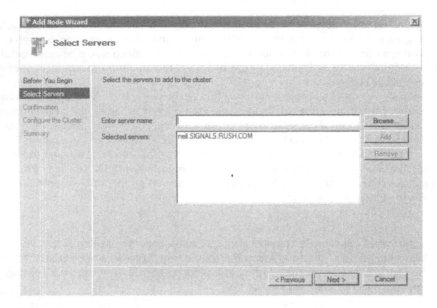

Figure 8-22. *Dialog for entering the node(s) to be added*

6. On the Confirmation dialog, as shown in Figure 8-23, click Next.

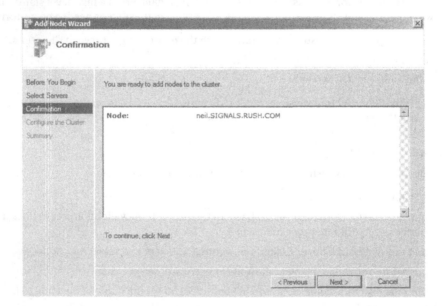

Figure 8-23. *Confirmation dialog for adding a node*

7. On the Summary dialog, click Finish. Note the warnings displayed in Figure 8-24. It is indicating that you now need to get SQL Server configured properly on that node.

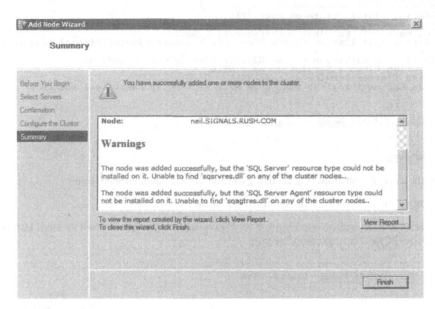

Figure 8-24. *Configuration warning*

8. If node that was added had a new operating system installed on it, run the Add Node operation as described in the section "Add Nodes to the Instance" in Chapter 6. If you are adding the node to the cluster as the result of a problem where it had to be evicted (see the next section), you may not have to do an Add Node operation; you may be able to run the *Repair* option of SQL Server Setup. Repair will do things like fix the registry and configuration values. I had success with this during testing, however, you may need to run a full Add Node operation if this does not work.

Note More information on repairing a SQL Server installation can be found at http://msdn.microsoft.com/en-us/library/cc646006.aspx.

---

9. Verify that SQL Server recognizes the new node. Follow the instructions in the section "Verify the Configuration" in Chapter 6.

10. Test failover of all resources to the new node.

Using cluster.exe

To add a node to a Windows failover cluster using cluster.exe, use this command:

```
cluster <cluster name> /ADDNODE /NODE:<node name>
```

A sample is shown in Figure 8-25. You must then perform steps 8 through 10 from the previous section.

```
C:\Windows\system32>cluster W2K8RTMFC /ADDNODE /NODE:"NEIL"
Configuring node NEIL
----------------------------------------
 12% Validating cluster state on node NEIL.
 25% Getting current node membership of cluster W2K8RTMFC.
 37% Adding node NEIL to Cluster configuration data.
 50% Validating installation of the Microsoft Failover Cluster Virtual Adapter o
n node NEIL.
 62% Validating installation of the Cluster Disk Driver on node NEIL.
 75% Configuring Cluster Service on node NEIL.
 87% Starting Cluster Service on node NEIL.
100% Waiting for notification that node NEIL is a fully functional member of the
cluster.
```

Figure 8-25. *Successful completion of an added node*

Using PowerShell

Adding a node using PowerShell is done using the cmdlet Add-ClusterNode. Enter

Add-Clusternode *<node name>* -Cluster *<cluster name>*.

A sample execution is shown in Figure 8-26. You must then perform steps 8 through 10 from the "Using Failover Cluster Management" section.

```
PS C:\> Add-ClusterNode TOMMY -Cluster STYX

Name                                                                  State
----                                                                  -----
tommy                                                                 Up
```

Figure 8-26. *Adding a node via PowerShell*

Evicting a Node

Evicting a node is literally removing a node from the failover cluster. Evicting a node is an administrative task, but not one that should be done on a regular basis. Evicting all nodes will destroy the entire cluster configuration. You should only evict a node from a Windows failover cluster when a problem is encountered and it needs to be removed from the cluster configuration to be fixed. This section will show how to evict a node using Failover Cluster Management, cluster.exe, and PowerShell.

Note Unlike some previous versions of SQL Server, removing a node in Windows without doing anything in SQL Server first does not cause any harm to the SQL Server instance.

Using Failover Cluster Management

The following steps demonstrate how to evict a node using Failover Cluster Management:

1. Start Failover Cluster Management.

2. Expand the Windows failover cluster tree and also expand *Nodes*.

3. Select the node to be evicted, right-click, select *More Actions*, and then select *Evict*.

4. At the confirmation prompt as shown in Figure 8-27, select the option to evict the node. If the node was successfully evicted, it will no longer appear in Failover Cluster Management.

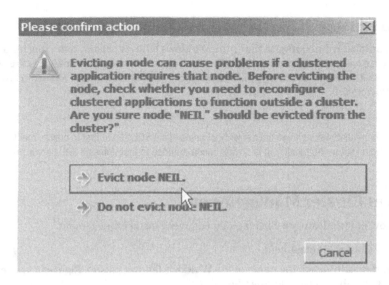

Figure 8-27. *Eviction confirmation dialog*

Using cluster.exe

To evict a node to a Windows failover cluster using cluster.exe, use the command cluster <cluster name> node <node name> /EVICT. A sample execution is shown in Figure 8-28.

```
C:\>cluster W2K8RTMFC node NEIL /EVICT
Evicting node 'NEIL'...
```

Figure 8-28. *Evicting a node using cluster.exe*

Using PowerShell

Evicting a node using PowerShell is done using the cmdlet Remove-ClusterNode. Enter

Remove-Clusternode <node name> -Cluster <cluster name>

A sample execution is shown in Figure 8-29. Note that it prompts to confirm the deletion of the node. If you do not want to be prompted, add -Force to the execution.

```
PS C:\> Remove-Clusternode TOMMY -Cluster STYX

Remove-ClusterNode
Are you sure you want to evict node tommy?
[Y] Yes  [N] No  [S] Suspend  [?] Help (default is "Y"): Y
PS C:\> Get-ClusterNode

Name                                                              State
----                                                              -----
dennis                                                            Up
```

Figure 8-29. *Evicting a node using PowerShell*

Destroying a Cluster

If you just want to completely unconfigure the entire Windows failover cluster, removing it node by node is one way, but an easier way introduced for the first time in Windows Server 2008 is the ability to destroy the cluster all at once. This section will show you how to do it both via Failover Cluster Management and PowerShell.

Caution I do not recommend destroying a cluster without uninstalling SQL Server first to ensure that there will be no errant entries hanging out in the registry. It is always recommended to first uninstall SQL Server properly.

Using Failover Cluster Management

This section will show how to destroy a cluster using Failover Cluster Management.

1. Start Failover Cluster Management.

2. In the left-hand pane, select the name of the Windows failover cluster. Right-click, select *More Actions*, and then select *Destroy Cluster*.

3. On the Please confirm action dialog, as shown in Figure 8-30, confirm that you want to delete the cluster configuration. By default, the selected option will be to not destroy the cluster.

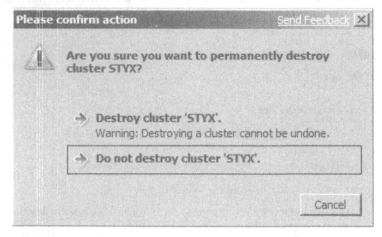

Figure 8-30. *Confirmation of destroying the failover cluster*

Using PowerShell

Destroying a cluster using PowerShell is done via the cmdlet `Remove-Cluster`. Enter

`Get-Cluster <cluster name> | Remove-Cluster -CleanupAD`

`CleanupAD` is an optional parameter, but it ensures that Active Directory is properly cleaned up during the removal of the cluster. As with removing a node, you can specify the optional parameter `Force`, which will not prompt you to confirm the cluster's destruction. The example shown in Figure 8-31 does not use `Force`.

```
PS C:\> Get-Cluster STYX | Remove-Cluster -CleanupAD

Remove-Cluster
Are you sure you want to completely remove the cluster STYX?
[Y] Yes   [N] No   [S] Suspend   [?] Help (default is "Y"): _
```

Figure 8-31. *Destroying a cluster using PowerShell*

Changing Domains

Changing a domain for a Windows Server 2008–based failover cluster is not supported by Microsoft. This is clearly documented in Knowledge Base article 269196 (http://support.microsoft.com/kb/269196). To change domains in a supported fashion, you will have to completely uninstall all clustered applications (including SQL Server), uncluster the Windows nodes (or just destroy the cluster as shown in the previous section), and then do what it takes to change domains for each node. Then and only then can you recluster the Windows nodes and reinstall SQL Server 2008. If this policy changes, it will be noted in the aforementioned Knowledge Base article.

Clustered SQL Server Administration

Besides tasks that involve both Windows and SQL Server for administration, there are certain administrative tasks that are SQL Server–specific and different than what would be done on a standalone SQL Server instance. This section will show those various tasks and how to perform them.

Changing the Service Account or the Service Account Passwords

To change a service account for a clustered instance of SQL Server 2008, you must use the SQL Server Configuration Manager utility. The following steps are the process by which you will change a service account or service account password for any one of the SQL Server–related services in a failover cluster. While the process is basically the same as that for a standalone SQL Server instance, there are a few subtle differences:

- Never manually change the service accounts outside of SQL Server Configuration Manager because the change needs to be properly applied to all nodes underneath the covers.

- Changing a service account or its password requires that all of the nodes participating in the cluster are online while the change is made. If any of the cluster nodes are offline, you will have to apply the change when the nodes that were once offline enter an online state.

- At some point, the SQL Server service will have to by cycled for the change in account and/or password to take effect. The change can be applied without restarting the service, but you should plan for an outage to occur.

- Remember that there are dependencies for SQL Server services. For example, when you cycle SQL Server in a cluster, SQL Server Agent will stop and will not automatically restart. You must manually restart SQL Server Agent after cycling SQL Server.

1. Ensure that all nodes of the cluster participating in the instance are online.

2. From the Start menu, select *All Programs*, then *Microsoft SQL Server 2008*, then *Configuration Tools*, and finally *SQL Server Configuration Manager*.

3. When SQL Server Configuration Manager opens, select *SQL Server Services*. You will see a list of services on the right. A sample is shown in Figure 8-32.

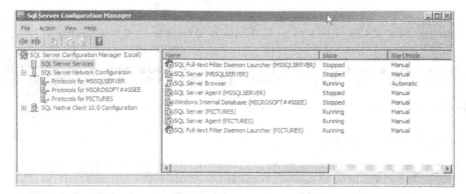

Figure 8-32. *Main display of SQL Server Configuration Manager*

4. Double-click the service to change, or right-click it and select *Properties*. You will now see a dialog similar to the one in Figure 8-33, which shows the current service account information. Change the information and click OK. You will then see the prompt, as shown in Figure 8-34. Click Yes. Once the service is restarted, you will be returned to the main SQL Server Configuration Manager dialog.

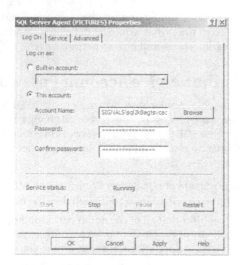

Figure 8-33. *Service account information for a SQL Server service*

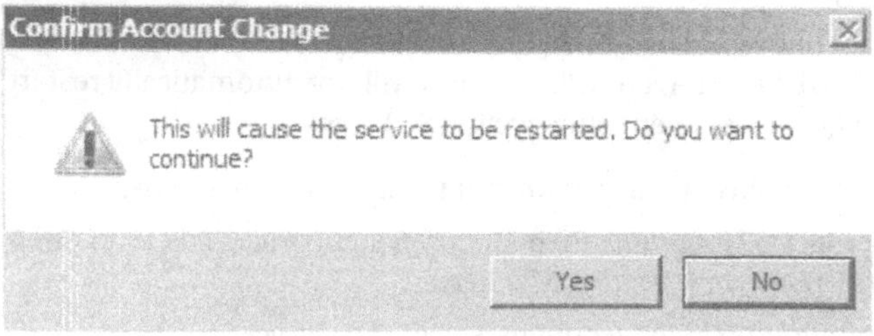

Figure 8-34. *Restart prompt*

Managing Performance with Multiple Instances

One of the more difficult things to do when it comes to the configuration and administration of a failover cluster is ensuring the performance of all instances in the cluster post-failover. This was discussed in Chapter 5 in the section "Memory and Processor." Here, I will show you how various tools and methods can assist you in this task.

Configuring Memory for a SQL Server 2008 Instance

As noted in Chapter 5, there are three main ways you can set memory for an instance:

- Set a fixed maximum
- Set a fixed minimum and let SQL Server manage everything on top of that
- Allow all memory to be dynamic

This section will demonstrate how to set memory using the recommendation of a fixed total amount of memory for a SQL Server instance using SQL Server Management Studio and Transact-SQL.

Note Remember that if you are still using a 32-bit version of Windows with a 32-bit version of SQL Server, you will need to configure the switch /PAE in boot.ini and enable AWE memory in each SQL Server instance to use more than 4 GB of memory.

Using SQL Server Management Studio

If you prefer to use SQL Server Management Studio, open the properties for the instance itself and select the Memory page. To set a fixed amount of memory, you must set both the minimum server memory and maximum server memory to the same value. SQL Server requires the amount to be entered in megabytes (MB). The example shown in Figure 8-35 sets a fixed memory size of 8 GB for the instance MOVING\PICTURES.

Figure 8-35. *Setting a fixed amount of 8 GB for a SQL Server instance*

Using Transact-SQL

To set a fixed amount of memory using Transact-SQL, it is done with the *min server memory* and *max server memory* options of the system stored procedure sp_configure. First, you must ensure that all options are able to be shown. The following example sets a SQL Server instance to use a fixed amount of 8 GB. As mentioned in the previous section, SQL Server needs these options to be set in MB.

```
sp_configure 'show advanced options', 1;
GO
RECONFIGURE;
GO
sp_configure 'max server memory', 8192;
GO
RECONFIGURE;
GO
sp_configure 'min server memory', 8192;
GO
RECONFIGURE;
GO
```

Using Windows System Resource Manager to Constrain Processor Utilization

Windows System Resource Manager is an effective way to control the percentage of processor utilization a given process on a cluster node can consume. If you want to set processor affinity, use the *affinity mask* option of sp_configure for 32-bit SQL Server instances, and *affinity64 mask* for 64-bit SQL Server instances. In my experience, processor affinity is not used very often since it constrains which physical processors an instance can use. It is much better to set a percentage of the processors. Following are the steps to use WSRM to constrain processor utilization by SQL Server instances.

■**Caution** Never use WSRM to restrain anything other than the percentage of processor a SQL Server instance can use. Use SQL Server for everything else unless noted. Also, do not use WSRM for the sake of using it; only configure WSRM if you need to.

---

1. Verify that Windows System Resource Manager has been configured as a feature using Server Manager. If it has not been added as a feature, follow the instructions in the section "Add Features in Server Manager" in Chapter 3 to add it as a feature.

2. From the Start menu, select *Administrative Tools*, and then *Windows System Resource Manager*. You will see a display similar to the one in Figure 8-36.

3. Select *Process Matching Criteria* and then *New Process Matching Criteria*. Click Add, as shown in Figure 8-37.

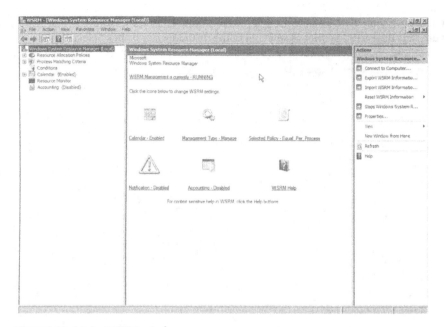

Figure 8-36. *Main WSRM window*

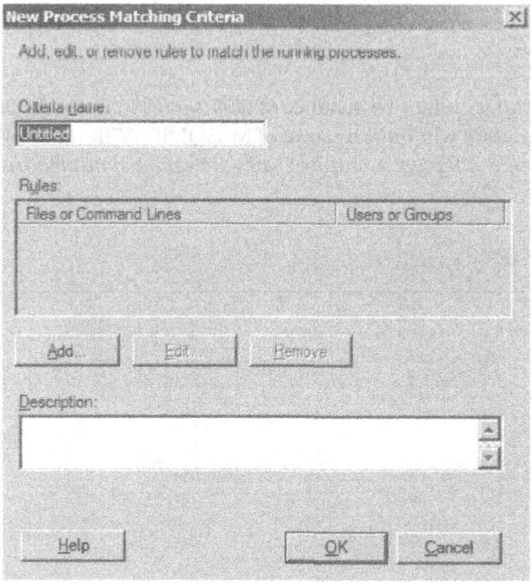

Figure 8-37. *New Process Matching Criteria dialog*

4. On the Add Rule dialog, select the *Files or Command Lines* tab, as shown in Figure 8-38. Make sure that Registered Service is selected in the dropdown, and click Select.

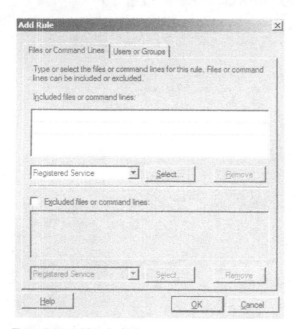

Figure 8-38. *Add Rule dialog*

5. On the Add Registered Services dialog, select an instance of SQL Server that will be managed. A default instance of SQL Server 2008 will have a name of MSSQLSERVER (as shown in Figure 8-39), and a named instance will have a name of MSSQL$<*part of named instance after slash*>.

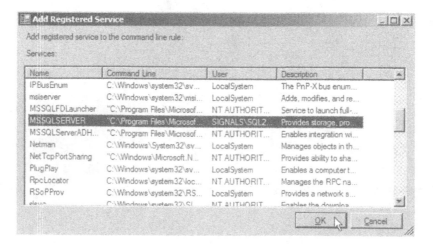

Figure 8-39. *Add Registered Service dialog*

6. When finished, you will see something like the dialog in Figure 8-40. Click OK.

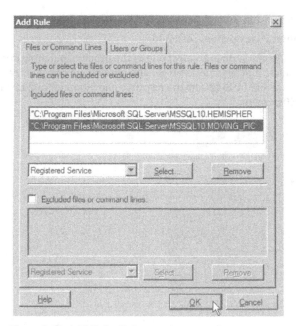

Figure 8-40. *Add Rule dialog again*

7. Repeat steps 4 through 6 for all instances that will be managed.

8. Add a name for the process matching criteria, and click OK. You should see a screen like that in Figure 8-41.

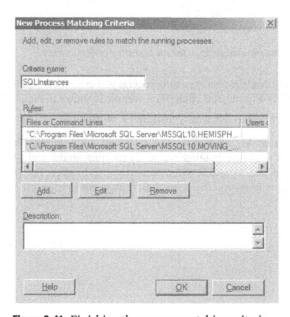

Figure 8-41. *Finishing the process matching criteria*

9. Select *Resource Allocation Policies* and then *New Resource Allocation Policy.*

10. On the New Resource Allocation Policy dialog, click Add.

11. On the Add or Edit Resource Allocation dialog, select one of the process matching criteria that you created in the dropdown, and set a percentage. The percentage cannot exceed 99 percent. The sample shown in Figure 8-42 sets the resource allocation for one instance of SQL Server not to exceed 40 percent.

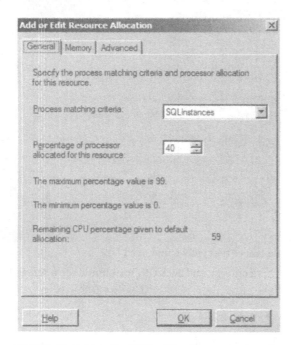

Figure 8-42. *Setting the CPU utilization percentage for an instance of SQL Server*

12. Repeat steps 9 and 10 for all instances/process matching criteria you created. When finished, give the resource allocation policy a name and click OK. A sample is shown in Figure 8-43.

13. Repeat steps 1 through 11 on all nodes. WSRM only manages a single node.

At this point, the policy is not activated. My suggestion is to manually enable it only when you are in the failover condition unless more than one instance is already running on the node. You can also set the policy to run based on a schedule, as well as when certain events happen. For example, if you select *Conditions* as shown in Figure 8-44, you can then choose an event to trigger the WSRM policy.

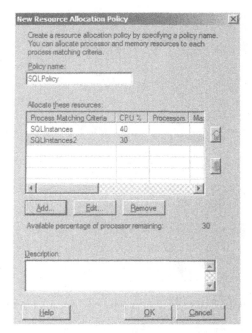

Figure 8-43. *Completed resource allocation policy*

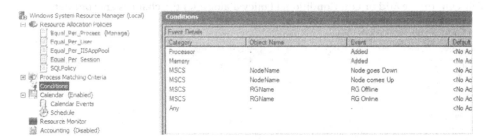

Figure 8-44. *WSRM conditions*

To edit the policy associated with a condition, perform the following steps:

1. Right-click *Conditions* and select *Add/Edit Conditional Policies*.

2. On the Add or Edit Conditional Policy dialog, select the one you want to change, and click Edit.

3. Change the properties for the condition. The sample shown in Figure 8-45 will trigger the SQLPolicy if the node GEDDY fails. Click OK.

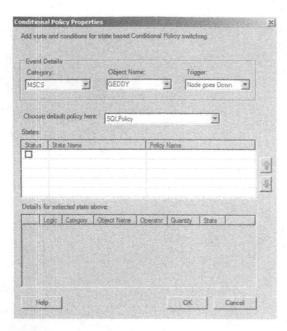

Figure 8-45. *Setting WSRM conditions*

4. Click OK on the Add or Edit Conditional Policy dialog after the changes are complete. An example is shown in Figure 8-46.

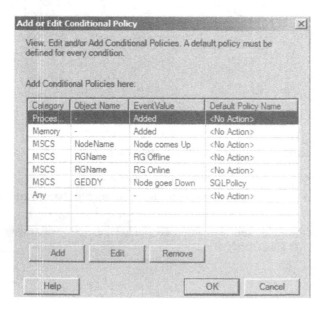

Figure 8-46. *Completed condition modification*

Using Resource Governor

New to SQL Server 2008 is Resource Governor. It is useful for identifying and controlling workloads within a particular instance; it does not know anything about other instances or their workloads. Similar to WSRM, Resource Governor cannot constrain disk I/O resources (like WSRM), so you will need to think about I/O in a different way. For more information on how to configure Resource Governor, see the topic "Resource Governor How-to Topic" in SQL Server 2008 Books Online.

Uninstalling a Failover Clustering Instance

Like running Setup for a new installation, removing an instance is also a node-by-node, instance-by-instance affair. This section will demonstrate how to properly remove a SQL Server 2008 failover clustering instance from a Windows failover cluster.

Under Windows Server 2008, when a clustered application is fully removed, all of its now unused storage goes back into the general storage pool (i.e., the Available Storage resource group) for reuse.

■**Tip** When removing a node, and finally uninstalling the entire failover clustering instance, it is best to remove the nodes that do not own the SQL Server 2008 instance first, and remove the node that owns the instance last. This will give you the maximum uptime of the instance. Removing a node does limit your failover options, so if the instance is still in use, be cognizant of that fact.

Using the SQL Server Setup User Interface

This first set of instructions will show how removing a node is done using SQL Server Setup. Here is the process to follow:

1. From your installation media, run setup.exe.

2. When the SQL Server Installation Center dialog appears, select *Maintenance*, and then *Remove node from a SQL Server failover cluster*, as shown in Figure 8-47.

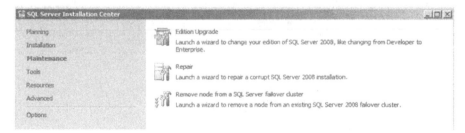

Figure 8-47. *Node removal option*

3. On the Setup Support Rules dialog, as shown in Figure 8-48, click Next.

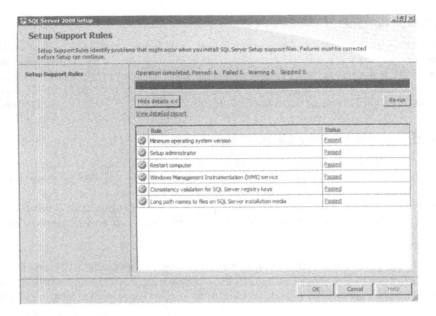

Figure 8-48. *Setup Support Rules dialog*

4. Setup will now perform further checks, as shown in Figure 8-49. Click Next.

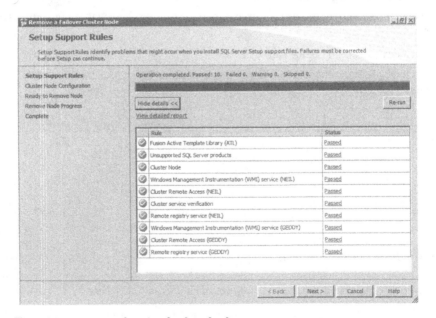

Figure 8-49. *Setup performing further checks*

5. On the Cluster Node Configuration dialog, shown in Figure 8-50, select the instance to remove the node from. Click Next.

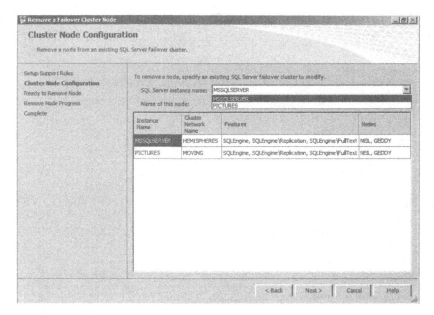

Figure 8-50. *Cluster Node Configuration option*

6. Click Remove on the Ready to Remove Node dialog, as shown in Figure 8-51.

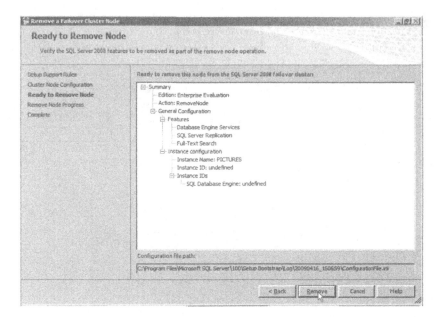

Figure 8-51. *Ready to Remove Node dialog*

7. If the node removal is successful, the Remove Node Progress dialog will appear, similar to the one in Figure 8-52.

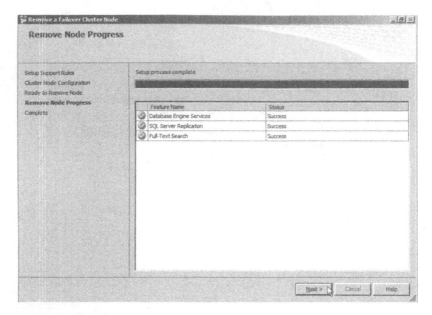

Figure 8-52. *Remove Node Progress dialog*

8. Click Close on the Complete dialog, as shown in Figure 8-53.

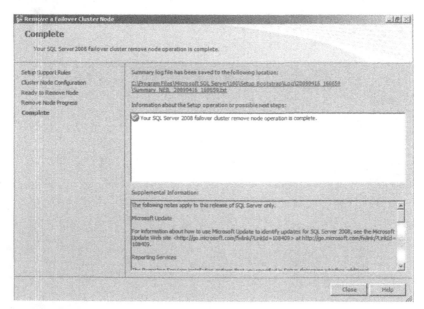

Figure 8-53. *Complete dialog*

Using the Command Line

Removing a node using a command line–based option is similar to everything else done previously in the book. The syntax is straightforward. The things you need to do are use an ACTION of RemoveNode and set a value for INSTANCENAME. Anything else, such as how you want to see progress, would be optional. A sample statement that would perform a silent removal (no pop-ups) but show the results of what is going in the log while removing a default instance would look like this:

```
setup /ACTION=RemoveNode /INSTANCENAME=MSSQLSERVER /INDICATEPROGRESS /Q
```

You can also create an INI file with the right commands and execute it with the CONFIGURATIONFILE switch, but this one is so short it is most likely not worth it unless you have a lot of nodes and you want to copy the same file to all nodes.

Changing the IP Address of a Failover Clustering Instance

You are allowed to change the IP address of the SQL Server 2008 failover clustering instance. To change it, you use the proper cluster administration tool for your version of Windows that is deployed. This section will show how to perform the task in Failover Cluster Management, cluster.exe, and PowerShell.

Unfortunately, changing the IP address for a clustered SQL Server instance will require you to schedule some sort of outage. The IP address itself can be changed dynamically, but for the change to take effect, the IP address resource for the SQL Server instance needs to be restarted. That means that SQL Server will be offline while the IP address is restarted and before you manually restart it.

Note Changing the IP address is dynamic from a pure network perspective, but you still may need to manually flush the DNS cache for each server that is accessing the SQL Server or Analysis Services instance that had its IP address changed If you need to access it more quickly than the time it takes to refresh your network. To flush the DNS cache, in a command window, enter ipconfig /flushdns. Then enter ipconfig /registerdns to refresh the DNS on that particular server.

Using Failover Cluster Management

The following steps will show you how to change an IP address for SQL Server or Analysis Services using Failover Cluster Management:

1. Start Failover Cluster Management.

2. Expand the tree for the Windows failover cluster, expand *Services and Applications*, and select the resource group with the SQL Server instance.

3. In the center status window, expand the instance Network Name resource (shown in Figure 8-48 as *Name: HEMISPHERES*) and you will see the IP address, as shown in Figure 8-54.

Figure 8-54. *IP address of a clustered SQL Server resource*

4. When the properties for the IP address are displayed, as shown in Figure 8-55, change the *Address* value to the desired new IP address and click OK. As shown in Figure 8-56, you will be informed that changing the IP address will require a restart of the resource. That means that all subsequent resources dependent on the IP address (the Network Name and all SQL Server–related resources) will have to be restarted as well. As noted earlier, you can opt to restart the resource at another time.

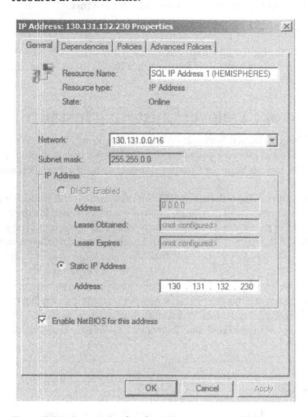

Figure 8-55. *Properties for the SQL Server IP address resource*

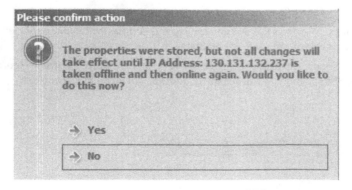

Figure 8-56. *Prompt informing you of the need to restart for the IP address change*

5. If you selected *Yes* on the dialog shown in Figure 8-56, you will now have to restart SQL Server. In Failover Cluster Management, select the resource group that contains the SQL Server resources, right-click, and select the option *Bring this service or application online*.

Using cluster.exe

To change the IP address using cluster.exe, follow these steps:

1. Open a command window.

2. At the command prompt, enter the command cluster *<cluster name>* resource. A sample execution is shown in Figure 8-57. This will show you a list of the resources in the cluster. In this example, the IP address resource names are SQL IP Address 1 (HEMISPHERES) and SQL IP Address 1 (MOVING).

```
C:\>cluster W2K8RTMFC resource
Listing status for all available resources:

Resource               Group             Node       Status
-------------------    --------------    ------     ------
Cluster Disk 1         Cluster Group     GEDDY      Online
Cluster Disk 2         HEMISPHERES       NEIL       Online
Cluster Disk 3         HEMISPHERES       NEIL       Online
Cluster Disk 4         HEMISPHERES       NEIL       Online
Cluster Disk 5         MOVING\PICTURES   GEDDY      Online
Cluster IP Address     Cluster Group     GEDDY      Online
Cluster Name           Cluster Group     GEDDY      Online
HEMISPHERES            HEMISPHERES       NEIL       Online
SQL IP Address 1 (HEMISPHERES) HEMISPHERES      NEIL        Online
SQL IP Address 1 (MOVING) MOVING\PICTURES   GEDDY        Online
SQL Network Name (MOVING) MOVING\PICTURES   GEDDY        Online
SQL Server             HEMISPHERES       NEIL       Online
SQL Server (PICTURES)  MOVING\PICTURES   GEDDY      Online
SQL Server Agent       HEMISPHERES       NEIL       Online
SQL Server Agent (PICTURES) MOVING\PICTURES   GEDDY        Online
```

Figure 8-57. *List of resources in the Windows failover cluster*

3. To show the current IP address for the resource you want to change, enter the command cluster *<cluster name>* resource *<resource name>* /priv. A sample execution and its output are shown in Figure 8-58.

```
C:\>cluster W2K8RTMFC resource "SQL IP Address 1 (HEMISPHERES)" /priv

Listing private properties for 'SQL IP Address 1 (HEMISPHERES)':

T  Resource                  Name                     Value
-- ----------------------    ----------------         ------------------------
FTR SQL IP Address 1 (HEMISPHERES) LeaseObtainedTime       (No Value)
FTR SQL IP Address 1 (HEMISPHERES) LeaseExpiresTime        (No Value)
SR SQL IP Address 1 (HEMISPHERES) DhcpServer             255.255.255.255

SR SQL IP Address 1 (HEMISPHERES) DhcpAddress            0.0.0.0
SR SQL IP Address 1 (HEMISPHERES) DhcpSubnetMask         255.0.0.0
S  SQL IP Address 1 (HEMISPHERES) Network                Cluster Network
 1
S  SQL IP Address 1 (HEMISPHERES) Address                130.131.132.230

S  SQL IP Address 1 (HEMISPHERES) SubnetMask             255.255.0.0
D  SQL IP Address 1 (HEMISPHERES) EnableNetBIOS          1 (0x1)
D  SQL IP Address 1 (HEMISPHERES) OverrideAddressMatch   0 (0x0)
D  SQL IP Address 1 (HEMISPHERES) EnableDhcp             0 (0x0)
```

Figure 8-58. *Showing the private properties of the IP address resource*

4. To change the IP address, use the Address private property. To change the subnet mask, use the SubnetMask private property. The syntax would be cluster *<cluster name>* resource *<resource name>* /priv Address=*<new IP address>*. If you are also changing the subnet mask, use the command cluster *<cluster name>* resource *<resource name>* /priv SubnetMask=*<new subnet>*. A sample execution and its output are shown in Figure 8-59.

```
C:\>cluster W2K8RTMFC resource "SQL IP Address 1 (HEMISPHERES)" /priv Address=13
0.131.132.250

System warning 5024 (0x000013a0).
The properties were stored but not all changes will take effect until the next t
ime the resource is brought online.
```

Figure 8-59. *Renaming the IP address using cluster.exe*

5. As shown in Figure 8-59, the change will not take effect until the resource is restarted. Because the IP address is the most fundamental resource in the resource group, restart the entire group. First, enter the command cluster *<cluster name>* group *<resource group name>* /OFFLINE. Then bring it back online with cluster *<cluster name>* group *<resource group name>* /ONLINE. An example is shown in Figure 8-60.

```
C:\Windows\system32>cluster W2K8RTMFC group HEMISPHERES /offline

Bringing resource group 'HEMISPHERES' offline...

Group                     Node              Status
-----------------------   ---------------   -------
HEMISPHERES               GEDDY             Offline


C:\Windows\system32>cluster W2K8RTMFC group HEMISPHERES /online

Bringing resource group 'HEMISPHERES' online...

Group                     Node              Status
-----------------------   ---------------   -------
HEMISPHERES               GEDDY             Online
```

Figure 8-60. *Restarting the cluster group with a renamed IP address*

Using PowerShell

To change the IP address using PowerShell, follow these steps:

1. Start PowerShell for your version of Windows Server 2008.

2. Use the cmdlet Get-ClusterResource to see a list of the resources in the Windows failover cluster. Enter Get-ClusterResource -Cluster *<cluster name>*. An example of the execution and output is shown in Figure 8-61.

```
PS C:\> Get-ClusterResource -Cluster W2K8RTMFC

Name                       State        Group                ResourceType
----                       -----        -----                ------------
Cluster Disk 1             Failed       Cluster Group        Physical Disk
Cluster Disk 2             Online       HEMISPHERES          Physical Disk
Cluster Disk 3             Online       MOVING\PICTURES      Physical Disk
Cluster Disk 4             Online       PERMANENT\WAVES      Physical Disk
Cluster Disk 5             Online       Available Storage    Physical Disk
Cluster IP Address         Online       Cluster Group        IP Address
Cluster Name               Online       Cluster Group        Network Name
SQL IP Address 1 <HEM...   Online       HEMISPHERES          IP Address
SQL IP Address 1 <MOV...   Online       MOVING\PICTURES      IP Address
SQL IP Address 1 <PER...   Online       PERMANENT\WAVES      IP Address
SQL Network Name <HEM...   Online       HEMISPHERES          Network Name
SQL Network Name <MOV...   Online       MOVING\PICTURES      Network Name
SQL Network Name <PER...   Online       PERMANENT\WAVES      Network Name
SQL Server                 Online       HEMISPHERES          SQL Server
SQL Server <PICTURES>      Failed       MOVING\PICTURES      SQL Server
SQL Server <WAVES>         Online       PERMANENT\WAVES      SQL Server
SQL Server Agent           Online       HEMISPHERES          SQL Server Agent
SQL Server Agent <PIC...   Offline      MOVING\PICTURES      SQL Server Agent
SQL Server Agent <WAVES>   Online       PERMANENT\WAVES      SQL Server Agent
```

Figure 8-61. *List of resources in the Windows failover cluster*

3. To show the current IP address for the resource you want to change, enter Get-ClusterResource <*resource name*> -Cluster <*cluster name*> | Get-ClusterParameter. A sample is shown in Figure 8-62.

```
PS C:\> Get-ClusterResource "SQL IP Address 1 <MOVING>" -Cluster W2K8RTMFC | Get-ClusterParameter

Object                     Name                Value                   Type
------                     ----                -----                   ----
SQL IP Address 1 <MOV...   Network             Public Network          String
SQL IP Address 1 <MOV...   Address             130.131.132.237         String
SQL IP Address 1 <MOV...   SubnetMask          255.255.0.0             String
SQL IP Address 1 <MOV...   EnableNetBIOS       1                       UInt32
SQL IP Address 1 <MOV...   OverrideAddressMatch 0                      UInt32
SQL IP Address 1 <MOV...   EnableDhcp          0                       UInt32
SQL IP Address 1 <MOV...   LeaseObtainedTime   1/1/0001 12:00:00 AM    DateTime
SQL IP Address 1 <MOV...   LeaseExpiresTime    1/1/0001 12:00:00 AM    DateTime
SQL IP Address 1 <MOV...   DhcpServer          255.255.255.255         String
SQL IP Address 1 <MOV...   DhcpAddress         0.0.0.0                 String
SQL IP Address 1 <MOV...   DhcpSubnetMask      255.0.0.0               String
```

Figure 8-62. *Showing the properties of the IP address resource*

4. To change the IP address, enter Get-ClusterResource <*resource name*> -Cluster <*cluster name*> | Set-ClusterParameter Address <*new IP address*>. If you are also changing the subnet mask, enter Get-ClusterResource <*resource name*> -Cluster <*cluster name*> | Set-ClusterParameter Subnet Mask <*new subnet mask*>. A sample execution and its output are shown in Figure 8-63.

```
PS C:\> Get-ClusterResource "SQL IP Address 1 <MOVING>" -Cluster W2K8RTMFC | Set-ClusterParameter Ad
dress 130.131.132.230
PS C:\> Get-ClusterResource "SQL IP Address 1 <MOVING>" -Cluster W2K8RTMFC | Get-ClusterParameter

Object                     Name                Value                   Type
------                     ----                -----                   ----
SQL IP Address 1 <MOV...   Network             Public Network          String
SQL IP Address 1 <MOV...   Address             130.131.132.230         String
SQL IP Address 1 <MOV...   SubnetMask          255.255.0.0             String
SQL IP Address 1 <MOV...   EnableNetBIOS       1                       UInt32
SQL IP Address 1 <MOV...   OverrideAddressMatch 0                      UInt32
SQL IP Address 1 <MOV...   EnableDhcp          0                       UInt32
SQL IP Address 1 <MOV...   LeaseObtainedTime   1/1/0001 12:00:00 AM    DateTime
SQL IP Address 1 <MOV...   LeaseExpiresTime    1/1/0001 12:00:00 AM    DateTime
SQL IP Address 1 <MOV...   DhcpServer          255.255.255.255         String
SQL IP Address 1 <MOV...   DhcpAddress         0.0.0.0                 String
SQL IP Address 1 <MOV...   DhcpSubnetMask      255.0.0.0               String
```

Figure 8-63. *Removing a node as an owner of the Network Name resource*

5. Since the change is not dynamic and all resources depend on the IP address, the entire group must be brought offline and then online. First, enter the command Stop-ClusterGroup `<resource group name>` -Cluster `<cluster name>`. Then bring it back online with Start-ClusterGroup `<resource group name>` -Cluster `<cluster name>`. An example is shown in Figure 8-64.

```
PS C:\> Stop-ClusterGroup "MOVING\PICTURES" -Cluster W2K8RTMFC

Name                        OwnerNode                                    State
____                        _____                                    _____
MOVING\PICTURES             geddy                                      Offline

PS C:\> Start-ClusterGroup "MOVING\PICTURES" -Cluster W2K8RTMFC

Name                        OwnerNode                                    State
____                        _____                                    _____
MOVING\PICTURES             geddy                                       Online
```

Figure 8-64. *Restarting the cluster group with a renamed IP address*

Renaming a Failover Clustering Instance

You can rename a SQL Server 2008 failover clustering instance, but realize there is a limitation: as with SQL Server 2005, if you are using a named instance, you can only rename the part before the slash. Consider this example: you have deployed a named instance of SQL Server 2008 called GRAND\ILLUSION. You could change the GRAND portion, but not ILLUSION. If you need to rename the entire instance, that would require a full uninstall and reinstall of SQL Server. It pays to do the necessary work up front so that you can avoid situations where you need to rename your SQL Server instances.

Unlike like changing an IP address, changing the Network Name resource is dynamic. However, if you do not have dynamic DNS in your environment, the network or security administrator will need to manually update the DNS entry. Also realize that all applications or desktops that connect to the SQL Server instance will need to be updated accordingly if they connect to it by name.

This section will show you how to rename your clustered instance of SQL Server or Analysis Services using Failover Cluster Management, cluster.exe, and PowerShell.

▓ **Note** Similar to the note mentioned earlier when changing an IP address, you may need to manually flush the DNS cache on a server or workstation connecting to the newly renamed SQL Server instance.

Using Failover Cluster Management

To change the name using Failover Cluster Management, follow these steps:

1. Start Failover Cluster Management.

2. Expand the tree for the Windows failover cluster, expand *Services and Applications*, and select the resource group with the SQL Server instance.

3. In the center status window, double-click the name found under Service Name. An example was shown earlier in Figure 8-54.

4. When the properties for the Network Name are displayed, change the value in the *DNS Name* field. The example in Figure 8-65 changes the name from HOLDYOURFIRE to HEMISPHERES. Click OK.

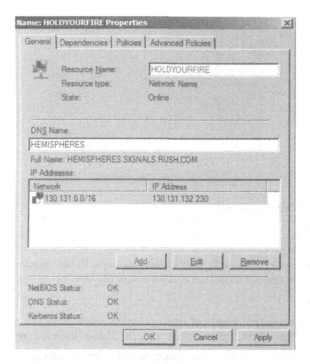

Figure 8-65. *Properties for the SQL Server Network Name resource*

5. You will then be prompted to confirm the change in name and advised that the clients will need to be updated, as shown in Figure 8-66. Select *Yes*.

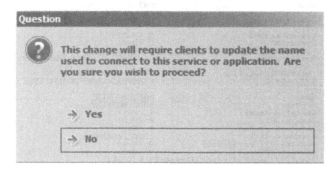

Figure 8-66. *Prompt to confirm the name change*

6. When finished, the instance will be renamed. In Failover Cluster Management, not only is the instance renamed, but the resource group/application name is also automatically updated, as shown in Figure 8-67.

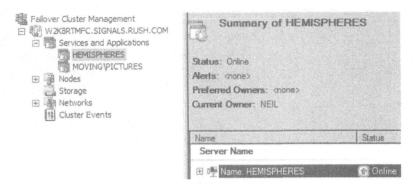

Figure 8-67. *Successful renaming operation*

Using cluster.exe

To change the name address using `cluster.exe`, perform the following steps. Unlike Failover Cluster Management, changing the name will require an outage if you use `cluster.exe`.

1. Open a command window.

2. At the command prompt, enter the command `cluster <cluster name> resource`. A sample execution is shown earlier in Figure 8-57. This will show you a list of the resources in the cluster.

3. To see the current name of the Network Name resource, enter the command `cluster <cluster name> resource <resource name> /priv`. A sample is shown in Figure 8-68.

```
C:\>cluster W2K8RTMFC resource "HOLDYOURFIRE" /priv

Listing private properties for 'HOLDYOURFIRE':

T   Resource            Name                        Value
--  ------------------  --------------------------  ---------------------------
BR  HOLDYOURFIRE        ResourceData                01 00 00 00 ... (260 byte
s>
DR  HOLDYOURFIRE        StatusNetBIOS               0 (0x0)
DR  HOLDYOURFIRE        StatusDNS                   0 (0x0)
DR  HOLDYOURFIRE        StatusKerberos              0 (0x0)
SR  HOLDYOURFIRE        CreatingDC                  \\W2K8DC.SIGNALS.RUSH.COM

PTR HOLDYOURFIRE        LastDNSUpdateTime           4/16/2009 5:10:38 PM
SR  HOLDYOURFIRE        ObjectGUID                  e98a9df5d680c74fb0d4f596c
b621da1
S   HOLDYOURFIRE        Name                        HOLDYOURFIRE
S   HOLDYOURFIRE        DnsName                     HOLDYOURFIRE
D   HOLDYOURFIRE        RemapPipeNames              1 (0x1)
D   HOLDYOURFIRE        RequireDNS                  0 (0x0)
D   HOLDYOURFIRE        RequireKerberos             1 (0x1)
D   HOLDYOURFIRE        HostRecordTTL               1200 (0x4b0)
D   HOLDYOURFIRE        RegisterAllProvidersIP      0 (0x0)
D   HOLDYOURFIRE        PublishPTRRecords           0 (0x0)
D   HOLDYOURFIRE        TimerCallbackAdditionalThreshold 5 (0x5)
```

Figure 8-68. *Private properties for a Network Name*

4. You cannot modify the name while the resource is online using `cluster.exe`; if you try, you will see the error shown in Figure 8-69. Take the Network Name resource offline. Use the command `cluster <cluster name> resource <resource name> /offline`.

```
System error 5019 has occurred (0x0000139b).
The operation could not be completed because the cluster resource is online.
```

Figure 8-69. *Error if the Network Name resource is online*

5. To change the name of the SQL Server or Analysis Services instance, use the command cluster `<cluster name>` resource `<resource name>` /PRIV DnsName=`<new instance name>`. You will not get a confirmation if it was successful.

6. I also recommend changing the resource group name to match the new name. To do this task, use the command cluster `<cluster name>` group `<resource group name>` /RENAME:`<new group name>`. A sample and its output are shown in Figure 8-70.

```
C:\>cluster W2K8RTMFC group "MOVING\PICTURES" /RENAME:ALLAN\PICTURES

Renaming resource group 'MOVING\PICTURES'...

Group                        Node                Status
--------------------------   -----------------   -------
ALLAN\PICTURES               GEDDY               Offline
```

Figure 8-70. *Renaming the resource group*

7. Bring the resource group online with the command cluster `<cluster name>` group `<group name>` /online.

Using PowerShell

To change the name address using PowerShell, follow the steps in this section. As with cluster.exe, you cannot modify the Network Name without taking the resource (and SQL Server) offline.

1. Start PowerShell for your version of Windows Server 2008.

2. Use the cmdlet Get-ClusterResource to see a list of the resources in the Windows failover cluster. Enter Get-ClusterResource -Cluster `<cluster name>`. An example of the execution and output was shown earlier in Figure 8-61. In this case, you are looking for resource types of Network Name.

3. To show the current name for the resource you want to change, enter Get-ClusterResource `<resource name>` -Cluster `<cluster name>` | Get-ClusterParameter. A sample is shown in Figure 8-71.

```
PS C:\> Get-ClusterResource "SQL Network Name (HEMISPHERES)" -Cluster W2K8RTMFC | Get-ClusterParamet
er

Object                       Name                Value                   Type
------                       ----                -----                   ----
SQL Network Name (HEM...     Name                HEMISPHERES             String
SQL Network Name (HEM...     DnsName             HEMISPHERES             String
SQL Network Name (HEM...     RemapPipeNames      1                       UInt32
SQL Network Name (HEM...     RequireDNS          0                       UInt32
SQL Network Name (HEM...     RequireKerberos     1                       UInt32
SQL Network Name (HEM...     HostRecordTTL       1200                    UInt32
SQL Network Name (HEM...     RegisterAllProvidersIP  0                   UInt32
SQL Network Name (HEM...     PublishPTRRecords   0                       UInt32
SQL Network Name (HEM...     TimerCallbackAddition...  5                 UInt32
SQL Network Name (HEM...     ResourceData        (1, 0, 0, 0...)         ByteArray
SQL Network Name (HEM...     StatusNetBIOS       0                       UInt32
SQL Network Name (HEM...     StatusDNS           0                       UInt32
SQL Network Name (HEM...     StatusKerberos      0                       UInt32
SQL Network Name (HEM...     CreatingDC          \\W2K8DC.SIGNALS.RUSH... String
SQL Network Name (HEM...     LastDNSUpdateTime   6/1/2009 8:40:50 AM     DateTime
SQL Network Name (HEM...     ObjectGUID          09b865de39c0ac4d8ad84... String
```

Figure 8-71. *Showing the properties of the Network Name resource*

4. Take the resource group offline with Stop-ClusterGroup `<resource group name>` -Cluster `<cluster name>`.

5. To change the name address, enter Get-ClusterResource *<resource name>* -Cluster *<cluster name>* | Set-ClusterParameter DnsName *<new instance name>*. A sample execution and its output are shown in Figure 8-72.

```
PS C:\> Get-ClusterResource "SQL Network Name (HEMISPHERES)" -Cluster W2K8RTMFC ! Set-ClusterParamet
er DnsName ALLAN
PS C:\> Get-ClusterResource "SQL Network Name (HEMISPHERES)" -Cluster W2K8RTMFC ! Get-ClusterParamet
er

Object                        Name                  Value                   Type
------                        ----                  -----                   ----
SQL Network Name (HEM...      Name                  ALLAN                   String
SQL Network Name (HEM...      DnsName               ALLAN                   String
SQL Network Name (HEM...      RemapPipeNames        1                       UInt32
SQL Network Name (HEM...      RequireDNS            0                       UInt32
SQL Network Name (HEM...      RequireKerberos       1                       UInt32
SQL Network Name (HEM...      HostRecordTTL         1200                    UInt32
SQL Network Name (HEM...      RegisterAllProvidersIP 0                      UInt32
SQL Network Name (HEM...      PublishPTRRecords     0                       UInt32
SQL Network Name (HEM...      TimerCallbackAddition... 5                    UInt32
SQL Network Name (HEM...      ResourceData          (1, 0, 0, 0...)         ByteArray
SQL Network Name (HEM...      StatusNetBIOS         0                       UInt32
SQL Network Name (HEM...      StatusDNS             0                       UInt32
SQL Network Name (HEM...      StatusKerberos        0                       UInt32
SQL Network Name (HEM...      CreatingDC            \\W2K8DC.SIGNALS.RUSH... String
SQL Network Name (HEM...      LastDNSUpdateTime     1/1/0001 12:00:00 AM    DateTime
SQL Network Name (HEM...      ObjectGUID            09b865de39c8ac4d8ad84... String
```

Figure 8-72. *Renaming a SQL Server instance with PowerShell*

6. To rename the resource group to match the newly changed name, enter

```
$group = Get-ClusterGroup <resource group name> -Cluster <cluster name>
$group.Name = "<new resource group name>"
```

An example is shown in Figure 8-73.

7. Bring the resource group online with Start-ClusterGroup *<resource group name>* -Cluster *<cluster name>*.

```
PS C:\Windows\system32> Get-ClusterGroup -Cluster W2K8RTMFC

Name                          OwnerNode                               State
----                          ---------                               -----
HEMISPHERES                   neil                                    Offline
MOVING\PICTURES               neil                                    Offline
PERMANENT\WAVES               geddy                                   Online
Cluster Group                 neil                                    Online
Available Storage             alex2                                   Online

PS C:\Windows\system32> $group = Get-ClusterGroup HEMISPHERES -Cluster W2K8RTMFC
PS C:\Windows\system32> $group.Name = "ALLAN"
PS C:\Windows\system32> Get-ClusterGroup -Cluster W2K8RTMFC

Name                          OwnerNode                               State
----                          ---------                               -----
ALLAN                         neil                                    Offline
MOVING\PICTURES               neil                                    Offline
PERMANENT\WAVES               geddy                                   Online
Cluster Group                 neil                                    Online
Available Storage             alex2                                   Online
```

Figure 8-73. *An example of renaming a SQL Server instance with PowerShell*

Patching a SQL Server 2008 Failover Clustering Instance

Applying a patch to a clustered SQL Server 2008 instance is different than what you have done in previous versions. As you know, in previous versions all nodes were patched at once. This is not possible in SQL Server 2008. That is not necessarily a bad thing, since some did have problems with that updating method, and it goes hand-in-hand with the change to the main installation procedure. Microsoft is recommending a rolling upgrade approach that at a high level works this way:

• Exclude nodes as possible owners from that particular instance (or instances) of SQL Server that will be upgraded. Microsoft recommends that you remove half of the nodes, but if you have an odd number of nodes, half is not possible.

- Apply the update to the nodes that were removed.
- Add the excluded nodes back as owners.
- Fail the SQL Server instance over to one of the upgraded nodes.
- Exclude the nodes as possible owners that were not upgraded and upgrade them.
- Add those excluded nodes back as possible owners.

One huge change that should be pointed out is that with SQL Server 2008, a service pack can be cleanly removed. Prior to SQL Server 2008, there was really no way to uninstall a SQL Server service pack from a SQL Server instance, and you pretty much had to do an uninstall and reinstall. From an availability perspective, this new ability is huge.

■**Tip** A SQL Server 2008 update as tested with SQL Server 2008 Service Pack 1 allows you to apply it to multiple instances on a given node at the same time (which is different from operations such as installing a new instance, where it is an instance-by-instance, node-by-node affair). My recommendation is that if you can schedule things properly, update as many instances (if not all of them) at once to minimize downtime. However, realize that there are multiple things that will influence that decision, which include but are not limited to application support for said update, coordination of multiple groups and applications for downtime, and tolerance of the business for updating multiple items at once.

The following subsections will show you how to apply an update to a clustered SQL Server or Analysis Services instance by demonstrating the installation of SQL Server 2008 Service Pack 1.

Rolling Update Step 1: Excluding Nodes As Possible Owners

This section will show you how to remove nodes safely from a clustered instance if you are applying an update to that instance.

Using Failover Cluster Management

To exclude nodes using Failover Cluster Management, perform these steps:

1. Start Failover Cluster Management.
2. Expand the tree for the Windows failover cluster, expand *Services and Applications*, and select the resource group with the SQL Server instance.
3. In the center status window, double-click the name found under Service Name.
4. Select the *Advanced Policies* tab.
5. Under *Possible Owners*, deselect the nodes that you would like to apply the update to. An example is shown in Figure 8-74. As noted earlier, Microsoft recommends you remove half of the nodes. If possible, try to leave at least one node for failover, so at a minimum, leave two selected. Deselecting nodes allows you to update them while giving you the option to retain high availability since there will be more than one node to fail over to. If you have an odd number of nodes, you may not be able to do half, so ensure that at least the node currently owning the instance is selected. Even if you have a two-node cluster, deselect one node. Click OK.

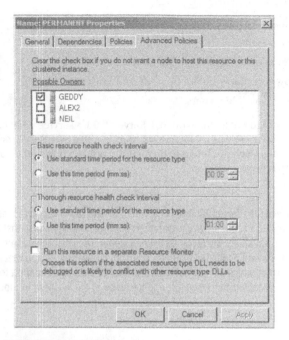

Figure 8-74. *Deselected nodes*

Note If you try to deselect the node that currently owns the SQL Server or Analysis Services resources, you will see the error dialog shown in Figure 8-75.

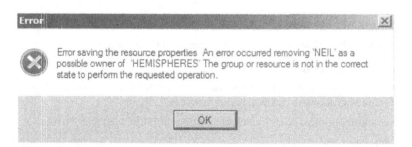

Figure 8-75. *Error if deselecting the node owning the resources*

6. If you are going to be updating more than one instance at a time, perform steps 2 through 5 for each instance.

Using cluster.exe

This section is similar to the previous one, except it will show you how to remove nodes using `cluster.exe`.

1. Open a command window.

2. At the command prompt, enter the command cluster *<cluster name>* resource to see the possible Network Name resources.

3. To see a list of the possible owners of an instance's Network Name resource, enter the command cluster *<cluster name>* resource "*<Network Name resource name>*" /listowners. An example is shown in Figure 8-76.

```
C:\>cluster W2K8RTMFC resource "SQL Network Name (PERMANENT)" /listowners

Listing possible owners for resource 'SQL Network Name (PERMANENT)':
Possible Owner Nodes
--------------------
GEDDY
NEIL
ALEX2
```

Figure 8-76. *List of owners of the Network Name resource*

4. To remove an owner from the Network Name resource, enter the command cluster *<cluster name>* resource "*<Network Name resource name>*" /removeowner:*<node to remove>*. If the resource has spaces, you will need to encase it in double quotes. An example is shown in Figure 8-77.

```
C:\>cluster W2K8RTMFC resource "SQL Network Name (PERMANENT)" /removeowner:NEIL

Removing 'NEIL' from possible owners of 'SQL Network Name (PERMANENT)'...


C:\>cluster W2K8RTMFC resource "SQL Network Name (PERMANENT)" /listowners
Listing possible owners for resource 'SQL Network Name (PERMANENT)':
Possible Owner Nodes
--------------------
GEDDY
ALEX2
```

Figure 8-77. *Removing a node as an owner of the Network Name resource*

5. Repeat step 4 for all nodes that need to be removed.

Using PowerShell

Use the following steps to remove possible owners using PowerShell:

1. Start PowerShell for your version of Windows Server 2008.

2. Use the cmdlet Get-ClusterResource to see a list of the resources in the Windows failover cluster. Enter Get-ClusterResource -Cluster *<cluster name>*. An example of the execution and output was shown earlier in Figure 8-61. In this case, you are looking for resource types of Network Name.

3. To show the current name for the resource you want to change, enter Get-ClusterResource *<resource name>* -Cluster *<cluster name>* | Get-ClusterOwnerNode. A sample is shown in Figure 8-78.

```
PS C:\> Get-ClusterResource "SQL Server (PICTURES)" -Cluster W2K8RTMFC | Get-ClusterOwnerNode
ClusterObject                                       OwnerNodes
-----------                                         ----------
SQL Server (PICTURES)                               {alex2, geddy, neil}
```

Figure 8-78. *List of possible owner nodes*

4. To change the possible owners, enter Get-ClusterResource *<resource name>* -Cluster *<cluster name>* | Set-ClusterOwnerNode "*<list of possible owners separated by commas>*". Unlike cluster.exe, the possible owners on the list are the actual owners you want to be able to own the SQL Server resources. Exclude the ones that will get the SQL Server update. A sample execution and its output are shown in Figure 8-79.

```
PS C:\> Get-ClusterResource "SQL Server (PICTURES)" -Cluster W2K8RTMFC | Set-ClusterOwnerNode "GEDD
Y"
PS C:\> Get-ClusterResource "SQL Server (PICTURES)" -Cluster W2K8RTMFC | Get-ClusterOwnerNode
ClusterObject                                       OwnerNodes
-----------                                         ----------
SQL Server (PICTURES)                               {geddy}
```

Figure 8-79. *Successful removal of possible owners*

Caution Make a note of all the nodes you remove whether you use Failover Cluster Management, cluster.exe, or PowerShell. You will have to add them in later.

Rolling Update Step 2: Installing a SQL Server 2008 Update

This section will show the steps on how to install an update (in this case, SQL Server 2008 Service Pack 1) on a clustered instance.

Using the Setup User Interface

Follow these instructions to install an update using the Setup interface:

1. Download the appropriate update that matches the version of SQL Server 2008 you have deployed. For example, if you have the x64 version of SQL Server 2008, download the update that is for an x64 processor. Place the update in a central location or on the node to be updated.

2. Log onto the node that will be updated with an account that has administrative privileges in the cluster.

3. Run the update by double-clicking the file that you downloaded.

4. Setup will first run a series of checks. If there are any warnings, investigate them. If you do not deselect any nodes (as shown in Rolling Update Step 1) and execute the update on the node owning the SQL Server resources, you will see the message shown in Figure 8-80. Applying an update in the fashion to cause the dialog in Figure 8-80 is essentially doing it the way you did for clusters prior to SQL Server 2008, and you do not get any advantage of a rolling upgrade. If everything looks fine, click Next.

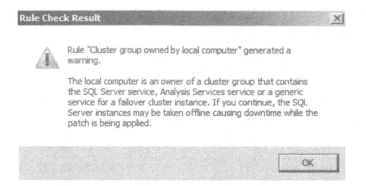

Figure 8-80. *Warning if the node owns the SQL Server clustered resources*

5. On the License Terms dialog, shown in Figure 8-81, select the *I accept the license terms* check box and click Next.

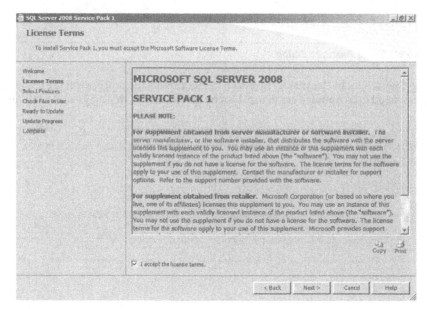

Figure 8-81. *License Terms dialog*

6. On the Select Features dialog, select what you want to update. Anything that has already been updated will have a grayed-out check next to it, as shown in Figure 8-82. In that example, the common files and the default instance were already updated to Service Pack 1, but the named instance was not. As you can see, you can select more than one instance to update at the same time.

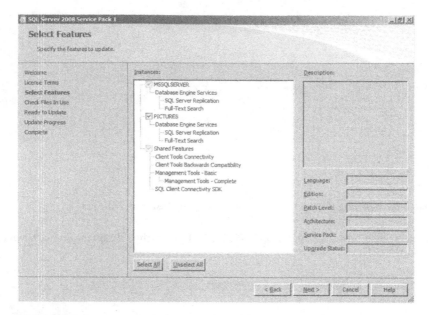

Figure 8-82. *Select Features dialog*

7. On the Check Files In Use dialog, as shown in Figure 8-83, the process will see if any of the files that need to be updated are in use. If some files are in use, this may cause a reboot. Click Next.

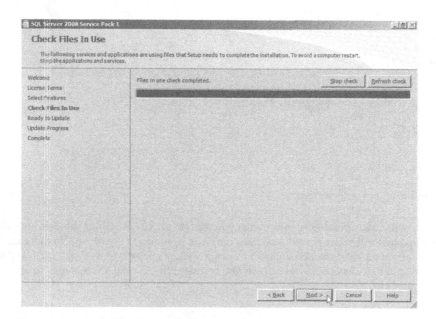

Figure 8-83. *Check Files In Use dialog*

8. On the Ready to Update dialog, shown in Figure 8-84, click Update.

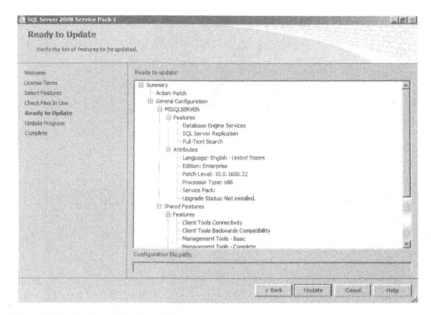

Figure 8-84. *Ready to Update dialog*

9. When the update is finished installing, it will appear similar to the dialog shown in Figure 8-85. Click Next.

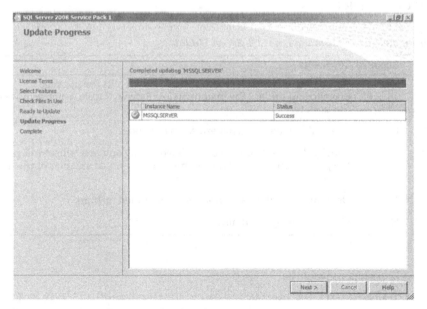

Figure 8-85. *Successfully completed update*

10. On the Complete dialog, shown in Figure 8-86, click Close.

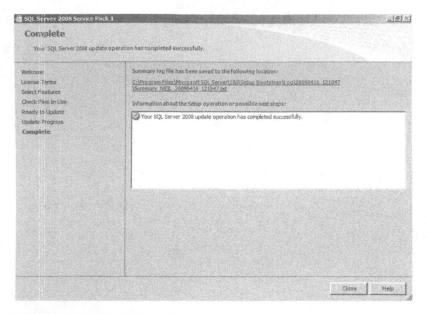

Figure 8-86. *Complete dialog*

Using the Command Line

To install an update via the command line, you run the executable of the package with the possible parameters shown in Table 8-1.

Table 8-1. *Parameters for a Command Line SQL Server Update*

Parameter	Required	Comments
Action	Yes	This can have either a value of Patch, which tells the package to execute and update the instance(s), or Remove Patch, which removes the update.
AllInstances	No	Install the patch to all instances on the node.
Instancename	No	Specify the instance(s) to be updated if only one or a subset will get the patch. Separate instance names with commas and do not use any spaces.
Quiet	No	Do a quiet install in a completely unattended fashion.
Qs	No	Shows the progress dialog.

Some sample executions would be

```
SQLServer2008SP1-KB968369-x64-ENU.exe /Action=Patch /InstanceName=MSSQLSERVER,WAVES
```

```
SQLServer2008SP1-KB968369-x64-ENU.exe /Action=Patch /AllInstances /quiet
```

■Tip If you have to remove a patch using the command line, use a value of RemovePatch for the Action parameter.

Rolling Update Step 3: Adding Excluded Nodes

Once the update has been applied to the nodes that were deselected, you must add them back so that SQL Server can fail over to them again.

Using Failover Cluster Management

Following are the steps to add the nodes back in using Failover Cluster Management:

1. Start Failover Cluster Management.

2. Expand the tree for the Windows failover cluster, expand *Services and Applications*, and select the resource group with the SQL Server instance.

3. In the center status window, double-click the name found under Service Name.

4. Select the *Advanced Policies* tab.

5. Under *Possible Owners*, select the nodes that were already updated. If there are other nodes to be updated, deselect the others you wish to now update, and repeat Rolling Update Steps 1 through 3 until all nodes are updated. Click OK.

6. If you are going to be updating more than one instance at a time, perform steps 2 through 5 for each instance.

Using cluster.exe

This section is similar to the previous one, except it will show you how to add nodes using cluster.exe. Here is the process to follow:

1. Open a command window.

2. To add an owner from the Network Name resource, enter the command cluster *<cluster name>* resource "*<Network Name resource name>*" /addowner:*<node to remove>*. If the resource has spaces, you will need to encase it in double quotes. An example is shown in Figure 8-87.

```
C:\>cluster resource HEMISPHERES /addowner:GEDDY
Adding 'GEDDY' to possible owners of 'HEMISPHERES'...
```

Figure 8-87. *Adding a node as an owner of the Network Name resource*

3. Repeat step 2 for all nodes that need to be added.

4. To verify that the owners were added properly, enter the command cluster *<cluster name>* resource "*<Network Name resource name>*" /listowners.

Using PowerShell

Use the following steps to include possible owners using PowerShell:

1. Start PowerShell for your version of Windows Server 2008.

2. To change the possible owners, enter Get-ClusterResource *<resource name>* -Cluster *<cluster name>* | Set-ClusterOwnerNode "*<list of possible owners separated by commas>*". Use the names of the nodes that were already updated for the list of possible owners.

Caution When you get to the point where the only node (or one of the only nodes) left to update is the one owning the SQL Server or Analysis Services resources, you will have to schedule an outage because you will need to manually fail the resources over to one of the already upgraded nodes. Once the original node owning the resources has been updated, you can either choose to fail the resources back, which will cause yet another outage, or leave them on the node they are currently running on.

Summary

You have planned for and installed both Windows and SQL Server failover clustering, and in this chapter, learned how to administer the unique aspects of a Windows Server 2008–based SQL Server 2008 failover cluster, which differs from a standalone implementation. At this point, there is nothing else you need to know from a day-to-day standpoint of dealing with your clustering implementations. The next and final chapter of this book is going to discuss virtualization and how it fits into the world of SQL Server failover clustering.

■■■

CHAPTER 9

Virtualization and Failover Clustering

Outside of the normal virtualization of names and IP addresses that happens when you cluster Windows and SQL Server, until now I have avoided discussing what most people associate these days with the term *virtualization*: taking a physical server and making it a virtual machine (VM), or *guest*, under software designed to host virtualized servers. Virtualization software uses what is known as a hypervisor to do the virtualization. Popular virtualization platforms include Microsoft's own Hyper-V feature, which is built into Windows Server 2008, and VMware's ESX server. This chapter will discuss where virtualizing SQL Server deployments may (or may not) fit into your IT department's virtualization strategy, and how virtualization can be achieved.

SQL Server Failover Clustering and Virtualization Support

When I initially wrote this section and sent it out for review, Microsoft did not support deploying SQL Server in a failover clustering configuration where the cluster nodes were guests under a hypervisor. As I was editing and trying to finish the book, Microsoft did a 180-degree turn on its stance, and now supports guest failover clustering (both SQL Server 2005 and SQL Server 2008) under virtualization even in a production environment as long as the guest VMs serving as nodes are running a version of Windows Server 2008. This means that SQL Server 2000 as well as older operating systems (such as Windows Server 2003) would not be supported as valid cluster configurations under virtualization. Knowledge Base article 956893 (http://support.microsoft.com/KB/956893) now reflects this updated status.

Considerations for Virtualizing Failover Clusters

Now that Microsoft supports virtualizing failover clusters with SQL Server, there are some things you must think about and consider before you choose this road as your deployment strategy. This section will discuss the aspects of virtualization that you need to consider.

Choosing a Virtualization Platform

Guest failover clustering is supported under Windows Server 2008 with Hyper-V, Windows Server 2008 R2, and some third-party hypervisors. Non-Microsoft hypervisors must appear as part of the Windows Server Virtualization Validation Program (SVVP). The SVVP is a list of approved hypervisors that you can use and get full Microsoft support. The SVVP is not unlike previous versions of Windows where you had to check the entire cluster solution to see if it was in the Windows Server Catalog or Hardware Compatibility List. More information on the SVVP and the list of supported hypervisors can be found at http://www.windowsservercatalog.com/svvp.aspx.

> ■Note Another potential option for a hypervisor is Microsoft Hyper-V Server 2008 (and the forthcoming Hyper-V Server 2008 R2). I have not used or seen it, but it is a basic virtualization platform that does not have the full virtualization features of Windows Server 2008 or Windows Server 2008 R2. More information and a comparison chart with the other versions of Windows Server 2008 can be found at http://www.microsoft.com/hyper-v-server/en/us/default.aspx.

Determining the Location of Guest Nodes

Technically, you can configure both guest nodes under the same hypervisor. As I see it, that is a bit problematic. Yes, you gain availability for your SQL Server instances, but you are essentially negating the one big thing that clustering prevents: a single point of failure from a server perspective. If the hypervisor fails, you would lose both nodes. Is that really the configuration you want? I would place the guests that will function as nodes on separate hypervisors to ensure that the server with the hypervisor will not be a single point of failure.

Since clustering is about redundancy, can you ensure that the virtual network cards or HBAs are using different paths on the underlying physical hypervisor? If not, that is a good reason not to either do failover clustering with guests, or split the nodes over different hypervisors. Virtualized failover clusters using guests are subject to all of the same rules that clusters configured on physical servers would have to adhere to.

> ■Caution Although from what I can tell it should be a supported configuration if it passes validation, I would never mix virtual machines and physical servers as nodes of the same cluster. I would either make all of your nodes physical servers, or guests under a hypervisor.

Performance

One of the biggest concerns for many when it comes to virtualization is performance. At this point, performance for virtual machines can be close to, if not the same as, many physical server configurations. If you are a DBA, realize that virtualization is not a fad, nor is it going away, so you need to work with your counterparts to determine if the SQL Server deployments you are doing should be virtualized. To that point, there are definitely some considerations that will affect that decision.

Most hypervisors do limit the number of processors that the guest can be configured with. Realize that when you configure a virtualized server with N processors, you are not necessarily getting N processors. To the guest, it appears that way, but in reality, you are getting access to up to that amount of processor power, but it is shared among all of the other virtual machines. This is why more often than not, deployments that are not very resource intensive tend to better for virtualization. I am not saying that heavily used SQL Server deployments are impossible under virtualization, but I would suggest testing before using that configuration.

Memory is similar to processor, although it is not as much of a concern. With most hypervisors, when you configure a virtual machine to use M gigabytes of memory, it will consume that much under the hypervisor. That means that the server that functions as the hypervisor will generally have a lot of memory. You do have to also realize that virtualization has overhead. For example, if you configure a guest to use 8 GB of memory, it is really 8 GB plus whatever overhead of virtualization is imposed by the hypervisor. This is why servers functioning as hypervisors generally have a lot of memory in them.

Arguably the biggest concern for virtualizing nodes will be disk I/O. Whether you are using iSCSI in the node or virtual HBAs, underneath the covers, all of the guests are sharing the hypervisor's I/O architecture. As has been mentioned numerous times, I/O is the key to a good portion of SQL Server performance. The easiest way to get better performance from guests is to configure them to use physical disks, not ones that are virtualized through the hypervisor. You still may be sharing some of the underlying disk functionality of the hypervisor to access those disks, but using "real" hardware where you can in this case provides a big benefit since you have full bandwidth of the disk.

Licensing

Many will virtualize to reduce cost, but remember that you need to license SQL Server and Windows for each guest. If you choose SQL Server 2008 Enterprise Edition and license all of the processors in the server with the hypervisor, you can configure SQL Server on any number of virtual processors under that one physical server. This would arguably be the cheapest option. If you do not purchase an Enterprise Edition license for the hypervisor, you will need to license each guest separately. For more information, consult http://www.microsoft.com/sqlserver/2008/en/us/licensing-faq.aspx. For Windows, consult http://www.microsoft.com/licensing/about-licensing/virtualization.aspx as well as http://www.microsoft.com/WindowsServer2008/en/us/hyperv-calculators.aspx.

■**Note** The issue of which applications and deployments are best suited for physical hardware and which can be done using virtualized hardware is discussed in various SQL Server consolidation whitepapers. At the time of writing this chapter, I'm writing the technical consolidation whitepaper for SQL Server 2008, which I hope will be out in the summer of 2009. Other good papers that you should read are "Running SQL Server 2008 in a Hyper-V Environment: Best Practices and Performance Considerations" (http://download.microsoft.com/download/d/9/4/ d948f981-926e-40fa-a026-5bfcf076d9b9/SQL2008inHyperV2008.docx), "Green IT in Practice: SQL Server Consolidation in Microsoft IT" (http://msdn.microsoft.com/en-us/architecture/dd393309.aspx), and "SQL Server Consolidation at Microsoft" (http://technet.microsoft.com/en-us/library/ dd557540.aspx).

Windows Server 2008 R2 and Virtualization

Another option for clustering SQL Server guests is new to Windows Server 2008 R2. If you cluster Windows Server 2008 R2–based nodes, Microsoft provides support for failover of virtualized guests under those physical clustered nodes if Hyper-V is configured. If a node goes down, the hosted guest will fail over to another node automatically, not unlike physical Windows failover clustering with a clustered SQL Server instance on it. There are four scenarios for a guest failover with Windows Server 2008 R2 and Hyper-V:

- The node experiences an unplanned failure, and the virtual machine (VM) may have been doing some processing. There could be data loss in the failover, and the VM is started on another node at the point of failure.

- The resource group containing the VM is manually failed over to another node. In this case, the VM will be stopped gracefully and brought up on the other node with no data loss.

- Instead of moving a whole group, you want to just move a single VM to another node for hosting. Hyper-V under Windows Server 2008 supports *Quick Migration*. With Quick Migration, it is a graceful move (similar to moving an entire resource group), and the clients using the VM may experience a brief interruption.

- Finally, Hyper-V under Windows Server 2008 R2 has a new feature for VMs called *Live Migration*. This is a planned move from one node to another where no downtime will be incurred and is totally transparent to end users and applications. Obviously this is a very desirable scenario.

Note To enable Hyper-V, you must add it as a role to the server. See the section "Step 3: Add Features and Roles" in Chapter 3. Your processor must also support virtualization as part of its hardware (either AMD-V or Intel's VT, both set in BIOS), as well as data execution protection (AMD: no execute bit; Intel: XD execute disable).

Unfortunately, Windows Server 2008 R2's release candidate was literally released as I was writing this chapter, so I was not able to test either a Quick or Live Migration with Hyper-V and clustered nodes as hosts for VMs. However, you can see in Figures 9-1 and 9-2 how everything integrates. Figure 9-1 shows where you would make the VM available in a utility called System Center Virtual Machine Manager (SCVMM). More information on SCVMM can be found at http://www.microsoft.com/systemcenter/virtualmachinemanager/en/us/default.aspx. Figure 9-2 shows in Failover Cluster Manager where you have the Live and Quick Migration ability. Thanks to Microsoft for providing the screenshots.

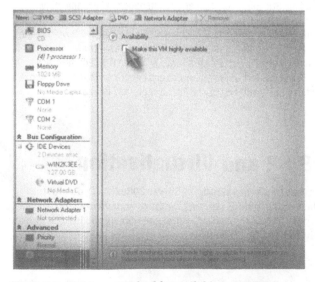

Figure 9-1. *Making a VM highly available in SCVMM*

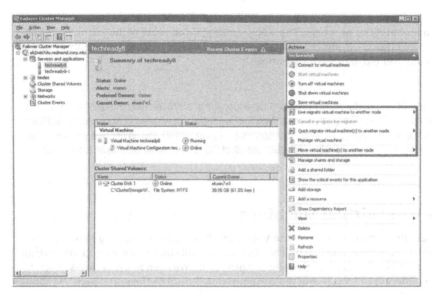

Figure 9-2. *VM migration features in Failover Cluster Manager*

How does one of the migration options (Quick or Live) fit into a longer-term picture for your SQL Server deployments? If you are getting a lot of pressure to virtualize SQL Server, and you need to make the VMs highly available with minimal interruption, physically clustering Windows and using Hyper-V with Live Migration may be a way to get the best of virtualization and availability for guests that will work well as virtualized. I feel this is a better option than clustering guests under a hypervisor where you may not be able to guarantee redundancy for some components or have the hypervisor be a potential point of failure.

As good as they are, deploying virtualized guests under a clustered hypervisor with Quick Migration and Live Migration will probably never replace every physical cluster you planned or may plan on deploying, as some applications and deployments are better suited for physical hardware (a discussion outside the scope of this book), but they may provide a compromise with your IT department to allow clustering to be used to get highly available SQL Server deployments even if they are on VMs.

Of course, using Live Migration assumes you will be using Windows Server 2008 R2 and Hyper-V. Other virtualization technologies may offer similar functionality, so do your homework to understand how your SQL Server deployments can be made highly available if you are forced to use VMs in production. Chances are you will use some of the other native SQL Server technologies described in Chapter 1 in addition to any tools or features provided by the virtualization platform.

Creating a Virtualized Failover Cluster

I have been using virtualized clusters for nearly 10 years. I could not have done a lot of the talks or written the books and documents without virtualization to demonstrate and test failover clustering. My living arrangements do not have the proper electrical power or air conditioning to have my own server farm or SAN, nor can I afford to purchase that much equipment! Virtualization when used properly (even in production) is a good thing for IT, but it is not right in all cases.

In this section, I will show you how to create a self-contained and virtualized SQL Server failover cluster for development and test purposes. The steps, concepts, and some of the instructions can also be used for a production environment assuming that your choice of hypervisor is supported for creating guests in a failover clustering configuration.

Tip If you want to use 64-bit guests, your processor must support Intel's virtualization extensions (known as VT, and sometimes referred to as VT-x). VT support is something that is generally configured in a computer's BIOS. Most processors these days support VT, but some hardware vendors choose to lock VT and do not give you the option in BIOS to enable it. That means you can virtualize a cluster, but all of the guests would need to be running 32-bit versions of Windows.

Step 1: Create the Virtual Machines

Before you can do anything, you must create the VMs that will be used. You need a minimum of three VMs: one domain controller and two nodes. This section will show you how to create a virtual machine with VMware Workstation, and give you the proper information to use Hyper-V. Each of your VMs may have different processes, but the configuration should be the same. Each VM should have:

- At least one processor
- The proper amount of memory for the particular version of Windows
- One disk for the operating system (virtualized or physical)
- A display adapter
- A minimum of three network cards (one for the public network, one for the private/heartbeat network, and one for iSCSI) for the cluster nodes; two for the domain controller (one for the public network and one for iSCSI)
- A CD/DVD drive (virtualized or physical)

Caution In a production environment, you need full redundancy, meaning two domain controllers. You also would most likely not be placing the iSCSI target on the domain controller in production, so you may not need two NICs for a production domain controller. For a test or development scenario, it makes things easier, though.

Creating a Virtual Machine with VMware Workstation

To create a virtual machine with VMware Workstation, follow the steps in this section. The instructions are based on VMware Workstation 6.5.1.

Tip The instructions in this section, while not exactly the same (some of the Wizard screens are slightly different), are very close to what you would do if you were configuring a guest using VMware ESX Server.

---

1. Start VMware Workstation.

2. Under the File menu, select *New* and then *Virtual Machine*, or just press Ctrl+N.

3. On the Welcome to the New Virtual Machine Wizard dialog, as shown in Figure 9-3, select *Custom* and click Next.

Figure 9-3. *Selecting a custom VM configuration*

4. On the Choose the Virtual Machine Hardware Compatibility dialog, as shown in Figure 9-4, keep the default of the latest version of VMware Workstation. Click Next.

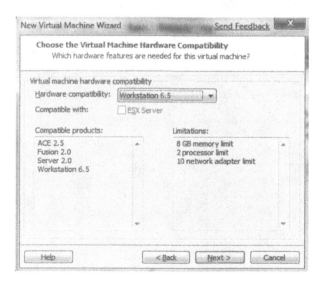

Figure 9-4. *Selecting the version of the VM*

5. On the Guest Operating System Installation dialog, as shown in Figure 9-5, select the option *I will install the operating system later.* Click Next.

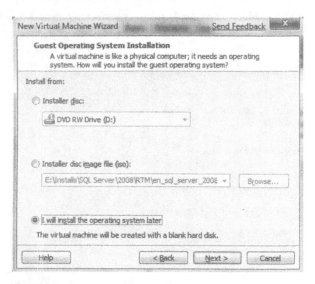

Figure 9-5. *Guest Operating System Installation dialog*

6. On the Select a Guest Operating System dialog, shown in Figure 9-6, select the guest's operating system configuration. VMware will configure certain defaults based on your selection. Click Next.

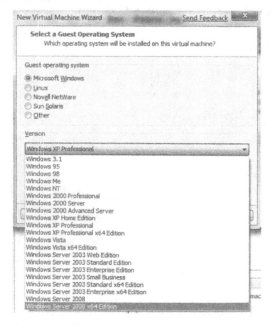

Figure 9-6. *Selecting an operating system for the VM*

7. On the Name the Virtual Machine dialog, enter a name that is easily identifiable for *Virtual machine name*, and change the location of the VM if necessary. An example is shown in Figure 9-7. Click Next.

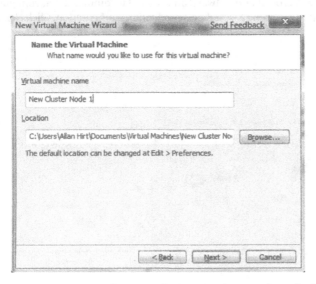

Figure 9-7. *Naming the VM and selecting where to place the files*

8. On the Processor Configuration dialog, as shown in Figure 9-8, select the number of processors the VM will use. For development and testing purposes, I always select one processor since I am not going to be needing extra horsepower, but you should select however many processors you need. The server-based products that can be used in production can generally support more than two processors per guest. Click Next.

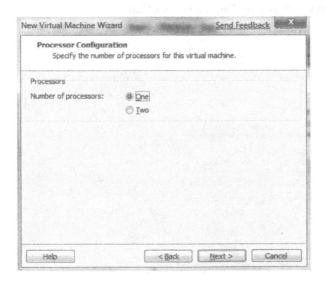

Figure 9-8. *Processor Configuration dialog*

9. Select the memory that the VM will use, as shown in Figure 9-9. The default for Windows Server 2008 is 1 GB (1024 MB). I have successfully run Windows Server 2008 VMs as cluster nodes with 512 MB since I generally run these on my laptop, but realize it is less than the memory recommended by Microsoft and VMware, and I do not recommend that configuration for production or servers that are going to emulate a production configuration. Click Next.

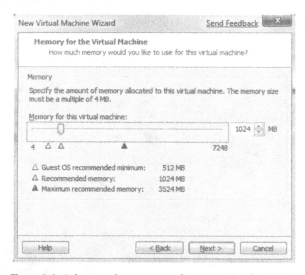

Figure 9-9. *Selecting the amount of memory for the VM*

10. On the Network Type dialog, shown in Figure 9-10, select the type of network that will be used with the initial virtual network card. I either select *Use network address translation (NAT)*, since you need to activate the install, or *Use host-only networking*, which means that the VMs can only see themselves. I use host-only networking because it isolates all of the virtual machines participating in the cluster configuration. Click Next.

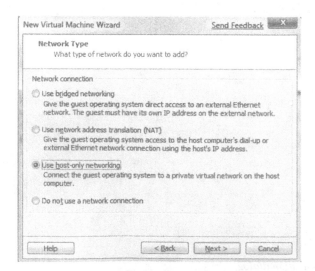

Figure 9-10. *Choosing a network to use with the first NIC*

Note If you select the NAT option, remember that after activating Windows, to set a static IP address for actual use in the guest, you must change the network configuration for that virtual NIC to host-only networking.

11. On the Select I/O Adapter Types dialog, the options will vary depending on the version of Windows you selected in step 6. The example shown in Figure 9-11 is for Windows Server 2008 x64. Click Next to continue.

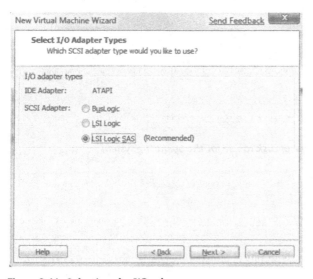

Figure 9-11. *Selecting the I/O adapter type*

12. On the dialog shown in Figure 9-12, you will be selecting which disk will be used to install the operating system. Since I am running on a laptop, I always use the default value of *Create a new virtual disk*. In a production environment or for better performance, I recommend using a physical disk, which would be just like if you put a real hard drive in a server. A virtual disk is just a disk file (like a Word document) that sits on your hard drive but contains the operating system and acts like a hard drive for the guest. Click Next.

13. On the Select a Disk Type dialog, as shown in Figure 9-13, choose the type of disk that the operating system will be installed on (*IDE* or *SCSI*). For development or test purposes, the disk type should not matter too much. Click Next.

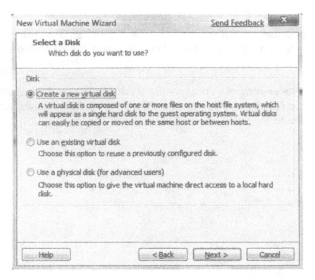

Figure 9-12. *Selecting the type of disk to use for the operating system*

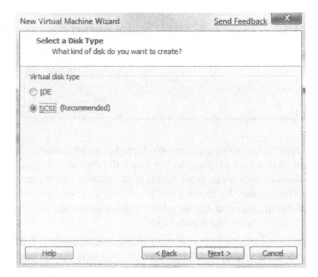

Figure 9-13. *Selecting a disk type*

14. On the Specify Disk Capacity dialog, shown in Figure 9-14, enter the size of the disk to use. The recommended value is the default. I always store everything in a single file, and do not allocate all the space at once since I may not wind up using it, and on a laptop, space can be precious. In a production environment, I would do the opposite: allocate all disk space so that you will not have any unwanted disk growths that negatively affect I/O performance. Click Next.

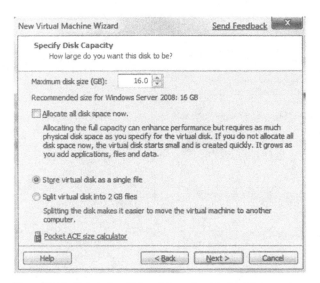

Figure 9-14. *Sizing the disk to be used with the VM*

15. The default name for the virtual disk file will be the name created in step 7, and will be created in the directory specified in that step. You can change these values if you wish, using the dialog in Figure 9-15. Click Next.

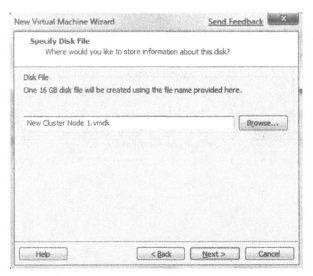

Figure 9-15. *Naming the virtual disk*

16. On the Ready to Create Virtual Machine dialog, as shown in Figure 9-16, click Customize Hardware.

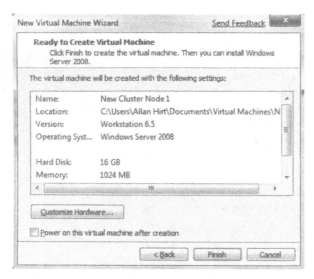

Figure 9-16. *Finalizing the configuration*

17. For the cluster nodes, add two more network cards to the configuration for a total of three, and one more for a total of two for the domain controller, and remove any unnecessary devices you will not be using such as the virtual sound card. Figure 9-17 shows what a base VM should look like. Click OK.

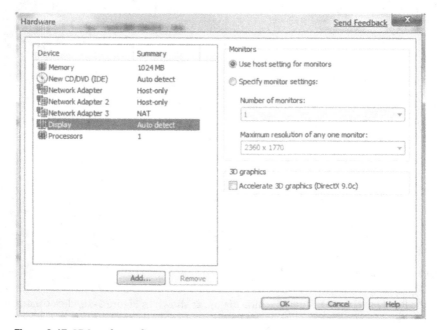

Figure 9-17. *VM node configuration*

18. For the one VM that will serve as the domain controller, you must also add additional virtual disks, which will become the shared disks since the domain controller in this configuration will also be the iSCSI target. That VM will look something like Figure 9-18. Click OK.

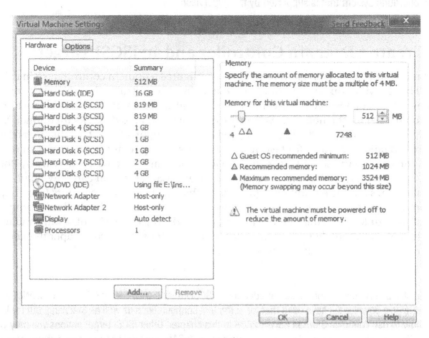

Figure 9-18. *Domain controller configuration*

19. On the Ready to Create Virtual Machine dialog, as shown earlier in Figure 9-16, click Finish.

Creating a Virtual Machine with Hyper-V or Virtual Server 2005 R2

You may choose to use one of the Microsoft options for virtualization. For instructions on how to configure a guest with Hyper-V, use the instructions found at http://technet.microsoft.com/en-us/ library/cc732470.aspx. To create a cluster for test or development purposes using Virtual Server 2005 R2 SP1 (which can be installed on Windows XP, Vista, or 7 and is a free download from Microsoft at http://www.microsoft.com/downloads/details.aspx?displaylang=en&FamilyID=bc49c7c8-4840-4e67- 8dc4-1e6e218acce4), use the instructions found at http://www.microsoft.com/technet/prodtechnol/ virtualserver/deploy/cvs2005.mspx to create the base VMs. Remember to have three network cards for the nodes themselves, and then use the instructions in this chapter to create the base disk config- uration with iSCSI.

Step 2: Install Windows on the VMs

Once the VMs are created, install the version of Windows Server in each of the guests. Since the instructions and screens will vary slightly depending on what version of Windows you are using, those steps will not be shown. How to install Windows is not shown in this book, but it is a simple process with fairly intuitive screens. If you are going to use VMware as your hypervisor, I recommend reading the whitepaper "Guest Operating System Installation Guide," which can be found at http://www.vmware.com/pdf/GuestOS_guide.pdf. It also outlines any specific problems and known issues you may have using VMware as a virtualization platform with Windows.

Note Remember that in a production environment with a supported hypervisor, only versions of Windows Server 2008 are supported with either SQL Server 2005 or SQL Server 2008. In a nonproduction environment, you can configure any operating system that is supported by the hypervisor.

Step 3: Create a Domain Controller and an iSCSI Target

I know that many of you are DBAs and have never configured a domain controller, so in this section I will be showing you how to not only set up a domain controller, but the iSCSI target as well. Using the VM that has two network cards, you will create a server that will serve as both the domain controller for the nodes as well as the host for the shared disks. As mentioned back in Chapter 2, Windows Server 2008 failover clustering only supports SCSI-3, so that means you need iSCSI-based failover clusters for testing. iSCSI has two components: a *target* and an *initiator*. The target is the host for the shared disks, and the initiator is the client. I use StarWind by Rocket Division (http://www.starwindsoftware.com/). It is a free iSCSI target you can download, but the free version does limit the number of hard disks that can be served to clients (see http://www.starwindsoftware.com/product-chart for a comparison of versions; if you don't configure multiple instances or MSDTC, the free version should work). If you do a lot of testing and use StarWind, I highly recommend purchasing a license since a license is much cheaper than buying a lot of clusters for development and testing purposes.

Tip You can also use Windows Storage Server 2008 as an iSCSI target. If you have an MSDN or a TechNet subscription, it is available as a download. I have used that for some test configurations as well as StarWind, but I will not be documenting how to use Windows Storage Server 2008 in this chapter. Other iSCSI target options you may want to look into are iSCSI Cake (http://www.iscsicake.com) and MySAN iSCSI (http://www.nimbusdata.com/products/mysan.php). I have not used either of those, but they seem to be viable alternatives if StarWind or Storage Server do not work for you.

Configuring Networking

Before you can configure either Active Directory or the iSCSI target, you have to configure the two network cards. The IP addresses must be static, and should be on completely different subnets/networks. For example, the Active Directory network card can have an IP address of 200.201.202.1, and the iSCSI network 30.31.32.1.

Configuring Active Directory

Follow these steps to configure an Active Directory forest for the cluster nodes to use:

1. From the Start menu, select *Run*, type **dcpromo**, and click OK.

2. On the Welcome to the Active Directory Domain Services Installation Wizard dialog, click Next.

3. On the Operating System Compatibility dialog, click Next.

4. On the Choose a Deployment Configuration dialog, select the option *Create a new domain in a new forest*, as shown in Figure 9-19. Click Next.

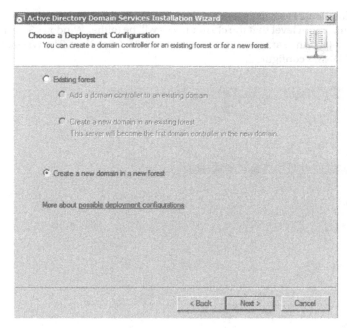

Figure 9-19. *Choose a Deployment Configuration dialog*

5. On the Name the Forest Root Domain dialog, enter a name for the domain. A sample is shown in Figure 9-20. Click Next. First, the Wizard will check to see if the name is in use, and then it will verify the NetBIOS name.

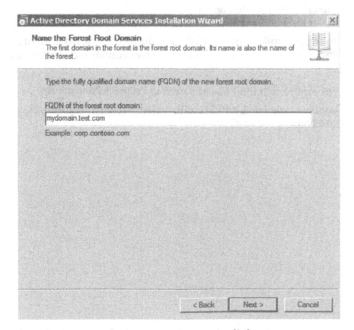

Figure 9-20. *Name the Forest Root Domain dialog*

6. On the Set Forest Functional Level dialog, select the functionality level of the Active Directory forest. Set it at the minimum level that the cluster nodes will be (either Windows Server 2003 or Windows Server 2008). An example is shown in Figure 9-21. Click Next. The Wizard will then check to see if DNS is configured.

Figure 9-21. *Set Forest Functional Level dialog*

7. On the Additional Domain Controller Options dialog, by default, as shown in Figure 9-22, the option *DNS server* will be checked if there is no DNS server configured already. Leave the default and click Next.

8. On the message relating to DNS that pops up, as shown in Figure 9-23, click Yes.

9. On the Location for Database, Log Files, and SYSVOL dialog, shown in Figure 9-24, you can accept the defaults. Click Next.

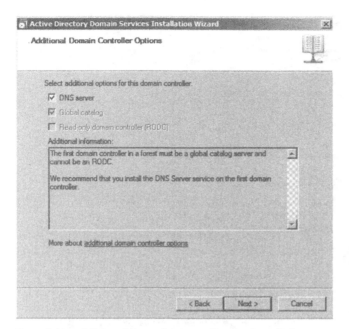

Figure 9-22. *Additional Domain Controller Options dialog*

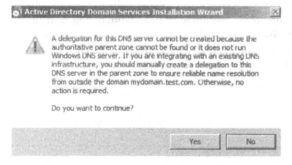

Figure 9-23. *Message relating to DNS dialog*

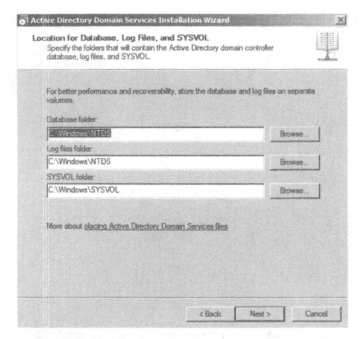

Figure 9-24. *Location for Database, Log Files, and SYSVOL dialog*

10. On the Directory Services Restore Mode Administrator Password dialog, enter a password. An example is shown in **Figure 9-25**. Click Next.

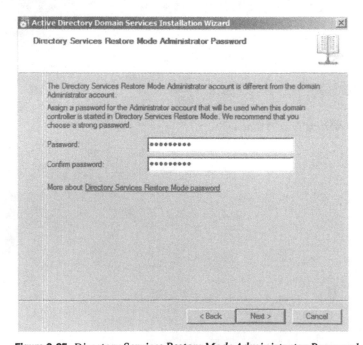

Figure 9-25. *Directory Services Restore Mode Administrator Password dialog*

11. On the Summary dialog, shown in Figure 9-26, click Next.

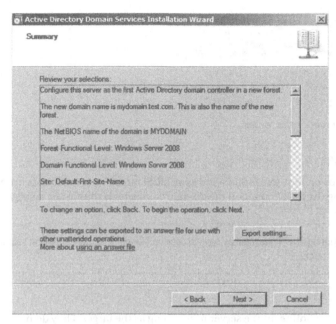

Figure 9-26. *Summary dialog*

12. On the Completing the Active Directory Domain Services Installation Wizard dialog in Figure 9-27, click Finish.

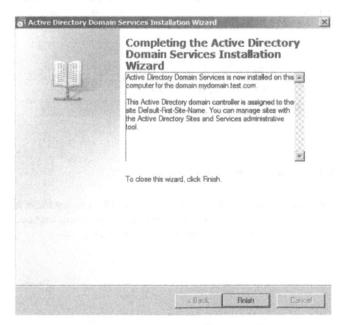

Figure 9-27. *Successful configuration of an Active Directory forest and DNS*

13. Click Restart Now, as shown in Figure 9-28, to activate the domain.

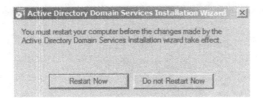

Figure 9-28. *Prompt to reboot the server*

Configuring the iSCSI Target

This section will show the steps on how to use StarWind as an iSCSI target for your virtual cluster. For development and test, putting the iSCSI target on the domain controller is the easiest configuration.

■ **Note** After installing and configuring StarWind, you may have to open up TCP ports 3260 and 3261 in your firewall for the nodes to be able to use the target.

---

1. Install StarWind.

2. Ensure that the disks are online on the server functioning as the target. They do not need to be formatted, but they do need to be recognized in Computer Management.

3. From the task bar, right-click the StarWind iSCSI target (it looks like a circle with three waves), and select *Start Management*.

4. Expand the root tree and *Connections*, as shown in Figure 9-29. You will notice that localhost:3260 is grayed out.

Figure 9-29. *Main StarWind initiator management utility*

5. Right-click localhost:3260, select *Connect*, and enter the password for the test login, as shown in Figure 9-30. The default password can be found in the StarWind documentation. I recommend changing the password (which can be done later in step 16).

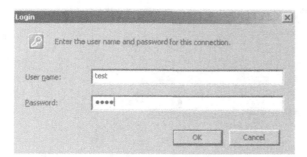

Figure 9-30. *Connecting to the initiator*

6. Right-click localhost:3260 now that you are connected, and select *Add Device*.

7. On the Device type selection dialog, choose the option *Disk Bridge device*, as shown in Figure 9-31, and click Next.

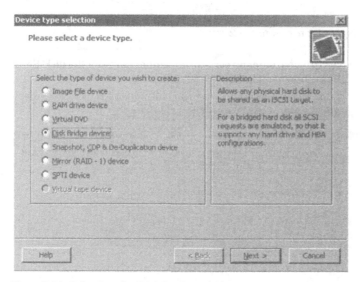

Figure 9-31. *Selecting the Disk Bridge option*

8. On the Disk Bridge device parameters dialog, select the disk to use. Make sure that only the option *Allow multiple concurrent iSCSI connections (clustering)* is selected, as shown in Figure 9-32. Click Next.

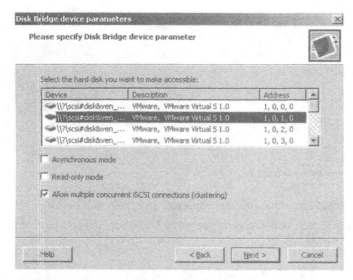

Figure 9-32. *Selecting a disk to add to the target*

9. On the iSCSI target name dialog, enter an easy-to-remember name for the disk. Ensure it has no spaces. An example is shown in Figure 9-33. Click Next.

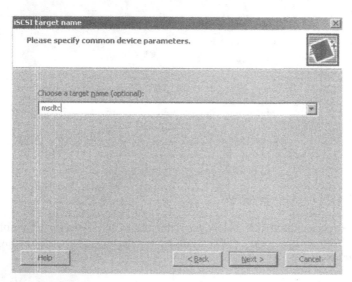

Figure 9-33. *Naming the disk*

10. On the Completing the Add Device Wizard dialog, as shown in Figure 9-34, click Next.

Figure 9-34. *Completing the Add Device Wizard dialog*

11. Once the disk is added to the target, click Finish on the dialog shown in Figure 9-35.

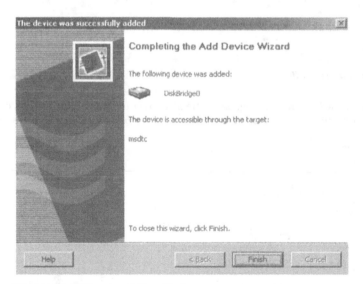

Figure 9-35. *Disk succesfully added*

12. Repeat steps 6 through 11 for all disks. When finished, it should look similar to Figure 9-36.

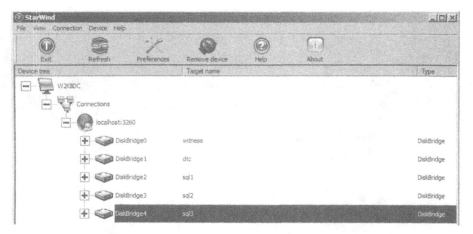

Figure 9-36. *Disks added to the target*

13. Right-click localhost:3260, and select *Access Rights*. On the Initiators Access Rights dialog, make sure that the default access policy is set to *Allow*, and click Add (see Figure 9-37).

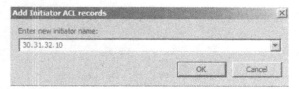

Figure 9-37. *Default access policy*

14. On the Add Initiator ACL records dialog, enter the IP address for one node's network card, which will be used to communicate with the target. An example is shown in Figure 9-38. Click OK.

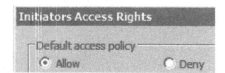

Figure 9-38. *Adding the node's iSCSI IP address*

15. Repeat steps 13 and 14 to add access for all nodes. When finished, click OK on the Initiators Access Rights dialog.

16. To change the username and password for the iSCSI target, or the IP address of the iSCSI target, right-click localhost:3260 and select *Edit Configuration*. You will see the dialog shown in Figure 9-39.

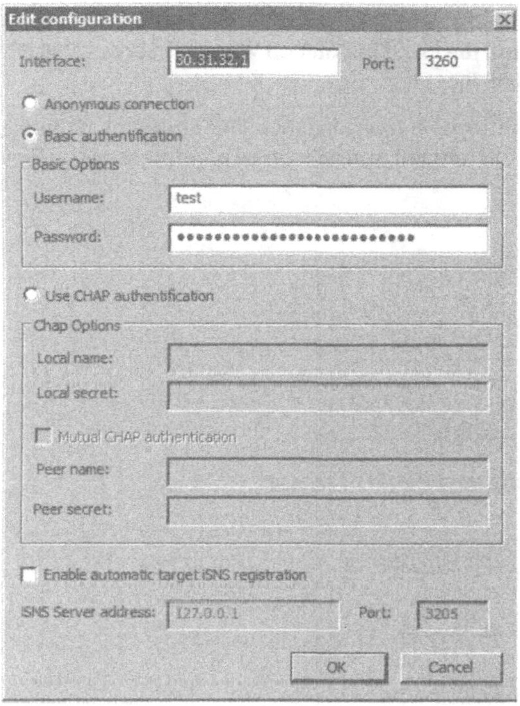

Figure 9-39. *Configuration of the iSCSI target*

Step 4: Configure the Cluster Nodes

Once the VMs are created, configure networking as per Chapter 3. Also remember to install any virtualization-specific tools that the host may require. For example, VMware Workstation has VMware Tools, which optimizes the guest by installing graphics and network drivers. Once those tasks are done, and before you do any disk work, the nodes have to recognize the disks. This section will show you how to configure the iSCSI initiator on each node. StarWind does have a free iSCSI initiator you can use; however, Windows Server 2008 has a perfectly good one built into the operating system that you can use as well. I will only show how to configure the one in Windows.

Tip If your VM will be running Windows Server 2003, you can download the Microsoft iSCSI initiator from http://www.microsoft.com/downloads/details.aspx?displaylang=en&familyid=12CB3C1A-15D6-4585-B385-BEFD1319F825.

Configuring the iSCSI Initiator

The instructions in this section will show you how to configure the Microsoft iSCSI Initiator to communicate to the iSCSI target you configured earlier.

Using Windows Server 2008 RTM

The steps that follow show how to configure the iSCSI initiator on Windows Server 2008 RTM. The next section will cover Windows Server 2008 R2.

1. From the Start menu, select *Administrative Tools*, and then *iSCSI Initiator*. If this is the first time you have run the Microsoft iSCSI Initiator, you will see the prompts shown in Figures 9-40 and 9-41. Click Yes on both.

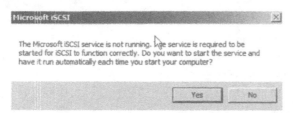

Figure 9-40. *Prompt to automatically start the iSCSI service*

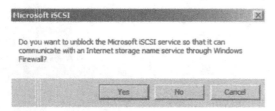

Figure 9-41. *Prompt to unblock the iSCSI ports*

2. On the iSCSI Initiator Properties dialog, select the *Discovery* tab. Click Add Portal.

3. On the Discover Target Portal dialog, enter the IP address or name of the iSCSI target. If the port is not the default (3260), also change that. A sample is shown in Figure 9-42. Click Advanced.

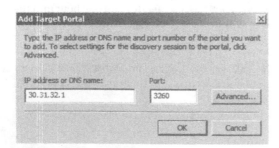

Figure 9-42. *Entering the iSCSI target*

4. On the Advanced Settings dialog, in the *Local adapter* dropdown, select the value *Microsoft iSCSI Initiator*, and in the *Source IP*, the IP address for the network card that will be used for iSCSI. An example is shown in Figure 9-43. Click OK.

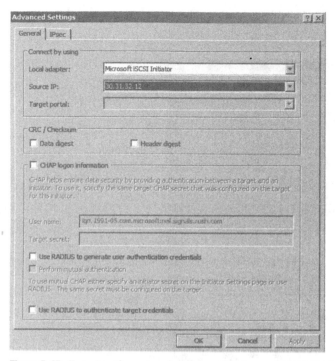

Figure 9-43. *Entering the network information to connect to the iSCSI target*

5. Click OK on the Discover Target Portal dialog. The target will now be shown, as in Figure 9-44.

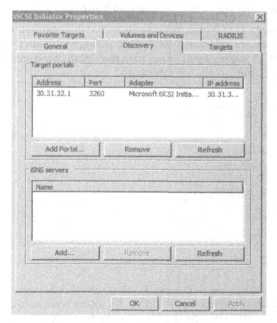

Figure 9-44. *Target added to the Initiator*

6. Select the *Targets* tab. All available disks will be displayed with a status of *Inactive*, as shown in Figure 9-45.

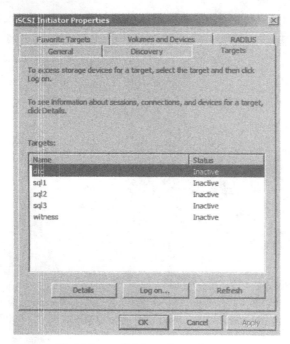

Figure 9-45. *Disks available to the node*

7. Select one of the disks in the *Targets* section of the tab, and click Log On.

8. On the Log On to Target dialog, make sure that *Automatically restore this connection when the computer starts* is selected, as shown in Figure 9-46. If you are using multipath I/O, check the box next to *Enable multi-path*. However, if you do not have multipath configured, do not select that option, as you will encounter errors. Click Advanced.

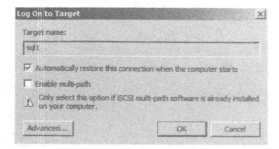

Figure 9-46. *Log On to Target dialog*

9. On the General tab of Advanced Settings, similar to step 4, select the value *Microsoft iSCSI Initiator* for *Local adapter*. For *Source IP,* select the IP address for the network card that will be used for iSCSI, and for *Target portal,* select the IP address of the target. An example is shown in Figure 9-47. Click OK.

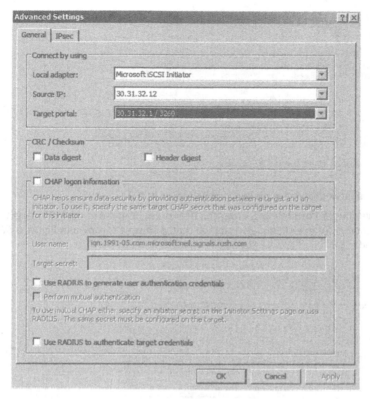

Figure 9-47. *Configuring the connection settings for the disk*

10. Click OK on the Connect To Target dialog. If the disk was successfully configured, it will have a status of *Connected*, as shown in Figure 9-48.

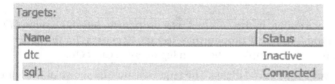

Figure 9-48. *Initiator successfully connected to a disk on the target*

11. Repeat steps 6 through 10 for each disk.

Using Windows Server 2008 R2

Microsoft changed the interface of the iSCSI initiator in Windows Server 2008 R2. The instructions in this section will cover that version of the Microsoft iSCSI Initiator.

1. From the Start menu, select *Administrative Tools*, and then *iSCSI Initiator*. If this is the first time you have run the Microsoft iSCSI Initiator, you will see the prompt shown in Figure 9-49.

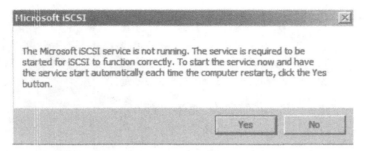

Figure 9-49. *Prompt to start the iSCSI service*

2. On the iSCSI Initiator Properties dialog, click Discover Portal.

3. On the Discover Target Portal dialog, enter the IP address or name of the iSCSI target. If the port is not the default (3260), also change that. A sample is shown in Figure 9-50. Click Advanced.

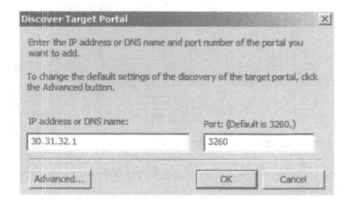

Figure 9-50. *Entering the IP address and port of the iSCSI target*

4. On the Advanced Settings dialog, in the *Local adapter* dropdown, select the value *Microsoft iSCSI Initiator*; and in the *Initiator IP* dropdown, select the IP address for the network card that will be used for iSCSI. An example is shown in Figure 9-51. Click OK.

5. Click OK on the Discover Target Portal dialog. The target will now be shown as in Figure 9-52. Select the *Targets* tab. All available disks will be displayed with a status of *Inactive*, as shown in Figure 9-53.

6. Select the *Targets* tab. All available disks will be displayed with a status of *Inactive*, as shown in Figure 9-53.

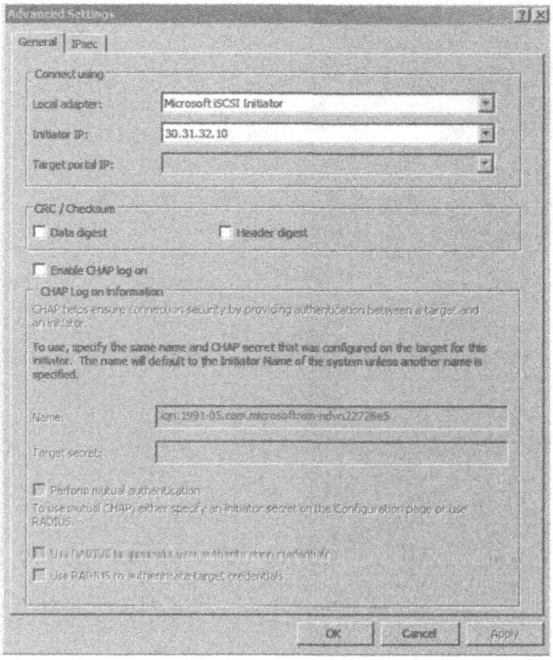

Figure 9-51. *Selecting the settings to connect to the target*

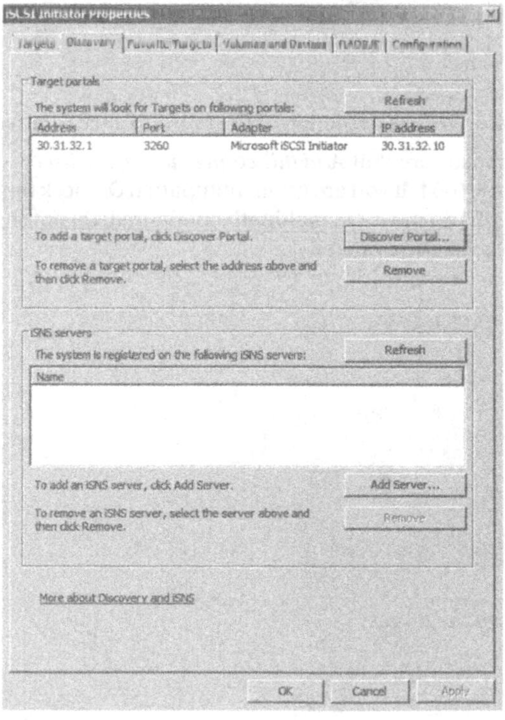

Figure 9-52. *Target added to the Initiator*

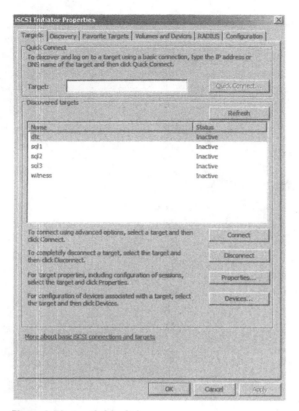

Figure 9-53. *Available disks*

7. Select one of the disks in the *Discovered Targets* section of the tab, and click Connect.

8. On the Connect To Target dialog, make sure that *Add this connection to the list of Favorite Targets* is selected, as shown in Figure 9-54. If you are using multipath I/O, check the box next to *Enable multi-path*. However, if you do not have multipath configured, do not select that option, as you will encounter errors. Click Advanced.

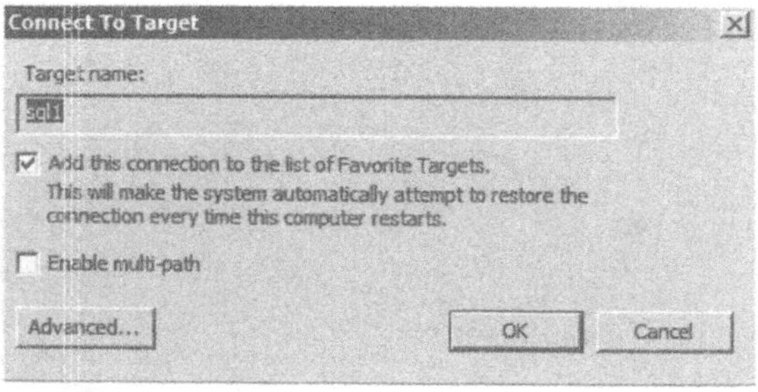

Figure 9-54. *Connecting to the disk on the target*

9. On the General tab of the Advanced Settings dialog, select the value *Microsoft iSCSI Initiator* for *Local adapter*; for *Initiator IP*, select the IP address for the network card that will be used for iSCSI; and for *Target portal IP*, select the IP address of the target. An example is shown in Figure 9-55. Click OK.

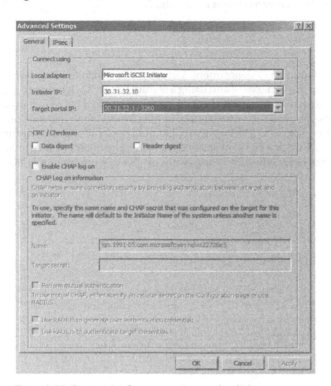

Figure 9-55. *Properties for connecting to the disk*

10. Click OK on the Connect To Target dialog. If the disk was successfully configured, it will have a status of *Connected*, as shown in Figure 9-56.

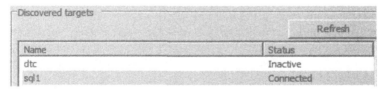

Figure 9-56. *Disk successfully connected*

11. Repeat steps 6 through 10 for each disk on the target.

Finishing the Windows Configuration and Cluster

At this point, you are ready to perform the preparation tasks for the failover cluster starting with the disk-related tasks in Chapter 3. Once you complete the node preparation, cluster Windows as shown in Chapter 4, and finally cluster SQL Server as shown in Chapter 6.

Summary

Virtualization is a powerful tool within an IT department. Virtualization and failover clustering can work together, either by clustering the hypervisor and using a feature like Live Migration to increase the availability of guests, or by clustering the guests themselves as you would if the virtual machines were physical cluster nodes. Whether you use virtualization or not in production depends on your requirements as well as your IT environment. Using virtualization in nonproduction environments is an idea I endorse wholeheartedly since it can give developers, DBAs, and other IT staff production-like configurations and sandboxes to try advanced things without affecting production or having to purchase additional hardware.

Index

You Need the Companion eBook

Your purchase of this book entitles you to buy the companion PDF-version eBook for only $10. Take the weightless companion with you anywhere.

We believe this Apress title will prove so indispensable that you'll want to carry it with you everywhere, which is why we are offering the companion eBook (in PDF format) for $10 to customers who purchase this book now. Convenient and fully searchable, the PDF version of any content-rich, page-heavy Apress book makes a valuable addition to your programming library. You can easily find and copy code—or perform examples by quickly toggling between instructions and the application. Even simultaneously tackling a donut, diet soda, and complex code becomes simplified with hands-free eBooks!

Once you purchase your book, getting the $10 companion eBook is simple:

❶ Visit **www.apress.com/promo/tendollars/**.

❷ Complete a basic registration form to receive a randomly generated question about this title.

❸ Answer the question correctly in 60 seconds, and you will receive a promotional code to redeem for the $10.00 eBook.

THE EXPERT'S VOICE™

Offer valid through 01/2010.